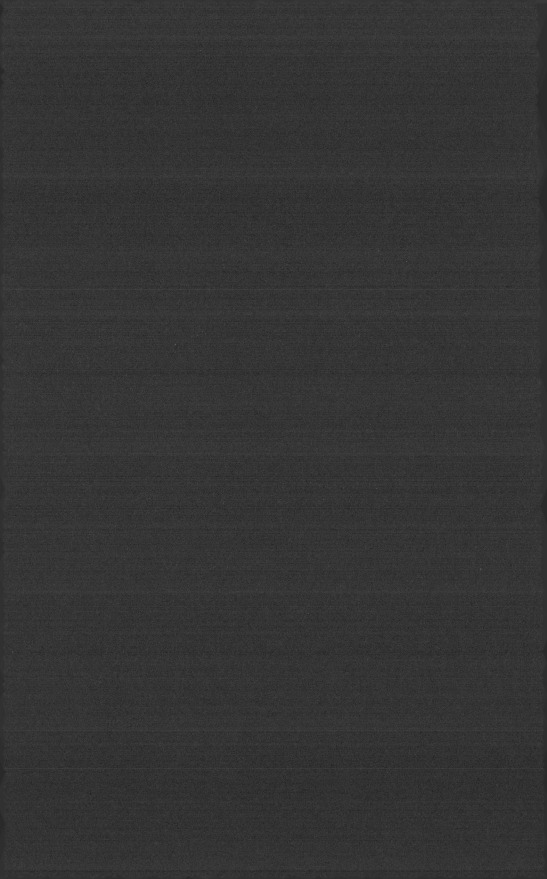

The British Library Studies in the History of the Book

THE ENGLISH
MEDIEVAL BOOK
Studies in Memory of Jeremy Griffiths

Jeremy Griffiths

THE ENGLISH MEDIEVAL BOOK

Studies in Memory of Jeremy Griffiths

Edited by
A. S. G. EDWARDS,
VINCENT GILLESPIE
and
RALPH HANNA

THE BRITISH LIBRARY

2000

© 2000 The Contributors

First published 2000 by
The British Library
96 Euston Road
London NW1 2DB

British Library Cataloguing in Publication Data
A CIP record for this book is available
from The British Library

ISBN 0 7123 4650 3

Designed by John Trevitt
Typeset by Norman Tilley Graphics, Northampton
Printed in England by St Edmundsbury Press, Bury St Edmunds

CONTENTS

Contents

NOTES ON CONTRIBUTORS

NORMAN BLAKE has recently retired as Professor of English Language at the University of Sheffield.

JULIA BOFFEY is Reader in the School of English and Drama at Queen Mary and Westfield College, University of London.

A. I. DOYLE is Honorary Reader in Bibliography and former Keeper of Rare Books at the University of Durham.

A. S. G. EDWARDS was most recently Helen Cam Fellow at Girton College, Cambridge.

VINCENT GILLESPIE is Reader in English Language and Literature at the University of Oxford and Fellow and Tutor in English, St Anne's College, Oxford.

RALPH HANNA is Professor of Palaeography at the University of Oxford and Fellow and Tutor in English, Keble College, Oxford.

CHRISTOPHER DE HAMEL is Director of the Department of Western Manuscripts, Sotheby's, London, and Librarian-elect of Corpus Christi College, Cambridge.

KATE HARRIS has been Librarian and Archivist to the Marquess of Bath at Longleat House since 1985 and was previously Lady Margaret Research Fellow in English at New Hall, Cambridge.

PEDRAG MILOVANOVIC is a rare-book dealer in Serbia.

LINNE MOONEY is Professor of English at the University of Maine, USA.

STEPHEN PARTRIDGE is Assistant Professor of English at the University of British Columbia, Canada.

DEREK PEARSALL is Gurney Professor of English at Harvard University. He was previously Professor and Co-Director of the Centre for Medieval Studies at the University of York.

KATHLEEN SCOTT, of Amherst, MA, is an independent scholar who works on the illustration and decoration of fifteenth-century English manuscripts.

ANDREW WATSON is Professor Emeritus of Manuscript Studies in the University of London at University College.

LIST OF PLATES

List of Plates

The editors and contributors are grateful to the various individual and institutional owners for permission to print these reproductions of manuscripts in their care.

ABBREVIATIONS

Adams   H. M. Adams, *Catalogue of Books printed on the Continent of Europe, 1501-1600, in Cambridge Libraries* (Cambridge, 1967)

BL   London, British Library

BMC   British Musem, *Catalogue of Books printed in the Fifteenth Century now in the British Museum* (London, 1909-)

Bodl.   Bodleian Library, Oxford

BRUC   A. B. Emden, *A Biographical Register of the University of Cambridge to A.D. 1500* (Cambridge, 1963)

BRUO   A. B. Emden, *A Biographical Register of the University of Oxford to A.D. 1500* (Oxford, 1957-9)

CUL   Cambridge University Library

DMC   P. R. Robinson, *Catalogue of Dated and Datable Manuscripts c. 737-1600 in Cambridge Libraries* (Cambridge, 1988)

DNB   *Dictionary of National Biography*

EETS   Early English Text Society

EPB   *Early Printed Books to the Year 1500 in the Library of Trinity Hall, Cambridge* (Cambridge, 1909), no. 1

GW   *Gesamtkataloge der Wiegendrücke* (Leipzig, 1926-38; Stuttgart, 1976-)

Hain   L. F. T. Hain, *Repertorium bibliographicum* (Stuttgart, etc., 1826-38)

Hamer   Richard Hamer, *A Manuscript Index to the Index of Middle English Verse* (London, 1995)

IMEP   *The Index of Middle English Prose* (Cambridge, 1984-)

IMEV   Carleton Brown & Rossell Hope Robbins, *The Index of Middle English Verse* (New York, 1943), with *Supplement* by Rossell Hope Robbins & John L. Cutler (Lexington, KY, 1965)

IPMEP   Robert E. Lewis, N. F. Blake & A. S. G. Edwards (eds), *Index of Printed Middle English Prose*, Garland Reference Library of the Humanities, vol. 537 (New York & London, 1985)

Ker   see *MLGB*

MET   *Middle English Texts* (Heidelberg, 1975-)

MLGB	N. R. Ker, *Medieval Libraries of Great Britain: a List of surviving Books*, 2nd edn (London, 1964) with *Supplement to the Second Edition*, ed. by Andrew G. Watson (London, 1987)
OCarm	Ordo Carmelitarum
SC	sale catalogue
SC	*A Summary Catalogue of Western Manuscripts in the Bodleian Library at Oxford*, 7 vols (Oxford, 1895-1953)
STC	A. W. Pollard & G. R. Redgrave, *A Short-Title Catalogue of Books Printed in England, Scotland and Ireland*, 2nd edn, begun by W. A. Jackson & F. S. Ferguson, completed by K. F. Pantzer (London, 1976-91)
STS	Scottish Text Society
UL	University Library
VCH	Victoria County History
WB	*Warren's Book*
\ /	enclose inserted letters
< >	enclose damaged words (inserted if deciphered)
[ ]	enclose undamaged but illegible words

JEREMY JOHN GRIFFITHS

5 June 1955 to 14 August 1997

An Address given at a Memorial Service in Thanksgiving for his Life
in The Chapel of St John's College Oxford
8 November 1997

Vincent Gillespie

It was, of course, a summer of unexpected deaths, of candles in the wind, of cards and flowers, of the struggle to express a deep sense of shock and loss. But for many of us the grieving began several weeks before the rest of the country woke up to sudden sadness. On 14 August, after fighting illness with dignity and determination, Jeremy was finally tricked into death by a cruel and unforgiving infection which was unrelated to the medical enemy he had eyed so steadfastly and fought so resolutely for the previous year. So for us, Diana's death was the opportunity to weep new tears of sorrow and anger at the cutting off of young life; a reinforcement of the sense of senseless loss and absence. An opportunity, more indirect, but still raw and powerful to revisit the feelings of impotence and numb anger at the cruelty of Fate; to wonder where in all this pain might be found the soothing pattern of Providence.

For myself, I spent much of the summer with a distorted version of a line from Chaucer's honest exploration of grief and consolation in *The Book of the Duchess* spiralling round in my head:

> 'He is ded!' 'Nay!' 'Yis be my trouthe!'
> 'Is that your los? Be God, hyt ys routhe!'

Day by day over the hot and airless weeks that followed, strikingly similar expressions of shock and reeling grief materialized on my computer screen as e-mails from round the world telegraphed the sense of loss and pain felt by Jeremy's many friends in the academic world, and especially in the manuscript studies community. This year, for many of us, August was the cruellest month.

Many of the ethereal messages that arrived spoke not only of sadness but of real and deep regret: regret at projects uncompleted; regret at huge promise somehow unfulfilled; regret at meetings, parties, and good gossip no longer to be enjoyed; regret, above all, at the end of a relationship with a man who was palpably special in his generosity of spirit and appetite for life, but who was also naggingly difficult to know well. One letter said: 'I think he was one of the nicest people I have ever met. I wish I had known him better', and I found myself agreeing with both statements.

1

There were many aspects to Jeremy's life – in a way there were many Jeremies. There was the Jeremy the *bon viveur* with a taste for Laphroaig; Jeremy the entrepreneurial dealer, trying to sell a Viking bucket; Jeremy the would-be politician and speech-writer; Jeremy the impulsive and unpredictable romantic, who approached Julie Pottle on Holkham beach out of the blue, and picked a real winner as her support and love for him over the last year showed; Jeremy the war-correspondent; Jeremy the sybarite; Jeremy the lead character in the *Cheers*-like cast of *The Duke of Cambridge* bar in Oxford; Jeremy the connoisseur and scholar of beautiful things: our last conversation was about art history in general and Kathleen Scott's great census in particular. Perhaps we all have our own Jeremy, and I can only try and do justice to the one I knew best.

I suppose I must have met him first in the late seventies in one of those lung-kippering sessions in Malcolm Parkes's room in Keble. Malcolm was Jeremy's supervisor and had been my undergraduate tutor. Already Jeremy was being talked about in hushed tones as a young man who KNEW THINGS. There was a style and certainty, an intellectual elegance and professional panache that lent authority to what he said. There was also an intentness in his listening, even then, that made you feel that maybe you KNEW THINGS too. He was good at moving relationships forward very quickly so that you felt as if you had been friends for years. And yet, despite this, to many of us he remained something of an enigma.

The basic facts of his life are straightforward enough. He was born in Aberdare, Glamorgan, in June 1955. After Papplewick School in Berkshire and Canford School in Dorset, Jeremy spent three years at Leamington College in Warwickshire. From there in 1973 he went to the University College of North Wales in Bangor, reading English. In 1976 he took a First Class Honours degree in English, winning the John F. Danby Memorial Prize. (His father tells me that he was very anxious to get a First to match the First in languages gained by his mother at Cardiff. Typical Jeremy: he loved a challenge!) After a one-year M.A. course at Bangor, Jeremy enrolled as a graduate student at Oxford in 1977, joining Jesus College in solidarity with his Welsh background.

Before long, Jeremy was an established figure on the Oxford scene, being appointed to College Lecturerships at Lincoln College and, from 1981, at St John's College, which was the beginning of the close and fond relationship with St John's (and its books and manuscripts) that continued to his death. In 1984, Jeremy, already identified as a major rising star in the firmament of manuscript studies, was appointed to a full-time lecturership in English at Birkbeck College in the University of London. He resigned from Birkbeck in 1988 to pursue business interests in the rare book trade, including extensive consultancy and cataloguing work for most major dealers.

Jeremy's time at Birkbeck was both formative and revealing of his attitude to academic life. He was always hugely idealistic, whether about projects (which sometimes didn't happen), people (who sometimes let him down), or partnerships (which sometimes stopped working). Going to Birkbeck was a function of his idealism about academic life: he chose to go into full-time teaching in a department with a history of educational out-reach, despite the fact that he had also in 1984 been elected to the Fulford Junior Research Fellowship at St Anne's College, Oxford. He rejected full-time research for the admittedly better paid but also much more demanding world of a teaching department. But by 1988 he was disillusioned by what he increasingly felt to be a faction-alized and narrow-minded world when compared to the idealism and range of his own objectives. By contrast he looked back on his time at St John's with great affection, an affection that was renewed and deepened by the warmth of the college's welcome when he agreed to undertake a new catalogue of their manuscripts.

But Birkbeck had bruised him, and his attitudes to academic life were there-after always ambivalent. Part of him contrasted his own long working days and sometimes precarious existence as a freelance with the apparently secure and seemingly less stressful world of his academic friends (though he also noticed the pressures of academic life inexorably increasing in recent years). He sought the company and friendship of independent scholars and of dealers and booksellers (some of whom were very big players in the corporate world). But another part of him idealistically longed for the fellowship and community of the republic of letters, and envied those of us who were more centrally part of it than he felt himself to be.

The irony of this is that Jeremy often did more to facilitate that academic community by his hospitality and his skills as an academic impresario than he could ever have realised. Because he was a dreamer of big dreams, he often inspired others to embark on projects beyond the parochial quick-fix level of much academic research in this world of bibliometrics and research assess-ment. So many contacts were made over lunch or dinner. So many projects launched in heated discussion over the second or third bottle, when anything seemed achievable. When he was not 'oonlie begetter' of such big ideas, he often served as midwife or wetnurse at later stages. I have a small anthology of typically punctilious cards and letters from Jeremy, usually beginning 'I very much enjoyed our lunch/dinner/drinks yesterday' and going on to recall and elaborate some scheme or some arcane discussion of a manuscript or text which he alleged had taken place at a point in the meal when I wasn't sure I knew my own name, never mind the identity of the second hand in the third quire.

I'm sure I'm not alone in having valued the whetstone keenness of Jeremy's questioning in such circumstances. Long-held truisms were challenged; sacred cows not just slaughtered but served up fricasseed and garnished. All this done with such impeccable courtesy and charm, with the skill of a forensic scientist: 'It seems to me that …' the invariable opening to a long, eloquent, passionate and entirely plausible rereading or cogent challenging of some common area of interest. He had a low boredom threshold, which led him to want fresh challenges and new projects, but also gave him the energy to revisit old ideas with new vigour: even his own thesis shows signs of substantial revision in its latest recension.

Most of this was achieved outside the academy. He acted as an *agent provocateur*, a catalyst, sometimes a voice from a distant discourse of commerce – what E. M. Forster described as the world of telegrams and anger – where the accuracy and acuity of his judgements were as vital to his professional success as a dealer as the accuracy of the tolerances in the machines designed by his father were to the success of the family firm (of which Jeremy became managing director in 1994). Yet in some ways, despite the energy he put into his dealing and consultancy work, and his intrigued and increasing engagement with the world of precision engineering, part of him longed, I think, to be back in academic life. Collegiate living suited him: it offered an almost perfect paradigm of fellowship, common purpose, and Athenian democracy, however much the reality differed from the ideal. Jeremy was magnetically drawn to corporate institutions, both as the subject of his academic study (as in his study of the Luton and Dunstable guild books; his interest in early Eton; or his fascination with John Blacman who after a life of business and politics retired to the cloister; or his study of merchants like Gilbert Maughfield), and in his own life as a member of St John's; as a liveryman of the Worshipful Company of Turners; as a Freeman of the City of London; as a Companion of the Guild of St George; or as a member of the Association Internationale de Bibliophilie or the Bibliographical Society. He was interested in the distinctive culture of small communities: the close-knit group of scribes who copied the early Chaucer and Gower manuscripts; or fifteenth-century guilds and mercantile milieu; or monastic scriptoria.

Jeremy had an anthropologist's ability to see the minute particulars and the big picture simultaneously, and to know how to relate the two. He was an incisive cultural historian of the present as well as the past. Above all he was never slow to recalibrate and reassess his academic judgements. 'I've been thinking a lot about this,' he would say, 'and it seems to me that …' He was equally quick to reconfigure himself and his own views on life. Michael Mitchell of Libanus Press, who printed today's order of service in Jeremy's distinctive personal livery of Oxford blue and turquoise, and who knew at first hand Jeremy's exacting standards of typography and ink colour, claims that Jeremy's business card changed every time they met, and indeed he was often fine-tuning his public persona as was perhaps necessary for someone who operated in such diverse worlds. Always beautifully groomed, invariably in jacket and tie, one could notice subtle changes in his personal style. One of his looks was 'the gentleman scholar': all double cuffs and bow ties. Another was 'the entrepreneurial yuppie', filofax and mobile phone (and sometimes Porsche) much in evidence. I used to tease him about being a master of disguise, a sort of Pink Panther of the manuscript world. And some of his adventures, not least in the Yugoslavian civil war, only served to reinforce that Bulldog Drummond or Richard Hannay quality about his life.

4

This protean, almost restless quality in Jeremy was one of the reasons why so many people felt that they wanted to know him better than they did. It was not unusual for Jeremy to disappear from one's life for six months, only for that instantly recognizable voice to reappear on the end of a phone line suggesting lunch the next day. And despite six months' silence, the conversation would pick up without a beat. He loved spontaneity: life was never dull when he was around. A meeting with Jeremy might involve being transported in one of his unfeasibly large and glamorous cars, driven quite astonishingly quickly by a man who often seemed to be simultaneously sending a fax, making a phone call, and replacing a tape in the cassette machine. Ralph Hanna made a vow never again to look at the speedometer of any car driven by Jeremy. And what taste he had in restaurants: elegant, understated, and often outstanding. He truly was a legend in his own lunchtime.

But stylish, enjoyable, and impressive though such occasions were, there was always hard talk and serious manuscript business to be done. It was typical of him that he insisted that the seminar we ran at St Anne's on Authors Scribes and Owners of Middle English Texts (which was intended to prime the pump for an ambitious bio-bibliographical index) had to be followed by a PROPER reception. Sherry and peanuts wouldn't do: had no style. It had to be proper canapés and decent wine because he wanted to give people a chance not only to hear a good paper but also to talk about it later. The real work was often done at the party or at dinner afterwards. Very Jeremy that, and very effective in encouraging extended, thoughtful, and open discussion about books and manuscripts. The exchange and accumulation of knowledge was what mattered, but doing it in style didn't hurt either.

Jeremy cared passionately about manuscripts, not because of their value or marketability (though he was skilled at that part of the job as well) or indeed because he wanted to possess them, but for the knowledge each object gave us, the new pieces for the great cultural jigsaw puzzle that he was constructing in his head or in the truly massive card-index system he developed. That was why he never minded parting with books or manuscripts: as long as he had extracted the information he wanted, it was largely irrelevant who owned them. This is why he was so keen to describe and catalogue. It was also why he was so interested in country-house collections and in individual collectors. The trust he generated and the advice he gave allowed him access to the artifacts. Many of his published pieces deal with unfamiliar books from unfashionable collections, or books in transit between collections, blinking shyly in the unaccustomed light of academic scrutiny. Not that he shied away from big issues: his thesis confronts head on the huge problems of Chaucer's text, while he had amassed substantial material on the manuscripts of Gower and of the Statutes of the Realm. Jeremy's visual memory for hands was prodigious; his skill in dating and classification was always precocious and seemed likely to become virtuosic. He could join in the medievalist's favourite game of cite the shelfmark, but few of us knew the books as intimately as he often did.

His friends have undertaken to ensure that as many as possible of his unfinished projects reach publication, and I have no doubt that when that process is completed Jeremy will be confirmed among the front rank of historians of the medieval book. In particular, Ralph Hanna is exploring ways of publishing the thesis in book form. And in an act of great far-sightedness and generosity, which reflects and partly explains Jeremy's own generous nature, his parents and Julie have donated the bulk of his wonderful working collection of reference books to the library of the English Faculty of the University of Oxford. The books will be kept together and will form the core of a new collection to be developed in a room dedicated to the History of the Book. Fittingly, they will be shelved alongside many of the books of another great archaeologist of the medieval book, Neil Ker. Each new generation of Oxford graduate students will have the opportunity of learning the arts of codicology and palaeography from the Griffths Collection, assembled by Jeremy with such care and discrimination and used by him with such acuity and telling effect. Indirectly, therefore, his books will help to build and cement that community of medievalists about which he cared so deeply, just as his publications, past and future, will help to inform it. Moreover, Jeremy's parents have endowed the university with a graduate scholarship in memory of Jeremy, dedicated to help a graduate student working on the History of the Book in England before 1625. Fittingly, that scholarship will be held at his beloved St John's College.

All of us have been provoked, prompted, or primed by Jeremy over the years. Of course one wishes he had written more, or at least finished more. But I recall Erasmus saying of an English contemporary that he had not written more for fear of writing ill. Something of that same anxiety afflicted Jeremy, I think. I have a theory that scholars become like the texts they work on. Writers on *Piers Plowman* often find themselves going through three (or is it four?) drafts; writers on Gower elaborate their apparatus and commentary; and, of course, writers on Chaucer fail to finish their projects. Jeremy was, it is true, a procrastinator on a quite heroic scale, having perhaps assimilated something of Chaucer's resistance to easy closure and glib resolution. Jeremy's thesis confronts truly massive questions of textual authority and huge quantities of manuscript evidence about, for example, the textual tradition of the Statutes of the Realm. I'm sure it will be a major addition to an increasingly important debate.

His list of publications is by no means insignificant, especially for someone who was having to earn a living at the same time. His Roxburghe Club editions of De Worde's *Speculum Peccatoris* and the Tollemache *Book of Secrets* distil great learning into little space. And his editorship with Derek Pearsall of that seminal volume *Book Production and Publishing 1375-1475* gave us an invaluable guide to an increasingly exciting area of study. I remember two rib-achingly funny and back-achingly long days during which Jeremy knocked into shape my chapter for that book. Not a sentence went unchallenged, not an assertion unquestioned with that courteous and disarming frankness that made it almost

impossible to take offence. 'I have to say', he would begin, prior to demonstrating that one was making a point that was simultaneously illiterate,
ignorant, and erroneous.

But it was, of course, in *English Manuscript Studies* that Jeremy's editorial
and entrepreneurial flair found a true and happy home. Peter Beal tells of
Jeremy's characteristic vision, his drive and determination for it to succeed; his
meticulous attention to detail and to the big picture of an argument in his sub-
editing; not to mention his willingness to offer financial support to the fledgling
venture. *EMS* meant a lot to Jeremy – he remembered it in his will – and I am
sure his vision and energy will ensure that it survives as an enduring monu-
ment to his impact on the geography and topography of the subject.

His proliferation of projects and commissions was a function of his idealistic
enthusiasm to be of assistance. He loved to be needed, and it sometimes seemed
to me that he was driven by a need to be accepted as a credible member of the
republic of letters, of the family of medievalists. Like Malory's Lancelot, he
always needed a new quest to test his reputation and burnish his prowess. His
direct achievements are already notable and will in time appear more so as more
completed projects appear. But his indirect contribution to the subject was
huge, both as a catalyst and as a collaborator, as is witnessed by the number of
friends willing to complete projects on his behalf. Like Lancelot, in that other
fellowship, he was 'the curtest knyght that ever bare shelde and the godelyest
persone that ever cam emonge prees of knyghtes and the mekest man and the
jentyllest that ever ete in halle'. He was, of course, a hugely respected and
admired scholar: I think he knew that and deeply valued it. I hope he also knew
how much many of us loved him as a person, and how much we miss him now.
May he rest in peace.

TRAVELS WITH JEREMY

Pedrag Milovanovic

Jeremy's career as a bookseller was not well known to his academic colleagues, and the special circumstances of my meetings and travels with Jeremy might remind us of his remarkable character.

A little-known, even somewhat mysterious part of Jeremy's life was connected with Yugoslavia. Without wishing in the slightest to be indiscreet, I would like to make a small contribution for the biography of Jeremy Griffiths, to say a few words that will shed more light on his rich and, sadly, all too short life. Also, I wish to relate several anecdotes and in that way I hope to add to Jeremy's bibliography of uncompleted works and projects.

The fact is that, among foreign lands, Yugoslavia was the one where Jeremy travelled most during the last six years of his life. He spent more time there than in any other foreign country, even more time than in the Virgin Islands. Jeremy Griffiths' first trip in Yugoslavia began during the war in Croatia, one of Yugoslavia's six republics. It was at that time that he wrote an article for *The Independent*, which this newspaper was very eager to publish on two pages of its Sunday edition.

As a man guided by curiosity, but also fairness, Jeremy Griffiths wished to obtain a full picture of the Yugoslav conflict, to follow up his Croatian trip by going to the other side. He took the decision to visit Serbia. It was then that he and I met in Belgrade. While he was there, he wrote another article, on the same subject-matter, but written from the Serb side of the battlefield. I am, alas, one of the very few persons to have ever read the article. Even though, compared with the previous one, it was no less honest, responsible, eloquent, inspired as well as professional (for Jeremy had precisely all these qualities), the article was never published. First *The Independent*, and later *The Guardian*, refused to print it.

As is often the case when events bring people together, Jeremy and I met and established a rapport. The first days of our friendship were spent on the article Jeremy was writing, but also in many hours of talk. I realized almost immediately, within minutes of our first conversation, that before me was a man with a wealth of unrestrained abilities, abilities which touched each other, complemented each other, and overtook each other. He required an interpreter, a guide to take him to the field of battle, he needed contacts with various officials for interviews, a brief analysis of Yugoslav wines, and Glagolitic and Bene-ventan manuscripts; and so on. At the end of his first visit he left with a pile of rarities in exchange for his business card.

A mere ten days later Jeremy returned to Belgrade.

Thus began our six-year-long friendship over which no shadows ever fell, a friendship during which many mutual visits and countless telephone conver-sations took place, and joint projects and plans took shape. I can say, without any exaggeration, that for me this was a time of deep meaning, and also of good omens, something that a terrible fate cut short.

Despite the lack of success of his previous war article, Jeremy was restless. His persistence and thoroughness and a deep interest in Yugoslavia made sure of that. Three years later he decided to go to Bosnia, to Republika Srpska. I was aware of the conditions and dangers of such a trip, not least because I myself was in the 1980s a war correspondent in El Salvador, and I thus knew the hazards of war journalism. So I tried to dissuade him from embarking on such a journey. But my effort was in vain. As he would not give up, I reluctantly made preparations for the trip, deciding to accompany him. Jeremy, however, eventually postponed the departure date because of commitments elsewhere. In the meantime, the war in Bosnia was coming to an end.

Only a few months before his illness, Jeremy told me that he had just begun to write a novel about, he said, and I quote him, 'a Briton who arrives in Yugo-slavia as a journalist and experiences a self-discovery'.

Let me now turn to Jeremy's last trip to Yugoslavia, and also say a few words about manuscripts and unfinished projects. The plan for Jeremy's longest and, as it turned out, last visit to Yugoslavia was a tour of Serb medieval monasteries and a spot of pike fishing. However, as the weather conditions were very bad, events took a very different turn. Jeremy himself later described them and the atmosphere on the trip, as a compilation of three films: *Day After*, *The Name of the Rose*, and *Indiana Jones*.

After several days and many roadside adventures, we drove to Kotor, better known as Cattaro, the oldest town in present-day Yugoslavia. We carried two incunabula from Cattaro's first printer, intending to present them to the monks at Cattaro monastery for a swap. We were exceptionally well received, staying the night there. The librarian-monk was overwhelmed with joy on seeing the incunabula. In fact, they were the only two copies in the country, so we could ask for anything we wanted in exchange. In a library exceeding one hundred thousand volumes, we had to look for something appropriate. In a stormy night we sat in the library, going through the catalogue, expecting valuable old publications. But it was a small offprint from the 1970s that caught Jeremy's attention, published in Toronto, Canada. The author was Virginia Brown. Jeremy showed it to me, saying: 'I wonder what this thing is doing here.' We looked at each other meaningfully and the day after we asked the librarian whether there were any Beneventan leaves in the library. 'Of course,' he said, 'you can have them if you want.' We left the monastery with outstanding Beneventan leaves from the tenth century.

The next day we went to a beautiful small island in the Bay of Cattaro. Some call it the Queen of the Adriatic. It is in fact an artificial island, created in the seventeenth century through very hard and persistent work of the faithful. There we looked at the church treasury and the lapidarium, and then went for a walk. Next to the church was this huge stone table supported by two bent baroque figures, looking very strained by the load they carried. Jeremy said to me: 'Pedja, I think we have here a historic discovery, for this is not just a stone table, we are at this moment looking at the last remaining document about two greedy book dealers who are taking away the largest and the most valuable book in the world.' An argument then developed as to whether the book was printed or a manuscript. 'It makes no difference,' Jeremy said, 'in any case the book explains the secret of perpetuum mobile.'

Jeremy's sincere and passionate interest in the history of writing often inspired me to embark on near-impossible missions to find scarce letters (alphabets). He and I discussed, among other matters, the so-called 'Culture of Vinca', a five-thousand-years-old culture in Serbia. A significant number, over thirty different signs have been discovered on pieces of Vinca pottery, and a controversy exists as to whether those signs are letters or not. This came after Jeremy had found a small piece of metal, of uncertain origin, which had nothing except one or two little scratches. We called this 'a very rare example of a manuscript with invisible alphabet'.

When, as a result of a major effort, I secured a small piece of pottery from the Vinca Culture which displayed the sign of the cross, I proudly showed it to Jeremy, keeping in mind his small piece of metal of which he was so proud. He carefully examined my little ceramic piece and then said: 'Pedja, I believe you have not understood the problem. A small cross does not mean a great deal, but it would be magnificent if we had two small crosses.'

On another occasion he and I were debating the value of an incunabulum which had damage to the first page. I tried to moderate his view about the damage in relation to the value of the incunabulum. Jeremy then took pen and paper, saying: 'Hold it, I have to write down this most interesting thesis.' And he wrote it, and I quote what he wrote: 'Treat loss of first page as no problem. Front page is just like any other.' He told me: 'I shall consult some of my colleagues before I study and publish a work about this problem.'

Before I relate the next anecdote, I wish to draw attention to one of Jeremy's, in fact two, important but uncompleted projects. Namely, Jeremy had begun work on a dictionary with the working title of *Names of Places in Imprints*. After a while the idea occurred to him that he should perhaps also, though he was not quite sure, do a dictionary of all Latin place-names in Europe. Greatly respecting his work, at his suggestion I prepared that part of the dictionary that covered the Yugoslav region. Although Jeremy had asked only for names of places in imprints, I sent him at the same time Latin place-names because of his related project. He called me immediately when he received my manuscript, feigning anger: 'Listen, it is not fair of you to so meticulously do your part of the job and leave me to cope with the rest of the world. In fact, you could have done just one of the two subjects.' I asked which one. 'That is a good question,' he said, laughing.

I telephoned Jeremy several days after he had returned from his second operation, but I got only an answer machine. I left him a message to call me back. No return call came, however, although I was convinced Jeremy was at home. In order to entice him, I left the same message the following day, but I added these words: 'Jeremy, I have in front of me a Coptic manuscript from the second century B.C., and I simply have no idea what to do with it.' Just as I was imagining the expression on his face on receiving this message, the telephone rang. It was Jeremy. He said: 'Your friend is all ears, I have been transformed into one big ear. Tell me what the damn thing looks like!'

As well as his many professional talents, his most important human talent was to see humour in life. If I had to describe the time I spent with Jeremy Griffiths in just one sentence, I would say: 'He was the man with whom, in my life, I laughed most.' For that, in gratitude, I wish to say before all of you, 'Thank you, Jeremy.' But this gratitude will not be limited to spoken words. Jeremy's name will be noted in Serbia. I am currently working on a book, a very large monograph on engravings by European artists depicting Belgrade, from the sixteenth to the nineteenth centuries. The book will be published in Serbian and English languages, and it will be dedicated to Jeremy. The dedication will read: 'To Jeremy Griffiths, whose light is shining brightly.'

INTRODUCTION

Ralph Hanna

Jeremy's memorial service, with its centre-piece Vincent Gillespie's moving eulogy, occurred in St John's College Chapel late in the afternoon of Saturday, 8 November 1997. After an evening of reminiscence in Headington, organised by Linda L. Brownrigg and Kathleen Scott, we devoted the following day to remembering Jeremy in the way we most admired him, as a manuscript scholar. Brownrigg arranged a special convocation of 'The Oxford Seminar in the History of the Book to 1500', an organization of which Jeremy had been a founding and active member. We returned, at a Sunday hour our honorand would undoubtedly have found obscenely early, to St John's, which had meant so much to him, to talk about medieval English manuscripts. The following papers are developments from that occasion, supplemented with contributions from those precluded by time and distance from attending.

The essays, as the contributors below indicate in a variety of ways, have a single, yet diffracted focus. All of us write to issues in which we have been stimulated by our contact (and often our collaboration) with Jeremy. Any apparent lack of focus thus may be taken as deliberate, a testimony to the diversity of Jeremy's interests and the breadth of his understanding of what is involved in dealing with medieval manuscripts. The essays address a range of topics from the tiny (identification of scribal hands) to the grandiose (the status of the author in medieval English manuscripts).

One presentation from the November 1997 conference appears above. Always the consummate juggler, Jeremy, near the end of his life, went to Yugoslavia as a correspondent for *The Independent* – and ended up in the book trade again. In the course of his search for what was happening in the splintered republics, Jeremy made the acquaintance of a Belgrade book-dealer, Pedrag Milovanovic. Pedrag's account of the relationship, 'Travels with Jeremy', introduces us to a news correspondent equally invested in extensive searches for books in Glagolitic hands, often in long-unvisited Bosnian monasteries.

Jeremy was always a keen student of scribal hands. Indeed, much of his reputation – and the awe he inspired in many of us – rested on his immense skill in this area. For someone so young, he had handled an immense number of medieval books, many in situations of non-public availability – his ability to cajole the often reluctant 'rich and famous', e.g. the Wemyses of Wemys Castle, to allow him access to their usually closed collections was legendary. Moreover, his visual memory was incredibly acute. Jeremy collected (and was continually expanding) a file of English scribes whose hand is found in more than one manuscript. Inevitably incomplete, this remains an archive of almost legendary proportions, containing, for example, lists of fifty-odd genealogical rolls in a single London hand of *c.* 1480 or of twenty-five manuscripts of the *Statutes of the Realm* copied by one individual *c.* 1470-95 (the latter the subject of a chapter in Jeremy's as yet unpublished dissertation). It is thus no accident that several of us contribute papers on this issue.

Linne Mooney, now engaged in a book-length project on the status of scribes whose hand appears more than once, began the piece here published in full collaboration with Jeremy. Indeed, he first recognized the hand as being that of the prolific 'Hammond scribe', an important late-fifteenth-century inheritor of John Shirley archetypes, yet far from limited to Shirleyan topics in his copying. Mooney finds this figure at work in the arena of heraldry, a far cry from the Chaucerian and Lydgatian work which generally stirred interest in him.

Ian Doyle reveals a second book – or its fragments – by a culturally important scribe, heretofore known in but a single volume. This person copied a deviant and immensely interesting *Piers Plowman B* in Oxford, Corpus Christi College, MS 201 (now available in full CD/ROM facsimile). Doyle, a meticulous investigator of libraries, now identifies him with two bits of the first folio of a *Prick of Conscience* long ignored in a relatively obscure collection, Ushaw College. That the scribe's second book, like the first, is illustrated is a further matter of interest here.

Jeremy's unsubmitted thesis, among many other moments of brilliance, is particularly interested in mise-en-page. He routinely addresses questions like: 'How did scribes present texts? How did they they handle supertextual details, e.g. Gower's Latin glosses? What governed the choices they made?' Important to Jeremy's intervention in this issue was his sense that scribes frequently responded to and transmitted, not just textual detail, but the presentation forms of their exemplars. Thus, he was keen to suggest that, since all exemplars must at some level go back to an authorial copy, features of authorial textual presentation survive in some scribal books.

Stephen Partridge takes up this challenge in the most provocative of circumstances, the canonical text of Chaucer's *Canterbury Tales*. With a painstakingness Jeremy would surely have admired (and for which he as tutor and friend is partly responsible), Partridge develops evidence of the 'relative completeness' of two 'unfinished' *Canterbury Tales*. And he offers a surprising hypothesis thoroughly in keeping with arguments Jeremy made about, for example, the *Troilus* of Cambridge, St John's College, MS L.1.

As my various comments indicate, central to Jeremy's thesis are manuscripts of Chaucer and Gower. He was constantly intrigued by both authors and the vicissitudes which accompanied the production of their works. One development closely associated with the dissertation was Jeremy's collaboration (he was the most sociable of colleagues) with Kate Harris and Derek Pearsall on a 'descriptive catalogue' of Gower manuscripts. Like many of his projects, this has yet to reach completion.

Pearsall's contribution here promises that such will not be the case for much longer. The surviving collaborators will work to bring the project to conclusion. Pearsall announces this intention in a discussion of a heretofore undescribed *Confessio*, the lavish copy in London, British Library, MS Harley 3490. And this book generates further discussion on subjects Jeremy would have appreciated (see below), an important late-fifteenth-century book-collector and a widely dispersed atelier of illuminators.

Other essays here illuminate further issues associated with Chaucer and Gower. Tony Edwards reflects on an issue precocious at the time and central to the writing of both, the possibility of vernacular authori(ali)ty. Edwards examines book evidence to discover the extent to which fifteenth-century producers thought in terms of poems originating in authorial presences. And the current master of both Chaucer's text and Caxton's printing, Norman Blake, re-examines this conjunction of 'father'-figures. Just what did Caxton do when he revised his first edition of *The Canterbury Tales*?

Perhaps one reason why such a small proportion of Jeremy's active and extensive research achieved published form was a penchant for enthusiasm. Jeremy could become thoroughly captivated by problems less rigorous (and more task-centred) souls might well have let pass – or left as notes to themselves for a future study, while they concentrated on the job in hand. Yet these enthusiasms, digressions in terms of projects announced, were enormously productive and have gone far to stimulate others, as the present volume will attest.

One such enthusiasm was an interest in book provenance. In certain respects, this may have begun as a kind of financial necessity. When Jeremy set up as a book-dealer, he went about the task of acquiring stock with a rigour his mentor Malcolm Parkes would have admired. Jeremy went through every private collection described in the appendixes of *Historical Manuscripts Commission* volumes and noted every book he could not identify with a volume which had entered a public collection as the result of a subsequent sale. He then went off to Somerset House and traced the descent of estates (and with them, libraries) from the late Victorian moment documented in HMC to the 1980s. Contact with modern heirs, often several generations along, led to private treaties and to release to Jeremy's clientele of important volumes long out of scholarly ken. The 'Louth Chronicle' (the subject of Jeremy's fine, as yet unpublished, presentation at the 1991 York conference honouring Ian Doyle) and the 'Holloway fragment' of *Piers Plowman C* are two fruits of this book-trade enterprise.

But Jeremy loved hunting provenances, far more than simple commercial considerations demanded. In his thesis, for example, he wrote very nearly as much about the fate of his *Statute* scribe's books, their later ownership and descent, as he did about the codicology of selected volumes. And, as this collection demonstrates, this enthusiasm certainly influenced those who knew him best and who write in his honour here.

Fully a third of our essays fall squarely in this area of study. Julia Boffey inflects an interest in books associated with an individual, whether patron or author, with considerations of genre, 'the household book'. In the process, she reveals a great deal about the Sinclairs, patrons of Oxford, Bodleian Library, MS Arch. Selden. B.24, and their interests. In contrast, Ralph Hanna attempts to open a literary history predicated on professional affiliation. Here the generally unrecognized efforts of Austin Canons and their adherents appear as a rambunctious set of thoroughly diverse productions, extending well beyond what might be construed predictable interests in parochial literature and history.

The three remaining essays address provenance through the productive topic of library history. Vincent Gillespie, in the process of editing the sixteenth-century Syon Abbey catalogue for the 'Corpus of British Medieval Library Catalogues', considers what history might be constructed from its entries. He innovatively considers the catalogue, not just as record of acquisition or reading, but as potentially revelatory of Syon literary activity. Andrew Watson, master of the genre, reveals another sixteenth-century collector, Robert Hare, through a survey of his surviving books, both print and manuscript. And Kate Harris, the Longleat librarian and engaged in a catalogue and history of the medieval manuscripts in the collection, reveals a Jeremy-like meticulousness in her archivally based reconstruction of activities in the Longleat library during the 1710s.

Another of Jeremy's fascinations remains rather covert in the published work. Only his essay on the illustrations to *Confessio amantis* would reveal to the outer world that he was a sucker for any book with pictures. Indeed, work on his catalogues for St John's College, Oxford and for Christ Church bogged down almost at the gate, since Jeremy chose first to describe selected illuminated books, and he found himself utterly mesmerised by them. His meticulous work with, for example, St John's, MS 94 (John Lacy O.P. of Newcastle's Hours, the subject of a fine unpublished paper) or Christ Church, MS 101 (Thomas Wolsey's lectionary) consumed long hours and prevented him from moving through the collections with the speed he had initially envisaged.

Two essays here, one initially intended as a full collaboration with Jeremy, address these interests. Christopher de Hamel, a master of fragments, takes up pieces of a book which once passed through the hands of the great fourteenth-century connoisseurs of illumination, the Bohuns. Kathleen Scott, who had planned to publish her paper in concert with our honorand, describes and places the artistic programme of the so-called 'Luton guild book', an important and revealing work of the early sixteenth century.

Our volume, regrettably, does not include one piece we should have liked to publish, from a potential contributor who could not be present at the November 1997 seminar. Jeremy's long-time friend, the professor/collector Toshiyuki Takamiya, has been unable to provide the contribution we had hoped for, 'Hilton's *Mixed Life* in the Hopton Hall MS' (sold Sotheby's, 5 December 1989, lot 89; now at Takamiya's home university, Keio in Tokyo). Even in the absence of a paper, he has remained, however, an important contributor to the volume. His generous subvention has allowed us to illustrate essays appropriately, a further fitting memorial to Jeremy Griffiths.

A NEW BOHUN

Christopher de Hamel

Jeremy Griffiths had an endearing habit, which we all share, more or less, of promising a publication with enthusiasm and then moving so rapidly on to the next project that the earlier commitment was somehow never quite finished. I myself can certainly outmatch Jeremy in this practice. What follows is a note on an unknown Bohun manuscript which I found in 1990. Jeremy convinced me to write it up for *English Manuscript Studies*, and of course I willingly agreed and did nothing. But it gets worse. I showed the manuscript at that time to Lynda Dennison and to Nicholas Rogers, both of whom generously sent me very extensive notes for my projected article (information I could never have discovered myself), and yet I still did nothing. This final piece owes most of its actual information to the kindness of both those scholars, especially Dr Dennison, and should really appear under joint names or, in greater detail, under hers alone.

The manuscript now belongs to the private library of an English medieval castle. It is a small octavo, 193 leaves, 153 mm × 93 mm, in rather battered London panel-stamped binding of the early sixteenth century, attributable to the stationer, Julian Notary.[1] The volume is formed from parts of two books bound together. 109 of the leaves are fifteenth-century; and 84 leaves are from the fourteenth century. Both parts are certainly English. The core of the volume (fols 3-111) comprises a Sarum Book of Hours, with the Office of the Virgin, Penitential Psalms and Litany, the Office of the Dead, the Commendation of Souls, and other prayers. So far this is all relatively straightforward. It becomes slightly more unusual as it then continues with a Calendar with astronomical information and tables made out for the years 1430-1462, a table of eclipses, a rather fine moving volvelle showing the phases of the moon and the signs of the zodiac, a drawing of the astronomical man, and other astrological notes. The style of illumination is entirely consistent with the dates on the tables, and these 109 leaves are English work of around 1430.

The first two leaves, however, and the 82 leaves at the end are from a very much finer and more beautiful manuscript, written on thin and high-quality parchment. The script is in 23 lines of a very compressed gothic hand in brown ink, within a tall and narrow written-space of 95 mm × 46 mm. The leaves form only a portion of an earlier manuscript and are neither quite complete nor all bound in their original order. The first bifolium is folded back to front, and once opened with the present fol. 2, including a half-page miniature of the Betrayal of Christ, for Matins in the Hours of the Cross (Pl. 1). The leaves also include approximately two hundred large 3-line illuminated initials of excellent quality in soft colours and delicately tooled burnished gold. Eight of these include coats of arms, and herein lies the fascination.

The arms occur in the following order. Those on fol. 2^v and again on fol. 111^r (*gules, 3 lions passant guardant or*) are the royal arms of England before 1340. They doubtless represent Edward I, king of England 1272-1307. His daughter, Princess Elizabeth (1282-1316), married Humphrey de Bohun (*c.* 1276-1322), fourth earl of Hereford and Essex, in 1302. The second coat of arms is on fol. 108^r, also royal: *azure, a semé of fleurs-de-lys or and gules, 3 lions passant guardant or, quarterly*. This quartering with the fleurs-de-lys occurs in the royal arms after Edward III had laid claim to France in 1340. The arms are, in fact, shown in reverse, as if at this time the formula was still not entirely familiar. Edward III was first cousin to all three main members of the Bohun family when our manuscript was made: Humphrey de Bohun (sixth earl of Hereford, d. 1361) and his two sisters Eleanor (d. 1363) and Margaret (d. 1391). Two identical coats-of-arms follow on fol. 112^r: *azure, a bend argent between 2 cotises and 6 lions rampant or*. These are actually the arms of the Bohun family itself, shown twice. The double appearance presumably represents both Humphrey de Bohun (fourth earl, d. 1322) and his younger surviving son Humphrey (sixth earl, d. 1361). Then follow his sisters. The arms at the top of fol. 113^v are *or, a chief indented azure*. These are the arms of the Butlers, earls of Ormond. In 1327 Eleanor de Bohun had married James Butler, Earl of Ormond (d. 1338). The arms below are *or, 3 torteaux, a label of 3 points azure*. These are Courtenay, earls of Devon. In 1325 Margaret de Bohun had married Hugh de Courtenay, earl of Devon (d. 1377). The final coat of arms here is smudged (fol. 114^r), but includes *argent, a chevron gules*. The overall evidence is completely clear. The manuscript was made for the family of Humphrey de Bohun, who died unmarried in 1361, and his two sisters. It shows all their arms (after 1327), and those of their father, grandfather, and first cousin (after 1340). It may have been made for the personal use of one of them, or as a gift from the family to someone else.

It needs no emphasis here that the Bohun family patronage of manuscripts was by far the most important and intriguing of fourteenth-century England.[2] The Bohun manuscripts have traditionally been divided into two principal groups, those associated with Humphrey de Bohun, towards the middle of the fourteenth century, and those from the circle of Mary de Bohun (d. 1394) around the time of her marriage to Henry Bolingbroke, the future Henry IV, in 1380. The present manuscript is a new addition to the earlier group, which includes Vienna, Österreichische Nationalbibliothek, Cod.1826*, London,

British Library, MS Egerton 3277, and the first campaigns in Oxford, Exeter College, MS 47. All the coats of arms in the new manuscript occur also in these three books, and in the Bohun Psalter in Vienna the arms of Edward III are similarly and wrongly painted back-to-front.[3]

I now rely especially on the advice of Dr Dennison. She tells me that the illuminator of the new manuscript is almost certainly the painter she calls 'Hand A' of the Bohun Psalter in Vienna. As she has shown elsewhere, the same illuminator contributed to two other manuscript Psalters, Bodleian Library, MS Douce 131, and Brescia, Biblioteca Queriniana, cod.A.V.17, and he illuminated a charter dated 1343 now in Cambridge University Archives, Luard *33a.[4] She dates the whole group of manuscripts to the 1340s, just before the Black Death. For various reasons, including the fact that the charter concerns the chancellor of Cambridge University, she suggests that the artist may have worked in Cambridge.

The Bohun portion of the new manuscript is only a fragment. It includes the opening of the Hours of the Cross, and was doubtless part of a complex Book of Hours rather than simply a Psalter. Several of the other Bohun manuscripts survive as fragments, including pieces now in Copenhagen, Pommersfelden and Lichtenthal.[5] The present book has 23 lines of text: so do the Vienna and imperfect Exeter College manuscripts, but the dimensions are not the same. The script, however, extremely closely resembles that of the Vienna book, and might be the work of the same scribe working on a smaller scale.

Vienna Cod.1826* includes prayers originally made out for use by a male petitioner called Humphrey. Before it was modified, the new Bohun had some prayers for use by a woman but in general form, with the user's name generically as 'N', e.g. 'da michi N. famula tua victoriam' (fol. 123^r). There are prayers for use in childbirth (fol. 115^r). Many prayers and rubrics are in French, a feature which occurs commonly (though by no means universally) in books for use by women. One prayer has a note that it was composed by the pope in 1330 (fol. 180^v); the arms of Edward III, however, date the book to not earlier than 1340. If the prayer for use in childbirth is anything more than a standard inclusion, the book was not made for Humphrey, the sixth earl (d. 1361), who never married, or for his sister Eleanor, whose husband had died in 1338, but might have been appropriate for their sister Margaret, whose husband lived until 1377, having given her eight sons and nine daughters. Childbirth certainly figured in that household.

Very briefly, the text here comprises: the end of a suffrage to St Julian (fol. 2^r); the Hours of the Cross (fol. 2^v), preceded by an offer of one year and 40 days' indulgence promised by John XXII (pope 1316-34); prayers on the Passion and Wounds of Christ (fol. 112^r); a prayer in French 'Aorrez soiez nous seinte crois ...' (fol. 115^r), preceded by a note that the Virgin gave the prayer to a holy man with advice that whoever says it three times a day will not die unconfessed and that a woman who uses it five times during childbirth will deliver her child safely; other prayers, including suffrages to St Christopher

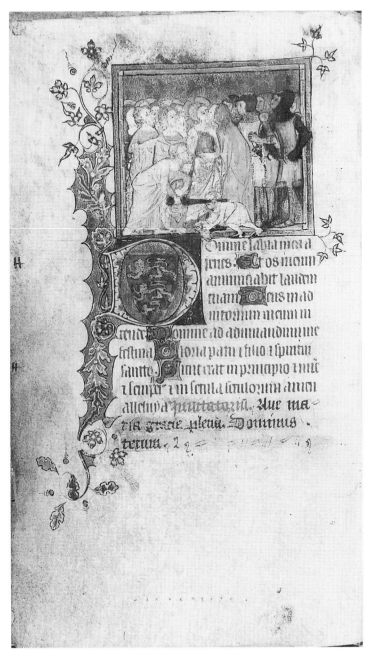

Pl. 1. Psalter, England, s. xiv-xv.

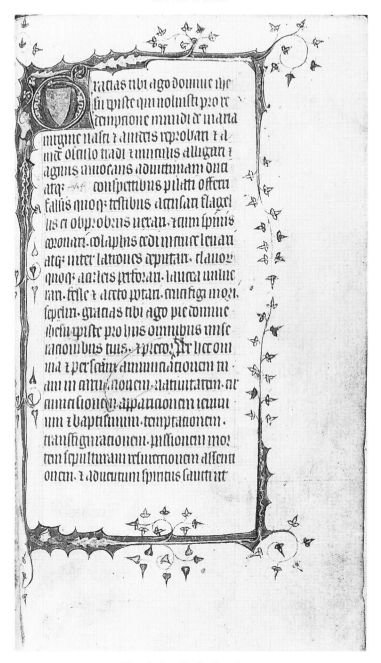

Pl. 2. Psalter, England, s. xiv-xv.

(fol. 117ʳ); a prayer 'Deus misereatur nostri ...' (fol. 121ᵛ), preceded by a long rubric explaining its use before going on a journey, '*et quant vous alez devant Roy, Prince, Comite ou baron ou devant ascun autre home si troveres honour*', or at sea; a prayer to the Virgin, 'Mater digna dei ...' (fol. 123ᵛ), preceded by a rubric saying it helped a very ill cleric in Aragon who by use of the prayer was able to confess before his death, '*& fu cel miracle provee a loundres*'; a prayer ascribed to St Anselm (fol. 224ʳ); a reading from St John's Gospel (fol. 225ʳ) and prayers to St John; many prayers on the Cross and the Passion, including one sent by Pope Leo to King Charles of France to prevent death by snake bite or ship-wreck (fol. 130ʳ); the Psalter of St Jerome (fol. 137ᵛ), useful for those at sea or during time of war; prayers to the Virgin and to God, including 'Beau sire deus si verraiment cum vous preistes char de la virgine marie ...' (fol. 151ᵛ), attributed to Pope Innocent; astrological explanations of each of the 30 phases of the moon, in two long cycles ('Leiur de la primiere lune a totes fesances est profitable ...', fol. 152ʳ, and 'La primiere lune est covenable totes choses de comencer ...', fol. 162ʳ), with extensive advice on predicting deaths and avoiding dangerous undertakings during the various months of the year and days of the week, and such advice as '*Coment poet home savoir si un home moroit avant un autre*' (fol. 172ʳ) and human characteristics compared with those of animals – bold as a lion, handsome as a tiger, noble as an elephant, etc. (fol. 174ʳ); the Litany of the Virgin (fol. 175ʳ); the Gospel Sequences (fol. 178ʳ); a prayer 'Salve ihesu xpiste qui te sub panis ...' (fol. 180ᵛ), which pope John XXII composed in the year of grace 1330, and other prayers including the *O intemerata*, also ascribed to John XXII (fol. 182ᵛ); and the Gradual Psalms (120 to 133) (fol. 185ʳ).

The Bohun family manuscripts were evidently dispersed early in their history, and at least three were sold from the estate of Humphrey, the sixth earl, in 1362.[6] The Bohun castle was at Pleshy, in Essex. The new manuscript left the possession of the family, but it evidently did not move far. A portion of it was still in circulation eighty years later, and was evidently judged sufficiently interesting or beautiful to be worth preserving as a component of a new book. The first bifolium was folded back to front, and its last lines were rewritten so that it joins up exactly (and correctly) with the *Venite* in the new text of Matins from fol. 3ʳ. By this means the artist has given himself a ready-made opening miniature. The fifteenth-century portion is also emblazoned with coats of arms in the opening initials of each of the Hours of the Virgin from Lauds onwards, all with the charge *gules, 3 chevrons argent*, crossed in each case with the arms of other families. The principal arms in every large initial are those of the family of Baud, of Corringham, Essex, and of Little Hadham, over the border in adjacent Hertfordshire. I owe this identification entirely to Mr Nicholas Rogers, who suggests that the new patrons might well have been Thomas Baud, who died in 1449, and his wife Margery.[7] They lived mainly at Little Hadham. The church there is dedicated to St Cecilia and the principal manor of Little Hadham belonged to the bishops of Ely.[8] The very short section of

Suffrages included in Lauds ends with St Etheldreda, patron saint of Ely (fol. 17^v), and St Cecilia (fol. 18^r). The last two names in the Litany are SS Cecilia and Etheldreda (fol. 43v).

NOTES

1 Cf. J. B. Oldham, *Blind Panels of English Binders* (Cambridge, 1958), p. 34; with his RO.13 on the upper cover and HE.30 on the lower cover (pls. XXXIX and XXII).

2 See esp. M. R. James & E. G. Millar, *The Bohun Manuscripts, A Group of Five Manuscripts Executed in England about 1370 for Members of the Bohun Family* (Oxford, Roxburghe Club, 1936); L. F. Sandler, 'A Note on the Illuminators of the Bohun Manuscripts', *Speculum*, 60 (1985), 364-72; L. F. Sandler, *Gothic Manuscripts, 1285-1385*, II (London, 1986) (*A Survey of Manuscripts Illuminated in the British Isles*, V), esp. nos 133-8, pp. 147-59; *Age of Chivalry, Art in Plantagenet England 1200-1400*, ed. by J. J. G. Alexander & P. Binski (London, 1987), esp. nos 686-9, pp. 501-3; and L. E. Dennison, 'The Stylistic Sources, Dating and Development of the Bohun Workshop, ca. 1340-1400', unpublished PhD thesis, University of London (1988). Dr Dennison's work involves redating some of the Bohun manuscripts, as in her thesis, appendix VII (iii), pp. 341-3, which will be published in her 'Egerton MS 3277: A Fourteenth-Century Psalter-Hours and the Question of Bohun Family Ownership', *Family and Dynasty in the Middle Ages, Proceedings of the 1997 Harlaxton Symposium*, ed. R. Eales (Stamford, forthcoming). Dr Dennison's endless patience in furnishing me with information has become almost as great an embarrassment as my failure to deliver the article to Jeremy. I am much in her debt. For the genealogy of the Bohun family, cf. G. E. C[okayne], *The Complete Peerage*, 13 vols in 12 (London: St Catherines, 1910-89), esp. VI, pp. 467-72.

3 Cf. esp. Dennison, 'Stylistic Sources', appendix X, pp. 362-70.

4 L. E. Dennison, '"*The Fitzwarin Psalter and its Allies*": a Reappraisal', in *England in the Fourteenth Century, Proceedings of the 1985 Harlaxton Symposium*, ed. by M. Ormrod (Woodbridge, 1985), pp. 42-66, esp. pp. 49-56.

5 It may be that all three were once part of the same book, disassembled, like the present manuscript, at an early date (cf. F. Heinzer, 'Un témoin inconnu des *Bohun manuscrits*': le ms.2 des archives de l'abbaye de Lichtenthal', *Scriptorium*, 43 (1989), pp. 259-66).

6 Sandler, 'Bohun Manuscripts', p. 366.

7 He refers me to W. Minet, 'The Baud Family of Corryngham and Hadham Parva', *Transactions of the Essex Archaeological Society*, n.s., 10, iii (1907), 165; and J. Foster, *Some Feudal Coats of Arms* (London, 1901, reprinted Bristol, 1984), p. 15.

8 V.C.H., *Hertfordshire*, IV (London, 1914), pp. 53-4; this reference too I owe to Mr Rogers.

AUGUSTINIAN CANONS AND MIDDLE ENGLISH LITERATURE

Ralph Hanna

THIS PRELIMINARY ASSAY deviates from manuscript studies per se to matters of general ecclesiastical and literary history. Yet my topic is peculiarly appropriate to this occasion. In our last conversation in March 1997, Jeremy and I chatted about Augustinian canons and their books; he directed me to his fine note, in which he assesses the evidence that a *Canterbury Tales* manuscript copied by John Brode belonged to the house of Augustinian canons at Plympton, Devonshire.[1] And of course, Jeremy the bookseller was an acute student of provenances; few of us have made such profitable use of Somerset House in tracing the dispersal of books – including, as I'll mention, a couple of volumes with Augustinian associations.

My proposition is this: past study of later medieval English literature, however profitably, has concentrated far too narrowly on the activities of one religious order. Following Ian Doyle's foundational dissertation, scholars have focused on the Carthusians and their relationships, mainly as instructors in practical contemplation, with those I can describe only as the posh and power-ful.[2] But the study of English regular clergy and vernacular writing might well be more broadly directed: I here join a developing, but still very nascent, group of voices urging a reassessment of the religious orders and vernacular com-position by assembling evidence for the large vernacular literary involvement of that order with the most houses in England, the Augustinian or black canons.

I take the term 'Augustinian' in its usual, although broad, acceptation. It includes not simply the main order but two small groups which followed the so-called 'rule of St Augustine' – the community of Arrouaise, with houses concentrated in Lincoln diocese and including Bourne (Lincolnshire) and Lilleshall (Shropshire); and the Victorines, with a few foundations, in the main around the Severn, represented by St Augustine's, Bristol, and Wigmore (Herefordshire). These small groups lost any connection with the French mother houses of their order after 1215, and their patterns of life became indistinguishable from the highly localized uses of other Augustinian houses – although they did not, until 1518, attend the general provincial councils of the order. But with one obvious exception, I exclude from my study Gilbertine canons and the white canons, the order of Premontré.[3] I also ignore the unrelated order of Austin Friars (O.E.S.A.) and with it authors like John Capgrave, William Flete, and John Waldeby.

As I suggest, I have been preceded in this area – by Thomas Heffernan, Helen Spencer, and now especially Teresa Webber.[4] My predecessors have concentrated their suggestions in one area, sermon studies or homiletics. In doing so, they have drawn attention to three important groups of texts, the cycle of readings put together by Ormm, a late-twelfth-century Arrouasian from Bourne; the anonymous Yorkshire *Northern Homily Cycle*, identified as Augustinian by its gospel pericopes; and the *Festial* of John Mirk, prior of Lilleshall toward 1390 – the last two texts of considerable diffusion.[5]

Because of the nature of Augustinian foundations, sermon materials are a promising place to look for texts associated with the order. Although in a general way 'monastic', canons routinely had an extramural service commitment; originally part of a bishop's *familia*, they served churches and administered hospitals.[6] Available statistics about Augustinian endowments indicate a continuing heavy dependence on income from parish churches appropriated to individual houses: the 1535 *Valor ecclesiasticus* showed that 36 per cent of Augustinian income came from spiritualities, while the figure for all monastic establishments (swelled by the *inclusion* of the Augustinians) is but 19 per cent. On this basis, Augustinians were two to three times more likely to have nominal responsibility for the *cura animarum* than other regular clergy.[7]

These statistics reflect peculiarities of Augustinian history, both the nature of the institutions and ongoing problems of historical interpretation. Early foundations associated with Henry I's court were typically well funded (and usually developed into the largest and most influential priories). But thereafter, the initial endowment of Augustinian houses was heavily skewed in favour of income derived from dependent parish churches, usually ones fairly close to the house. At its foundation in 1143, for example, St Mary's in the Fields, Leicester, was bankrolled with the advowson of all the parish churches in the city.[8]

With this income came responsibilities, and it is a moot (and central) issue of Augustinian history how well the canons fulfilled these. Did they actually exercise parochial duties? Or were they indifferent possessioners who farmed their churches and lived off the tithes, while poorly paid vicars took care of the parishioners? From this vexed issue, there has frequently emerged an image of Augustinians as uninterested in things intellectual and spiritual, perhaps the most poorly regulated of late-medieval religious orders.[9]

But such criticisms may only draw attention to certain peculiar institutional norms. Founding a house of canons was easy and, consequently, a form of gentry piety 'on the cheap', the upwardly mobile could simply toss together a handful of advowsons as an endowment. As a result, a great many priories were chronically underfunded and incapable of any very sustained development, economic or intellectual.[10] Equally, many houses were very small, and even the largest would have found it difficult to serve continuously a great many churches. For constitutions of the order required that a canon resident at a church should have a *socius*, and at some point such dispersed pairs of canons would impair the priory's ability to perform its domestic ritual.[11]

Yet simultaneously one must admit that the surviving evidence for Augustinian Latin literary composition is at best sporadic, and most of it is early. Among the two thousand plus British Latin authors in Richard Sharpe's *Handlist*, only sixty-three were affiliated with the order. The Augustinians produced but a single major intellectual figure, indeed one who professed late, after a lengthy career in the schools, Alexander Nequam (d. 1217). But he did have contemporary colleagues, and Anne Lawrence's fine study of early Bridlington (East Yorkshire) book-production and library records indicates substantial enthusiasm for at least Robert 'scriba's biblical scholarship.[12]

On the other hand, the canons never really got their projected Oxford college off the ground. That institutional failure might, however, reflect the order's decentralization and concommitant tendencies to localism, as well as cost problems. And the failure might be balanced by a number of canons, small but substantial, known to have been Oxford scholars. Again, the surviving English register of Osney abbey may have been prepared because no one in the house could any longer deal with the original documents.[13]

Augustinian vernacular authors, while they may not show high learning of a university stripe, certainly express an educational interest belying many modern critiques. One might well interpret Augustinian preaching collections as one way of addressing constraints on the *cura animarum*. If the canons could not personally administer dependent parishes, they could do so by proxy, through books provided for the aid of the vicars who actually served. Certainly, Mirk's œuvre, which includes instructional materials for priests in both Latin and the vernacular, offers ample evidence for such an interest in improving clerical performance.[14]

Further, one can extend the list of Augustinian vernacular preachers. Two other figures, both associated with the Leicester house, have left extensive records of public performance. One, Philip Repingdon, survives for us only by report and in Latin representation; he preached two incendiarily Lollard sermons in spring 1382, both now lost, and later, probably preceding his successful career as abbot of Leicester and cardinal-bishop of Lincoln, achieved notoriety as a preacher more orthodox. His sermons survive in a form more extensive than he can have delivered them, possibly to serve as models or cribs for other preachers.

The second figure represents an anomalous category to which I'll return, the Augustinian hanger-on. William Swinderby 'heremita', a self-designated prophet and Lollard itinerant with a career which lasted more than a decade, was for some time a boarder at St Mary's; we actually know most about him from his trial before Bishop John Trefnant of Hereford in 1392.[15]

But preaching scarcely exhausts the Augustinian religious oeuvre. I merely mention the greatest English Augustinian author, Walter Hilton of Thurgarton (Nottinghamshire). Michael Sargent has demonstrated how his *Scala perfectionis* was transmitted under Carthusian auspices. But it also appears in one very important miscellany, ignored in Doyle's survey of monastic book production – the three volumes, originally one: British Library, Add. MS 10052 + Huntington Library, MS HM 112 + Add. MS 10053, certainly from Holy Trinity, Aldgate., London. And the Augustinian nuns of Campsey (Suffolk), whose surviving books indicate a heavy investment in vernacular materials, owned a copy of the *Scala*, now Cambridge, Corpus Christi College, MS 268.[16]

I will also mention only in passing *Ancrene Riwle* and its satellites, the 'Katherine Group' and 'Wohunge Group'. Perhaps the best evidence (other than linguistic) for taking seriously E. J. Dobson's arguments for composition at Wigmore is the early association of copies with Augustinian houses. Cambridge, Corpus Christi College, MS 402, of course, belonged to Wigmore (but was a donation of *c*. 1300).[17] British Library, Cotton MS, Cleopatra C.VI was donated by Matilda de Clare, refounder of the house, to the Augustinian nuns of Canonsleigh (Devon); as I'll show in a moment, the book contains corrections indicating a second copy of the work available there, as well as at least the transmission of vernacular sermons and *materia praedicandi*. R. M. Wilson thought Lambeth Palace MS 487, with one 'Wohunge Group' text at the end of late-twelfth-century homilies (part shared with Cambridge, Trinity College, MS B.14.52), apt to have been a Llanthony book, and a quotation from the *Riwle* appears in an early-fourteenth-century Latin rule from the Augustinian house in Dublin.[18] Of course, provenance and origins are not necessarily connected.

Late associations of the *Riwle* may suggest some further Augustinian activities. At Canonsleigh (thus post-1284), a scribe (Dobson's D) writing the language of western Norfolk not only corrected the text of the Cleopatra manuscript (including partial supply of missing materials) but filled blank spaces in the book with Middle English texts. These include three sets of verses (IMEV 1820, 1917, 2285), all mono-rhymes of a sort useful for sermon divisions, and a Middle English sermon (IPMEP 552). And he made roughly identical additions to another Canonsleigh book, Cambridge, Trinity College, MS B.1.45, fols 1-42 (omitting one set of verses and adding a note at the end of the prose). There was more blank space available to him in this volume, significantly Latin and Anglo-Norman sermons, however; the scribe had room for a further sermon (which takes as its text another lyric, the scrap 'At wrestling my lemman I ches', IPMEP 432). Another house scribe, in this case of south-west Midland origins, *c*. 1300, made brief Latin additions to Scribe D's additions, as well as providing, in the originally separate second part of the book (the 'Rule of St Augustine' with commentary), another bit of verse – the unique signs of death poem 'When my eyes mist' (IMEV 3998).[19]

A huge book, surprisingly ignored, Cambridge, Magdalene College, MS Pepys 2498, may belong linguistically at the site of a major Augustinian house, Waltham (Essex), suburban London. Its revised version of *Ancrene Riwle*, 'The Recluse', has been asserted to be Lollard, although the manuscript, dated by Neil Ker *c.* 1375, is probably too early to reflect Wycliffite influence. This volume is a central testimony to a pre-'Trinity Gower' London book production;[20] it communicates an extensive group of texts translated from Anglo-Norman of the previous century, all of them devoted to varying forms of biblical explanation. These include Robert of Gretham's *Mirror*, a sermon cycle derived from Gregory's homilies on the gospels; an Apocalypse with commentary; and a Psalter with commentary. This book contains also some short odds and ends, a unique diatesseron (in part fusing the ps.-Bonaventuran *Meditations* with a more conventional text), a gospel of Nicodemus, and the prose 'Complaint of our Lady'.[21]

The imponderable is to know how to ascribe this material. The scribe was clearly a professional: although Pepys 2498 is an extremely large book, the scribe found time to copy two other books. And works both within and outside Pepys 2498 may appear dissociated from Augustinian authorship: Bodleian Library, MS Laud Misc. 622 includes the romance *Alisaunder*, for example.

But one such work may represent no chance accretion. British Library, Add. MS 17136, in comparable London language, looks to be slightly older than Pepys (there's some evidence that the book might predate 1349). It shares with Pepys the glossed prose Psalter, but in a separate booklet the scribe also provides the unique copy of poems ascribed to a non-London figure, William of Shoreham, vicar of Chart (Kent). Shoreham was certainly not an Augustinian, but a secular; he had been appointed mass-priest to the nuns of Malling (Rochester diocese) on 3 May 1299. But the MS rubrics significantly describe his new parish as 'Chart iuxta Ledes'; when he was instituted (3 January 1320), Shoreham was designated vicar in an appropriated church – his patrons the Augustinian canons of Leeds.[22]

Shoreham's poems resemble what one would hope constituted the programme in a dutiful Augustinian parish. They are firmly instructional, versified introductions to those basic Christian concepts which Archbishop Pecham had enjoined every priest to teach his parishioners. Shoreham explains the sacraments, Pater Noster, decalogue, and Seven Deadly Sins, as well as providing a Marian lyric and an account of the fall and redemption. From the rubrics in the MS, one gathers that he died at Chart, *c.* 1327-33.

But Augustinian writing is far from limited to such religious subjects, and includes a heavy investment in historical and learned writing. This emphasis, of course, corresponds to the most outstanding Latin literary contributions of the order. Henry Knighton of Leicester would be the best-known example, but before the fourteenth century William of Newburgh and Walter of Guisborough, as well as the lesser-known John of Hexham and Thomas Wykes, had also compiled chronicles.[23] This emphasis continued in English texts. Leaving out of account for a moment Robert Manning, I would single out three works of extensive circulation, given usual Middle English patterns for productions of this type. In each case, however, such circulation probably represents the efforts of aristocratic patrons, rather than Augustinian authors.

To compose the alliterative *Siege of Jerusalem* would have required a library of a monastic stripe, including Josephus and Higden, for example. Its most recent editors believe the text reflects activities at Bolton (North Yorkshire) in the 1370s or early 1380s. Princeton University Library, MS Taylor Medieval 11 had a now illegible Bolton *ex libris*, and the only known copy of the poem's French source produced in England (Bodleian Library, MS Fairfax 24), also belonged to Bolton. With nine surviving copies, *The Siege* is the most widely dispersed alliterative poem excepting *Piers Plowman*; the editors consider this dispersal, which included the metropolis, probably the work of Bolton's (and the poem's) patrons, the Clifford earls of Skipton.[24]

Andrew of Wyntoun was prior of the Augustinian house, St Serf's or Portmoak in Loch Leven, Kinross, from 1395 until his death in 1424. Between 1407 and 1420, at the insistence of Sir John of Wemyss, he compiled the *Original*, a verse chronicle largely dependent on Peter Comestor. The poem, which occupies six fat STS volumes, survives in nine copies and a brief excerpt.[25] One of these, alas a scribal version of *c.* 1500, acquired a century after the Dissolution – it was in the library of the Augustinians of Cambuskenneth, near Stirling – still belongs to the family whose ancestor patronized Andrew, at Wemyss Castle – I think. For Jeremy Griffiths, the book-dealer/Schøyen scout, saw and photographed this book several years ago.

Wyntoun seems to have shared inferentially Augustinian-transmitted source materials with an even more prolific Scots historian. Between 1441 and 1447, Walter Bower, prior of Inchcolm (on another island, this one in the Firth), wrote an expansion/continuation of John of Fordun's *Chronica*, the *Scoti-chronicon*. Like Wyntoun, Bower was patronized by a laird, Sir David Stewart of Rosyth. Both a fair-copy with authorial corrections and a copy from it (datable 1471-2), also from Inchcolm, are among the surviving manuscripts.[26]

Bower is almost totally a Latin historian. But he delights in inserted verse effusions, and seven of these are in Scots. Perhaps predictably, the verses resemble those useful for sermon divisions; perhaps also predictably (Augustinians were, after all, Latinate clerics), the most extensive of these vernacular bits are concentrated within a clerical set piece, a revelation of women's deviance.[27]

Perhaps the most overtly learned of Augustinian authors remains only a name – and a work in twenty-three manuscript copies. According to colophons, in 1410 one 'capellanus Johannes' translated into English rime royal Boethius's *Consolation of Philosophy*, with chunks of Nicholas Trivet's commentary; he used Chaucer's prose as at least an initial basis.[28] The print edition produced in 1525 at the Benedictine press in Tavistock (Devon) includes acrostic verses extant in no manuscript; these identify John as John Walton of Osney (presumably from the modern Jericho, since the abbey held lands in then suburban Walton, Oxfordshire) and his sponsor as Elizabeth Berkeley-Beauchamp, the daughter of the great Gloucestershire patron and the wife of Richard Beauchamp, an earl of Warwick famed as 'the flower of English chivalry'. Jeremy also examined (and negotiated transit to Oslo of) an outstanding copy of this text, the quite handsome volume then owned by H. R. Pratt; in the late fifteenth century it belonged to Thomas Hyngham, the monk of Bury responsible for copying the Macro Plays.[29]

Finally, Augustinians were modestly invested in vernacular science. At least two canons left English works on alchemy, in one case quite extensive. Much of George Ripley of Bridlington's œuvre – he died in 1490 – probably survives only in Latin translation in continental books, but four English poetic works occur in eight to twenty-five copies each. The otherwise unknown John Snell of Wigmore is associated with two brief texts.[30]

From these secular writings I move to some rather anomalous activities which exhibit Augustinians in proximity to the *saeculum*, encouraging persons I would call 'Augustinian groupies'. Early local customaries indicate two categories of privileged long-term 'guests' in Augustinian houses. At Barnwell (Cambridgeshire) about 1200, the almonry did not simply dispense charity to a chosen number of the poor but also provided living space for 'permanent chaplains'. The priory also had a pension plan; 'stacionarii', elderly canons felt to be past chapel duties, were allowed to retire and live untroubled by themselves, apparently in the infirmary.[31]

This much would explain the position of the poet John Audelay, apparently put out to grass in his blind old age to serve a L'Estrange family chantry in Haghmond priory (Shropshire). His poems appear in a book which has attracted substantial recent interest, Bodleian Library, MS Douce 302. Audelay's relationship to the entire volume is moot, but he at least planned fols 1^r-22^v. These leaves demarcate a separate 'liber vocatu[s] concilium conciencie aut scala celi et vita salutis eterni'. And this collection is commended, not to Audelay's secular patrons, the L'Estranges, but his Augustinian hosts; the poems are described as prepared 'ad exemplum aliorum in monasterio de Haghmon'.[32] Whatever one should make of the remainder of the volume, this portion, dated 1426, forms an effort advanced and au courant – albeit in a different key, comparable with contemporary author anthologies like Hoccleve's autographs and with scribal anthologies devoted to 'authors' like Cambridge, University Library, MS Gg.iv.27 and British Library, Add. MS 16165.[33]

This last volume might have been produced in any variety of locales, but, as Jeremy indicated in a fine article synthesizing materials on his surviving books, John Shirley (1366-1456) was an Augustinian hanger-on of some type.[34] Augustinian regulations presuppose that priories might entertain visitors, not in some liminal area reserved for hospitality, but in the refectory, where they would share meals with the canons. And in practice, there's evidence for unprofessed guests as long-term 'boarders'. Moreover, Augustinian foundations in urban areas often were endowed with tenements and engaged in 'property management' to achieve a return on investment.[35] Shirley's renting shops from St Bartholomew's, Smithfield, London, exemplifies the second behaviour, but the evidence probably suggests a more intimate relationship.

Any assessment of Shirley at St Bartholomew's must explain details that extend well beyond merely being a lessee. First, Shirley owned Cambridge, Gonville and Caius College, MS 669*/666, copied by the most prolific identified Augustinian scribe, John Cock (fl. 1421-68). The contents of this volume merit some notice. They at least indicate Augustinian transmission, even if not actual production, of Middle English religious classics: Rolle's *Form of Living* and translations of his *Emendatio vitae* and the ps.-Bonaventuran *Meditationes passionis Christi*. But the translations here are not those common in Middle English, which might suggest the restricted circulation of texts produced within the order. The *Emendatio vitae* occurs elsewhere only in Edinburgh, University Library, MS 93, a book put together from a variety of (quite cosmopolitan) sources. And the Bonaventura translation is the mid-fourteenth-century Passion narrative, eventually driven out of circulation by the Carthusian Nicholas Love's more extensive representation of the source.[36] In addition to this book, as Jeremy pointed out, Cock also transcribed chunks of two St Bartholomew's cartularies.

But equally, Shirley's relationship with Cock may have exceeded anything simply professional. Along with the master of St Bartholomew's hospital, Cock was an executor of Shirley's will. Moreover, Shirley's work appears in certain respects – whatever else it may be – firmly Augustinian. For example, British Library, MS Harley 7333 is a huge Chaucerian miscellany probably copied at St Mary's in the Fields, Leicester – in part from Shirley archetypes; is it reasonable to assume that these were transmitted through ordinal, rather than general book-trade, channels?[37] And Shirley certainly produced his own 'original writings' while at St Bartholomew's. These three prose translations, communicated in a scribal copy, British Library, Add. MS 5467, were all probably compiled *c.* 1440 (the date in a colophon at fol. 97). To what extent might they – or Shirley's customarily 'clergial' rubrics – have influenced the florid translation of St Bartholomew's foundation documents composed toward 1500 and appended to the Latin originals in British Library, Cotton MS, Vespasian B.XI?[38]

Shirley and his enigmatic associations with St Bartholomew's may be paralleled in the careers of two other named authors. John Gower spent a substantial period as a tenant of the Augustinian priory of St Mary Overy in Southwark. Although the Macaulay-Fisher thesis that he frequented the house to use its library and scriptorium has been largely discredited by other explanations of apparent revisions in Gower manuscripts, Augustinian connections seem nonetheless worth pursuing. For example, a copy of Gower's *Chronica tripartita* appears in the extensive late-fifteenth-century library catalogue from Leicester, perhaps another case of transmission by ordinal channels.[39]

Similarly, John Harding the historian spent a substantial part of his writing career (after 1434) serving his Umfraville patrons as chastelain of Kyme (Lincolnshire). The locale probably included nothing very much more than the castle and the neighbouring Augustinian priory. Again, Harding's reliance on Latinate history of a sort likely to be found in an Augustinian house suggests possible links between order and author.[40]

Passing beyond such direct attestations to Augustinian authors, a trio of works has some possible, although uncertain claim, to Augustinian authorship. One might be associated with Leicester, again: the verse 'Prick of Love', a translation of Edmund Rich's *Speculum ecclesie*, has an enthusiastic reference to Henry, duke of Lancaster, author of the Anglo-Norman *Livre de seyntz medicines*. In this case, he is heralded for his construction of a secular college, 'the New Work', in Leicester. But the poem claims no affiliation with that institution, and, as earl of Leicester, Henry was also a major and active benefactor of the Augustinian priory St Mary's.[41]

Ignorantia sacerdotum is an encyclopedic manual of religious instruction composed for priests not capable of using Lyndwood's *Constitutions* to learn their duties directly from the Latin of Archbishop Pecham. At one point its author, probably writing in the 1440s, refers to his 'lord seynt Austin', which may indicate his status as canon – and one filling a function for non-Latinate clerics like Mirk had done for both Latin- and English-literate. *Ignorantia* is, in the main, derived from another work, the more lay-oriented derivative of *Somme le roi* called *Disce mori*; Doyle, in a brief discussion, thinks it at least possible that the same author might be responsible for both.[42]

In this essay, I've consciously restricted myself to authorship. But one should recognize that a vast amount of 'secondary' evidence for Augustinian involvement with Middle English literature survives in books associable with OSA houses.[43] And one example (my third possible) would imply Augustinian involvement in an as yet unmentioned form of parochial instruction, the drama.

Our knowledge of the oldest surviving English moral play, 'The Pride of Life', is entirely dependant upon a most peripheral variety of Augustinian transmission. The text we receive is intimately associated with the Priory of Holy Trinity, Dublin. It was written by two scribes (one perhaps from dictation), on the dorse of a roll bearing priory accounts for 1343-4. The work is certainly Anglo-Irish, with affinities to the poetic language of British Library, MS Harley 913; yet given that at least half a century separates composition and record, there is no assurance the play originated with the order.

But the copying of itself implies some interest in producing a morally instructive text (and should make one consider how much surviving Middle English drama might reflect similar religious locales). Yet the non-literary environment of 'The Pride of Life' scarcely seems conducive either to the text being available or usable for production (the Holy Trinity archive survived relatively intact until 1922). On the other hand, a following member of the roll (together with a substantial portion of the play) has been lost; perhaps blank spaces on superannuated rolls seemed to someone an appropriate surface for a script which could be passed among players.[44]

As I have indicated, this paper provides an interim listing. Thus I offer only a few suggestions of a range of possible Augustinian work. These anonymi lack any clear ties to Augustinian authors and identifying them will depend upon isolating features which resemble works of certain Augustinian origin. One example: although Anglo-Norman may often have functioned in England as 'nuns' Latin', a learned language appropriate for women, reliance on local French texts, especially after 1350, may also mark Augustinian work. (That view would, of course, support contentions that this is the ultimately anti-intellectual order, although such interests would derive from the proscriptions included in very old conciliar regulations which forbade speaking English in the cloister but allowed French beside Latin.)[45] One striking feature of surviving Augustinian books is the heady percentage in the vernacular, including Anglo-Norman.

Here one should recall the extensive Anglo-Norman source texts behind Pepys 2498; and one might consider the activities of another Augustinian hanger-on, Robert Manning, by profession a Gilbertine, but from Bourne, an Arrouasian site. Indeed, Manning felt fondly enough about the place to dedicate *Handling Sin* (1303) to the men of Bourne. Both Manning's undisputed works translate Anglo-Norman authors, William of Waddington and Pierre Langtoft (the latter another Augustinian canon and historian).[46] Or consider *The Siege of Jerusalem*, dependent on French, as well as learned Latin: in addition to a copy of the poem and the only surviving English manuscript of the French source, Bolton also owned a French Mandeville (now British Library, MS Harley 212).

So what lies ahead is a good deal of slog through promising texts and manuscripts looking for more definitive signs of Augustinian provenance. Certainly, on the basis of its reliance on a regulars' library, its French source material, as well as its historical – and biblical historical – bent and its undoubted usefulness for parochial instruction (some copies supplement their history with an appended penitential book), *Cursor Mundi* would appear a promising quarry. Moreover, in what may be the oldest, if fragmentary, copy, Edinburgh, Royal College of Physicians, *Cursor* appears bound together with a very early copy of an Augustinian work, the *Northern Homily Cycle*.[47]

Another promising candidate again represents an example of a Yorkshire 'bible for lay-persons'. In this case, the so called 'Surtees Psalter', one need not look far for Augustinian connections. One copy, in the trilingual British Library, MS Harley 1770, belonged to the Augustinian priory at Kirkham (North Yorkshire). This verse scriptural translation resembles those in Shirley's Caius College 669*: the text proved of minimal use after the mid-fourteenth century, its transmission almost totally restricted to north-western Yorkshire once Rolle's more extensive and scholarly prose text became available.[48] Such truncated circulation histories may characterize a wider range of Augustinian texts.

Obviously enough, at some point any such discussion will enter an area of rank speculation. But even restricting the discussion to the named Augustinian figures I have mentioned above produces a healthy list of vernacular authors. One might well argue that English literature gained through the very absence of Augustinian Latinate intellectual work. However backward, when compared to the sophisticated involvement of other orders, the black canons seem scarcely to have been idle. And their influence on English spiritual life – in the case of Mirk and Hilton, one which extended well into the sixteenth century through print – should be recognized for its breadth and extent.

NOTES

1 See 'New Light on the Provenance of a Copy of the *Canterbury Tales*, John Rylands Library, Eng. 113', *Bulletin of the John Rylands University Library*, 77 (1995), 25-30. For a description of the book, see John M. Manly & Edith Rickert, *The Text of the Canterbury Tales*, 8 vols (Chicago, 1940), I, pp. 349-55.

2 A. I. Doyle, 'A Survey of the Origins and Circulation of Theological Writings in England ...', 2 vols (unpublished Cambridge University Ph.D. thesis, 1953). Michael G. Sargent has perhaps been most assiduous in following Doyle's lead; cf. the number of studies devoted to Carthusianism in the volume he edited, *De Cella in Saeculum: Religious and Secular Life and Devotion in Late Medieval England* (Cambridge, 1989), and his 'The transmission by the English Carthusians of some late medieval spiritual writings', *Journal of Ecclesiastical History*, 27 (1976), 225-40.

3 See David M. Robinson, *The Geography of Augustinian Settlement in Medieval England and Wales*, 2 vols (Oxford, 1980), I, p. 55; and A. Hamilton Thompson, *History and Architectural Description of the Priory of St Mary, Bolton-in-Wharfdale*, Surtees Society 30 (1928), p. 9.

　　H. E. Salter, *Chapters of the Augustinian Canons*, Oxford Historical Society 74 (1920), 277-9 prints a listing of OSA houses *c.*1360 from British Library, Add. MS 38665; it includes houses of all three groups, but indiscriminately marks former Arrouasian and Victorine houses 'Arras', apparently to indicate generically institutions not attending councils. For the 1518 submission of the head of the Arrouasians, see p. 136.

4 See, respectively, 'The Authorship of the "Northern Homily Cycle": the Liturgical Affiliation of the Sunday Gospel Pericopes as a Test', *Traditio*, 41 (1985), 289-309, esp. p. 307; *English Preaching in the Late Middle Ages* (Oxford, 1993), pp. 61-2, 384-5, nn 171-4; and 'Latin devotional texts and the books of the Augustinian canons of Thurgarton Priory and Leicester Abbey in the late middle ages', *Books and Collectors 1200-1700; Essays Presented to Andrew Watson*, ed. by James P. Carley & Colin G. C. Tite (London, 1997), pp. 27-41.

5 For Ormm (ignored in IPMEP, although he writes in a highly regularized offspring of Aelfrician rhythmic prose), who survives in the unique Bodleian Library, MS Junius 1, see M. B. Parkes, 'On the Presumed Date and Possible Origin of the Manuscript of the "Ormmulum"', rep. in his *Scribes, Scripts and Readers: Studies in the Communication, Presentation and Dissemination of Medieval Texts*, ed. by Partols Selbst (London, 1991), pp. 187-200.

　　The Northern Homily Cycle exists in seventeen copies (IMEV Sup. , p. 522), its constituent items indexed separately; the vast majority date from a century and a quarter after composition. See Saara Nevanlinna, *The Northern Homily Cycle: the Expanded Version in MSS*

Harley 4196 and Cotton Tiberius E viii (Helsinki, 1972); Maryann Corbett, 'An East Midland Revision of the *Northern Homily Cycle*', *Manuscripta*, 26 (1982), 100-7; James R. Sprouse, 'The Textual Relationships of the Unexpanded Middle English Northern Homily Cycle', *Manuscripta*, 33 (1989), 92-108.

For Mirk's *Festial*, see IPMEP 734, which lists something approaching forty copies; Martin F. Wakelin, 'The manuscripts of John Mirk's *Festial*', *Leeds Studies in English*, n.s. 1 (1967), 93-118; Alan J. Fletcher, 'Unnoticed Sermons from John Mirk's *Festial*', *Speculum*, 55 (1980), 514-22. Richard Beadle extends Wakelin's analysis, 'Middle English Texts and their Transmission, 1350-1500: some Geographical Criteria', in *Speaking in Our Tongues*, ed. by Margaret Laing & Keith Williamson (Cambridge, 1994), pp. 69-91 (81-2). Fletcher, 'John Mirk and the Lollards', *Medium Aevum*, 56 (1987), 216-24 argues Mirk wrote the sermons for use at St Alkmund's, Shrewsbury; and on that use, see Susan Powell, 'John Mirk's *Festial* and the Pastoral Program', *Leeds Studies in English*, n.s. 22 (1991), 85-102. In addition to the manuscripts, there are twenty-three early Renaissance prints. See also Richard Sharpe, *A Handlist of the Latin Writers of Great Britain and Ireland before 1540* (Turnholt, 1997), pp. 284-5.

6 See Christopher N. L. Brooke, 'Monk and Canon: Some Patterns in the Religious Life of the Twelfth Century', *Studies in Church History*, 22 (1985), 109-29 (122-4).

7 The statistics come from Robinson, 1, 117, 172, a figure subject to local variations. For example, the papal taxation of 1291 found that Yorkshire houses derived 68 per cent of their income from spiritualities (117). In the *Valor*, each convent, on average, drew income from about seven churches, a total which would represent something like one-eighth of all English parish churches (Robinson 1, 210-12).

8 On the proximity of churches, see Robinson, 1, 206 (in Lincoln diocese, in the early thirteenth century, about 60 per cent were within ten miles of the house); on the foundation of Leicester, see Thompson, *Bolton*, p. 18.

9 Cf. the Benedictine condescension of David Knowles, *The Religious Orders in England, volume II: The End of the Middle Ages* (Cambridge, 1957), p. 361.

10 See R. W. Southern, *Western Society and the Church in the Middle Ages* (Harmondsworth, 1970), pp. 244-8; and the sympathetic comments of Jane Herbert, 'The Transformation of Hermitages into Augustinian Priories in Twelfth-Century England', *Studies in Church History*, 22 (1985), 131-45, especially pp. 143 (seconding Southern) and 134, 138 (where she outlines the cost to a priory of engaging in intellectual pursuits).

11 On serving churches and the need for a *socius*, see Salter's edition of the constitutions imposed by Benedict XII in 1339, ch. 13, pp. 240-3. Critical treatments include Thompson, *Bolton*, pp. 16-34, 47-9, 62, 99-108 (on Bolton's late decision to start serving at least some of its churches); Thompson, *The English Clergy and their Organization in the Later Middle Ages* (Oxford, 1947), pp. 117-22; J. C. Dickinson, *The Origins of the Austin Canons and their Introduction into England* (London, 1950), p. 136 on the smallness of many houses (as few as three canons, not the expected thirteen) and pp. 214-54 passim; and R. A. R. Hartridge, *A History of Vicarages in the Middle Ages* (Cambridge, 1930), pp. 164-75.

12 I am grateful to Richard Sharpe for producing a list of Augustinian authors from his database; for Nequam and Robert, see *Handlist*, pp. 51-3 and 526-8, respectively. On learned canons (and Nequam), see R. W. Hunt, 'English Learning in the Late Twelfth Century', *Transactions of the Royal Historical Society*, 4th ser. 19 (1936), 19-35 (31-4); and Hunt, ed. & rev. Margaret Gibson, *The Schools and the Cloister: the life and writings of Alexander Nequam, 1157-1217* (Oxford, 1984), pp. 9-12 for Nequam's conversion. Lawrence's study, 'A Northern English School? Patterns of production and collection of manuscripts in the Augustinian houses of Yorkshire in the twelfth and thirteenth centuries', appears at *Yorkshire Monasticism: Archaeology, Art, and Architecture*, ed. by Lawrence R. Hoey, British Archaeological Association Conference Transactions 16 (Leeds, 1995), pp. 145-53.

13 Opinions on black canons at Oxford vary. Evangeline Evans presents as a particularly dispiriting history efforts to meet canonical obligations and provide a university house of study,

in 'St Mary's College in Oxford for Austin Canons', *Oxfordshire Archaeological Society Report*, 76 (1931), 367-91. But Simon N. Forde offers more extensive, although perhaps not numerically overwhelming, evidence for learned canons in 'The Educational Organization of the Augustinian Canons in England and Wales and their University Life at Oxford, 1325-1448', *History of Universities*, 13 (1994), 21-60. See also David Postles's assessment of early Osney learning and the later register (published in EETS 133 and 144), 'The Learning of Austin Canons: the Case of Oseney Abbey', *Nottingham Medieval Studies*, 29 (1985), 32-43.

14 See 'Instructions for Parish Priests' (IMEV 961), in seven copies, most recently edited by Gillis Kristensson (Lund, 1974); and Alan J. Fletcher, 'The Manuscripts of John Mirk's *Manuale Sacerdotis*', *Leeds Studies in English*, 19 (1988), 105-39, a large Latin text which survives in thirteen copies.

15 On Repingdon, see Sharpe, pp. 437-8, with a list of eleven surviving manuscripts (and as many lost ones). Only a small bit of Forde's extensive Birmingham dissertation has ever been published, 'Theological Sources Cited by Two Canons from Repton: Philip Repyngdon and John Eyton', *Studies in Church History*, subsidia 5 (1987), 419-28. On Swinderby, see James Crompton, 'Leicestershire Lollards', *Transactions of the Leicestershire Archaeological and Historical Society*, 44 (1969), 11-44 (18-22); and Anne Hudson, *The Premature Reformation* (Oxford, 1988), pp. 73-6, with references to the Trefnant register.

16 For the Hilton canon, see Valerie M. Lagorio & Michael G. Sargent with Ritamary Bradley, 'English Mystical Writings', ch. 23 of the revised Wells *Manual*, 9, 3430-8; Sharpe, pp. 735-6. IPMEP 255 lists forty-eight manuscripts of the *Scala*, and there were five early prints (the fifteen copies of Thomas Fishlake's Latin translation fall outside the scope of the volume). See Sargent, 'Walter Hilton's *Scale of Perfection*: the London Manuscript Group Reconsidered', *Medium Aevum*, 52 (1983), 189-216. Doyle, 'Book Production by the Monastic Orders in England: Assessing the Evidence', in *Medieval Book Production: Assessing the Evidence*, ed. by Linda Brownrigg (Los Altos Hills, 1990), pp. 1-19, discusses the fitfulness of Augustinian work at pp. 12-13; the principal Augustinian scribe he discusses is John Cock, whom I mention below. One volume of a long-awaited new edition of Hilton, book 2 by S. S. Hussey, is forthcoming from the Early English Text Society.

17 See E. J. Dobson, 'The Date and Composition of *Ancrene Wisse*', *Proceedings of the British Academy*, 52 (1966), 181-208, and *The Origins of 'Ancrene Wisse'* (Oxford, 1976) – and Bella Millett's demurrers, 'The origins of *Ancrene Wisse*: new answers, new questions', *Medium Aevum*, 61 (1992), 206-28. The first frontispiece to EETS 249 reproduces Corpus Christi 402, fol. 1, with the priory's *ex libris* including a record of the donation to Wigmore 'ad instanciam fratris Walteri de Lodel' senioris tunc precentoris'.

18 On Cleopatra and Matilda de Clare, see EETS 267 (1972), xxi-ii, xxv-ix. On Lambeth 487, see EETS 241 (1958), xi. On the Dublin rule, see Hope Emily Allen, 'Further Borrowings from "Ancrene Wisse"', *Modern Language Review*, 24 (1929), 1-15 (1-2).

19 For Dobson's scribe D, see the plates at EETS 267 (1972), 316-17 (the supply leaf), 110-11 (the two versions of the first sermon), and the discussion, especially pp. cxlii-iv, clviii. For his language, see Angus McIntosh, 'The Language of the Extant Versions of *Havelok the Dane*', *Medium Aevum*, 45 (1976), 36-49 (38-40). For the second Trinity scribe, see EETS 267, cxlv, cxlix n2; Dobson overlooks a hand, very similar to Scribe D's, which writes IMEV 2286 (a versified decalogue) between 'At wrestling' and the second scribe's Latin.

20 I refer to the book at the centre of Doyle and M. B. Parkes's argument in 'The Production of Copies of the *Canterbury Tales* and the *Confessio Amantis* in the Early Fifteenth Century' in *Medieval Scribes, Manuscripts and Libraries: Essays Presented to N. R. Ker*, ed. by Parkes & Andrew G. Watson, (London, 1978), pp. 163-210. But evidence for a scribal community centred in producing copies of the English *Mirror* comes from other books in comparable language – British Library, MS Harley 5085, and Glasgow, University Library, MS Hunter 250 (U.4.8). And the Pepys scribe copied the *Apocalypse* a second time, in BL, MS Harley 874.

21 For the scribal dialect, see EETS 274 (1976): xvii-iii. On the *Mirror*, see Thomas G. Duncan, 'The Middle English *Mirror* and its Manuscripts', in *Middle English Studies Presented to*

Norman Davis, ed. by Douglas Gray & E. G. Stanley (Oxford, 1983), pp. 115-26; and Kathleen Marie Blumreich Moore, 'The Middle English "Mirror": an Edition Based on Bodleian Library, MS. Holkham Misc.40 …', Michigan State University Ph.D. diss., 1992 (*Dissertation Abstracts International*, 53 [1992], 3598A). The other texts of Pepys 2498 are IPMEP 584 (a dozen copies), 114, 530, and the texts published subsequent to IPMEP by C. William Marx & Jeanne F. Drennan, eds, *The Middle English Prose Complaint of Our Lady and Gospel of Nicodemus*, MET 19 (1987) (three copies each).

22 For the appointment to Malling, see *Registrum Roberti Winchelsey*, ed. by Rose Graham, 2 vols, Canterbury and York Society 51-2 (1952-6), I, 346-7; the appointment to Chart appears in the unpublished register of Walter Reynolds, fol. 27. The seven poems are edited in EETS e.s. 86 (1902); the sixth, a Marian lyric, appears to be ascribed to Grosseteste.

23 See respectively, Sharpe, pp. 172, 794, 735, 263, and 695.

24 IMEV 1583; for the tiny fragment from a ninth manuscript, Exeter, Devon Record Office 2507, see Michael Swanton, 'A Further Manuscript of *The Siege of Jerusalem*', *Scriptorium*, 44 (1990), 103-4. On the transmission, see my 'Contextualizing *The Siege of Jerusalem*', *Yearbook of Langland Studies*, 6 (1992), 109-21 (115-18).

25 IMEV 399, 2697. See further Donald Kennedy, in the revised Wells, *Manual* 8, 2905 [55].

26 There are six manuscripts of the full version and at least three of an authorial abridgement; the autograph is Cambridge, Corpus Christi College, MS 171, the copy the earl of Moray's MS (MLGB, p. 104). See the nearly complete edition, ed. D. E. R. Watt et al., 8 vols of a projected 9 (Aberdeen, subsequently Edinburgh, 1987-).

27 For a full list of verse in Bower, see IMEV Sup. , p. 535, s.v. 'Fordun': for the antifeminist materials, see Watt et al., eds., 7:344/76-81 (IMEV 299.8; misindexed, since the incipit is 'At', i.e. 'That'); 348-50/73-82 (IMEV 3492.5); and 352/21-2 (IMEV 3742.5).

28 See I. R. Johnson, 'Walton's Sapient Orpheus', in *The Medieval Boethius: Studies in the Vernacular Translations of 'De Consolatione Philosophiae'*, ed. by A. J. Minnis (Cambridge, 1982), pp. 139-78.

29 IMEV 1597; see the reproduction of materials unique to the print, EETS 170, pp. xliii-iv. In 'Sir Thomas Berkeley and His Patronage', *Speculum*, 64 (1989), 876-916 (899-902), I argued that Walton is not responsible for the Vegetius translation produced for Berkeley. See further Ian Johnson, 'New Evidence for the Authorship of Walton's Boethius', *Notes and Queries*, 241 (1996), 19-21; and Jeremy's 'Thomas Hingham, Monk of Bury and the Macro Plays Manuscript', *English Manuscript Studies*, 5 (1995), 214-19.

30 See Sharpe, pp. 131-3 and 320. For Ripley, see IMEV 595 (about twenty-five copies), 1364.5 (eight copies; MS 7 is now Huntington Library, MS HM 30313), 3721 (twelve copies), and 4017 (about ten copies); the as yet unpublished prose is handlisted at IMEP 11:98-9. One of Snell's texts is listed at IMEP 11:38, the second (Cambridge, Trinity College, MS R.14.45, fols. 9ᵛ-13ʳ) ignored by the editor.

31 See *The Observances in Use at the Augustinian Priory of S. Giles and S. Andrew at Barnwell, Cambridgeshire*, ed. by John Willis Clark (Cambridge, 1897), p. 175, on permanent chaplains allowed to live in the almonry; and pp. 212-15, on 'stacionarii'. On this priory and its foundation, see W. H. Frere, 'The Early History of Canons Regular as illustrated by the foundation of Barnwell Priory', in *Fasciculus J. W. Clark Dicatus* (Cambridge, 1909), pp. 186-216.

32 See EETS 184 (1931):149; MLGB, pp. 112, 273 associates Douce 302 with a canon of Launde (Leics.) who got it as a gift from one Wyatt, a minstrel of Coventry. On Audelay, see especially Michael Bennett, 'John Audley: Some New Evidence on his Life and Work', *Chaucer Review*, 16 (1982), 344-55; and most recently, Eric Stanley, 'The Verse Forms of Jon the Blynde Awdelay', in *The Long Fifteenth Century: Essays for Douglas Gray*, ed. by Helen Cooper & Sally Mapstone (Oxford, 1997), pp. 99-121. On the prose works at the conclusion of the manuscript, evidence for Augustinian transmission of religious materials, see Susannah Greer Fein, 'A Thirteen-Line Stanza on the Abuse of Prayer from the Audelay MS', *Medium Aevum*, 63 (1994), 61-74 (an extract from Rolle's *Form* with inserted verse; cf. Cambridge, Corpus Christi

College, MS 387, a Rolle psalter which belonged to John Coleman, prior of Lesnes (Kent)); and A. I. Doyle, '"Lectulus noster floridus": An Allegory of the Penitent Soul', in *Literature and Religion in the Later Middle Ages: Philological Studies in Honor of Siegfried Wenzel*, ed. by Richard G. Newhauser & John A. Alford (Binghamton, NY, 1995), pp. 179-90.

33 See further A. S. G. Edwards's discussion of 'Fifteenth-Century Author Collections' elsewhere in this volume.

34 See 'A Newly Identified Manuscript Inscribed by John Shirley', *Library*, 6th ser. 14 (1992), 83-93. I have attempted to dissociate the Additional manuscript from Shirley's other activities; see 'John Shirley and British Library, MS. Additional 16165', *Studies in Bibliography*, 49 (1996), 95-105 (99-101).

35 Cf. Salter's conciliar acta, p. 24: no secular persons should eat with canons, 'nisi que onestate et deuocione sua pensata fuerint admisse de prouidencia prelatorum', a regulation repeated in the rules for visitation (*c*.1518), p. 202. But this legislation encompasses stays a good deal more protracted than just sharing dinner and predates the conciliar record; cf. Thompson's account of the 1280 Bolton visitation, p. 73. On real estate management, see *The Cartulary of Holy Trinity Aldgate*, ed. by Gerald A. J. Hodgett, London Record Society Publications 7 (1971), xvi-xx and passim; Postles, 'The Austin Canons in English Towns', *Historical Research*, 66 (1993), 1-20.

36 For this translation of Bonaventura, see Elizabeth Zeeman (Salter), 'Continuity and Change in Middle English Versions of the *Meditationes Vitae Christi*', *Medium Aevum*, 26 (1957), 25-31. To Salter's list of six manuscripts, add the further OSA copy in Princeton University Library, MS Taylor 11, fols 97^r-104^v. One might note a similar text with a black canons provenance, the English *Infantia salvatoris* at British Library, MS Harley 2399, fols 47^r-64^r, from Bodmin (Cornwall).

37 In addition to this copy, described by Manly & Rickert (cited above, n. 1), 1, pp. 207-18 (and by Barbara Cline, in an unpublished University of Washington dissertation), and John Brode's, a third *Canterbury Tales* manuscript has an Augustinian provenance. Manchester, Chetham's Library, MS 6709, a sequence of saints' lives, including the tales of the Prioress and Second Nun, was copied in March 1490 by William Cotson of the Dunstable house; see Manly & Rickert, 1, 82-4, a reference I owe to Tony Edwards. Manly & Rickert (1, 342) also ascribed Longleat, Marquis of Bath MS 257 to the Augustinian priory of Hempton (Norfolk), but their evidence seems to me uncompelling.

38 Shirley composed IPMEP 56 (a *Secreta secretorum* translation; the source, with his *ex libris*, survives as Cambridge, University Library, MS Ff.i.33), IPMEP 569 (the assassination of James I), and the still unpublished translation of Jacques le grand's *Livre de bonnes meures* (one of four Middle English translations, again derived from Ff.i.33, cf. IPMEP 820). For the St Bartholomew's history, see EETS 163 (1923): is it, perhaps, like the Osney cartulary, a testimony to the difficulty of the original document? Certainly the author shows minimal facility at changing Latin lexicon and word-order to English.

There are two recent editions of Shirley's chronicle on James I; see Margaret Connolly, '*The Dethe of the Kynge of Scotis*: a New Edition', *Scottish Historical Review*, 71 (1992), 46-69; and Lister M. Matheson, *Death and Dissent: Two Fifteenth-Century Chronicles* (Cambridge, 1998), pp. 1-59.

39 See, following G. C. Macaulay, John H. Fisher, *John Gower: Moral Philosopher and Friend of Chaucer* (London: Methuen, 1965), pp. 58-60, 93; and the criticisms of Peter Nicholson, 'Poet and Scribe in the Manuscripts of Gower's *Confessio Amantis*', in *Manuscripts and Texts: Editorial Problems in Later Middle English Literature*, ed. by Derek Pearsall (Cambridge, 1987), pp. 130-42; and M. B. Parkes, 'Patterns of scribal activity and revisions of the text in early copies of works by John Gower', in *New Science out of Old Books: Studies in Manuscripts and Early Printed Books in Honour of A. I. Doyle*, ed. by Richard Beadle & A. J. Piper (Aldershot, 1995), pp. 81-104.

40 The standard biographical account is still Charles Lethbridge Kingsford, 'The First Version of Hardyng's Chronicle', *English Historical Review*, 27 (1912), 462-82; see also IMEV 710

(fifteen copies) and A. S. G. Edwards, 'The manuscripts of John Harding's *Chronicle*', in *England in the Fifteenth Century*, ed. by D. Williams (Woodbridge, 1987), pp. 75-84; I owe a great deal to the researches of Christine M. Harker, whose edition of Harding's Arthuriana is forthcoming from MET.

41 IMEV 974, with two manuscripts; see EETS o.s. 98 (1892):273 (lines 163-8).

42. *Ignorantia sacerdotum* is unique to Bodleian Library, MS Eng. th. c.57; for a full bibliography of discussions, see IMEP 12:9; and Doyle, 'Lectulus' (cited above, n. 32), pp. 183-5. Vincent Gillespie suggests to me, however, that the author could well have been a Bridgettine of Syon, where the Augustinian Rule was in use; see now Edward Jones, 'Jesus College Oxford, MS 39: Signs of a Medieval Compiler at Work', *English Manuscript Studies*, 7 (1998), 236-48.

43 Among such volumes (the full list is fairly readily retrievable in Ker's MLGB), I simply mention Bodleian Library, MS Douce 372; Oxford, University College, MS 181; and Cambridge, University Library, MS Add. 2823 (the last not in MLGB and a reference I owe to Tony Edwards).

44 IMEV 2741, ed. by Norman Davis, EETS s.s. 1 (1970), 90-105 (and see further pp. lxxxv-vi, xcvi). One might note, however, that until well into the modern period acting scripts were divided into rolls with individual parts (hence the surviving form of the fragment 'Dux Moraud'). Tony Edwards points to two other poetic texts, one unique, transmitted in Augustinian account rolls,in this case from Bicester (Oxon.); see V. J. Scattergood, 'An Unpublished Middle English Poem', *Archiv*, 203 (1967), 277-82.

45 See Salter (cited above, n. 3), pp. 14 and 17.

46 Matthew Sullivan collects materials indicating, *inter alia*, Mannyng's continuing associations with Bourne (as well as the Augustinian house at Barnwell); see 'Biographical Notes on Robert Mannyng of Brunne and Peter Idley, the Adaptor of Robert Mannyng's *Handlyng Synne*', *Notes and Queries*, 239 (1994), 302-4.

47 See IMEV 2153; three additional copies have only the penitential book (IMEV 694). There is now a full study: John J. Thompson, *The 'Cursor Mundi': Poem, Texts and Contexts* (Oxford, 1998). For the important earlier studies of Sarah M. Horrall, see p. 189, as well as J. J. Lamberts, 'The "Proloug" to *Cursor Mundi*, vv. 1-270', *Neophilologus*, 68 (1984), 292-316.

48 IMEV 3103, with six copies; ed. by C. Horstman, *Yorkshire Writers*, 2 vols (London, 1895-96), 2, 130-273.

USHAW COLLEGE, DURHAM, MS 50

Fragments of the Prick of Conscience, *by the same Scribe as Oxford, Corpus Christi College, MS 201, of the B Text of* Piers Plowman

A. I. DOYLE

AMONG Jeremy Griffiths's projects was one, together with Angus McIntosh, for a list of scribes, named and unnamed, whose hands had been recognized in more than one Middle English manuscript, of which he sent me a twenty-seven page draft in April 1992, and to which I kept promising him and Angus to make additions and amendments, and apologizing for my failure to do so. I hope it will be possible, with the help of Linne Mooney and others interested, to publish a revised list, which of course can only be a first essay of an indefinitely expansible repertoire. As closer study of groups of medieval manuscripts increases there will be a growing number of proffered identifications of individual hands, on good or not-so-good grounds, which must at least be noticed, if only with queries or caveats. Well-founded attributions of scribal resemblance in the making or early augmentation or annotation of two or more manuscripts are one of the most promising ways of placing them temporally and geographically, but we must beware of wishful thinking and rushing beyond simple observations. The following instance seems to me to be certain, and of special interest because involving a unique prologue of one major poem and a very idiosyncratic copy of another, though the implications must remain speculative until still other pieces of work by the scribe or artists are recognized, and therewith possible connections with specific originators.

In 1989 Dr Jan Rhodes brought to my attention two pieces of the first leaf of a copy of the *Prick of Conscience* in the library of Ushaw College, Durham, now MS 50.[1] They are of membrane of moderate quality, roughly rectangular (though with rounded corners), measuring at their maxima 142 × 111 and 144 × 111 mm, respectively from the upper and lower halves of the leaf. The lower left corner (viewed from the recto) of the upper piece has been cut off obliquely and the rounding of the others, designedly it seems, was perhaps for their use as stiffeners in a semi-limp binding, since there are no marks of stitching or pasting on them. The lower piece however has been folded about half-way horizontally and is badly rubbed and soiled near that line on the verso, more broadly on the recto, but there are no such marks on the upper piece. Neither piece shows any signs of provenance. No book or document at Ushaw

Pl. 1. Oxford, Corpus Christi College, MS 201, top half of fol. 1ʳ. By permission of the President and Fellows. Reproduced approximately two-thirds actual size.

has yet been identified from which the pieces may have come. The dismemberment of the manuscript probably took place in the sixteenth or seventeenth century, though discarding and re-use did happen quite often in the Middle Ages.

The two pieces contain (apart from a few letters cropped at the ends or beginnings of lines) almost all the text of lines 1–55 of the *Prick of Conscience* (according to the numeration of the only edition),[2] but lines 4 and 42 were lost in the bisecting and trimming, lines 27 and 28 are in reverse order, 31–2 are wanting and 33–4 repeated between 42 and 43. Line 1 is that of the East Midland or Southern Recension of the *Prick* (IMEV 3429), but it is preceded by an otherwise unrecorded passage[3] under the rubricated heading *Incipit prologus De Stimulo Consciencie* (see Pl. 2):

> Alle þat will knowe / þe sciens\<e>
> What ys þe prikke / of Consy\<ense>
> Turne 30ure hertis / holly i\<?...>
> & y will shewe it 30w / ei\<?...>
> But to manye men / þis let\<...>
> To lewed men / but to n\<?...>
> For Clerkis know\<e i>tt / in h\<...>
> & lewede men / no þyng know\<...>
> & for lewede men / þis is s\<?...>

44

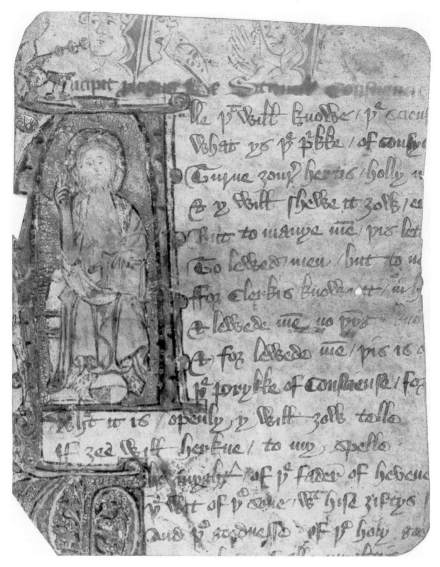

Pl. 2. Durham, Ushaw College, MS 50, top half of fol. 1ʳ. By permission of St Cuthbert's College, Ushaw. Reproduced actual size.

þe Prykke of Consciense / for <...>
What it is / openly y will ȝow telle
If ȝee will herkne / to my spelle

I rapidly recognized the hand of the copyist as being the same as that of Oxford, Corpus Christi College, MS 201, a peculiar copy of the B-text of *Piers Plowman* (compare Pls 1 and 2).[4] It is a practised anglicana of the late four-teenth or early fifteenth century, quite current though with many letters separately formed, of similar appearance although of somewhat different size in the two manuscripts. There is no pricking or ruling visible, either for frames or lines, on the Ushaw pages. Allowing for the lost line of text on each, the height of the writing space must have been very near that of Corpus (243 mm approx.), the width narrower for the shorter verses of the *Prick* (*c*. 100 mm, Corpus 110 mm). Ushaw however had only 33 and 35 written lines on its pages, whereas Corpus ranges from 37 to 45 within its simple frame ruling.[5] Ushaw thus is more amply spaced and the size of writing larger. The original measure-ments of the Ushaw leaf may have been about the same as those of Corpus: at least 293 × 173 mm (approximately 10½ × 7 inches); copies of the *Prick* are not uncommonly narrower than those of *Piers*, since the verse lines are shorter, but Corpus has suffered marginal cropping of its sidenotes and is consequently narrower in proportions than is normal for *Piers Plowman*.[6]

Of the features which agree between the writing of the two manuscripts, the most individual are the circular left-hand hook below the 2-like **r** (Pl. 1 line 3 'world', l. 4 'morwe', l. 7 'boorne'; Pl. 2 line 9 'for'); the very noticeable crossing of the downstroke and upstroke of the sigma or 6-like **s** (Pl. 1 l. 1 'was', l. 2 'shrowdes'; Pl. 2 l. 3 'ys'; Pl. 3 ll. 1, 2 'as'); and the common use of the *and* sign at the beginning of lines (Pl. 1 ll. 3, 8; Pl. 2 ll. 5, 9, 10).

Medial v, for consonantal **u**, is conspicuous in Ushaw and predominant in Corpus (Pl. 1 l. 4 'malverne', l. 10 'mervelous'; Pl. 2 l. 14 'hevene').[7] The shape of ȝ (yogh) is the same, and spellings with it (e.g. Pl. 1 l. 12 'heyȝ'; Pl. 2 l. 4 'ȝoure', ll. 5, 12 'ȝow', l. 13 'ȝee', l. 15 'ȝiftys'; Pl. 3 l. 1 'wyȝs'). Most of the other spellings (e.g. 'nowht') also agree with the linguistic profile of Corpus (LALME 6110), placed in central Essex.[8] But the rhyming of 'tane' with 'alane' (lines 23-4) must survive from the northern original of the *Prick*.

The opening rubric (partly oxidized) of Ushaw 50 (Pl. 2) is in textura, not clearly the same as that used for Latin quotations throughout Corpus, which appears to be the work of the main scribe; the three enlarged ascenders are decorated with four heads, one at least (on the right) probably of a woman, and on the verso (Pl. 3) one similar black ascender in the top margin has a head of a lion ornamented with red, and adjacent a bearded male head and another man's head with his hand and shoulders in a cowl (probably a religious), clearly by the same talented hand, possibly that of the scribe himself. The heads are cropped at the top by at least 5 mm. There are similar human and animal heads on two top-line ascenders in Corpus 201 (fols 11ʳ and 76ᵛ) and a tinted sketch of a stork holding an empty scroll below the Explicit on fol. 93ʳ.[9]

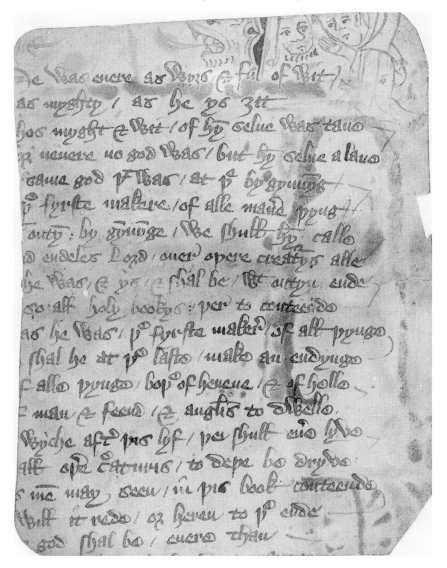

Pl. 3. Ushaw College MS 50, top half of fol. 1ᵛ. By permission of St Cuthbert's College, Ushaw. Reproduced actual size.

The first page has a ten-line inhabited initial A showing Christ enthroned (with wounds in his feet, on each side of a terrestrial globe), holding an open book with his left hand and raising his right hand with two fingers extended in admonition. His facial details and hair are drawn and tinted very sensitively, with perhaps an expression of sadness. He has a pink halo and a blue and pink garment, now faded, on a rubbed and cracked gilt background. The letter is formed of a darker rose pigment with relieving ornament and is framed and attached to a gold bar in the left margin. Below it is a four-line similarly illuminated initial T in blue, occupied by leaf-buds of pink. The bar-border terminates with a straight spray of oxidized trefoils in the lower margin. Corpus 201 has a similar opening eleven-line inhabited initial A showing the narrator, also attached to an L-shaped illuminated bar-border with budding leaves and a straight spray with trefoils. In both manuscripts the style is rather of the later fourteenth than early fifteenth century.[10] Dr Kathleen Scott has been kind enough to compare slides of Ushaw 50 with Corpus 201 itself. After reporting in detail on the similarities and differences she concludes: 'On the whole I would have to say that they are probably not by the same artist. The *Prick* artist is really more accomplished and even looks somewhat later, though that could be simply because he is better.' She does not say (but it is implied by a reference in her *Survey* to Corpus)[11] that the two inhabited initials are unlike the best metropolitan work of the period shortly before and after 1400 and so may be provincial, but, like the borders, they are not amateurish in execution.

There is another decorated initial on the lower half of the Ushaw first page, a three-line B of red, its cross-bar ending in a fleur-de-lys, with buff or void ornament. At the top of the verso of the leaf (Pl. 3) the first line-initial H is enlarged and stroked with red.

Whatever the status of the scribe, who did not employ a formalized anglicana as found the textual sibling of Corpus (Bodleian Library Rawlinson poet.38 with British Library, MS Lansdowne 398) and other copies of *Piers Plowman* of the same period, it appears that more than minimum expense was taken to finish both Ushaw and Corpus and that the necessary skills were available. Ushaw 50 is the only recorded copy of the *Prick of Conscience* with a pictorial illustration and there is only one other (Douce 104) of *Piers Plowman*.[12] It is notable too that the scribe in both cases copied or created abnormal texts.[13] The remarkable number of singleton leaves in Corpus (two in each quire up to the last which has four) suggests either an uncommon shortage of membrane for this period and area, or the repeated cancellation of textual mistakes. The latter would be unusual yet not unlikely, in view of the large number of unique variants which occur in the extant leaves.[14]

NOTES

* A previous version of this description is included, with colour reproductions of Ushaw MS 50, in a CD-rom of Corpus Christi 201 edited by Robert Adams, Hoyt Duggan, Eric Eliason, Ralph Hanna and Thorlac Turville-Petre.

1 As a fragment, not described with other Ushaw holdings by N. R. Ker & A. J. Piper, *Medieval Manuscripts in British Libraries*, IV (Oxford, 1992), 505-51; nor by Robert E. Lewis & Angus McIntosh, *A Descriptive Guide to the Manuscripts of the Prick of Conscience*, Medium AEvum Monographs n.s. 12 (Oxford, 1982)

2 Ed. by Richard Morris (Berlin, 1863).

3 Not IMEV 1193, 3428-9, nor in the Supplement or Lewis & McIntosh.

4 Described in *Piers Plowman: the B Version*, ed. by George Kane & E. Talbot Donaldson (London, 1975), p. 8; C. David Benson & Lynne S. Blanchfield, *The Manuscripts of Piers Plowman: the B-Version* (Cambridge, 1997), pp. 98-101, 207-27.

5 Ralph Hanna has found that the number of lines per page varies greatly, up to as many as 45 in the first three quires but thereafter closer to 37-8 lines.

6 A reduced facsimile of fol. 8^v is in Benson & Blanchfield, p. 98, showing passus Explicit and Incipit and a coloured initial with pen-work decoration but no marginalia.

7 Professor Duggan has given me precise figures for this.

8 Angus McIntosh and others, *Linguistic Atlas of Late Mediaeval English* (Aberdeen, 1986), I, 152; III, 118.

9 It has been suggested that the bird is a pelican and so a later mark of ownership by Corpus Christi.

10 Benson & Blanchfield describe the Corpus inhabited initial as an I; but the first word is 'Al', a grammatically acceptable variant not noted by Kane & Donaldson, nor by A. V. C. Schmidt, *Piers Plowman, Parallel Text Edition*, I (London, 1995). W. W. Skeat in his first edition of B (EETS OS 38, 1869), p. xxviii, recognized the 'A', as a mistake, but only Ralph Hanna, *Pursuing History: Middle English Manuscripts and Their Texts* (Stanford, 1996), p. 315 n. 19, has noticed the whole word, as a characteristic peculiarity of this copy.

11 *A Survey of Manuscripts Illuminated in the British Isles: Later Gothic Manuscripts 1390-1490* (London, 1996), II, 67.

12 See Kathleen Scott, *Survey*, I, 35; 'The illustrations of *Piers Plowman* in Bodleian Library MS Douce 104', *Yearbook of Langland Studies* 4 (1990), 2-86.

13 Kane & Donaldson, pp. 165-72.

14 Ralph Hanna observes that in the last quire the scribe has cannibalized his own blank half-sheets and supplied another: 'if not shortage a strange economy would seem indicated'.

MINDING THE GAPS

Interpreting the Manuscript Evidence of the Cook's Tale *and the* Squire's Tale

STEPHEN PARTRIDGE

THE ATTENTION paid to the manuscripts of Chaucer's *Canterbury Tales* over the last two decades is a prime example of the expansion of manuscript studies and the field's increasing influence on contemporary understanding of medieval literature. Numerous books and articles on the manuscripts and textual tradition of the *Tales* represent virtually all aspects of the recently renewed study of the medieval codex. They have radically reconsidered what the manuscripts might tell us about Chaucer's own intentions for his work; they have garnered new evidence for the early reception of the *Tales*; and they have shed light on the processes of medieval book production. Moreover, it has become increasingly common for those primarily concerned with literary scholarship and criticism to draw on the manuscripts' evidence for their arguments, and to acknowledge the challenges they may present to our interpretation of the *Tales*.[1]

The *mouvance* of those *Canterbury Tales* generally regarded as unfinished, the Cook's and the Squire's, has been remarked upon with particular frequency, in contexts which illustrate the varying kinds of attention the manuscripts are receiving.[2] Daniel Mosser has cited the variant forms of these tales as prime examples of the manuscript variation that can best be represented by an electronic edition.[3] Other discussions tend to be of one of two types. On the one hand, bibliographical and textual studies have hypothesized about the nature of the exemplars from which early scribes worked. The two unfinished tales seem to provide particularly rich evidence for the difficulties some scribes had in deciding how to make use of their exemplars in presenting the *Tales* as a book.[4] On the other hand, several studies consider the manuscript evidence, to widely varying extents, in the course of arguments which are primarily literary in nature. Thus, for example, John Burrow has surveyed the reception history of these tales and Chaucer's two other apparently unfinished poems, the *House of Fame* and the *Legend of Good Women*, partly to determine what we may know of Chaucer's own intentions for them.[5] The earliest major studies of the *Cook's Tale* draw on the manuscript evidence in their titles and arguments;[6] two more recent articles examine in detail one particularly interesting fifteenth-century response to that tale.[7] Similarly, two extended studies of the *Squire's Tale*, while concerned primarily with other aspects of the tale, have highlighted the manuscripts' evidence that scribes were uncertain or disagreed about how to proceed after the final surviving lines.[8]

These studies suggest, first, that understanding how the scribes treated these tales is significant for any hypothesis about the early history of the *Tales*, and second, that awareness of the manuscript context is particularly important in interpreting the *Cook's Tale* and the *Squire's Tale*. Yet although the manuscript evidence for these tales has frequently been cited in passing or in part, there has been no comprehensive outline of that evidence, and the lack of one has sometimes given rise to questionable assumptions and even errors of fact. In what follows I aim to provide such an outline. Re-examining the full history of these two tales reveals certain patterns in scribal treatment of them. Awareness of these patterns can, in turn, lead us to re-evaluate the evidence of individual manuscripts of the *Tales*, including some of the most important ones. Thus I aim to go beyond merely observing the fact of manuscript variation, or examining particular variants in isolation, and instead seek to make generalizations about scribal behaviour and the likely direction(s) of variation.

My discussion, which will grow progressively more conjectural and contentious, will be in several parts. I want to begin by reviewing which manuscripts include the *Cook's Tale* and the *Squire's Tale*, in part to reconsider how often they were purposely omitted from the tale-collection. Next, I will survey those places where we can most clearly identify and interpret scribal variation in the treatment of these tales; as part of this survey, I will consider a few particular manuscripts in detail. My goal here is not only to offer a concise summary of certain kinds of information, but also to provide some context for what follows. Then, I will consider two more ambiguous features of the manuscript tradition: the practice of leaving blank space after one or both of these tales, and the notes about their unfinished state which appear in a few manuscripts. I will argue that these features, generally understood as the products of scribes' work on individual codices, actually possessed a kind of textual status in the fifteenth century. I will suggest, moreover, that recognizing this, along with other facts about scribal practice, should lead us to consider seriously the possibility that these features originated with Chaucer himself rather than with the scribes. Finally, I will suggest how the evidence for these tales might help us understand two aspects of the early history of the *Canterbury Tales*: the shape of the lost manuscripts from which the earliest surviving codices were made, and the condition of the text when it left Chaucer's hand.

Before beginning, I want to make explicit the assumptions which underlie my discussion. First, I am sympathetic to Burrow's argument that because so many scribes, editors, and other readers have agreed over several centuries that the tales as we have them are unfinished, we must be sceptical of more contemporary assertions that they are in fact complete.[9] Second, I accept David Seaman's arguments that Chaucer did not intend 'The Words of the Franklin to the Squire' as an interruption of the *Squire's Tale*; thus the incompleteness of the tales I am considering differs from that of the two interrupted tales, *Sir Thopas* and the *Monk's Tale*.[10] Third, I believe that the fact that the *Cook's Tale* survives in most manuscripts of the *Tales* provides the best evidence about Chaucer's own intentions for the tale at the point he ceased work on it, and outweighs arguments from the text that Chaucer meant to cancel it.[11] All three of these assumptions reflect my inclination to examine the manuscripts' evidence before accepting any hypothesis about Chaucer's intentions, however ingenious, that is based solely on interpretation of his text. Similarly, I aim to interpret the details of that evidence, so far as possible, without prior commitment to a binding hypothesis about the transmission of the *Canterbury Tales*. For example, I do not make any *a priori* assumptions about whether or not Chaucer would have published the *Tales* in their present state, which is in some ways obviously incomplete, or about the form(s) in which they might have circulated either before or shortly after his death. Instead I simply make guarded use of the Manly & Rickert classification of the manuscripts, limiting my faith mostly to their judgements about which pairs or small groups of manuscripts were likely to have been copied from one another or from a common exemplar or archetype.[12] Finally, because we can fix the dates of almost all the surviving manuscripts only to within a specific quarter of the fifteenth century, or at best to within a decade, I assume that the relative chronology of manuscripts of similar date must remain a matter of conjecture. My hypotheses, therefore, do not depend on either a particular sequence of copying for the earliest manuscripts or a particular pattern of survival.[13]

THE MANUSCRIPTS OF THE *COOK'S TALE* AND THE *SQUIRE'S TALE*

Of the many *Tales* manuscripts, a significant number do not contain these tales. An initial outline of which manuscripts do and do not contain them will help establish a context for some of the numbers which appear later in this essay, and also will enable me to reconsider the question of how often the *Cook's Tale* and the *Squire's Tale* were actively suppressed.[14] Of the 82 manuscripts listed by Ralph Hanna III in the Textual Notes to *The Riverside Chaucer*, one contains only a brief excerpt from the *General Prologue* recorded from memory; seventeen others are anthologies of various kinds containing from one to five *Tales*, never the Cook's or the Squire's; and two are ambiguous cases. Regardless of whether these last two survive from complete codices or from anthologies, their evidence is so partial that we can draw no conclusions about the *Cook's Tale* or the *Squire's Tale* from them.[15] Five further manuscripts, to judge by their contents or their codicological features or both, represent complete codices, but are so partial that we cannot even make an informed guess about how their scribes would have handled the two incomplete tales.[16] Another two fragmentary manuscripts contain no direct evidence for these tales. Although the textual affiliations of what does survive are clear enough to permit a conjecture about how these manuscripts would have treated the Cook's and Squire's tales, such a hypothesis would not affect the larger argument I will pursue here, and so I will not include them in what follows.[17]

Two relatively complete manuscripts, Bodley 414 and Bodmer, lack both tales, probably because their shared exemplar did as well. But these omissions apparently resulted from accidents of transmission rather than from any purposeful suppression.[18] A further three copies preserve evidence only for one tale or the other. The very fragmentary manuscript divided between the John Rylands Library and the Rosenbach Foundation contains only the *Cook's Prologue* and the first few lines of his tale, and nothing of the *Squire's Tale*.[19] Northumberland, on the other hand, preserves only the *Squire's Tale*, and it seems impossible to determine whether it ever included the *Cook's Tale*, and if so, in what form.[20] Finally, Holkham Hall 667 seems never to have contained the *Cook's Tale*, but as in the case of Bodley 414 and Bodmer, this omission seems to have been accidental rather than intentional.[21] We therefore have evidence from 50 manuscripts for how the *Cook's Tale* was treated, and for the treatment of the *Squire's Tale*, from 51.[22]

While it may seem odd to devote so much space to establishing which copies do not even include the two tales on which I will focus, this survey draws our attention to a significant fact: the evidence for conscious suppression of the two incomplete tales is quite limited, perhaps surprisingly so. Such evidence can be found clearly only in the Paris manuscript, Jean d'Angoulême's copy. This manuscript never included the *Cook's Tale*. The *Squire's Tale* ends at V.28 and is followed by a comment which begins 'Ista fabula est valde absurda in terminis'. Both the interrupted tales are likewise abbreviated, *Thopas* after three stanzas and the *Monk's Tale* after four. That all of the incomplete tales are omitted or abbreviated suggests that their incompleteness was a major reason for Jean's lack of interest in them.[23] To Paris we might add one other instance of possible suppression of the *Squire's Tale*. This is not another complete copy of the *Tales* but rather Harley 1239, apparently intended as a collection of Chaucer's romances – *Troilus*, as well as five tales.[24] Given the generic focus of the collection, the omission of the *Squire's Tale* is surprising, and may well be due to the tale's incompleteness.

GAMELYN IN THE *CANTERBURY TALES*

Although outright suppression of these two tales is in fact rare, the manuscripts clearly show that some scribes (or their supervisors) were dissatisfied with the received text of these two tales, ending at I.4422 and V.672, respectively. Scribes responded more often by slightly abbreviating their text or by adding to it, and by far the most commonly occurring such interpolation is the romance *Gamelyn*. This survives in 25 fifteenth-century manuscripts as well as in two later copies. Almost always it immediately follows the complete Chaucerian text of the *Cook's Tale*, which breaks off just after two new characters have been introduced and a new phase in Perkyn Revelour's career has begun.[25] Accounts of *Gamelyn* sometimes imply that it was substituted for the *Cook's Tale* or its conclusion, but such language is misleading;[26] it is a supplement to the Chaucerian text, rather than a substitute for any part of it. Although scribal passages linking the *Cook's Tale* and *Gamelyn* create a fiction of substitution, by having the Cook suggest he is interrupting at I.4422 a story which exists in some complete form (even if only in his head), there is no evidence at all that Chaucer himself ever proceeded any further; in fact, some manuscripts preserve positive assertions that he did not.[27]

Nor is there persuasive evidence that *Gamelyn* has any connection with Chaucer, even as a piece of source material which he intended to rewrite for some pilgrim such as the Yeoman.[28] Despite the number of copies, *Gamelyn* is largely confined to manuscripts which fall into two of the Manly & Rickert groups: *c*, which includes such early manuscripts as Corpus 198 and Lansdowne 851, and *d*, a group which appears to have its origins late in the first quarter of the fifteenth century, and to derive for the most part from the same 'ancestor' or archetype as the *c* manuscripts. Exceptions are copies which show clear evidence of drawing together material from more than one manuscript group, including *cd*; the most significant of these is Harley 7334.[29] *Gamelyn* does not appear in most of the manuscripts which are generally considered most reliable, such as Hengwrt, Ellesmere, Gg.4.27, Dd.4.24, and Egerton 2726.[30] Thus it appears that an early scribe or 'editor' inserted *Gamelyn*, largely unmodified, to repair a perceived deficiency in a copy of the *Tales* which turned out to be the archetype of a large number of the surviving codices.

The evidence suggests that in this copy *Gamelyn* followed I.4422 without any transition. But this state of the text is preserved in only seven manuscripts.[31] This is not terribly surprising; the insertion, by itself, of *Gamelyn* provides a complete tale for the Cook but does little or nothing to conceal the discontinuity at the end of Chaucer's *Cook's Tale*. There were several other attempts to do so. In one manuscript, Lansdowne, the Cook interrupts himself, announcing that the rest of Perkyn's story is too 'foule' to tell further, and briefly introduces the subject matter of *Gamelyn*. This scribe was working from a set of exemplars which lacked transitions or prologues in several other parts of the *Tales* as well, and the transition from the *Cook's Tale* to *Gamelyn* is one of several pieces of text supplied by the scribe to 'finish' the text he had inherited. By supplying links in some places and providing new headings for Chaucerian text in others, the scribe created a work where prologues and tales alternate with absolute regularity.[32] The manuscript also conceals the loose end of the *Squire's Tale*; V.671-2 are suppressed, and in eight added lines the Squire explains that because his tale is becoming so long, he will wait until he takes another turn in the pilgrims' game to finish it. This solution exemplifies the local nature of many of the scribal additions to these tales and the *Canterbury Tales* as a whole. Although the scribe has read the text with some attention (his addition echoes some of Chaucer's own language), the Lansdowne scribe has made no attempt to address other kinds of discontinuities which are less obvious and would require more extensive intervention in his text. For example, neither the Squire nor any of the other pilgrims takes a second turn at tale-telling in Lansdowne, nor has the scribe supplied tales for those described in the *General Prologue* to whom Chaucer never assigned a tale. The scribe's systematic work on the links and the structure of the *Tales* actually makes clear how superficial was his effort to present a 'complete' text of the work.

A briefer transition between the *Cook's Tale* and *Gamelyn* survives in thirteen manuscripts, and probably also appeared in another three which have lost leaves since the fifteenth century.[33] As in Lansdowne, the *Cook's Tale–Gamelyn* link is again one of a comprehensive set of scribal additions to the text designed to conceal its unfinished state. These additions distinguish the Manly & Rickert group *d*, and so apparently have their origins in the archetype(s) from which those copies derive. Although this effort to finish the text is closely parallel to that of the Lansdowne scribe, we cannot be certain that the Lansdowne scribe and those who prepared the *d* archetype knew of each other's work, because apparently neither manuscript drew directly on the language of the other's added passages.[34]

GAMELYN AND OTHER SOLUTIONS TO THE COOK'S TALE IN PARTICULAR MANUSCRIPTS

While *Gamelyn* is present in many manuscripts, the example of Lansdowne illustrates the value of looking at individual copies in more detail in order to understand scribal practice. In what follows, therefore, I will look more closely at how several scribes incorporated *Gamelyn* into the *Tales*, or arrived at other ways of repairing or concealing the unfinished state of the *Cook's Tale*. First, I will examine certain codicological features of Christ Church, Bodley 686, and Harley 7334. Then, I will go on to review the scribal ending to the tale which survives in Chicago and Rawlinson 141, and finally will discuss an altered position for the tale in Additional 35286, one which was probably shared by Harley 7335.

Christ Church offers a straightforward instance of a scribe acquiring *Gamelyn* from a supplemental exemplar. In his first stage of copying the scribe left the remainder of a quire blank after I.4422, and then went on to begin the *Wife of Bath's Prologue* in a new quire. He apparently copied the rest of the *Tales*, again leaving the remainder of a quire blank after the *Squire's Tale*, before discovering another exemplar which did contain *Gamelyn*. In a separate stage of work he copied the romance on the blank leaves left after I.4422 and then on an additional quire of half the usual length, inserted to accommodate the remainder of *Gamelyn*. What the scribe of Christ Church 152 has done is not extraordinary. The practice of comparing multiple exemplars to obtain the most complete text possible was of course quite common among scribes of

Middle English literary manuscripts, and perhaps especially so when they were copying a popular work such as the *Canterbury Tales* for which exemplars may well have been easily available.[35] Christ Church 152 is particularly important for understanding treatment of the *Cook's Tale*, however, because it provides evidence for two important kinds of scribal practice – not only the provision of *Gamelyn*, but also, in the first stage of copying, the leaving of blank space after the tale, a pattern which will be discussed in more detail below.

Bodley 686 likewise provides two kinds of evidence about the transmission and reception of the *Cook's Tale*. In this manuscript the tale has been expanded by about 40 lines, including a 12-line conclusion which administers what the interpolator regarded as poetic justice to Perkyn and his disreputable friends:[36]

> What thorowe hymselfe and his felawe that sought,
> Unto a myschefe bothe they were broght.
> The tone y-dampned to presoun perpetually,
> The tother to deth for he couthe not of clergye.
> And therfore, yonge men, lerne while ye may
> That with mony dyvers thoghtes beth prycked al the day.
> Remembre you what myschefe cometh of mysgovernaunce.
> Thus mowe ye lerne worschep and come to substaunce.
> Thenke how grace and governaunce hath broght hem a boune,
> Many pore mannys sonn, chefe state of the towne.
> Ever rewle the after the beste man of name,
> And God may grace the to come of the same.

Because two recent studies have been devoted entirely to this manuscript's version of the tale, I do not want to revisit its content, but the codicological features of Bodley 686 do demand some attention here.[37]

Most previous descriptions have overestimated the number of hands in this manuscript. In fact, only one scribe is responsible for essentially all of Bodley 686.[38] But his writing, and the shade of his ink, vary in a way that shows he did not copy the manuscript in sequence. Although his writing is rather variable throughout the manuscript, there is an especially marked difference between the writing on fols 1–54 and 56–95, and the writing which appears in corrections on these folios, in the text on fol. 55 (which contains the revised form of I.4383-4422), and on fols 96 et seq. (Pls 1–2).[39]

These variations in the scribe's writing are important for the present discussion because they show that the scribe, apparently uncertain about how to finish the *Cook's Tale*, at first copied only I.4365-82 to the bottom of fol. 54ᵛ, left fol. 55 blank, and then went on to begin Fragment II in a new quire. Later – apparently at the same time as he made corrections to other folios copied in this first stint – he returned to finish the *Cook's Tale* not with *Gamelyn*, to which he apparently did not have access, but with an expanded and revised version of I.4383-4422.[40] This *remainiement* contains not only the roughly 40 added lines but also frequent and purposeful revisions of Chaucer's own lines. By contrast, the eighteen lines of the tale copied in the first stint contain only

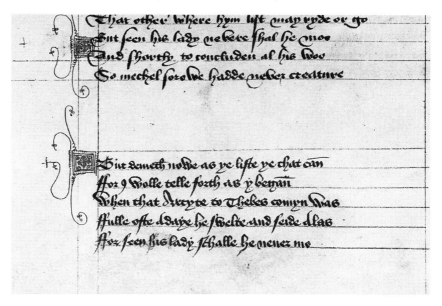

Pl. 1. MS Bodley 686, fol. 17ᵛ. Reproduced by permission of the Bodleian Library, Oxford. Reproduced 81 per cent.

a few minor variants of commonplace kinds, which probably do not result from any conscious intervention by the scribe. This difference suggests that the *remainiement* had not been ready when he was engaged in his first stint of copying, and that the need to fill exactly the blank space left by the scribe, the recto and verso of fol. 55, was one determinant of that *remainiement*'s length and thus of its content. In other words, one of the motivations for its presence, perhaps as important as any interest in completing the text, was a desire for codicological neatness, a need to avoid either a blank space between tales or an inserted leaf.[41] Despite this attempt at disguise, however, Bodley 686, like Christ Church, clearly attests to two scribal practices, leaving blank space after the *Cook's Tale*, as well as using interpolation to solve the difficulties the tale presented.

Another manuscript, Harley 7334, long an object of controversy among those concerned with Chaucer's text, provides similar, if again somewhat obscured, evidence for the practice of making Fragment I physically disjunct from the rest of the text and beginning Fragment II on a new quire. Here the *Cook's Tale* ends at I.4414 – 'And þus þe ioly *prentys* had his leue / Now let hy*m* ryot al the night or leue' – so the tale takes the form of a simple anecdote which relates the riotous life and dismissal from employment of Perkyn Revelour, without ever introducing Perkyn's friend, his wife who 'swyved for hir sustenaunce', or the next stage in Perkyn's career. As a conclusion, I.4413-14 do not conform to the patterns of closure in the other *Tales*, but the Cook's

58

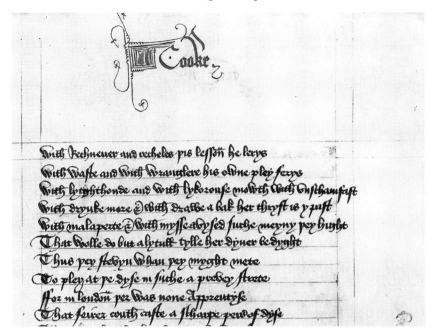

Pl. 2. MS Bodley 686, fol. 55ʳ. Reproduced by permission of the Bodleian Library, Oxford. Reproduced 79 per cent.

apparent bidding of farewell to Perkyn offers a plausible end to the brief narrative and a kind of transition to *Gamelyn*. Here, as in Lansdowne and the *d* manuscripts, this adjustment to the end of the *Cook's Tale* is part of a larger pattern of scribal interference in the text.[42]

Several features argue that the scribe copied to this point, left the remainder of the quire blank, and then took up copying the *Man of Law's Tale* and perhaps the rest of the text, returning to *Gamelyn* only later. *Gamelyn* begins at the top of fol. 59ʳ, the third leaf of a quire of eight, continues to the end of this quire, and then concludes on a quire of six leaves, unique in this manuscript.[43] *Gamelyn* ends on the 27th line of fol. 70ᵛ, and is followed by eleven blank lines. This last leaf of the quire does not contain a catchword, and Fragment II begins at the top of fol. 71ʳ, the first leaf of a new quire. The irregularly sized quire, the failure to move immediately to the next part of the text after the end of *Gamelyn*, the coincidence of textual and bibliographical boundaries, and the lack of a catchword make it clear that *Gamelyn* was not copied after the *Cook's Tale* and before Fragment II, but rather in a separate stage of work.[44]

At least two possible explanations for why the scribe arranged his work in this way suggest themselves. Which one we prefer will depend partly on how we interpret the note which appears after I.4413-14 at the bottom of 58ᵛ, in a script often used for catchwords in Harley 7334, and which is possibly in the hand of the main scribe: 'Icy come*n*cera le fable de Gamelyn'.[45] This might suggest that the scribe first left the remainder of the quire blank after copying to near the end of the *Cook's Tale*, before going on to begin Fragment II on a new quire; only much later in his work on the *Tales* did he hit on the idea of inserting *Gamelyn*, either on his own or by consulting another manuscript which did so. If this is the case, the scribe has worked in much the same way as the scribe of Christ Church.

But although Christ Church provides one model for understanding the progress of copying in Harley 7334, this is not the only possible hypothesis. We might instead explain the unique note about 'le fable de Gamelyn' by connecting it with another unique feature, the manuscript's abbreviated form of the *Cook's Tale*. Thus the note at the bottom of fol. 58^v may record a decision to begin *Gamelyn* 'ici' – that is, after I.4413-14, which are squeezed on one line at the bottom of the page – rather than a simple decision to include *Gamelyn*. That is, the scribe of Harley 7334 might have proceeded in a way similar to that of the copyist of Bodley 686. While the interruption in copying and the 'ici comencera' note argue the scribe waited to finish the *Cook's Tale* because he was uncertain how he would do so, it is much harder to draw definite conclusions about the focus of that uncertainty; he may have been uncertain about how to effect a transition from the *Cook's Tale* to *Gamelyn*, rather than unsure about whether or not *Gamelyn* would be included.[46]

We may mention more briefly two further ways of 'solving' or disguising the incompleteness of the *Cook's Tale*. A four-line conclusion which, like that in Bodley 686, brings the tale's characters to an exemplary bad end appears in Chicago and in Rawlinson 141:

> And þus w*ith* hordam and briberie
> Togeder þei vsed tyl hanged hye
> For who so euel byeth shal make a sory sale
> And þus I make an ende of my tale.

Because Rawlinson 141 seems to have been largely copied from the Chicago manuscript, we can plausibly attribute these lines to the scribe of the latter copy.[47]

A final way of responding to the unfinished state of the *Cook's Tale* was to move the tale to a later position in the manuscript, where it was apparently expected to receive less notice. In Additional 35286 the final four tales, with their prologues, are the Manciple's, Cook's, Canon's Yeoman's, and Parson's. The deviser of this arrangement probably placed the *Cook's Tale* in this particular position because the Cook is referred to in the *Manciple's Prologue*, where the Host calls on him to tell a tale before the Cook proves himself too inebriated to do so. Such attention to the text probably also explains the omission of the two lines which in most manuscripts appear at the beginning of the *Canon's Yeoman's Prologue*; these refer back to the 'life of St Cecile', and so omitting them would have been an easy way to remove an obvious inconsistency.[48] Yet such attempts to provide a superficial 'finish' to the text did not proceed very far, for the *Cook's Prologue* in Additional 35286 still refers back to the Reeve, and the *Parson's Prologue* still names the Manciple as the immediately preceding tale-teller. The manuscript thus exemplifies the kind of partial and local finishing that we have seen in, for example, Lansdowne. This solution to the *Cook's Tale* may well have been devised not for Additional 35286, but for its exemplar. The closely related and now fragmentary Harley 7335 no longer includes the *Cook's Prologue* and *Tale*, but in what survives Fragment II follows immediately after the *Reeve's Tale*. While we cannot be absolutely certain, it seems most likely that the *Cook's Tale* does not appear in its usual position in Harley 7335 because here too it was placed instead after the *Manciple's Tale*. Given that Additional 35286 dates from early in the second quarter of the fifteenth century, and that both copies are often of relatively high accuracy, it is quite possible that this order was devised early in the history of the *Tales'* transmission.[49]

THE SQUIRE'S TALE

The *Squire's Tale* provoked less extensive scribal activity than did the Cook's.[50] The interpolation devised by the scribe of Lansdowne is designed not to finish the tale but only to explain why it suddenly breaks off. The only other manucript which might be said to include an interpolation is Christ Church, where a second scribe added Hoccleve's Marian miracle 'The Sleeveless Garment' as a *Plowman's Tale* on blank leaves originally left after the *Squire's Tale*. Although lines unique to this manuscript link this *Plowman's Tale* to the pilgrimage, they do not link it to the preceding *Squire's Tale*.[51]

Scribes probably perceived less need for radical solutions to the state of the *Squire's Tale* because most of them had access to a linking passage which looked back to the tale as well as forward to the one which followed. In eleven manuscripts this passage is the 'Wordes of the Franklin to the Squier, and the Wordes of the Hoost to the Franklin' familiar from most modern editions as V.673-708.[52] In 21 manuscripts there appears a modified form of this passage which introduces the *Merchant's Tale*.[53] Thus there are relatively few copies where the *Squire's Tale* is followed immediately by a tale or prologue which does not refer back to the Squire or his tale – though among those few copies, there is striking variation in what that subsequent text is.[54]

Indeed, it is generally true that even though there is less interpolation than at the end of the *Cook's Tale*, there is still considerable variation at the end of the *Squire's Tale*. This may well be because the tale stops in mid-sentence and just after a major transition in the narrative, marked in some manuscripts as the beginning of 'tercia pars'. The manuscripts differ according to several factors; the fact that one cannot use any combination of these factors to classify the manuscripts argues that scribes introduced many of these variants rather freely. For example, the tale stops in some copies at V.670, the end of 'Secunda

Pars', but in others at V.672. Of the eighteen that stop at V.670, at least eight probably derive this feature from a shared archetype.[55] But variation even among closely related manuscripts suggests that scribes frequently suppressed V.671-72 in an effort to disguise the tale's fragmentary state.[56] Of those witnesses which do include V.671-2, surprisingly few have any Incipit for 'tercia pars', though such an Incipit appears in most modern editions.[57]

The manuscripts also vary according to whether they have an Explicit beside or after the final lines of the tale, and if so, whether this Explicit is for the tale or for 'Secunda Pars'. For example, of those copies which continue to V.672, twelve contain an Explicit for 'Secunda Pars' but not for the tale;[58] of these, five place the Explicit in the margin, four after V.670, and three after V.672.[59] On the other hand, twelve of the witnesses which continue to V.672 contain an Explicit for the tale but not for 'Secunda Pars'.[60] Royal 18 C.ii and Sloane 1685, in general closely related, are divided among these two groups of twelve, further evidence that scribes introduced variants rather freely at the end of the *Squire's Tale*. Those manuscripts where the tale stops at V.670 are similarly divided among those which contain an Explicit only for 'Secunda Pars' and those which contain one only for the tale.[61] A few copies, whether they end at V.670 or V.672, contain Explicits for both 'Secunda Pars' and the tale, while others contain them for neither.[62]

THE GAPS

The preceding has made clear that the received text of the *Cook's Tale* and the *Squire's Tale* was often perceived as a problem which needed to be addressed. The solutions, while generally local in nature, reflect repeated scribal intervention. Even when we take into account other kinds of scribal interpolation and editing, such as providing links between tales, the amount of this intervention is striking. In what follows I want to propose that the scribes were responding to a bibliographical anomaly as well as (and as much as) a textual one. To argue this, I will show how many manuscripts leave blank spaces after one or both of these tales. I want to argue that these do not represent separate responses by many scribes to the incomplete texts of these two tales, but rather are a traditional feature; the majority of scribes, in leaving blank spaces, were following their exemplars. In fact, the bibliographical discontinuity may well have come to the scribes' notice first, and drawn their attention to the incompleteness of their text. The pattern of attestation for these blank spaces suggests that they were introduced into the textual tradition very early. Indeed, they may well have prompted even the earliest textual responses, such as the insertion of *Gamelyn*.

There are a handful of witnesses for the practice of leaving blank space after the *Cook's Tale*. In three manuscripts the scribe copied to I.4422, provided no Explicit to the tale, and left the remainder of the quire blank before going on to the next piece of text. In Ellesmere this text was the opening of Fragment II, 'the wordes of the Hoost'. In Hengwrt likewise scribe B went on to the opening of Fragment II, although later a set of four quires containing Fragment III was placed after the quire in which the *Cook's Tale* ended.[63] In Christ Church the *Wife of Bath's Prologue* follows the *Cook's Tale*. In a fourth manuscript, Dd.4.24, the scribe left 13 lines blank after I.4422, at the bottom of fol. 53^v; an Explicit for the *Cook's Tale* and an Incipit for the 'prologus Legisperiti' appear at the top of fol. 54^r, and then Fragment II begins. While the scribe did not leave space to the end of a quire – fol. 53 is the fifth leaf in a quire of 24 – his treatment of the ending of this tale is unusual for this manuscript, particularly in the delay before the Explicit. With these four manuscripts we can associate two more, both discussed in detail above. The first of these is Bodley 686, which like Ellesmere, Hengwrt, and Christ Church, attests to the practice of treating Fragment I as physically independent from the rest of the text – even though in Bodley 686 the scribe has added lines to the *Cook's Tale* to fill the blank space he originally left at the end of that quire. The second is Harley 7334, where Fragment I likewise is physically separable from the rest of the manuscript – though this is the variant form of Fragment I which includes *Gamelyn*.

Although the number of manuscript witnesses to the leaving of blank space after the *Cook's Tale* is relatively small, their significance, I would argue, exceeds their number. First, in evaluating the numbers, we must remember that *Gamelyn*, and scribal lines linking the *Cook's Tale* to it, entered the textual tradition early in the fifteenth century and were copied, probably with little reflection, into many manuscripts thereafter. As a result, the textual uncertainty which the blank spaces both reflect and allow for does not exist in roughly half the surviving codices. Therefore, we should count the six copies I have discussed out of the remaining 27 rather than out of 50.[64] In addition, all six draw on exemplars which reflect the earliest history of the *Tales*. This is most obviously true of Hengwrt, Ellesmere, Harley 7334, and Dd.4.24, all copied within the first quarter (and possibly the first decade) of the fifteenth century. It is likewise true of the much later but highly accurate Christ Church, and of Bodley 686, copied with indifferent accuracy and frequent editing from sound exemplars. Moreover, these six witnesses leaving space after the *Cook's Tale* are in other ways quite different, and thus we cannot treat this feature as if it were isolated in a small corner of the textual tradition.

The fact that blank space appears after this tale in witnesses which are all in some sense 'early' but also textually distinct suggests that this space was an ancient feature of the textual tradition, which most likely antedated all of the surviving witnesses, and also a feature which scribes tended to resist. That resistance was expressed either by one or more of the strategies discussed above – interpolation, abbreviation, or removal to a less visible position in the manuscript – or, more simply, by closing up the blank space. There is an obvious commercial explanation for such resistance: if the codicological gap drew the text's incompleteness to the attention of the scribes themselves, then they could have expected it to affect their customers in the same way, and so they would have been eager to erase the tell-tale sign. Such resistance would explain the early appearance of *Gamelyn*. It would also explain the situation in such manuscripts as Gg.4.27 and Egerton 2726, otherwise generally comparable in their contents and accuracy to those copies which contain blank spaces, and all the others where scribes proceeded from the *Cook's Tale* to the following text without leaving any blank space.

Before reflecting further on the implications of this hypothesis, I would like to consider the *Squire's Tale*. Here the evidence forms similar patterns, though it is if anything clearer than for the *Cook's Tale*. To begin with, blank spaces follow the *Squire's Tale* in a much larger number of manuscripts, fourteen. The end of this tale coincides with the end of a quire in five manuscripts: Christ Church, Harley 1758, Harley 7335, Hatton, and Rawlinson 149.[65] The scribes have achieved a very similar effect in two further codices. In Additional 35286, because only a few lines of the *Squire's Tale* remained after the conclusion of one quire at fol. 130^v, the scribe appears to have reserved not an entire quire, but only a single leaf (or bifolium) for the remainder of the tale. When the manuscript was bound, this leaf was attached – perhaps after a second, blank leaf of the bifolium had been cut away – to the following quire, on which the scribe had begun the remainder of Fragment V.[66] The scribe of Rawlinson 223 seems to have worked in a similar way, writing the final lines of the *Squire's Tale* (to V.670) on fol. 89 and attaching it to the preceding quire of twelve.[67] In all seven of these manuscripts, the scribe kept open the possibility of adding some undefined amount of additional text, on however many leaves were needed to accommodate it, right up to the point when the manuscript was bound. In another seven manuscripts, scribes left blank space after the *Squire's Tale* which did not extend to the end of a quire: Corpus 198, Dd.4.24, Ellesmere, Fitzwilliam, Hengwrt, Holkham, and Trinity R.3.3.[68]

Lack of an Explicit, another sign of the text's incompleteness, is likewise more common for the *Squire's Tale* than for the *Cook's Tale*. Of these fourteen manuscripts which leave blank space after the *Squire's Tale*, Dd.4.24 and Hatton are the only two which include an Explicit for the tale. In Dd.4.24 it is combined with a note that this is 'as meche as Chaucer made', and in Hatton the Explicit appears only after the considerable blank space which follows V.672.[69] In addition to most of those in the group of fourteen leaving blank space, a further eleven manuscripts also lack an Explicit for the *Squire's Tale*.[70]

As is the case with the *Cook's Tale*, the manuscripts leaving blank space after the *Squire's Tale* include several of the chief witnesses; here too we find Hengwrt, Ellesmere, Christ Church, and Dd.4.24, and to these we may add Corpus 198, Additional 35286, and Harley 7335. But the remaining manuscripts are important, too, because they show clearly how the practice of leaving blank space persists in the midst of considerable variation in the text.[71] Blank space is left after the *Squire's Tale* whether it ends at V.670 or V.672, and whether it is followed by the authentic form of V.673-708, by the scribally emended version which introduces the Merchant, or by another piece of text entirely, such as the *Wife of Bath's Prologue* or the *Second Nun's Prologue*. The pattern of witnesses argues that we can explain the presence of these blank spaces as we did those following the *Cook's Tale*, as a derived feature which entered the textual tradition very early, and which some scribes preserved but others resisted. The more generations of copying behind a given codex, therefore, the less likely this feature was to be preserved.

When we consider the tales together, we have enough data to make some observations and conjectures about scribal practice. We find very similar treatment of the *Squire's Tale* in manuscripts which are closely related, such as Additional 35286 and Harley 7335, and Hatton and Rawlinson 149. In these cases there can be little question, I think, that the scribes were imitating their exemplars, rather than leaving such spaces independently.[72] Once we have recognized this possibility, moreover, it is hard to see why the spaces in other copies should not be interpreted similarly. Apparently the gaps were granted a certain authority, as if, without any contradictory indication, some scribes were ready to follow their exemplars by including a gap at the end of one or both tales. One clear piece of evidence for such a view of the scribes' attitude is the fact that in a number of manuscripts they left gaps which had little or no practical value. Where this space at the end of a tale coincides with the end of a quire, it has, at least potentially, a practical purpose: scribes reserved the option of inserting additional text of any length, if it should either come to hand or be written specifically in order to conceal the text's incompleteness. Yet in several manuscripts, where scribes left blank space only to the bottom of a recto or the end of a folio, this seems to have been merely a vestige of the larger space, inserted for the sake of fidelity to an exemplar, rather than a serious attempt to leave open the option of rearranging or inserting text.

A few particular cases suggest that scribes might have been less likely to leave the remainder of the quire blank if the end of the *Cook's Tale* or the *Squire's Tale* fell early in the quire. Thus, for example, the scribes of Additional 35286 and Rawlinson 223, as discussed earlier, copied the last lines of the *Squire's Tale* on a single leaf or bifolium, rather than setting aside an entire quire for them. The decision of the scribe of Dd.4.24 to leave only limited blank spaces after both tales may well be explained by the fact that he was using unusually long quires of 24 leaves. Moreover, in both Hengwrt and Ellesmere, Scribe B left space to the end of a quire after the *Cook's Tale*, where to do so required leaving only a few lines blank, or part of a verso and a single leaf.[73] But when he came to the end of the *Squire's Tale*, in both manuscripts Scribe B left blank only most of a verso, quite possibly because this part of the text falls relatively early in a quire in both of his manuscripts. If scribes did indeed decide whether to leave space to the end of a quire, or a smaller space, on the basis of how much vellum might have to be expended on the gap, then this suggests that they were rarely if ever thinking seriously about inserting additional text. They imitated end-of-quire spaces if that was easy, but otherwise they included a space which acknowledged the authority of their exemplars but did not really allow for possible future adjustments to the text.[74]

Paradoxically, then, at a point where a manuscript may seem to have the most bibliographical texture – where the scribe seems, on first glance, most clearly to be manipulating the format of his book – that format may be essentially a traditional feature inherited from the exemplar. What appears to be a feature of the individual codex may instead be, in effect, a textual feature. We should not suppose that scribes imitated this feature unthinkingly. The variations in text around the gaps, as well as the variations in the physical structure of the manuscripts, argue that the ends of these two tales drew careful attention from the scribes. Yet a scribe's exact motives in creating or preserving such a space may remain opaque to us. If the primary reason for allowing such spaces in the surviving manuscripts was their presence in the scribe's exemplars, then there is no real basis for imagining that in a particular manuscript they are a sign that a scribe was weighing whether or not to include *Gamelyn*, for example, or was otherwise uncertain about what text he would copy after the *Cook's Tale* or the *Squire's Tale*. Such conjectures have been made about, for example, the Ellesmere manuscript.[75] But is it really plausible to suppose that such a fundamental issue would not have been resolved in the careful planning that M. B. Parkes demonstrates took place before Ellesmere was copied? Rather than signs of scribal indecision, the gaps in Ellesmere, otherwise so finished a manuscript, seem the most extraordinary sign of the authority this format must have carried in the tradition.[76]

NOTES ON THE TEXT

Next I want to consider the notes which attribute the unfinished state of the *Cook's Tale* and the *Squire's Tale* to Chaucer himself. Here, as with the gaps, the pattern of evidence suggests that the scribes reproduced, revised, and suppressed a feature which entered the tradition very early. The similarity of these notes makes clear that they represent a unified tradition, rather than independent scribal annotations. Although they survive in only a few manuscripts, their presence in textually dissimilar codices argues that their tradition antedates Hengwrt, the earliest surviving manuscript to preserve such a note. In addition, the pattern of variation in the ways the notes are placed and in their relationship to more conventional Explicits suggests they would have been particularly vulnerable to omission as copies of the *Tales* were produced. Moreover, we can well suppose that scribes may have actively suppressed notes that Chaucer 'made no more' in order to disguise the text's incompleteness. While it may seem, at first, equally possible to imagine one or more scribes introducing such claims about Chaucer's activity into the textual tradition, comparisons with other Middle English manuscripts and printed books suggest that scribes were in fact likely to make more conservative remarks when faced with an apparently imperfect text. Finally, variations in the word-order of the notes that Chaucer 'made no more' resemble those which scribes imposed on Chaucer's text, and thus provide some positive evidence that the notes originated not with the scribes but with Chaucer himself.

It will be best to begin by describing the evidence from which I will make this series of arguments. The best-known comment on these tales' unfinished state is, of course, that in Hengwrt: 'Of this Cokes tale maked Chaucer na moore'. This appears in the margin beside the space the scribe had left on fol. 57ᵛ.[77] The ink in which this note is written differs from that used for the text of Fragment I, which suggests it was added at a later stage of work.[78] Explaining why the scribe might have waited before adding this note may well be a significant part of any hypothesis about how the Hengwrt manuscript was produced. But we cannot arrive at an adequate explanation by considering Hengwrt in isolation.[79] Instead we must take account of the fact that three other manuscripts contain notes so similar that they are clearly part of the same tradition as Hengwrt's. Unlike Hengwrt's, however, all these notes appear in the text column rather than in the margin:

Egerton 2864, fol. 64ᵛ: Chaunces maad no moor of the cookis tale
      Heer bigynneth the *prologe* of þe S*ergeauntis* tale of Lawe
Harley 7333, fol. 60ʳ: Off þis tale chauncier made namore
      Nowe this eondithe here þe cookes tale and nexste
      Folowyng begynneþe þe prologe of þe man of lawes tale
Physicians, fol. 78ʳ: Of this Cookes tale makith Chauncer nomore (as text)
      Here endith the Cookes tale
      The prophemye of the Manne of Lawes tale.

Although in one place the Manly/Rickert edition characterizes these as 'all, perhaps, copying Hg', this remark cannot be given serious consideration; it flatly contradicts the editors' other statements about the relationships of these manuscripts, which they elsewhere assign to several distinct groups.[80] The more plausible explanation is that these codices share the note through derivation from a common archetype, which must have been very early indeed in order to precede Hengwrt in the textual tradition.

One may well ask why Manly and Rickert preferred their own rather offhand conjecture to this hypothesis. The explanation, I think, lies in the tendency – reflected in their own statements as well as in those of subsequent scholars – to approach the complex problems which the textual tradition of the *Tales* poses by focusing first and most intently on Hengwrt and other early surviving manuscripts, and then turning to the voluminous evidence of the larger tradition only after broad fundamental conclusions have been reached. As a result, in this instance and in others, those hypothesizing are obliged to interpret the evidence of later manuscripts, which they already assume to be less worthy of attention, in a way that does not disrupt the theories they have based on a few early codices. The present study's perhaps over-exhaustive investigation of what appear to be a few minor details of the textual tradition is intended, in part, to illustrate how differently the evidence may be interpreted when one approaches it without prior commitments to a particular view of Hengwrt or any other witness.

One might, nevertheless, still wish to explain why, in Hengwrt, the scribe wrote the note on the *Cook's Tale* in a later stage of work. But one can imagine various reasons why he might have done so if, as I have proposed, he was deriving that note from an exemplar. One reason might be that the note was derived from a supplemental exemplar which came to hand only later in the process of copying. Or we could connect this note with other evidence in Hengwrt of editorial sophistication contemplated but rejected; it appears that the scribe (or his supervisor), after departing from his exemplars at some points, or leaving blank spaces which allowed him the option of departing from them, ultimately decided to go back and reproduce those exemplars as closely as possible. We can find such evidence, for example, in his returning at a later stage to write 'and prestis thre' at I.164, and 'Manciple' in the first line of the *Parson's Prologue*. Both readings are universally attested in the other manuscripts of the *Tales*, and so are difficult to attribute to the specific circumstances in which Hengwrt was produced. Along the same lines, I would argue, we best explain the *presence* of the statement that Chaucer made 'na moore' by referring to the larger textual tradition and thus to the exemplars of Hengwrt – though the evidence that it was written later than the text of the *Cook's Tale*, together with other physical features like those I have briefly described here, may tell us much about how the scribe made use of his exemplars in producing this codex.

Similar notes accompany the *Squire's Tale* in five manuscripts. These are less uniform in their language than those on the *Cook's Tale*. In Physicians, the only manuscript to have notes at the ends of both tales, the wording and treatment of the two notes are very similar (fol. 109[v]):

Of this Squyers tale Chauncer makith nomore (written as text)

Explicit fabula Incipit prologus Mercatoris

The other notes do not seriously contradict the possibility that the note, when it entered the tradition, was worded in this way; but if it was, it has been subject to more scribal abbreviation and emendation than that on the *Cook's Tale*. A couple of manuscripts do, however, retain what was probably the original placement of the note in the margin. In New College, for example, a note that 'Chaucer made no more' appears in the margin beside V.625 on fol. 78[v], although the text continues to V.672, where follows a conventional Explicit (fol. 79[v]):[81]

Here endith the Squieris tale

Begynnynge of the Marchauntis Prolog'

The note's position at V.625 may be derived from an archetype of 45-48 lines to a page in which the note was inadvertently moved in copying from the right page of an opening to the left.[82] That this note's position at V.625 in New College resulted from displacement in an exemplar is supported by the appearance of a similar note after V.672 in Princeton, a closely related manuscript (fol. 60[v]):[83]

Squyers tale for Chawser made no more
And here begynnyth the Marchaunte his prolog.

In Northumberland, a note that 'Chawcere made noo end of this tale' appears beside the Explicit at V.349, where the *Squire's Tale* ends in this manuscript:

Here endith the Squyer his tale
And here begynnyth the Marchant his prologg.

In Dd.4.24 the tale ends at V.670, and is followed immediately by 'Explicit secunda pars'; a few lines below appears:

Here endith the Squyers tale as meche as Chaucer made.

Finally, in Caxton's second print of the *Tales*, V.672 is followed by a note which, to judge by the word 'nomore', seems to be part of the same tradition as those which appear in the five manuscripts:

Ther is nomore of the Squyers tale
The wordes of the Frankeleyns

In this part of the text Caxton clearly was drawing on a manuscript to supplement his first edition, which did not contain the Squire-Franklin link, and he apparently obtained this statement about the *Squire's Tale* from that source.

As was the case with the notes on the *Cook's Tale*, these notes appear in witnesses which otherwise are quite different and, according to Manly & Rickert, are not closely related, aside from the pair New College and Princeton.[84] They appear in copies where the *Squire's Tale* may end at V.670 (Dd.4.24), V.672 (New College, Princeton, Physicians), or even V.349 (Northumberland), and where what follows may be the Squire-Franklin link (V.673-708; in Caxton's second edition, and clearly once in Dd.4.24, though now lost), that link as altered to fit the Merchant (in Physicians and Northumberland), or even the genuine *Merchant's Prologue* (in New College and Princeton). This distribution argues against any attempt to see the history of these notes as one in which the surviving witnesses derive from one another. Instead it seems that they, like the notes to the *Cook's Tale* and the gaps, are vestiges of a stage in the transmission of the *Tales* when such notes were more common than they are in the surviving manuscripts.

There are, of course, some significant differences in the evidence for the gaps, on the one hand, and that for the notes, on the other. To begin with, the notes coincide with the gaps in only two copies, Hengwrt and Dd.4.24 – though, perhaps significantly, these are two early and generally reliable manuscripts. In addition, the evidence for the notes is at first glance weaker than that for the gaps, both in terms of absolute numbers of witnesses, and because the direction of variation is clearer for the gaps. They are well attested in earlier and more accurate manuscripts, while the later manuscripts reflect the scribal tendency to eliminate such gaps. The notes, on the other hand, are attested in only two of the earliest manuscripts, and otherwise seem dispersed rather randomly through the textual tradition. Yet the greater scarcity of the notes can be understood if we look at certain patterns in the scribes' treatment of them and of Incipits and Explicits more generally.

What can be observed at the ends of these two tales is a process of regularizing the Incipits and Explicits that characterizes the history of the *Tales* as a whole. As discussed above, while the best manuscripts often lack Explicits for these two tales, scribes apparently added them as the textual tradition evolved, so the treatment of these tales would conform more closely to that of others. More generally, the scribes tended to make the entire text conform to a strucure of prologues alternating with tales, and thus would either omit or emend Incipits and Explicits which survive in some of the best manuscripts but do not conform to this pattern. For example, links introduced as the 'Wordes of the Host' in Ellesmere, Hengwrt, and some other manuscripts were identified as prologues; in addition, scribes preceded the early heading to the *Retractions*, 'Here taketh the makere of this book his leve', with a more conventional statement that 'Heere endeth the Parson's Tale'.[85] We see the same process at work in these comments on the unfinished state of the *Cook's Tale* and the *Squire's Tale*. In Hengwrt the note appears instead of an Explicit; strictly speaking, the same is true also of Egerton 2864, New College, and Caxton's second printing. But in the remaining copies these notes appear together with the more usual kinds of Explicits.

We can also observe a scribal tendency to regularize the placement of these notes by bringing them from the margins into the text column. Once this happened, they may have been perceived as merely anomalous and extraneous information within the Explicits, and we can easily imagine a subsequent stage in transmission to have been further regularization through simple removal of the statements that 'Chaucer made no more'.[86] Princeton and New College demonstrate even more clearly why these notes were likely to be deleted in the course of transmission. In Princeton the placement of the note beside an Explicit puts the two into competition, in effect, and New College's incorrect placement of the marginal 'Chaucer made no more' shows how little attention a scribe might pay to such a note once his copy included an Explicit.

In order to understand why, in general, the gaps survive in some manuscripts but not in others, we can only speculate about the scribes' motives and their apparently differing judgments about what their patrons and readers might accept. On the one hand, the notes may have been a more unusual feature of these books, since, as Hanna has pointed out, the gaps in Hengwrt and other manuscripts would have resembled those which frequently resulted from the 'booklet' production of codices.[87] As a reader or potential buyer inspected a copy of the *Tales*, the gaps may not have always drawn attention to themselves as signs that something was irregular in the text at this point. The notes, however, would have done so, and for that reason may have been more subject to suppression.[88] On the other hand, some scribes apparently valued the information the notes provided and wished for this reason to preserve them, even as they made various kinds of changes to the adjacent *ordinatio* and text – including closing up the bibliographical gaps present in their exemplars.

THE AUTHORITY OF THE NOTES AND GAPS

A modern student of Chaucer's text finds puzzling the scribes' apparent decision to suppress notes which authorize the text's discontinuity at the ends of these two tales – which state definitely that despite these tales' unconventional lack of closure, a reader should trust the manuscript before him or her. Yet this reaction simply draws attention to the contrast between two different ways of measuring completeness. We are accustomed to the idea that it is important to distinguish what an author such as Chaucer wrote from what others may have added to it, and thus our sympathies are with the notes which mark the boundaries of what Chaucer wrote. But the overall evidence of the tradition, as surveyed in the first part of this essay, suggests that those producing the manuscripts were often more concerned with giving the tales plausible conclusions and links, rather than with the exact boundaries of Chaucer's 'making'. Familiarity with the ways scribes treated the *Cook's Tale* and the *Squire's Tale*, and indeed the *Canterbury Tales* more generally, has the effect of highlighting how distinctive are the notes which state that Chaucer 'made no more'. If the scribes transmitting this text clearly were not always over-scrupulous about authenticity, is it wise to assume that these notes are scribal?

Another way to evaluate the manuscript notes about these two tales is to compare them with other remarks that appear where printers and scribes are faced with somewhat similar situations. Let us begin with the early printings of the *Tales*. In his second edition Caxton had followed V.672 with a note probably derived from the manuscript he had used to correct his first edition: 'Ther is nomore of the Squyers tale'.[89] This note, making no reference to Chaucer, is more ambiguous than those in the manuscripts, and Wynkyn de Worde transformed it into a note clearly about the printer's own search for copy rather than about Chaucer's authority for the state of his text: 'There can be founde no more of this forsayd tale whyche I have ryght dilygently serchyd in many dyuers scopyes'.[90] Thynne apparently derived the note in his *Works* of 1532 from de Worde's: 'There can be founde no more of this foresaid tale / whiche hath ben sought in dyvers places'. It is worth emphasizing that even in his imposing 'authorizing' edition of Chaucer, Thynne does not claim Chaucer's authority for his incomplete text. Should we suppose then that Scribe B or any other early scribe of the *Tales* would have done so on his own initiative?

We might compare the note in de Worde's and Thynne's editions with those in some manuscripts of other Middle English works. Here we find scribes making similar assertions about their good-faith efforts to provide 'complete' texts, though their explanations focus on the imperfections of their exemplars, rather on their attempts to repair these. For example, in a book of receipts and other medical writings, copied in 1528, one John Reed, 'at two points where the text seems confused ... takes pains to point out to the reader that he is not responsible for the confusion'.[91] Reed in both cases attributes the imperfection of his text, which he believes will be apparent to his reader, to his exemplar: 'I follow my copy word for word', he states on fol. 61[r], and 'I followed my copy' on fol. 64[r].[92] Kathleen Scott cites a 'somewhat fussy direction' by the copyist of a *Brut* chronicle who acknowledges some of the text is missing and suggests that if the book's owner finds it, it should be written out 'in þe henderend of þis boke or in þe forþerend of it whene he gettes þe trew copy'.[93] The situation of this scribe is not entirely parallel to that the Chaucer scribes found themselves in, but it is significant that the *Brut* scribe makes no attempt to authorize the incompleteness of his text. Instead, he makes an appeal to the 'trewe text' against the authority of his immediate exemplar.[94]

More similar to the notes in de Worde's and Thynne's printings of the *Tales* is one of John Shirley's notes in Cambridge, Trinity College, MS R.3.20, which focuses on his own activity and the state of his exemplar: 'Shirley kouþe fynde no more of þis copye'.[95] Another comment in the same manuscript, howver, is more like those in Hengwrt and other *Tales* manuscripts because it invokes the poet's authority for the condition of the scribe's text: 'Of this balade Dan John lydgate made no more'.[96] Yet this note cannot be taken as evidence that the Hengwrt note is of a typical scribal kind. Rather it is so close, in language and word order, to the notes on the *Cook's Tale* and the *Squire's Tale* that it must be derived from them, either through Shirley or through Lydgate himself. In support of the former possibility, we might recall that one of the manuscripts containing the *Cook's Tale* note is Harley 7333, in which the *Tales* (and several other texts) derive from Shirleian exemplars; evidently Shirley had seen such a note. On the other hand, Lydgate reproduces the language of Chaucer's works so closely and so often that we could also easily imagine the origins of this note lie with him. Lending some support to the latter possibility is the presence of a virtually identical note in another manuscript of the Lydgate poem.[97]

This evidence from the printed editions of the *Tales* and from manuscript copies of other Middle English texts draws our attention, in the first place, to the simple but important fact that the manuscript notes on the *Cook's Tale* and the *Squire's Tale* assert nothing about the processes that produced the manuscripts, such as a search for additional copy. Instead, they concern Chaucer's activity as the author of these tales. Second, the evidence of how scribes behaved when confronted with apparent imperfections in their texts lends no support to the notion that a scribe of the *Tales* might have added a statement that 'Chaucer made no more' on his own initiative.[98] These two points, in turn, argue that we should give credence to the notes as the best explanation for why the tales survive in their present form, rather than suppose that these two tales were once complete but exist as they do because the remainders were lost through accident or conscious suppression.[99]

There is a further question about the authority of the notes and gaps, beyond that of whether they give us reliable information about Chaucer's own work and intentions. This question concerns the *origins* of the notes, as well as of the gaps which suggest the text is discontinuous at the ends of the *Cook's Tale* and the *Squire's Tale*. Might their *presence* be a Chaucerian aspect of the work? While any conjecture about this issue must be speculative, the arguments I have made so far lead me to infer that the answer to this question is yes. The notes and the gaps entered the textual tradition very early, and were copied with varying degrees of frequency and fidelity by the scribes of the surviving manuscripts.[100] Moreover, their presence cannot be casually attributed to typical scribal practice. Logically, there appears to be no reason why we should not extend the inferred chain of copying of these features back to the very origins of the textual tradition in Chaucer's own working manuscript of the *Tales*. Of course, a hypothesis that the *Tales* were arranged and 'finished' after Chaucer's death by one or more 'literary executors' would be a way to explain the notes and the gaps. But as I have attempted to show, the evidence of scribal habits through the entire textual tradition does not suggest that these specific features are scribal in origin.[101]

While so far my arguments have been primarily negative – that the notes and gaps cannot be assumed to be scribal – there is also some positive evidence to support the idea that they derive from Chaucer himself. The exact details of how they might have made their way into the textual tradition must remain uncertain, as do so many things about Chaucer's interactions with 'Adam scriveyn'. But observing the variations these notes were subject to in transmission draws our attention to certain Chaucerian features of their language:

> Hengwrt: Of this cokes tale maked Chaucer na moore.
> Physicians: Of this Cookes tale makith Chauncer nomore.
> Harley 7333: Off þis tale chauncier made namore.
> Egerton 2864: Chaunces maad no moor of the cookis tale.
> Physicians: Of this Squyers tale Chauncer makith nomore.
> Princeton: Squyers tale for Chawser made no more.
> New College: Chaucer made no more.
> Northumberland: Chawcere made noo end of this tale.
> Dd.4.24: Here endith the Squyers tale as meche as Chaucer made.

While the word order in Hengwrt and Physicians is sharply inverted, the other copies apparently reflect scribal normalizing of that word order.[102] That is, these notes underwent variation similar to that which Chaucer's verse was subject to; B. A. Windeatt identifies such normalizing of word order as a very frequent kind of scribal response to Chaucer's language in *Troilus*.[103] That scribes treated these notes in the same way as they did Chaucer's verse does not necessarily prove that they too are Chaucer's, but the scribes' modifications of them highlight the notes' extraordinary syntax, a feature which helps make the note in Hengwrt so memorable.[104]

The notes are also consistent with another aspect of Chaucer's practice, his attempts to define his canon. The lists of his own works in the *Prologue* to the *Legend of Good Women* and in the *Retraction* represent one approach to that task, as Chaucer claims credit, albeit in self-deprecating contexts, for his 'makings'. Yet Chaucer also famously expresses anxiety about his loss of control over his texts when he turns them over to scribes for copying, in 'Adam Scriveyn' and at the end of *Troilus and Criseyde*. We can well imagine that he might have added the notes that he 'made no more' of the *Cook's Tale* and the *Squire's Tale* out of the same anxiety, this time not about 'mismetering' or corruption but rather about wholesale scribal addition to his text of the *Tales*. As the history of interpolation and other scribal intervention I have discussed here shows, such fears would have been well founded.

We may well ask if and why Chaucer would have released into the scribal medium unfinished tales which would have been particularly subject to interference. To consider this question raises the much broader one of whether Chaucer would have published the *Tales* in their present fragmentary form. Derek Pearsall has plausibly proposed that Chaucer may have devised the story-collection and its dramatic framework as a way of preserving a group of shorter pieces which otherwise might not have fared well in manuscript culture.[105] By collecting them in a larger work which filled an entire manuscript volume, Pearsall has argued, Chaucer hoped to increase their chances of survival. Though Pearsall does not extend this hypothesis to explain why Chaucer might have published the *Tales*, one certainly can do so. If Chaucer was anxious that the pieces collected in the *Tales* be disseminated, then there seems no reason to suppose he would have allowed them to remain on his desk pending some ideal state of completeness for the work as a whole.[106] And if Chaucer put into circulation a work that was obviously unfinished in so many other ways, for the sake of preserving the vast amount of work he had already completed, then he may well have been willing to include these two tales in their fragmentary state.

The leaving of gaps after these two tales is perfectly consistent with this model of Chaucer's dissemination of the *Tales*. If Chaucer's own intentions were incompletely realized, then his originals would likely have been in the form of a provisional codex, where the physical format gave him freedom to add and re-arrange material. Recent work on the booklet construction of Middle English manuscripts has highlighted the tendency of scribes to work in this way: to copy texts into a series of quires or multi-quire booklets while forestalling final decisions about contents or arrangement. We have much less evidence about how authors arranged their working originals and transmitted them to the scribes, but there seems to be no reason why we should not suppose that Chaucer worked in the same provisional way. The frequency with which scribes reproduced these gaps well into the fifteenth century supports the idea that 'Adam Scriveyn' may simply have imitated them from the copy Chaucer handed to him.

Thus those gaps are a sign not only, or even primarily, of the scribes' indecision but rather of Chaucer's own uncertainty about how he would proceed after I.4422 and V.672. There is no possible way to know what Chaucer may have had in mind. Perhaps these tales were to be interrupted, like *Sir Thopas* and the *Monk's Tale*. Or perhaps Chaucer would ultimately have cancelled the *Cook's Tale*. But the manuscripts tell us nothing about this possible future stage of Chaucer's intentions. Rather they argue simply that Chaucer, when he left the *Tales*, meant these two incomplete tales to be included and that he understood the text to be discontinuous where each of them breaks off. Though arguments of extraordinary ingenuity have been mustered to support the idea that the *Squire's Tale*, in particular, is either complete as it stands or is tactfully interrupted at just the right moment by the Franklin, the manuscript evidence argues that both Chaucer and the early scribes understood it differently from the complete tales, on the one hand, and the two clearly interrupted tales, on the other.[107]

Bibliographical hypotheses about the early history of the *Canterbury Tales* are not new. In fact, the theory that Chaucer left the tales or fragments on loose quires or booklets has become a common way to explain the inconsistencies in order and arrangement among even the earliest surviving manuscripts.[108] The popularity of such explanations has been fostered, I suspect, by increased awareness of booklet production as a scribal strategy, and particularly by intensive attention to the make-up of the Hengwrt manuscript of the *Tales*, where the scribe arranges his text in booklets and occasionally leaves blank space after tales. Yet the evidence I have gathered and discussed here argues this theory needs to be qualified. The surviving manuscripts do provide strong evidence for bibliographical discontinuities at the ends of the *Cook's Tale* and the *Squire's Tale*. Because blank spaces to the ends of quires followed these, Fragment I was physically independent from what followed, and the *Squire's Tale* (along with some amount of preceding material) was likewise separate from what followed it. At many other places in the *Canterbury Tales*, of course, there are clear discontinuities in the text; this is the whole basis for speaking of the work as a series of fragments. As the early and repeated provision of apocryphal linking passages makes clear, the scribes were often aware of these discontinuities and eager to respond to them. Yet there is little or no direct evidence that they were responding to *bibliographical* discontinuities at these points, as they clearly were when dealing with the *Cook's Tale* and the *Squire's Tale*. Instead, in most manuscripts (even in Hengwrt, and more so in other codices), most tales are copied continuously and across quire boundaries. The persistence of one kind of bibliographical disjunction, at the ends of the *Cook's Tale* and *Squire's Tale*, suggests that if such disjunctions at other points in the text played a significant role in the early transmission of the *Tales*, we would expect to see them preserved in the surviving manuscripts more often. But we do not.

This difference, I would argue, should make us reconsider whether Chaucer's own copy was thoroughly provisional; the bibliographical signs of uncertainty seem rather to have been restricted to these two specific points in the text. Thus while Chaucer's intentions may, like his working copy, have been open-ended at those particular places, his intentions for order and arrangement elsewhere may have been more stable, at least at the moment (or moments) when he released the text into the scribal medium. Much of the early scribes' subsequent uncertainty about the shape of the *Tales*, therefore, may have resulted from incomplete or inconsistent information in the text, rather than from codicological accidents or manipulation – even if exemplars remained unbound, as the habit of leaving space to the end of a quire after the two unfinished tales suggests.[109] While such use of unbound exemplars would have made possible the dizzying shifts in textual affiliation we observe in many extant manuscripts of the *Tales*, there may also have been – indeed, must have been, if scribes shifted exemplars within tales – some mechanism for preserving a stable order for those exemplars, and the decision to intervene in the text and rearrange the order would have been a distinct and conscious one. This broader set of implications for the arguments I have made here must, however, await further exploration elsewhere.[110]

NOTES

1 I discuss recent developments in the study of Chaucer manuscripts and provide a selective bibliography in 'Questions of Evidence: Manuscripts and the Early History of Chaucer's Works', in *Writing After Chaucer*, ed. by Daniel Pinti (New York, 1998), pp. 1-26. Although I have not, by any means, cited every point in which my arguments agree with or differ from theirs, in my approach and conclusions I am in dialogue with, for example, N. F. Blake, *The Textual Tradition of the Canterbury Tales* (London, 1985); Ralph Hanna III in several of the essays collected in his *Pursuing History: Middle English Manuscripts and Their Texts* (Stanford, 1996); Charles A. Owen, Jr., *The Manuscripts of the Canterbury Tales*, Chaucer Studies XVII (Cambridge, 1991); Derek Pearsall, *The Canterbury Tales* (London, 1985), esp. chs 1 and 2.

2 *Mouvance* is Paul Zumthor's term: 'By *mouvance* I mean to indicate that any work, in its manuscript tradition, appears as a constellation of elements, each of which may be the object of variations in the course of time or across space'; *Speaking of the Middle Ages*, trans. by Sarah White (Lincoln, Nebr., & London, 1986), p. 96, n. 49.

3 Daniel W. Mosser, 'Reading and Editing the *Canterbury Tales*: Past, Present, and Future (?)', *Text*, 7 (1994), 201-32. At present the *mouvance* of these two tales can be studied most conveniently in *The 'Canterbury Tales': Fifteenth-Century Continuations and Additions*, ed. by John M. Bowers (Kalamazoo, Mich., 1992).

4 For example, conjectures concerning the deliberations of the 'Ellesmere team' about how to handle the unfinished *CkT* appear in two essays in *The Ellesmere Chaucer: Essays in Interpretation*, ed. by Martin Stevens & Daniel Woodward (San Marino, Calif., & Tokyo, 1995): M. B. Parkes, 'The Planning and Construction of the Ellesmere Manuscript', pp. 41-7, and Ralph Hanna III, '(The) Editing (of) the Ellesmere Text', pp. 225-43. For a hypothesis about how the scribe of the Hengwrt MS handled this situation, see M. C. Seymour, 'Of This Cokes Tale', *Chaucer Review*, 24 (1990), 259-62.

5 John Burrow, 'Poems Without Endings', *Studies in the Age of Chaucer*, 13 (1991), 17-37.

6 E. G. Stanley, '"Of This Cokes Tale Maked Chaucer Na Moore"', *Poetica*, 5 (1976), 36-59; V. A. Kolve, 'The *Cook's Tale* and The *Man of Law's Introduction*: Crossing the Hengwrt-Ellesmere Gap', in *Chaucer and the Imagery of Narrative* (Stanford, 1984), pp. 257-96.

7 David Lorenzo Boyd, 'Social Texts: Bodley 686 and the politics of the *Cook's Tale*', in *Reading From the Margins*, ed. by Seth Lerer (San Marino, Calif., 1996), 81-97; Daniel J. Pinti, 'Governing the *Cook's Tale* in Bodley 686', *Chaucer Review*, 30 (1996), 379-88.

76

8 Elizabeth Scala, 'Canacee and the Chaucer Canon: Incest and Other Unnarratables', *Chaucer Review*, 30 (1995), 15-39; Kathryn L. Lynch, 'East Meets West in Chaucer's Squire's and Franklin's Tales', *Speculum*, 70 (1995), 530-51.

9 'Poems Without Endings', pp. 29-37. The final lines of the two tales do not conform to any of the usual forms of closure Rosemarie Potz McGerr has identified in most of the tales; 'Medieval Concepts of Literary Closure: Theory and Practice', *Exemplaria*, 1 (1989), 149-79.

10 '"The Wordes of the Frankeleyn to the Squier": An Interruption?', *English Language Notes*, 24 (1986), 12-18.

11 Such an argument is made by Martin Stevens in 'Malkin in the Man of Law's Headlink', *Leeds Studies in English*, NS 1 (1967), 1-5.

12 J. M. Manly & Edith Rickert, *The Text of the Canterbury Tales: Edited from all Known Manuscripts*, 8 vols (Chicago, 1940). For recent and cogent criticism of Manly and Rickert's understanding of the earliest surviving manuscripts, see Hanna, '(The) Editing (of) the Ellesmere Text' (cited above, n. 4). The *Canterbury Tales* project has announced plans to make all the textual evidence available in electronic format, on the model of *The Wife of Bath's Prologue on CD-ROM*, ed. by Peter Robinson (Cambridge, 1996), and thus promises a re-examination of the textual tradition, but I do not expect any conclusions drawn from that project to affect substantially the arguments I present here.

13 In *The Textual Tradition* (cited above, n. 1), Blake assumes and argues that Ellesmere was produced only after several others of the surviving manuscripts, an assumption shared by, for example, Hanna in '(The) Editing (of) the Ellesmere Text' (cited above, n. 4). But elsewhere in *The Ellesmere Chaucer: Essays in Interpretation* (cited above, n. 4), Kathleen Scott presents evidence that Ellesmere is somewhat earlier than has been previously assumed, and thus antedates, for example, Harley 7334; 'An Hours and Psalter by Two Ellesmere Illuminators', pp. 87-119. Her revised date would affect how we understand the production of Ellesmere and other early manuscripts.

14 I have not included Caxton's two printings of the *Tales*, usually accorded the status of manuscript witnesses, in this initial survey of the manuscripts. Both printings included *CkT* and *SqT* and will be referred to at a few specific points in what follows.

15 *The Riverside Chaucer*, ed. by Larry D. Benson (Boston, 1987), pp. 1118-19. Readers are referred to Hanna's Textual Notes for the manuscript sigla I employ here, and for full information about the locations and shelfmarks of the manuscripts. Ad⁴ preserves lines from the *General Prologue* description of the Parson, reconstructed from memory. The following manuscripts are anthologies containing selections from the *Tales*: Ar, Ct, Ee, Ha¹, Hl¹, Hl², Hl³, Hn, Ll¹, Ll², Np, Ph⁴, Pp, Ra⁴, Sl³, St, Tc³. Hl⁴ and Si are uncertain cases. The single leaf of Hl⁴ is perhaps more likely to survive from a complete copy of the *Tales*. Si seems to be unique among surviving manuscripts. It is not an anthology, because its only contents are four of the *Tales*; yet they are so well preserved that the manuscript does not appear to be the remnant of a complete copy. Rather, Si may represent the first stages of an effort to collect the *Tales* piecemeal, singly or in very small groups, as exemplars became available. The fact that the project did not progress very far argues against Owen's thesis in *The Manuscripts of The Canterbury Tales* (cited above, n. 1) that this was the method used to produce many more complete manucripts of the *Tales*.

16 These are Do, Ds², Kk, Me, and Pl. Do, Me, and Pl preserve parts of the *Tales* which never appear in the surviving anthologies; the single folio of Kk, and the two of Ds², resemble those of the expensive metropolitan vellum manuscripts of the *Tales* produced in the first half of the fifteenth century.

17 These are Ad² and Ph¹. Ad² is similar to Ht, and so probably would have contained *CkT* followed by a two-line transition and *Gamelyn*, and *SqT* followed by V.673-708, the Franklin's praise of the Squire, modified to introduce the *MerchT*. Ph¹ resembles Gg, and so probably *CkT* was followed immediately by Fragment II, and *SqT* by V.673-708, *FkPro*, and *FkT*.

18 The Manly & Rickert account (1: 59-61) suggests that this common exemplar missed out *MerchT* and *SqT* because while copying the scribe shifted exemplars, from a manuscript of the *a* type which placed them in the middle, to one of the *d* type which placed them very early. Having changed exemplars at a point in the text between these two possible positions, the scribe included them in neither stint of copying. *CkT* might have been omitted through the loss of leaves in the first of the manuscripts this scribe used, because the shared exemplar of Bo¹-Ph² also seems not to have invoked the first lines of Fragment II. For a lucid overview of Manly and Rickert's classification of the manuscripts, on which I draw in characterizing some of them as *a*, *b*, *c*, or *d*, see Hanna's Textual Notes to *The Riverside Chaucer* (cited above, n. 15), pp. 1119-21. In what follows I have used these symbols as rarely as was practical.

19 Because Ox is a *b* manuscript, it probably placed *MerchPro* and *MerchT* after *SqT*.

20 Manly and Rickert conclude that either II.1-98 or I.4325-4422 were never included in Nl (1: 387); I do not see any way to decide between these two possibilities.

21 Manly and Rickert (1: 284-87) argue persuasively that the scribe of Hk is making the best he can of very imperfect exemplars. In 'Additional 35286 and the Order of the *Canterbury Tales*', *Chaucer Review*, 31 (1997), 272-8, Simon Horobin asserts that *CkT* 'has been omitted deliberately in Ps, Hk, Bo¹, and Ph²', but does not present his evidence (p. 277, n. 6).

22 We can draw conclusions about how *CkT* was presented in one fragmentary manuscript, Ha⁵, even though neither *CkT* nor *CkPro* survives; see the discussion of tale-order in Ad³ below. Ph³ and Ra² include *Gamelyn* but not *CkPro* or *CkT*, but this appears to be simply the result of loss of leaves; the presence of *Gamelyn* justifies my inclusion of these two manuscripts in the following survey. Ha² also lacks *CkT* through loss of leaves, but the beginning of *CkPro* does survive in this manuscript, and so I include it as well.

23 This pattern is not obscured by the fact that in addition to these four, the two prose tales are absent and much of *CYT* has been omitted. The omission of the prose tales suggests Jean was interested primarily in Chaucer as a writer of verse rather than of prose, and is paralleled elsewhere, in Bo². A note following *CYT* states that 'maior pars istius fabule est pretermissa usque huc quia termini sunt valde absurda'. The pattern of omissions and abbreviations suggests Jean is using 'termini' to mean the endings of *SqT* and *CYT*, rather than 'the words or terms in which they are written', as argued by Paul Strohm in 'Jean of Angoulême: A Fifteenth Century Reader of Chaucer', *Neuphilologische Mitteilungen*, 72 (1971), 69-76, p. 73. Strohm's analysis of Jean's possible motives for his omissions, abbreviations, and comments overlooks the possibilities suggested here, which seem to me the most obvious ones.

24 These are the tales of the Knight, the Man of Law, the Wife of Bath, the Clerk, and the Franklin.

25 The discussion which follows, concerning whether and how manuscripts address the discontinuity between *CkT* and *Gamelyn*, mentions all the fifteenth-century copies of the latter. An eighteenth-century copy of *Gamelyn* from Ld¹ was inserted into En¹ (Manly & Rickert, 1: 134-35). Oxford, Bodleian Library, MS Ashmole 45, a composite manuscript, contains a copy of *CkT* and *Gamelyn*, of the sixteenth century or later, in an independent booklet of two quires. I have not yet been able to determine the textual affiliations of this copy. Bowers suggests that 'one eccentric, mutilated collection' places *Gamelyn* somewhere other than after *CkT*, but I am not sure which manuscript he means; *Continuations and Additions* (cited above, n. 3), p. 33. Ha⁴, in which *Gamelyn* follows a slightly abbreviated *CkT*, is discussed in more detail below.

26 Discussions of *CkT* and *Gamelyn* sometimes state or imply that the latter was substituted for the former or some part of it. See, for example, Bowers in *Continuations and Additions* (cited above, n. 3), p. 33; A. S. G. Edwards, 'Chaucer From Manuscript to Print: the Social Text and the Critical Text', *Mosaic*, 28 (1995): 1-12, p. 5; Tim William Machan, 'Chaucer's Poetry, Versioning, and Hypertext', *Philological Quarterly*, 73 (1994), 299-316, p. 301.

27 These scribal links, as well as the manuscript notes about Chaucer's own failure to complete the tale, are discussed separately later in this essay.

28 Bowers is the most recent proponent of this idea, in *Continuations and Additions* (cited above, n. 3), p. 33.

29 Others include Dl, Ii, Ry¹, and To. Ha⁴ will be discussed in more detail below.

30 Ch, which provides evidence both for *Gamelyn*'s absence from the best exemplars, and for the scribal practice of drawing on multiple exemplars for material, will be discussed in more detail below. The absence of text from the manuscripts I have listed here does not, in itself, prove the text is not genuine; the 'Epilogue to the Man of Law's Tale' is not in them, but it is, significantly, in the *b* group, which appears to be related only loosely to *cd* and does not contain *Gamelyn*.

31 These are Ch, Cp, Dl, Ld¹, Ry¹, Sl², and To. In the later copy in MS Ashmole 45, *Gamelyn* follows directly after I.4422.

32 Blake discusses La in *The Textual Tradition* (cited above, n. 1), pp. 119-22. For the texts of Lansdowne's added passages, see Bowers, *Continuations and Additions* (cited above, n. 3), pp. 43-6.

33 The link survives in Bw, En², Fi, Gl, Ht, Ii, Lc, Ld², Mg, Mm, Pw, Ry², and Sl¹; probably it was once also in Ha², Ph³, and Ra².

34 Richard Beadle presents intriguing testimony about yet another handling of the transition from *CkT* to *Gamelyn* in '"I wol nat telle it yit": John Selden and a Lost Version of the *Cook's Tale*', *Chaucer to Shakespeare: Essays in Honour of Shinsuke Ando*, ed. by Toshiyuki Takamiya & Richard Beadle (Cambridge, 1992), pp. 55-66. If the report of another manuscript version of *CkT* is to be trusted, I am much more inclined to attribute the variant to a scribe than to Chaucer himself.

35 Two other clear examples of such practice are Ha², where the scribe acquired apocryphal additions to *MerchT* from a supplemental exemplar and copied them into the margins, and Ln, where a second scribe acquired links and new information about tale-order by comparing manuscripts. For Ha² see Rosalind Field, '"Superfluous Ribaldry": Spurious Lines in the *Merchant's Tale*', *Chaucer Review*, 28 (1994), 353-67, especially pp. 357-8.

36 I cite Bowers' edition of these lines in *Continuations and Additions* (cited above, n. 3), p. 37.

37 These are Boyd, 'Social Texts: Bodley 686', and Pinti, 'Governing the *Cook's Tale*' (both cited above, n. 7). See my comments on Boyd's study in a review of the volume in which it appears: *Studies in the Age of Chaucer*, 20 (1998), 291-6.

38 Daniel Mosser's account of Bo² in *The Wife of Bath's Prologue on CD-ROM* (cited above, n. 12) departs from previous descriptions in attributing the entire manuscript to one scribe. The description by M. C. Seymour in *A Catalogue of Chaucer Manuscripts, vol. 2: The Canterbury Tales* (Aldershot, 1997), pp. 168-71, finds four scribal hands in the manuscript. I am grateful to Dr Malcolm Parkes for examining Bo² with me at length and confirming my initial judgement that it was written by one scribe.

39 In the former portion, the writing is rather rounded and the ink has dried to a solid black; in the latter, the scribe's writing contains more broken strokes and horns, and the ink has dried to a lighter brown shade. The identity of the hand is confirmed by the fact that in the folios after 96, the writing gradually reverts to the first kind, so that by fol. 107 it resembles that of fols 1-54 and 56-95. Thus the scribe's work conforms to a pattern seen fairly often in fifteenth-century manuscripts; as he began his second stint, perhaps after some time had elapsed, he imposed discipline on his own hand, writing more slowly to include more calligraphic features, but gradually reverted to writing in a way that was more familiar and presumably more rapid. See examples of both types of the scribe's writing in Pls 1 and 2. In correcting the first stint, the scribe provided ruled spaces at the bottoms of several folios to add lines he had missed out.

40 It is impossible to be certain whether the scribe himself, or a supervisor or patron, was responsible for the *remainiement* of I.4383-4422.

41 Owen points out that the ruling for fol. 55 allows for more lines than on other leaves, and that a few of the extra lines were left blank (*Manuscripts of the Canterbury Tales* (cited above, n. 1), pp. 25-6). While this may be evidence of imperfect communication between the scribe

and a supervisor, or simply of imperfect planning on the scribe's part, it does not present an obstacle to supposing, as I have, that the revision and expansion of *CkT* was intended to fill the blank space the scribe had left during his first stint.

42 The scribe's treatment of the 'Epilogue to the Man of Law's Tale' offers a close parallel to his practice with *CkT*. He suppressed the final 5 lines (II.1186-90), in which the speaker proclaims 'Ther is but litel Latyn in my mawe!', presumably in order to make plausible the manuscript's assignment of that speech to the Summoner, who according to the *General Prologue* (I.637-46) pretended to speak a great deal of Latin. See Mosser, 'Reading the *Canterbury Tales*' (cited above, n. 3), fig. 1, p. 215, for a photograph of fol. 58[v].

43 Most quires in Ha[4] are of eight leaves.

44 The scribe must have written *Gamelyn* before adding signatures to the quires, because their sequence takes account of the irregular quire added for the remainder of *Gamelyn*.

45 The scribe of Ha[4] also copied Cp and a number of other Middle English manuscripts, and is known as 'Scribe D' after A. I. Doyle & M. B. Parkes, 'The Production of Copies of the *Canterbury Tales* and the *Confessio Amantis* in the Early Fifteenth Century', in *Medieval Scribes, Manuscripts, and Libraries: Essays Presented to N. R. Ker*, ed. by M. B. Parkes & A. G. Watson (London, 1978), pp. 163-210. Of Ha[4], Doyle and Parkes state: 'The bulk of the manuscript was copied by Scribe D who was also responsible for all headings and running titles in red, and some of the catchwords and informal directions are in his informal hand' (p. 194, n. 73).

46 The 'ici comencera' note could be a direction (never carried out) for a formal Incipit for *Gamelyn*, rather than an instruction about where or whether to insert it. If this is so, however, we are still left with two possible scenarios for when including *Gamelyn* became part of the scribe's plan for Ha[4]. Blake, in *The Textual Tradition* (cited above, n. 1), pp. 110-11, also proposes that *Gamelyn* was present in the tradition before Ha[4] was copied, though I do not share his wish to assign the innovation to Cp.

47 I am not sure why Bowers attributes this conclusion instead to the scribe of Ra[1] (*Continuations and Additions* (cited above, n. 3), p. 33). Manly and Rickert (1: 357, 451) concluded that Ra[1] was 'possibly' copied from Mc, a conjecture my own work with the glosses in these manuscripts confirms, though my study also shows that Ra[1] must have had access to another exemplar as well.

48 The history which led to the removal of these two lines may well have been more complicated than my account suggests, for in Ad[3] the prologues and tales of the Second Nun and Canon's Yeoman are widely separated, the life of St Cecilia appearing between the tales of the Summoner and Clerk much earlier in the manuscript. This aspect of the ordering cannot be explained simply by the attempt to disguise the unfinished state of *CkT* and in fact may antedate the latter.

49 Mosser interprets the evidence of Ad[3] as I do here ('Reading the *Canterbury Tales*' (cited above, n. 3), p. 217), though he does not discuss the manuscript's similarities to Ha[5] and what they probably tell us about the origins of this placement of *CkT*. In 'Additional 35286 and the Order of the *Canterbury Tales*' (cited above, n. 21), Horobin argues that the manuscript's placement of *CkT* goes back to the early years of the fifteenth century. As I have argued here, such a conclusion is plausible. Horobin does not draw on the evidence of Ha[5] for an early origin for the *CkT* placement because he misunderstands its relationship to Ad[3]; he states that 'the ordering of this manuscript is derived directly from Ad[3]' (p. 278, n. 6), but their similarities are more likely due to a shared exemplar (Manly & Rickert 1: 42-3 and 233). An early date for Ad[3]'s placement of *CkT* does not justify, however, Horobin's apparent implication (p. 273) that it rivals or challenges the authority of the more usual position for *CkT*, which is overwhelmingly supported by the manuscripts. Horobin's interpretations of *CkT* are part of a larger argument about the development of the ordering and linking of *SNT* and *CYP*. This argument seems to me to strain the evidence, though, as I have acknowledged above, the position of *CkT* does not necessarily explain the omission of what is usually the opening couplet of *CYP*.

50 The evidence of the fifteenth century thus contrasts sharply with that of the sixteenth and seventeenth, when, as discussed by Burrow, the imaginations of writers such as Spenser, Lane, and Milton were provoked by *SqT*.

51 The evidence of scribal correction in these lines noted by Bowers is interesting, but does not justify the conclusion he draws from it, that the scribe 'was apparently copying from some exemplar in which the narrative had already been adapted as a supplementary Canterbury tale' (*Continuations and Additions* (cited above, n. 3), p. 25); the scribe may simply have been copying these unique stanzas from a rough copy prepared by a patron or supervisor.

52 These are Ad^1-En^3, Ad^3-Ha^5, Cn-Ma, El, En^1-Ds, Ld^1, and Ps. The passage also appears in this form in Cx^2, Pynson, and de Worde. It is virtually certain that the link also took this form in another four manuscripts, from which leaves are now missing: Bo^2, Dd, Gg, and Ha^4.

53 These manuscripts include Bw, Dl, En^2, Fi, Gl, Ha^2, Hg, Ht, Ii, Ld^2, Ln, Mm, Mg, Nl, Pw, Py, Ra^2, Ra^3, Ry^2, Sl^1, and Tc^1. Manly and Rickert assign many of these manuscripts to their group *d*. A similar link probably also has been lost from two further *d* manuscripts, Lc and Ph^3, which are now missing leaves.

54 Twelve manuscripts, along with Caxton's first printing, can be assigned to this category. In members of Manly & Rickert's *b* group (Cx^1-Tc^2, He-Ne, and Ha^3), along with Ry^1, *MerchPro* follows. In Mc-Ra^1, *ClPro* follows. In To, *PhyT* follows, and in Ch, *SNP* followed before the second scribe added a *Plowman's Tale*. *WBP* follows in two of the three *c* manuscripts (the third is La). Finally, in Hk, *MLP* (II.99) follows *SqT*. In a thirteenth manuscript, Se, the sequence was: the 8-line spurious link copied from La after V.670, then V.671-2, after the link, and then (after an Explicit and Incipit), *MLIntro* (II.1).

55 These are the manuscripts of Manly & Rickert's *a* group and related manuscripts: Dd-En^1-Ds^1, Cn-Ma, Ad^1-En^3, Ln.

56 For example, Ad^3 ends at V.672, but Ha^5 at V.670; Cp and Sl^2 end at V.672, but La, discussed above, at V.670. Manly and Rickert also conclude that a number of scribes must have suppressed V.671-2 independently (2: 297). There are two more extreme instances of truncation in Ps (at V.28) and in Nl (at V.349).

57 Such an Incipit appears only in Ch, El, Hg, Ht, Py, and Ra^2, as well as in Cx^2. These witnesses, however, include some of the most reliable ones.

58 Ch, Cp, El, Fi, Ha^2, Hg, Ld^1, Ld^2, Mm, Mg, Ra^2, and Ry^2; to these we may add Ht, where the Explicit for the tale appears only after a large blank space.

59 These are, respectively, Cp, Fi, Ha^2, Ra^2, Ry^2; Ch, El, Hg, Mg; and Ld^1, Ld^2, Mm.

60 These are Bw, Cx^1, En^2, Gl, Ha^3, He, Ii, Ne, Ry^1, Se, Sl^1, and Sl^2.

61 These are, respectively, Ad^1-En^3, Dl and Cn-Ma, En^1-Ds^1, La, Tc^2, To.

62 In the first group are Dd, Pw, and Py, along with Cx^2, which has a note that 'Ther is nomore of the Squiers tale'; in the second group are Ad^3-Ha^5, Hk, Ln, Mc-Ra^1, Ra^3, and Tc^1.

63 In El the scribe left blank 22 ll. on fol. 47^v and all of fol. 48. Scott ('An Illuminated Hours and Psalter' (cited above, n. 13), p. 94) points out that at this point in El there is also a change in limners and flourishers. In his first stint of work, the first scribe of Ch left 21 ll. blank after I.4422 on fol. 58^v, and left fols 59-61 blank. Later, apparently after obtaining another exemplar which included *Gamelyn*, he began that in the blank space and added a quire of 10 fols. (half the usual length in this manuscript) to accommodate the rest of *Gamelyn*. In Hg the scribe left about 10 ll. blank on fol. 58^v, the last of quire 8; later he returned to add a marginal note, which is discussed below. In addition to these three, there are a few other manuscripts which do not provide an Explicit, strictly defined, for *CkT*: Ad^3, En^3, Mc, Ra^1, and Tc^1. But En^3 provides a note, similar to Hg's, that 'Chaunces maad no moor of the Cookis tale', and in the other four manuscripts many tales lack Explicits. I make no attempt to survey the Incipits and Explicits, if any, the manuscripts containing *Gamelyn* provide at the transition from *CkT* to the romance.

64 For reasons which I hope are clear from the earlier detailed discussion, I arrive at this number by adding Ch and Ha^4 to the 25 manuscripts which have *CkT* but no fifteenth-century copy of *Gamelyn*.

65 In Ch the first scribe left blank part of fol. 228^v, after V.672, and all of fols 229-31, and then wrote the Incipit for *SNT* at the top of fol. 232^r. Later another hand added a 'Ploughman's Tale' (Hoccleve's 'Sleeveless Garment') and a prologue to fill most of this space. In Ha^2, the scribe left blank 11 ll. after V.672 on fol. 75^r, and all of fol. 75^v; in addition, clearly visible stubs after fol. 75 show the final two leaves of the quire were cut away, presumably because the scribe had originally left them blank. The Incipit for V.673-708, rewritten for the Merchant, appears at the top of fol. 76^r. Manuscripts Ha^5, Ht, and Ra^2 all resemble Ha^2. In Ha^5, V.670 falls at the foot of fol. 139^r; fol. 139^v is blank, and two blank leaves were cut away. At the top of fol. 140^r begins V.673-708, introducing the Franklin. In Ht, V.672 is the tenth line on fol. 83^v; the remainder is blank, and fol. 84, the last in the quire, is blank except for 'here endeth' at the foot of fol. 84^v. In addition, two stubs visible between fols 83-4 show that leaves were cut out here. The conjecture by Manly and Rickert that the central bifolium of the quire, originally an eight, was also left blank and then later simply removed is plausible but not subject to proof (1: 251). At the top of fol. 85^r are an Explicit for *SqT* and an Incipit for V.673-708, rewritten for the Merchant. In Ra^2, V.672 falls on the 27th line of fol. 44^r, and the remainder and the verso are blank; the following leaf, the last in the quire, was left blank and later cut out. The Incipit for V.673-708, rewritten for the Merchant, is at the top of fol. 45^r, and may have been added rather late in the production of this manuscript.

66 The quires in Ad^3 are regularly eights. Catchwords are visible on fols 130^v and 139^v; only one stub is visible between 139 and 140. Although it is possible, as Mosser proposes ('Reading the *Canterbury Tales*' (cited above, n. 3), p. 219), that the space after V.672 originally consisted of almost an entire quire of blank leaves, no evidence of this remains in the manuscript. Mosser's description of Ad^3 for *The Wife of Bath's Prologue on CD-ROM* (cited above, n. 12) accounts for fol. 131 as I do here.

67 See Mosser's description of Ra^3 for *The Wife of Bath's Prologue on CD-ROM* (cited above, n. 12).

68 Scribes sometimes left blank space to the end of a leaf, elsewhere simply to the bottom of a recto. In Cp, there are 18 ll. blank on fol. 99^v, and the Incipit for *WBP* appears at the top of fol. 100^r. In Dd, 36 ll. are blank after an explicit on fol. 127^r, and all of fol. 127^v is blank; the following leaf, which would have contained V.673-753, is lost. In El, 38 ll. are blank on fol. 122^v, and an Incipit for 'the wordes of the Frankelyn' appears at the top of fol. 123^r. In Fi, 22 ll. are blank on fol. 102^r, as is all of the verso; the Incipit for V.673-708, rewritten to introduce the Merchant, appears at the top of fol. 103^r. In Hg, the scribe originally wrote V.671-2 at the top of fol. 137^r, and left the remainder blank; later he returned to write V.673-708, rewritten for the Merchant, along with an Incipit in the blank space. In Hk, part of fol. 42^r and all of fol. 42^v are blank after V.670. In Tc^1, the scribe left 17 ll. blank in the right column of fol. 38^r, and later wrote the Incipit for V.673-708, rewritten for the Merchant, in the lower 8 ll.

69 There are actually two in Ht, a vague 'here endeth' at the bottom of fol. 84^v, the end of the quire, and a more specific Explicit at the top of fol. 85^r. Notes like that in Dd are discussed in more detail below.

70 These are Ad^1, Dl, En^3, Ld^1, Ld^2, Mm, Mg, Ry^2, Ln, Mc, and Ra^1. All except the last three do include an Explicit for 'secunda pars', and in those last three, as in Tc^1, the lack of Explicit is not unusual.

71 It is also revealing that the remaining seven witnesses include at least two others, Ha^2 and Ra^3, which, while not comparable to those I have listed here, seem to have been the products of relatively few generations of copying.

72 I can hardly do justice here to the strong impression of derivation from a shared model one receives when comparing these four manuscripts, Ha^2, and Ra^3.

73 See Doyle & Parkes, 'The Production of Copies' (cited above, n. 45), for the identification of the same hand in El and Hg and the scribe's designation as 'Scribe B'.

74 Another sign of the authority accorded these gaps, implicit from some of what has preceded, is the fact that scribes preserved them even as they were apparently making other adjustments to the text, for example in what followed *SqT*.

75 Mosser, 'Reading the *Canterbury Tales*', p. 214; Parkes, 'Planning and Construction', p. 47, n. 6; Hanna, '(The) Editing (of) the Ellesmere Text', p. 232 and p. 242, n. 25. (Cited above, nn. 3 & 4.)

76 Parkes ('Planning and Construction', pp. 44-5) makes the conjecture that the quire used as endleaves in El was originally planned for a continuation of *CkT*.

77 For what follows it will be important to keep in mind that the note is written beside the gap at the bottom of fol. 57ᵛ and not in that space.

78 The most thorough and conservative guide to Hg remains A. I. Doyle & M. B. Parkes, 'Paleographical Introduction' to *The Canterbury Tales: A Facsimile and Transcription of the Hengwrt MS with Variants from the Ellesmere MS*, ed. by Paul Ruggiers, The Variorum Edition of the Works of Geoffrey Chaucer, vol. 1 (Norman, Okla., 1979), pp. xix-xlix. Doyle and Parkes compare the lighter ink used for the note at the end of *CkT* to that used for the four quires containing Fragment III, which may have been among the last pieces of text copied for Hg (p. xxvii).

79 Seymour, 'Of This Cokes Tale' (cited above, n. 4), reflects most clearly the tendency to hypothesize about Hg without adequate reference to the evidence of other copies of the *Tales*.

80 Manly & Rickert, 2: 169, cited by Burrow in 'Poems Without Endings' (cited above, n. 5), p. 21. Note especially that while Manly and Rickert see a relationship between Py and Hg, they never state that the former is derived from the latter (1: 141).

81 By 'conventional' I mean similar to the Incipits and Explicits which typically mark the beginnings and endings of prologues and tales in the manuscripts.

82 Several of the surviving manuscripts generally contain about this many ll. to the page, such as Dd, El, Ha², and Mm.

83 Both He and Ne belong to the Manly & Rickert group *b*.

84 For the Manly & Rickert analysis of the textual groups for *SqT*, see 2: 288-97. My argument that the manuscripts I discuss are unlikely to derive their notes on the unfinished tales from one another does not require a thorough commitment to the details of the Manly & Rickert analysis.

85 Such an Explicit precedes the Incipit for the *Retr* in La, Mm, Pw, and Ry².

86 No copies of these manuscripts containing the notes actually survive; my point is to illustrate the processes that might have led to the absence of such notes in most of the surviving manuscripts.

87 Hanna compares Scribe B's work on Hg, in particular, to the 'booklet' method of production that was used for many Middle English manuscripts. As I have argued above, however, comparing the many manuscripts of the *Tales* makes clear that the gaps after *CkT* and *SqT* were not merely incidental outcomes of producing these manuscripts in booklets.

88 Scribe B's omission of this note in El, after including it in Hg, therefore does not have to be explained by Seymour's conjecture ('Of This Cokes Tale' (cited above, n. 4)) that the scribe in the meantime had learned Chaucer had in fact completed the tale. Rather, we can suppose either that the note simply was not in the El exemplars, or that Scribe B was conforming to what appears to have been a widespread pattern of scribal suppression.

89 The same note appeared in Pynson's 1492 *Tales*, which was based on Caxton's second printing.

90 The immediately following Incipit shows that de Worde had, in fact, sought out at least one manuscript as a supplement here to Cx², which served as his primary copytext. De Worde expands Caxton's 'The wordes of the frankeleyns' to 'The wordes of the frankeleyn to the squyre And the wordes of the hoste to the frankeleyn'. This is very similar to the Incipit in El: 'Heere folwen the wordes of the Frankeleyn to the Squier and the wordes of the Hoost to the Frankeleyn'. Only Ps gives possible additional manuscript evidence for such an elaborate Incipit for these lines; they are missing through loss of leaves in some of the manuscripts where the Incipits resemble El's, such as Bo², Dd, and Gg.

91 G. R. Keiser, 'MS Rawlinson A.393: Another Findern Manuscript', *Transactions of the*

Cambridge Bibliographical Society, VII (1980), 445-8, p. 446.

92 Cited by Keiser, 'MS Rawlinson A.393', p. 446.

93 The note appears in London, British Library, MS Egerton 650, fol. 111^r. Scott's discussion of it appears on pp. 147-8 of her article, 'Limning and book-producing terms and signs *in situ* in late-medieval English manuscripts: a first listing', in *New Science out of Old Books*, ed. by Richard Beadle & A. J. Piper (Aldershot, 1995), pp. 142-88.

94 The manuscripts of the *Tales* contain one scribal response to the unfinished state of *SqT* which is analogous to those I discuss in this paragraph, though more laconic; in Pw, the scribe wrote 'vacat' in the margin beside V.671-72.

95 Cited by Richard Beadle & Jeremy Griffiths in their 'Introduction' to *St John's College, Cambridge, MS L.1: A Facsimile*, Variorum Edition, Facsimile Series of the Works of Geoffrey Chaucer 3 (Norman, Okla., 1983), pp. xix-xxxii (p. xxviii); they in turn cite Aage Brusendorff, *The Chaucer Tradition* (Oxford, 1925), p. 209. The note in the St John's manuscript of *Troilus*, which provokes this discussion by Beadle and Griffiths, strikes me as more ambiguous than any of the notes they discuss, and those I cite, because it is in the passive voice, it does not refer explicitly to either author or copyist, and it employs the word 'made', which can refer to the activities of either: 'Her faileth thing þ^t is not yet made' (fol. 83^r). The closest parallel to this might be the note in Cx^2.

96 Cambridge, Trinity College MS R.3.20, p. 348, cited in Beadle & Griffiths, 'Introduction', p. xxviii, who cite Brusendorff, *Chaucer Tradition*, p. 222, n. 3.

97 London, British Library, MS Harley 2252, fol. 260^v; cited in Beadle & Griffiths, 'Introduction', p. xxviii, who presumably take it from Brusendorff, *Chaucer Tradition*, p. 222, n.3.

98 A conjecture intermediate between this one and what I have suggested would argue that a scribe might write such a note because he was reasonably certain it was an accurate statement. But this solution begs the question, I think, of how the scribe would have obtained such information; we might imagine a kind of scribal gossip in the book-making district in London, but the more probable source would have been a similar note in his exemplar or some other copy of the *Tales*.

99 In *The Canterbury Tales* (Oxford, 1989), Helen Cooper accepts Hg's note on *CkT* (p. 119) but considers the evidence of *SqT* more ambiguous (p. 218): 'There is no clue in the state of the manuscripts as to whether the tale was left unfinished or deliberately broken short, or indeed whether it simply lost the later pages of its original exemplar'. This conclusion seems to me to undervalue the evidence afforded by the notes in Dd and several other manuscripts.

100 One must consider seriously the possible authenticity of any feature which appears in one or more of the earliest manuscripts. The gap after *SqT* is attested in more manuscripts than is the 'Epilogue' to *NPT*.

101 Similarly, but more generally, careful attention to how scribes treated the *Tales* over the course of the fifteenth century does not support a hypothesis of centralized editorial control of the text in the early years of the century. For the most recent such hypothesis, see Seymour's 'Introduction' to *A Catalogue of Chaucer Manuscripts, vol. 2* (cited above, n. 38), pp. 1-30.

102 The pattern is less clear in Dd, perhaps because its Incipits and Explicits (like those of the *a* manuscripts generally) have undergone more extensive revision than those of most manuscripts.

103 'The Scribes as Chaucer's Early Critics', in *Studies in the Age of Chaucer*, 1 (1979), 119-41; see esp. pp. 136-8.

104 Quotation of the note in the titles of the articles by Stanley and Seymour (cited above, nn. 4, 6) may reflect a (perhaps unconscious) recognition of the note's distinctive, literary – i.e. Chaucerian – quality.

105 *The Canterbury Tales* (cited above, n. 1), pp. 32-3.

106 Pearsall, of course, has argued repeatedly and vigorously that Chaucer was so far from finishing the *Tales* that we should not imagine that he released them for copying; he is one of the most visible proponents of the notion that the *Tales* were published only after Chaucer's

death. William Kamowski argues that Chaucer and his audience were receptive to fragmentary works, in 'Trading the "Knotte" for Loose Ends: The *Squire's Tale* and the Poetics of Chaucerian Fragments', *Style* 31 (1967), 391-412, pp. 400-404.

107 Donald C. Baker provides a comprehensive review of criticism written before 1985 in *The Squire's Tale*, A Variorum Edition of The Works of Geoffrey Chaucer, Vol. II: The Canterbury Tales, Part 12 (Norman, Okla., 1990). For more recent statements that the Franklin interrupts the Squire see, for example, Seth Lerer, *Chaucer and His Readers* (Princeton, 1993), pp. 57, 74; Cooper, *The Canterbury Tales* (cited above, n. 99), p. 230; A. C. Spearing, *Medieval to Renaissance in English Poetry* (Cambridge, 1985), p. 37. For an erudite and complex argument that the tale as it stands is in important ways complete, see J. D. North, *Chaucer's Universe* (Oxford, 1988). In 'Poems Without Endings' (cited above, n. 5), Burrow expresses scepticism about such arguments. On the other hand, I am also sceptical of any suggestion that Chaucer was committed to leaving these tales incomplete and uninterrupted as part of a larger design for the *Tales*; McGerr in 'Medieval Concepts of Literary Closure' (cited above, n. 9) sees them as part of Chaucer's persistent resistance to closure. The definiteness of my conclusions here inevitably raises the question of whether we might extend them to the manuscript evidence of Chaucer's dream poems, where blank spaces sometimes also appear. I am reluctant to do so, for several reasons. First, the textual evidence is generally not as reliable, especially for the *Book of the Duchess* and the *House of Fame*. Second, there are no notes saying 'Chaucer made no more' (aside from Caxton's on *HF*, where he wants to acknowledge he supplied the ending). Finally, those dream poems are shorter poems appearing in miscellanies, and thus differ from the situation of these two tales, which are part of something much larger that was conceived and transmitted as a whole; with the tales it is harder to suppose an ending has simply been lost. Then again, if we entertain the idea that Chaucer had anything at all to do with how the dream visions and shorter poems were arranged in the miscellanies, it is possible that the provision of blank space after *HF* and *LGW*, and perhaps even within *BD*, may have begun with him.

108 For example, Helen Cooper invokes such a hypothesis to explain the variations in order among the tales of the Clerk, Merchant, Squire, and Franklin in 'The Order of the Tales in the Ellesmere Manuscript', in *The Ellesmere Chaucer* (cited above, n. 4), pp. 245-61, esp. p. 252. For rather different purposes, Hanna also proposes that sections of the text were sometimes physically independent, in '(The) Editing (of) the Ellesmere Text', esp. pp. 229-32.

109 If scribes imitated the end-of-quire spaces in their exemplars, this argues that the quire divisions were visible to them, and this in turn implies that the exemplars were not yet bound into continuous codices.

110 In '(The) Editing (of) the Ellesmere Text' (cited above, n. 4), Hanna concludes, on the basis of his reconsideration of a large portion of the text in the earliest surviving manuscripts, that the unit of transmission was often the quire or a small set of quires rather than the tale or some larger portion of the text. I first became acquainted with this hypothesis in my initial course on paleography, taught by Jeremy Griffiths in the summer of 1986 at Harvard. I continue to be grateful to Jeremy for directing me to the manuscripts of the *Canterbury Tales* as a topic for research, and for urging me constantly to be aware of scribal practices and of the physical make-up of manuscripts, particularly their discontinuities.

THE REDE (BOARSTALL) GOWER

British Library, MS Harley 3490

Derek Pearsall

Plans for 'A Descriptive Catalogue of the Manuscripts of the Works of John Gower' were laid some twenty years ago. It was, at the time, a new kind of venture in Middle English manuscript studies. There had before been descriptive lists of manuscripts of individual works, usually as part of the introduction to an edition of the work (like the extensive catalogue of the manuscripts of the *Canterbury Tales* in Volume I of the edition of the *Tales* by Manly & Rickert), though occasionally standing independently, like the catalogue of manuscripts of the *Prick of Conscience* by Lewis and McIntosh.[1] Sometimes, as in the examples cited, the descriptions of individual manuscripts were quite detailed, and concerned themselves with make-up, layout, decoration and other technical features of the codex, and with its provenance and later history, as well as with the kind of text it contained (usually the main object of interest). But there had been no full descriptive catalogue of all the manuscripts of all the works of a Middle English author such as has now been attempted by Seymour.[2]

A contract for the publication of the Catalogue was drawn up with Garland Publishing, the deadline for submission of camera-ready copy being 31 December 1980. The deadline came and went, but the project acquired new impetus when two younger scholars, Jeremy Griffiths and Kate Harris, joined in it with me as a collaborative venture. We divided the manuscripts among us (Jeremy taking Oxford, Kate Cambridge, and myself London, with the re-mainder distributed *ad lib*), and Jeremy Griffiths provided a model description (it was of Oxford, Bodleian Library, MS Bodley 902),[3] and the master-list of Gower manuscripts. The rationale of the work was variously understood, but it was essentially intended to mark a stage in the progress of the study of medieval English literary manuscripts, one in which they would be inves-tigated in terms of every aspect of their physical existence, the presumption being that everything about a literary manuscript, from the choice of material to write on and the kind of writing employed to the smallest comments and notes made by later readers, is significant to the understanding of the texts that it contains. The catalogue was also to provide a vehicle for the demonstration of the importance of selections and excerpts in the literary history of a text: there are a considerable number of manuscripts containing selections and excerpts from the *Confessio Amantis*, and Kate Harris, whose particular scholarly interest this was (and is), took over the description of all such manuscripts. There was also, in addition to the literary interests of literary scholars, the sense that a catalogue of a coherent body of manuscripts, examined thus in detail, would provide a cross-section, or core-sample, of the manuscript-production of a particular period, in this case the fifteenth century, which would be valuable for comparative purposes (for instance, with handwriting and decoration), in a way that the catalogue of a single collection or library, containing manuscripts more or less randomly accumulated, would not. A particular feature of the Gower catalogue, with this in mind, was to be the inclusion of photographs of manuscript-pages showing examples of all the hands represented in all the manuscripts, and of all the principal forms of decoration.

Work got under way, and well over half the descriptions were drafted. There were several meetings between the three collaborators and various points of difference were identified and compromises hammered out. The main issue was the degree of comprehensiveness that could be aimed at, from a practical point of view, given the constraints of publication. It was possible to think of different levels of detail appropriate to an analytic description, and of discussions of ownership-history that might carry on beyond the sixteenth century and become part of the larger history of taste and text-reception.

There was discussion too of the desirability of adding to the description of each manuscript of the *Confessio* two further features – a brief description of the language of the text in the manuscript, and a selective collation. Jeremy Smith of the University of Glasgow, who had a particular interest at the time in the spelling practices of different scribes copying the same well-stabilized text and the extent to which they modified or acquiesced in the spelling of their exemplars, did an essay on the language of the *Confessio* manuscripts, to be prefixed to the Catalogue, and also prepared brief notes on the language of a number of individual manuscripts. Meanwhile, the three cataloguers, for each manuscript of the *Confessio* that they examined, did a collation of all variants, orthographical as well as substantive, for five tranches of 200 lines each, taken from different parts of the poem, including areas of particular textual instability, making a total sample of 1000 lines. The purpose here was to provide further information about the textual affiliations of the manuscripts and in particular some answers to questions concerning the relationship between text-character and 'recension' (the term used by the editor of the standard text of the *Confessio*, G. C. Macaulay, to describe the different stages at which he presumed the poem to have existed, as evidenced in the presence or absence of references to Richard II and Chaucer, and other large aspects of content and arrangement).[4] In other words, did the different 'forms' or 'shapes' of the text of the poem – terms we preferred to use, hesitatingly, in order to avoid the implication of one-directional authorial revision present in 'recension' (an assumption made by Macaulay that Peter Nicholson was showing to be increasingly doubtful)[5] – correspond to the groupings of manuscripts that might be established by detailed collation of the minor aspects of textual variation?

Whether it was the complications introduced by this additional (and, as I now think, inappropriate) task we had set ourselves, or whether it was the formidable problems set by some of the Latin manuscripts (with multiple authorial revisions in several hands across several manuscripts),[6] or whether it was other factors, the project ground to a halt in the next few years and eventually stalled completely about ten years ago. From time to time, one or other of us would appear at a conference and comment on the 'progress' of the Catalogue, but in fact it wasn't making any.

Jeremy Griffiths's death has made Kate Harris and myself determined to bring the Catalogue to completion, if necessary by pruning some of its accumulated extras, while keeping the essentials. Having himself invested so much time and effort in it, Jeremy would have wanted this. It is what I shall be doing during the first year of my retirement, from January 2000, and as an earnest of that intention, and an appropriate contribution to the present volume, I include below the description of London, British Library, MS Harley 3490 as it exists now. There is considerable revision and updating from the description that I prepared ten years ago and that was seen by the other two collaborators, but there is more work to do before it appears in the Catalogue. Harley 3490 is not a manuscript that sets many problems of description, but it is interesting for the manner in which the scribe disposes the Latin apparatus of the *Confessio*, and specially interesting for the uniquely full and clear information it offers concerning provenance. The publication of this description in a volume which will be seen by so many experts in the field will also provide an opportunity for them to comment on the content and form of the description in a way that will be helpful for the making of the Catalogue (in preparing the present revised description, I have already received invaluable information from A. I. Doyle and Kathleen Scott). The inclusion of a photograph of fol. 11^r (Pl. 1), showing both script and decoration (Prol. 572-661), will demonstrate one of the important prospective uses of the Catalogue.

The description will be largely self-explanatory, but one or two points may need clarification. First, the identification of the 'form' of the text, though it does not use Macaulay's language, follows his classification: 'form' refers to 'recension', and 'group' to his division of the first and second recensions into groups, three for the first and two for the second. Also, 'major text-division' is used instead of Macaulay's 'chapter', and 'minor text-division' instead of his 'paragraph', so as to avoid the implications regarding content that are present in the modern terms. Also, the form of bibliographical reference, by author and date within the text, is the form that will be adopted in the Catalogue: the description is thus a 'quotation' within the context of the present volume. A

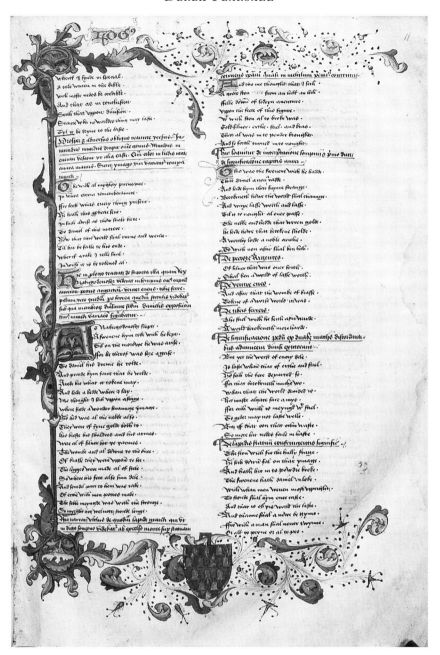

Pl. 1. London, British Library, MS Harley 3490, fol. 11^r.

last minor point: the headings in square brackets are inserted for the guidance of readers on the present occasion. They will not appear in the final Catalogue.

BL MS HARLEY 3490

London, British Library, MS Harley 3490.
Confessio Amantis (lacks ending) preceded by the *Speculum Religiosorum* of Edmund of Abingdon.
Oxford, 1450-60.

[CONTENTS]

I

(fols 1ra-6vb) The *Speculum Religiosorum* of Edmund of Abingdon (St Edmund of Abingdon, archbishop of Canterbury 1234-40).

(After table of contents and chapter heading for first chapter:) Videte vocacionem vestram &c. Verbum hoc apostoli <> propter nostram dilectionem amari propter nostram humilitatem ad celos mereamur exaltari./ Amen. Explicit Speculum beati Edmundi de pontiniaco.

Ed. Forshaw (1973), where this copy is discussed p. 4 and regularly collated as C or C3.

fol. 7 (last leaf of first quire) blank, except for later inscription (see below).

2

(fols 8ra-215va) *Confessio Amantis* Prologue 1 – VIII.3062*.

(After six-line Latin verse-heading, beginning 'Torpor hebes sensus scola parua minimusque' [*sic*: 'labor' is omitted after 'parua']:) Of hem that wryten vs before <> I haue it made for thilke same.

Book I (fol. 13vb), Book II (fol. 33ra), Book III (fol. 54ra), Book IV (Latin, fol. 71ra; English, fol. 71rb), Book V (fol. 94vb), Book VI (fol. 146ra), Book VII (fol. 161va), Book VIII (Latin, fol. 196va; English, fol. 196vb).

The text ends abruptly at VIII.3062*, two-thirds of the way down the first column of fol. 215^v, without explicit or explanation. Some 48 lines are missing, presumably through loss of leaf in an exemplar, though the lines with which the text concludes make a perfectly satisfactory ending in themselves.

Text: Form 1, group (b). [This corresponds to Macaulay's 'First Recension, (b) Intermediate'. New trial collations of the text of Harley 3490 (which is not a carefully copied text) against Macaulay's lists of variants show that it is indeed regularly with MSS of the first recension, but not at all regularly with MSS of the Intermediate group.]

[ILLUSTRATION]
No illustrations.

91

[decoration]

Each book is introduced, as is the Prologue, with a three-sided border, or demi-vinet, in gold, blue, red and green, opening from an elaborate 4-line or 3-line initial in the English text; Prol. 595 (fol. 11ra, the beginning of Nebuchadnezzar's dream) is similarly introduced. Column-borders (central demi-vinets) occur where the text-initial is in the right-hand column (viz. 13^v, 71^r, 94^v, 196^v). All ten decorated pages have coats of arms on a bracket in the middle of the lower border (for identification, see below).

Dr Kathleen Scott identifies two border-artists at work in Harley 3490, the one (Hand A) responsible for eight of the borders, the other (Hand B) for those on fols 94^v and 161^v. Hand A did three other dated manuscripts, Oxford, Exeter College, MS 58 (1452), MS 62 (1454) and MS 64 (1456), all with text of Hugh of St Cher made for Roger Keys, archdeacon of Barnstaple, with coats of arms in the lower border on a bracket as in Harley 3490, and all written by a continental scribe, William Salomon, working in Oxford. The owner of Harley 3490, Sir Edmund Rede (see later), evidently had his copy of Gower made in Oxford. The second border-artist (Hand B) is probably responsible for the decoration in BL, Cotton MS, Nero C.iii, a manuscript of Nicholas Upton's *De officio militari* which was owned also by Rede.

2-line (occasionally 3-line) pen-flourished initials, red on blue, introduce major and some minor text-divisions, and very occasionally Latin verse-headings and prose summaries; 1-line pen-flourished initials, red on blue, introduce minor text-divisions and a few Latin verse-headings and prose summaries. Paraphs, alternately red and blue, introduce most Latin verse-headings, prose summaries, short notes and speech-markers, Explicits and Incipits, and occasional minor text-divisions. Latin verse-headings, prose summaries, short notes and speech-markers are underlined in red. The top line of text often has quite extended flourishing, especially in the second half of the poem.

The same style of decoration is used in the *Speculum*.

[technical description: i, material and size of page; ii, foliation; iii, collation; iv, layout; v, handwriting and correction; vi, punctuation; vii, binding]

i   Parchment, 370×255 mm.

ii   fols i + 215. Modern foliation.

iii   Collation : i^8 wants 7, ii – xvii^8. Tiny catchwords are scribbled in a contemporary hand at fols 23^v, 31^v, 39^v, 47^v, and regularly thereafter.

iv   Written space 265×180 mm. 36-53 lines (of English verse) per column, 2 columns per page. The number of lines per column varies considerably because of the marked increase in the size of the script from Prol. (where 52/53 is normal) through Books i-iii to iv (42/44) to v (38/40); after this there is more effort at constraint (42/44) and even some squeezing (e.g. fol. 210^v, with 50 lines per column). There is also local variability due to pen-changes. Writing space is ruled in dry-point, but not lines. Running titles regularly appear, split across opening ('L' on verso, roman numeral on recto), decorated in blue with red pen-flourishing. The Latin verse-headings (except for the first) are written as prose, in column, underlined; the Latin prose summaries are written in column, underlined; shorter Latin notes and speech-markers are added at the end of the line with introductory paraph mark. Latin notes and speech-markers are occasionally omitted in the second half of the poem.

The decision to clear the margins of all Latin apparatus and to move the Latin prose summaries into the English text column (a common practice in *Confessio* manuscripts: see Echard 1998:18) produces some irregularities. Where there are Latin verse-headings, the summaries are simply run on after them without a break; where there are no Latin verse-headings but nevertheless clearly marked text-divisions, the summaries are correctly placed before the text-break, except for some occasions where the break comes in the middle of a couplet, in which cases the Latin prose summary is often inserted after the couplet (e.g. III.2439, fol. 69ra; IV.236, fol. 72va; IV.1039, fol. 77vb) and not at the point where the text-division was presumably marked in the exemplar (where the summaries were presumably in the margin). Columnization produces particular awkwardness where there is marginal Latin running commentary, as in parts of the Prologue or in the story of Constance in Book II (e.g. II.640, fol. 37ra; II.715, fol. 37va; II.751, fol. 37vb) or in the story of Apollonius in Book VIII, or where there is a frequency of short marginal Latin notes or *auctoritates*, as in Books VI and VII (e.g. VI.1513, fol. 155vb; VI.1569, fol. 156ra). Here, the continuous English text has necessarily to be broken into, though an attempt seems sometimes to be made to mitigate the arbitrariness of the procedure, as when the Latin prose summary is introduced before a line of English text that contains a key-word corresponding to one which also occurs among the opening words of the Latin (e.g. VII.2417, fol. 177vb; VII.4757, fol. 192va; VIII.805, fol. 202ra). There may, of course, have been no decisions of this or any other kind: the summaries may simply have been mechanically transferred into the column at the line which happened to be on a level with the beginning of the summary in the margin of the exemplar. In any of these cases where the English text is resumed at a more or less arbitrary point after the Latin prose summary, the resumption may be signalled as a text-division with the customary markers, whether 2-line or 1-line pen-flourished initials or paraphs (e.g., respectively, Prol.669 at fol. 11va, I.99 at fol. 14va, Prol.700 at fol. 11va).

V   Written by one scribe in a neat secretary book-hand of s.xv 2nd quarter. The Latin is written in a slightly larger version of the same script, which partly accounts for the tendency, noted above, for the script generally to increase in size (e.g. fol. 164^r). Forshaw (1973:4) associates the hand with that of Dublin, Trinity College, MS E.1.29 (519) (according to Dr A. I. Doyle, there are three hands in TCD 519, none of them the hand of Harley 3490), and takes the text of the *Speculum* in Harley 3490 to be a copy of the text in that manuscript, perhaps made in the same 'scriptorium'. There are some corrections, apparently in the scribe's hand, including the insertion in the margin of a line omitted at IV.811 (fol. 76rb). Lines are repeated and erased on fols 102va (V.1213-18) and 112ra (V.2731-4).

VI   The only punctuation is the raised *punctus* which is placed at the end of every line, and occasionally at the caesura.

VII   Sewn on 5 bands. Early nineteenth century red morocco on millboards, gold-tooled titles on spine: EDMUNDI\SPECULUM\RELIGIOSOR\J. GOWER'S\DIALOGUE\COD.SEC.XV\ MUS.BRIT.\BIBL.HARL.\3490\PL LXIX.I.

2° fo dirigatur vita mea temporalis in te finiatur et anima mea teipso.

[GENERAL COMMENTS]

A very large and spacious manuscript, with fine decoration. The presence of the *Confessio* in conjunction with the *Speculum Religiosorum*, a treatise for religious on the spiritual life of prayer and contemplation, is not easily explained: they are not readily compatible texts. Presumably the quire containing the *Speculum*, having been done in the same workshop and by the same scribe as the Gower, was bound up with it for convenience or protection. Forshaw (1973:4) suggests that the *Speculum* was 'chosen to fill up the first gathering', but separate gatherings do not usually need to be 'filled up'.

[ADDITIONS]

fol. 7ʳ   (across the middle of the page, which is otherwise blank) 'O com let vs humble ourselves and fall downe before the lorde'. s.xvii.

fol. 8ʳ   (above decoration, above first column) 'Jhon Gower'. s.xvii. See fol. 215ᵛ, below.

fol. 9ʳ   (outer margin, beside Prol.223)   'Preest*es* lyfe'.   s.xv.

(outer margin, beside Prol.241)   'Symonye'.   s.xv.

(outer margin, beside Prol.263)   'Couetyse'.   s.xv.

fol. 9ᵛ   (outer margin, beside Prol.312)   'Auarice'.   s.xv.

(outer margin, beside Prol.321)   'Slouthe'.   s.xv.

(inner margin, beside Prol.347)   'Enuye'.   s.xv.

fol. 98ʳ   (in a large hand, scrawled at the top, above first column, referring to V.539, on the jealousy of lovers) 'O dames Remorce'. s.xv/xvi.

fol. 215ᵛ (at bottom of first column, left vacant after end of text) 'Chaucer by writinge purchas'd fame/ And Gower gatt a worthy name/ Sweet Surrey suck't pernassus springs/ And wiatt wrote of woundrous things'. These are the first four lines of an 8-line poem that appears among the commendatory verses prefixed to a collection of Gascoigne's poems printed in London for Richard Smith in 1573 ('A hundreth sundrie flowres bounde vp in one small poesie', STC 11635) and again in 1575 ('The Posies of George Gascoigne Esquire', STC 11636), in the latter at sign. ¶¶¶¶ iijv; it is reprinted in Cunliffe (1907:I.29) and Spurgeon (1925:I.111). It is entitled 'The Printer in Commendation of Gascoigne and his workes', and concludes with praise of Rochfort and Gascoigne. The third quarto, printed by Abell Jeffes in 1587 (STC 11638), has 'Richard Smith' in place of 'The Printer' in the title. Wright (1972:199) associates this inscription with 'Jhon Gower', fol. 8ʳ, and says they are both in the hand of Lord William Howard, a later owner of the manuscript (see below).

fol. 215ᵛ (below and to the right of the added quatrain, in a different hand)   'W. Horner'. s.xvii/xviii (dated by Wright 1972:197).

[PROVENANCE]
The coats of arms painted in the lower borders have been identified as follows:

fol. 8ʳ   Azure three pheasants or   (REDE)

fol. 11ʳ   Vair three mascles gules   (MARMION of Checkenden, co. Oxon.)

fol. 13ᵛ   Per chevron gules and argent three unicorns' heads couped and counter-changed (JAMES)

fol. 33ʳ   Argent a lion rampant azure crowned armed and gutty or   (HAUDLO)

fol. 54ʳ   Argent a fess gules in chief two crescents gules at the base a hunting horn stringed vert   (FITZ-NIGEL)

fol. 71ʳ   Or fretty sable on a chief of the second three besants   (ST AMAND)

fol. 94ᵛ   Azure a fess or charged with a plate sable between three leopards' faces or   (DE LA POLE)

fol. 146ʳ   Azure an eagle displayed with two necks argent on its breast an escutcheon gules charged with a leopard's head or   (COTTESMORE of Baldwin Brightwell, co. Oxon.)

fol. 161ᵛ   as fol. 8ʳ

fol. 196ᵛ   as fol. 11ʳ

All these coats of arms are portrayed in the manuscript known as the Boarstall Cartulary, calendared and edited by H. E. Salter in 1930 (Salter 1930), at which time it was owned by the inheritor of the Boarstall estate, Major Henry Lancelot Aubrey-Fletcher, Lord-Lieutenant of Buckinghamshire, who had the manuscript temporarily deposited in the Bodleian Library for Salter's use. Salter does not reproduce the coats of arms, but blazons them, at the points at which they appear in the manuscript, in his footnotes at pp. 108, 118, 120, 123, 233, with the exception of Rede and Marmion, which he omits to blazon where they appear in the manuscript (p. 123), though he does give the blazon for the two coats from brasses in Checkenden church at p. viii. Salter also gives a full account of the family relationships that the coats of arms allude to (see pp. vii-xi, 1-3, 65, 70-4). The Cartulary was made for Edmund REDE the younger (1413-89) in 1444 and the years following. The coats of arms in Harley 3490, which was evidently made for him and/or decorated with marks of his ownership at about the same time, principally record his title to the Boarstall estate in Buckinghamshire, and the manner in which it was acquired.

The essential points may be briefly summarized. John de HAUDLO succeeded to the manor of Boarstall in 1299, having married Joan, daughter and heiress of John FITZ-NIGEL, in whose family it had been since the reign of Henry II. John de Haudlo, knighted in 1306, had by his first wife, Joan, a son Richard, born before 1315. who married in 1329 Isabella (d. 1361), daughter of John of ST AMAND. Richard died in 1343, before his father, leaving a son Edmund, born about 1339, who succeeded when his grandfather died in 1346. Edmund died without issue in 1355 and was succeeded by his sisters Margaret and Elizabeth, the latter of whom married Edmund DE LA POLE by 1359 and acquired all the Boarstall properties in 1366. Edmund was the brother of the Michael who became Earl of Suffolk, and he himself was knighted by 1358. By Elizabeth he had two daughters, Elizabeth (1362-1403) and Katharine (b. 1369), the latter of whom married Robert JAMES. The couple bought from

Elizabeth in 1394 the moiety of the estate that she would inherit at the death of her father, and when he died in 1419 they thus inherited the whole Boarstall estate. Their daughter Christina married in 1412 Edmund REDE, son of Cecilia Harlyngrugge and John Rede; Cecilia's mother was Alice MARMION, through whom she had title to a quarter of the Marmion estate at Checkenden. (She acquired another quarter from her sister Margaret; the moiety that had gone to Alice Marmion's sister Margery was finally acquired by Edmund Rede the younger from Richard Marmion in 1440 in exchange for the manor of Adwell.) Edmund and Christina had a son, Edmund (b. 1413), who succeeded to the property on the death of his father in 1430 and his mother in 1435. In 1434 he married Agnes, daughter of Sir John COTTESMORE of Baldwin Brightwell, famous as Lord Chief Justice of England (d. 1439).

Edmund Rede the younger, for whom the Boarstall Cartulary was made, was knighted in 1465 and died in 1489 (brief biography in Wedgwood 1936:711-12). He was sheriff of Oxfordshire and other counties on several occasions, J.P. in Buckinghamshire 1439-58, a King's Servant (1447), M.P. for Oxfordshire (1450-1), a prominent man in his district, and very busy in the acquisition of lands around Boarstall and Checkenden, on the borders of Buckinghamshire and Oxfordshire, in the 1430s (Kennett 1695:621-9). William de la Pole, earl of Suffolk (the husband of Alice Chaucer, and a distant cousin of Edmund Rede) was similarly active during the same period in the same area (Kennett 1695:627-9); Thomas Chaucer, Alice's father, who was likewise active in the area at an earlier period, 1410-17 (Salter 1930:10, 122-3, 266, &c.), was witness to a conveyance of land to Edmund Rede in 1434 (Kennett 1695:622; Salter 1930:49); Peter Idle (Idley), author of the verse *Instructions to his Son*, was witness to two land-conveyancings involving the Rede estate in 1461-2 (Salter 1930:40, 229).

Sir Edmund Rede's testament (in Latin) and will (in English), drawn up in 1487, are printed as an Appendix to the Cartulary (Salter 1930:286-95; for an English translation, see Weaver 1958:42-6), and show him to have been a man of education, judging from the number of his books, and a benefactor of Magdalen College, Oxford, at its foundation. Apart from Harley 3490 and the Boarstall Cartulary, one other manuscript is known to have been made for him, BL, Cotton MS, Nero C.III, a manuscript of Nicholas Upton's *De officio militari*, decorated with his coats of arms, and 'about the same period in similar style to the Gower' (Doyle 1983:176). Sir Edmund Rede left a substantial number of books to his son and heir William Rede, and some also to other legatees, a total of 24 books at least, including not only the usual prayer-books, service-books, psalters (one of which, of late thirteenth-century northern French origin, survives as Oxford, Christ Church, MS 98), law-books, and collections of statutes and charters, but also (as far as can be determined, and with the help of footnotes in Salter 1930 provided by M. R. James) a book of the chronicles of England ('librum Cronicorum Anglie', perhaps an English *Brut* chronicle, such as BL, Cotton MS, Galba E.VIII, which belonged to Leonard Rede, Edmund's grandson), Harding's *Chronicle*, a written copy (it is said to be 'written', and manuscript copying of printed books was not unusual) of Caxton's 1474 *Recuyell of the Historyes of Troye* ('Rakyll de Troye'), a book 'de obsessione Troge' (maybe the *De excidio Troiae* of Guido della Colonna, but perhaps

Lydgate's *Troy-Book*; *obsessio*, 'siege', is common enough in titles of books of Troy, and does not necessarily indicate that this is the English poem now commonly called *The Seege of Troye* nor the prose *Sege of Troy*), Nicholas Upton's *De officio militari* (most probably Cotton Nero C.III, mentioned above), Albertanus of Brescia's *De arte tacendi et loquendi*, a life of Alexander, a book of Bonaventure (probably Nicholas Love's translation of the pseudo-Bonaventuran *Meditationes vitae Christi*), a bestiary and herbal, the *Medulla grammatice* (a Latin vocabulary, like the *Promptorium Parvulorum*), and other books.

Edmund Rede bequeathed also two copies of Gower. One is the only book bequeathed to his wife Katharine (his second wife, whom he married in 1461), listed as 'unum librum vocatum Gower coopertum cum rubeo coreo' (p. 288). James thinks this may be Caxton's 1483 print of the *Confessio*, though it could be Harley 3490, despite the absence of mention of the *Speculum*. It was presumably, from the mention of its binding, a substantial book, and 'vocatum Gower' suggests that all or the bulk of the contents were by Gower; it would most likely be a copy of the *Confessio*.

The other Gower was left to his son and heir William and is listed as 'unum librum de Gower cum tractatu trium regum de Coleyn coopertum cum coreo albo' (p. 288). It is also possible that this is the present manuscript, even though the *Confessio* is no longer bound in white leather with the *Historia Trium Regum*: it would not be unusual for separate texts to be arbitrarily bound together and subsequently separated. The *Historia* may be a copy of one of the English translations of John of Hildesheim's Latin history, which was written between 1364 and 1375, or a copy of the Latin itself. Twenty manuscripts of the English prose-translation (ed. by Horstmann 1886) are listed in *IPMEP* (item 290), and the unique manuscript of the English verse-translation noted in *IMEV* (item *854.3, formerly *31) and by D'Evelyn (1970:630-1). The manuscripts of the Latin remain to be investigated: Horstmann lists 37 (1886:ix-xi), and several early prints, and editions of the German and Dutch versions list more manuscripts of the Latin.

However, it is by no means certain that this second 'Gower' is a copy of the *Confessio*. BL, MS Stowe 951, for instance, is one of the manuscripts containing the English prose-translation of the *History of the Three Kings*; it also contains the *Speculum vitae* of William of Nassyngton, ascribed in at least one manuscript (not Stowe 951) to Gower, and the unique copy of Quixley's English verse-translation (*IMEV* 4105) of Gower's *Traitié pour essampler les amantz marietz*, with the title *Exhortacio contra vicium adulterii* (Quixley names himself and Gower in his first stanza: see MacCracken 1909:40); it is in its original oak-boards, though the leather backing is modern. This might be Rede's second Gower.

[LATER OWNERSHIP]
Harley 3490 was in the collection of Lord William Howard (1563-1640) of Naworth Castle, co. Cumberland, and is recorded as being at Naworth ('*John Gower's* Old English Poems', with 'S.Anselmi Speculum Religiosorum. Fol.') in 1697, in the catalogue of Bernard (1697), Vol. II, Part 1, p. 14 (no. 611). This catalogue of Howard's manuscripts is reprinted in the edition of Howard's household books by Ornsby (1878:469-72, with Harley 3490 as the first item), along with other lists of manuscripts and printed books (473-87) still preserved (in

1878) at Naworth, among them a copy of Berthelette's 1554 reprint of his 1532 edition of the *Confessio* (sold as Lot 525 at Sotheby's, 28 October 1947), with an inscription signed by William Howard and dated June 28 1587. Wright (1972:199) says that the marginal notes on fols 8^r and 215^v in Harley 3490 are by Howard. Lord William Howard, who became a Catholic in 1584 and settled at Naworth in 1603, was a scholar, a considerable collector of books, and a friend of antiquaries such as Camden and Cotton. His household books record many purchases of books (e.g. Ornsby 1878:104, 121, 199, 203, 234, 256-8, 292-3) and one purchase of manuscripts (244), as well as expenses of binding. Unfortunately the titles of the books are not often mentioned. It is likely that Howard acquired the Gower by purchase, since he has no apparent links with the Rede family. Harley 3490 has no connection, as Macaulay (1901:II.cli) points out, with the Gower manuscript now in the Newberry Library, Chicago (Case + 33.5: see Saenger 1989:61), that belonged to the branch of the Howard family at what is now Castle Howard (Ornsby 1878:486). However, this Gower manuscript did once belong to Lord William Howard (he thus had three copies of the *Confessio* at Naworth) before it went to Castle Howard with a group of other manuscripts that included, interestingly enough (in connection with the list of books mentioned in Edmund Rede's will), Harding's *Chronicle* and Nicholas Upton's *De re militari* (Ornsby 1878:486-7). Harley 3490 was subsequently acquired by John Warburton (1682-1759), Somerset Herald, another redoubtable collector, and was purchased from him for the collection of Robert Harley, 1st Earl of Oxford, on 16 July 1720 (Wright 1972:199, 347; Wright 1966:I.58). The date is recorded in a note in Warburton's hand at the top right of fol. i^r.

[BIBLIOGRAPHY]
Edward Bernard (ed.), *Catalogi Manuscriptorum Angliae et Hiberniae* (Oxford, 1697).
Catalogue of the Harleian Manuscripts in the British Museum, 4 vols (London, 1808).
John W. Cunliffe (ed.), *The Complete Works of George Gascoigne*, 2 vols (Cambridge, 1907).
Charlotte D'Evelyn & Frances A. Foster, 'Saints' Legends', Part V of Albert E. Hartung (ed.), *A Manual of the Writings in Middle English 1050-1500*, vol. 2 (Hamden, Conn., 1970). No. 277 (pp. 630-1) is the *Three Kings of Cologne: Balthasar, Melchior, Caspar*.
A. I. Doyle, 'English Books In and Out of Court', in *English Court Culture in the Later Middle Ages*, ed. by V. J. Scattergood & J. W. Sherborne (London, 1983), pp. 163-81. Notes the Rede connection of Harley 3490 (p. 176).
Siân Echard, 'With Carmen's Help: Latin Authorities in the *Confessio Amantis*', *Studies in Philology*, 95 (1998), 1-40.
Helen P. Forshaw, S.H.C.J. (ed.), Edmund of Abingdon, *Speculum Religiosorum and Speculum Ecclesie*, Auctores Britannici Medii Aevi, III (London, 1973). Harley 3490 listed among manuscripts of the *Speculum*, p. 4.
Kate Harris, 'The role of owners in book production and the book trade', in *Book Production and Publishing in Britain 1375-1475*, ed. by Jeremy Griffiths & Derek Pearsall (Cambridge, 1989), pp. 163-99. Notes Harley 3490 among other manuscripts containing coats of arms integral with the decoration (p. 168).
C. E. Horstmann (ed.), *The Three Kings of Cologne*, EETS, OS 85 (1886).
IMEV. Carleton Brown & Rossell Hope Robbins, *The Index of Middle English Verse* (New York, 1943), with *Supplement*, by Rossell Hope Robbins & John L.Cutler (Lexington, KY, 1965).
IPMEP. R. E. Lewis, N. F. Blake & A. S. G. Edwards, *Index of Printed Middle English Prose* (New York, 1985).

White Kennett, *Parochial Antiquities Attempted in the History of Ambrosden, Burcester, and Other Adjacent Parts in Counties of Oxford and Bucks.* (Oxford, 1695).

G. C. Macaulay (ed.), *The Complete Works of John Gower, Vols II and III: The English Works* (Oxford, 1901). Description of Harley 3490, II.cxlii-iii.

Henry Noble MacCracken, 'Quixley's Ballades Royal (?1402)', *Yorkshire Archaeological Journal*, 20 (1909), 30-50.

[George Ornsby], *Selections from the Household Books of the Lord William Howard of Naworth Castle*, Surtees Society, vol.68 (1878, for 1877).

Paul Saenger, *A Catalogue of the Pre-1500 Western Manuscript Books at the Newberry Library* (Chicago, 1989).

H. E. Salter, *The Boarstall Cartulary*, Oxford Historical Society, vol. 88 (Oxford, 1930).

Caroline F. E. Spurgeon, *Five Hundred Years of Chaucer Criticism and Allusion 1357-1900.* In 7 parts, Chaucer Society, 2nd series, 48-56 (1914-24); in 3 vols (Cambridge, 1925).

J. R. H. Weaver & A. Beardwood (eds), *Some Oxfordshire Wills Proved in the Prerogative Court of Canterbury, 1393-1510*, Oxfordshire Record Society, 39 (1958).

Josiah C. Wedgwood, *History of Parliament: Biographies of Members of the Common House, 1439-1509* (London, 1936).

C. E. Wright & Ruth C. Wright (eds), *The Diary of Humfrey Wanley 1715-1726*, 2 vols (London, 1966).

Cyril Ernest Wright, *Fontes Harleiani: a Study of the Sources of the Harleian Collection of Manuscripts preserved in the Department of Manuscripts in the British Museum* (London, 1972).

[END OF DESCRIPTION OF MS HARLEY 3490]

NOTES

1 *The Text of the Canterbury Tales, edited on the basis of all known Manuscripts*, by John M. Manly and Edith M. Rickert, 8 vols (Chicago, 1940); Robert E. Lewis & Angus McIntosh, *A Descriptive Guide to the Manuscripts of the 'Prick of Conscience'*, Medium Aevum Monographs, new series, XII (Oxford, 1982). Gisela Guddat-Figge, *Catalogue of Manuscripts containing Middle English Romances* (Munich, 1976), is an example of a catalogue of the manuscripts of works belonging to a certain genre.

2 M. C. Seymour, *A Catalogue of Chaucer Manuscripts*, 2 vols (Aldershot, 1995, 1997).

3 His model is based on the descriptions in M. B. Parkes, *The Medieval Manuscripts of Keble College Oxford* (London, 1979), with appropriate modifications. See Parkes's account of 'The Form of the Entries', pp. xix-xxi.

4 *The Complete Works of John Gower, Vols II and III: The English Works*, ed. by G. C. Macaulay (Oxford, 1901).

5 See Peter Nicholson, 'Gower's Revisions in the *Confessio Amantis*', *Chaucer Review*, 19 (1984), 123-43, and 'Poet and Scribe in the Manuscripts of Gower's *Confessio Amantis*', in *Manuscripts and Texts: Editorial Problems in Later Middle English Literature*, ed. by Derek Pearsall (Cambridge, 1987), pp. 130-42.

6 The essay by M. B. Parkes, 'Patterns of Scribal Activity and Revisions of the Text in Early Copies of Works by John Gower', in *New Science out of Old Books: Manuscripts and Early Printed Books: Essays in Honour of A. I. Doyle*, ed. by Richard Beadle & A. J, Piper (Aldershot, 1995), pp. 81-121, has now tackled some of these particular problems, but it has also posed some new questions.

FIFTEENTH-CENTURY MIDDLE ENGLISH VERSE AUTHOR COLLECTIONS

A. S. G. EDWARDS

THE CONCEPT of 'authorial identity' has been held to be a problematic one for medieval vernacular writers. Tim Machan, for example, has recently advanced the view that such writers had no idea of the possible authority that might inhere in such an assertion of identity: it is, he tells us 'difficult if not impossible for a contemporary writer to acquire auctorial status'.[1] To some extent the force of this assertion depends on what one means by auctorial status. Machan himself points to some of the literary devices that medieval authors used to attempt to establish this status.[2] But it seems worth considering the extent to which such tendencies were adumbrated in fifteenth-century English literary manuscripts themselves at a time when, in the generations after Chaucer's death, the status of the vernacular, particularly the poetic vernacular, was rapidly rising. What do manuscript collections tell us about the degree of distinctiveness with which particular authors were perceived?

I am primarily concerned with the intimations of such a concept of authorial status in a codicological sense as evidenced in verse collections. I would like to comment briefly on a few manuscripts of such materials which seem to embody, in varying degrees, deliberate assemblage and presentation as author collections and to look at the different forms of compilation and presentation through which this apparent intention is enacted.

It is hard to point to much conscious bringing together of a range of authorially distinct collections in England before the early fifteenth century. Occasional names stand out – Laurence Minot's collection of historical poems in London, British Library, Cotton MS, Galba E IX, for example,[3] or BL, Add. MS 46919 (*olim* Phillipps 8336), which contains a number of lyrics by William Herebert;[4] but the problem of establishing secure criteria for canonicity generally prove too intractable to make attribution compelling, resricted as they must be to grounds of style. One thinks of Thomas Chestre and the rather desperate modern attempts to construct a canon of his writings on the criterion of shared awfulness,[5] or the once infinitely expandable oeuvre of Huchown of the Awle Ryale who seems at various points in the late nineteenth or early twentieth century to have been credited with almost all the surviving corpus of alliterative verse.[6] Even in collections that do seem to have some distinctive identity it is hard to establish that that identity is authorial rather than formal: it has never been conclusively established that all the unique alliterative poems in BL, Cotton MS, Nero A. X, are by the same author or that he did not write *St. Erkenwald*,[7] which occurs in a different manuscript.

This situation stands in obvious contrast to that in France where, as Sylvia Huot has brilliantly demonstrated, consciousness of the author was clearly reflected by the later fourteenth century in a multiplicity of lyric collections; this development seems to have begun much earlier.[8] In the case of longer French works this tendency can be seen in the collected writings of Christine de Pisan in the early fifteenth century.[9]

In England consciousness of such possibilities seems to have been slow to develop, even with the remarkable efflorescence of vernacular poetry associated with the reign of Richard II. The notion of a collected Gower does seem to find some early expression in Oxford, Bodleian Library, MS Fairfax 3, where the *Confessio Amantis* appears with other English poems and the *Traitié* and various Latin works.[10] A 'lyric Gower' is constructed in the 'Trentham' manuscript (BL, Add. MS 59495) where the *Cinkante Balades* occur with the *Traitié* and other shorter poems in Latin and English.[11] But such instances of attempts to represent the range of the Gowerian corpus seem very intermittent. Doubtless the bulk of the *Confessio* itself and its early establishing in a stable format, the double column one favoured by the D scribe, who copied six of these early copies, with only slight fluctuations in the number of lines, helped to establish its separate identity.[12]

The situation for Chaucer seems rather different. The conception of a distinct collection of his works does not seem to have commended itself readily to posterity. I say this in spite of the survival of Cambridge, University Library, MS Gg. 4. 27 which clearly represents an early attempt to encompass a number of Chaucer's works within a single collection, including, uniquely, both the *Canterbury Tales* and *Troilus*. The loss of opening and/or closing leaves for a number of works, like the *Canterbury Tales* and *Troilus*, does make generalization difficult, but it can be said that where complete texts exist in the manuscript there is no general consciousness of Chaucer's identity reflected in the attributions. The only works attributed explicitly to Chaucer are the lyric 'Lenvoy de Chaucer a Scogan' ('per G. C.'; fol. 7ᵛ) and the *Parliament of Fowls* (in a colophon; fol. 490ᵛ).[13] Moreover, this is not a closed collection in canonical terms. It includes Lydgate's *Temple of Glas* and other anonymous works.[14]

Nor is the sense of authorship any more precisely focused in other major manuscript collections of Chaucer. In the next largest after Gg. 4. 27, Bodleian Library, MS Arch. Selden. B. 24, prepared in Scotland at the end of the fifteenth or beginning of the sixteenth century, Chaucer attributions are both untypically extensive and conspicuous for their inaccuracy. Nearly half of the large number of works ascribed there to Chaucer are not by him.[15]

Elsewhere, there are only intermittent efforts in manuscripts to present

Chaucer in ways that suggests he is distinctive because of the range of his writings. In CUL, MS Ii. 3. 21, two of Chaucer's 'Boethian' lyrics, 'The Former Age' and 'Fortune' are intercalated with the appropriate metres to his *Boece*. In BL, Add. MS 10304, the *Boece* is joined by a later hand with a unique extract from the General Prologue and the lyric 'Truth', with a unique Envoy (both added on a flyleaf), to form a rather more extensive kind of Boethian vernacular anthology. But neither of these has any attribution. In contrast, the second of the two manuscripts that is now Cambridge, Magdalene College, MS Pepys 2006, combines Chaucer's prose tales, Melibee and the Parson's Tale, with a collection of lyrics, all of which are attributed.[16] But such closed authorial collections of Chaucer's works seem atypical: the more general anthologizing tendency was to mingle his own works with those of the emergent Chaucerian tradition, linking him with Hoccleve, Clanvowe, Roos, and particularly Lydgate.

The massive bulk of Lydgate's longer poems precludes their assemblage into collections in the main. Thus his longest work, *The Fall of Princes*, over 36,000 lines, always appears in complete form alone (it was, however, frequently excerpted in a variety of contexts).[17] His *Troy Book*, only slightly less long, is occasionally joined to his *Siege of Thebes*, reflecting traditional medieval collocations of the two histories.[18] A few manuscripts follow Lydgate's own cue and add his *Siege of Thebes* to the *Canterbury Tales*, to which it is an explicit continuation, thereby subsuming any concept of an author collection by different principles of compilation based on shared narrative principles.[19] But such collocations are intermittent and unsystematic.

Assemblages of Lydgate's shorter poems seem to have found their way into metropolitan publishing circles, probably in part through the activities of the mid-fifteenth century copyist John Shirley, and are reflected in large and well-known compilations, either from his own hand, like Bodleian Library, MS Ashmole 59,[20] or that seem to derive from his activities like BL, MSS Add. 34360 and Harley 2251.[21] Such collections are all London derived, most of them clearly connected to the commercial book trade. In all of them, however, Lydgate's works are once again linked to those by Chaucer and others.

Rather less remarked are collections of a different kind, which preserve Lydgate's shorter, primarily religious poems with varying senses of their distinctiveness, a few of which I would like to briefly mention. One of the earliest of these collections is in CUL, MS Kk. 1. 6. Its chief content is a copy of Eleanor Hull's translation of the Seven Penitential Psalms. But it also contains a parchment quire (fols 194^r-214^v), apparently a vestige of a once larger compilation, copied by Richard Fox of St Albans. This quire is exclusively verse and comprises eleven poems[22] which have been attributed with what seems to be very careful discrimination. Six of them are explicitly ascribed to Lydgate, in rubricated headings or colophons.[23] In addition, the final poem (IMEV 2784) breaks off imperfectly at the end of the quire, but is generally accepted as by Lydgate. The other four poems are not attributed.

Lydgate had died in 1449, at Bury St Edmunds, where he had been resident from the early 1430s, and Fox alludes to his death in one of his rubrics.[24] Fox himself died in 1454,[25] so these poems were obviously copied close upon Lydgate's death. Fox seems to have been in the habit of compiling such quires,[26] and it is worth speculating on the sources of his texts and the grounds for his very precise differentiation of Lydgate's poems from other, surrounding ones. Lydgate himself had had some links to St Albans: he had written his *Lives of SS Albon & Amphibel* for the abbot of the abbey there, John Whethamstede, in the early 1440s. Fox describes himself in his will as 'of the house of St. Alban, simple servaunt', and includes bequests of copies of lives of both St Alban and of St Edmund, patron saint of Bury St Edmunds, another of Lydgate's saint's lives,[27] one evidently written at Bury in the 1430s. It seems likely that Fox was able to pursue his literary avocation because of his institutional links, which may have afforded him direct access to copies of Lydgate's verses from his own monastery as well as verses by unidentifiable others, probably also local in derivation. In addition to being an author collection the Cambridge manuscript may also be a regional anthology.[28]

Other groupings of manuscripts may also reflect, in some measure, some ultimate authorial origins, possibly linked to Bury St Edmunds. For example, BL, Harley MS 2255, a parchment manuscript, is seemingly in some way connected with Lydgate's own monastery there.[29] Its contents are exclusively verse and comprise forty-five poems by Lydgate, all of which are separately numbered in the upper outer margin. These contents seem related to a greater or lesser extent to two other collections, Bodleian Library, MS Laud misc. 683 and Cambridge, Jesus College, MS 56. In Laud the contents are originally exclusively Lydgatean,[30] comprising thirty poems, of which thirteen occur in both the other manuscripts.[31] Jesus contains twenty-eight poems by Lydgate,[32] of which twenty-five are common to the Harley collection.[33] These collections are, at best, modestly decorated and seem to have been produced by scribes operating possibly fairly early in the third quarter of the fifteenth century outside London.

The extent of the correspondences in content seems unusual in such early, seemingly non-metropolitan collections of Lydgate's shorter poems. Clearly these three manuscripts reveal something about the circulation of collections of Lydgate's shorter poems in ways that reflect shifting senses of the distinctiveness of his verse. There seems to be no general insistence on his identity as author: many, but not all, of the poems in Harley are specifically ascribed to him; in Laud, the first and last poems in the collection are ascribed to Lydgate, but none of the intervening ones; while in Jesus, none is identified as by Lydgate, or anyone else. Although there is a shared core of common texts, these do not occur in the same order or even in any significant shared sequences.

It does not seem very easy to reconstruct the origins and transmission of such collections. It appears possible that they may initially have circulated as separate poems within a single environment, possibly, if there is any force to my arguments about Kk. 1. 6, Lydgate's monastery at Bury, and were gradually assembled and disseminated in larger posthumous groupings, in part by early amateur enthusiasts like Richard Fox, forms of activity that may have been institutionally sanctioned. But these institutional holdings may not have been preserved in any larger stable form of the kind we now think of as 'booklets', and hence survive in variant forms reflecting the arbitrary larger collocations of early compilers, collocations in which the notion of authorial identity may have become obscured or lost over time.

Other collections, some of them either clearly or probably non-metropolitan in origin, vary markedly in their sense of what is appropriate for representing the author. The only manuscript of John Audelay's poems survives in Bodleian Library, MS Douce 302, a parchment manuscript that begins imperfectly, of which thirty-five leaves remain, probably copied *c*. 1426, in a religious house in Shropshire. It has been argued that this is a manuscript in which 'the author had direct control of the volume'.[34] Quite how such control might have been exercised is not altogether clear, since Audelay was apparently blind. Certainly there is evidence of careful correction, possibly as a result of a corrector reading back poems to the author after initial transcription. Each poem is distinguished by red roman numerals in the upper margin to indicate the sequence.[35] The poems are differentiated in other ways: each is marked by four-line initials, infilled in red and with red penwork; as well there is careful rubrication of headings, divisions, and Explicits possibly by a different hand from the main scribe. Such relatively simple strategies create a coherent sense of this as a collection, as well as demonstrating the modest ambitions and possibly resources of its compilers.

One obvious way of emphasizing the distinctiveness of an author collection is through decoration. We get some sense of what this might have signified in BL, MS Harley 682, a parchment manuscript of 147 leaves, containing only the English poems of Charles d'Orléans. The manuscript has been quite carefully prepared, almost certainly for Charles himself:[36] the leaves have been regularly ruled (with the qualifications set out below), and bounded (pricking is still visible), with catchwords and signatures present. Space has been left for the insertion of a number of decorated or illuminated initials of between two and four lines. In addition, in the earlier portions of the text occasional spaces have been left (on, for example, fols 4ᵛ, 16ᵛ), possibly for the insertion of miniatures. Moreover the text has been quite carefully corrected at a number of points, with some lines partly erased and different versions inserted in the margin.

This evident attention to matters to do with construction, layout, and text stands in some contrast to other aspects of the manuscript's presentation. There are, for instance, no attempts to provide titles or attributions for any poems. More puzzling are some aspects of the layout of the text: up until fol. 60ᵛ the text is set out using the full page. Thenceforward, between fols 61 and 111 the text is usually presented using only the bottom half of the page, the top being generally left blank and, between fols 66 and 103 generally unruled.[37]

After this, from fols 111^v-147^r the manuscript is again ruled and written regularly using the full page.

These facts pose some intriguing if unresolvable problems. The question of the blank spaces is particularly difficult. What were they left for? Decoration, including illustration, seems the most likely possibility. The general lack of ruling in the upper parts of the page between fols 66 and 103 suggests such a plan. (They could perhaps have been for music, but there seems generally not enough room, and ruling would seem necessary.)[38] If so, these blanks hint at a scale of ambition unusual among Middle English verse collections and without precedent among lyric collections. Possibly Charles was influenced by earlier, elaborately decorated French lyric collections of the kind described by Sylvia Huot.[39] He was, of course, a noted bibliophile whose collecting interests have recently been linked to a number of de luxe English books including Cambridge, Corpus Christi College, MS 61, Chaucer's *Troilus and Criseyde*.[40] That he may have contemplated decoration on a comparable elaborateness of scale to that manuscript, and that it should have been even more comprehensively aborted, would be among the keener ironies of fifteenth-century manuscript production.

The seeming decorative aspirations of the Harley manuscript, albeit unfulfilled, have few parallels in other author collections of the period. The unique manuscript of Osbern Bokenham's *Legendys of Hooly Wummen*, now BL, Arundel MS 327, is one of the few that does reflect any significant degree of enhancement occasioned by any sense of the distinctiveness of its contents. The manuscript reflects at least two distinct stages of assemblage and decoration, in different places within East Anglia, the chief of which may have been Clare, in Suffolk, where Bokenham was resident at the Augustinian house.[41] It is a collection of legends which were initially composed separately for pious lay East Anglians. His manuscript differs from earlier hagiographical collections, like the *South English Legendary* or the *Northen Homily Cycle*, in its specificity of focus – only female saints are included – and clear authorial presence linking narratives. (Throughout, Bokenham declines to identify himself by name, but remains obtrusive in his anecdotal prologue and various prefaces.) This combined generic and gendered focus makes the manuscript unusual; evidently its commissioner felt that its distinctiveness should be signified by its careful decoration by accomplished provincial artists.[42]

A more modest non-metropolitan manuscript is CUL, MS Ee. 1. 12, a collection of carols and other poems by the Franciscan James Ryman, which survives uniquely in a parchment manuscript of some eighty leaves, presumably produced either at or under the auspices of the friary at Canterbury with which he was associated. This is best known as a carol collection, containing a quarter of the surviving carol corpus before 1550.[43] The texts are copied in a single small, neat hand. Each poem is prefaced by a title or heading in an accomplished display script in the same hand, generally, the burden or opening lines. Apart from the display script there is no attempt at decoration. The carols which begin the transcription are usually generously spaced. As the poems become lyrics they become more compressed (from fol. 53ᵛ) and the display script is used to distinguish the opening word or words of stanzas as well as for headings. It is impossible to know whether Ryman aspired to distinguish his collection in any more elaborate ways or simply had no access to the resources, material or artistic, to do so. The careful spacing and prominent headings may give some support to the view that 'he designed his poems to be sung by his preaching brothers and their audiences',[44] presumably to familiar tunes since there is no music in the manuscript.

What makes this manuscript particularly striking is its overall, quite self-conscious construction of as a collection. This construction is established by the final explicit in the scribe's display script:

> Explicit liber ymnorum / et cantorum quem com/posuit
> ffrater Iacobus / Ryman ordinis minorum / ad laudem
> omnipotentis / dei et sanctissime matris eius / marie
> omnique sanctorum Anno domini millesimo ccccm° xxxxij° (fol. 80ʳ)

This is an unusual statement, explicitly establishing that the integrity of the collection as a whole is based on single authorship. I know of no equivalent in fifteenth-century author collections.

Indeed, the unusualness of the colophon to the Ryman manuscript is thrown into greater relief when one turns from such a provincially produced manuscript to Thomas Hoccleve's autograph poems, produced in London, probably in the 1420s, by an accomplished professional scribe. Some of these poems survive in two manuscripts now in the Huntington Library, MSS HM 111 and HM 744. These manuscripts form a collection of his shorter poems, the first comprising only Hoccleve's poems (fols 1ʳ-47ᵛ), the second now bound with unrelated materials (of which it forms fols 25ʳ-68ᵛ).[45] This collection (I speak of them as a single assemblage) is particularly noteworthy given Hoccleve's own professional career as a scribe. But this scribal expertise is reflected only in a very limited way in the manuscript: texts are unruled and unbounded; there is little decoration beyond some slightly larger initials decorated with simple penwork. Given Hoccleve's evident links to the commercial book trade[46] it is curious that he did not seek any more elaborate form of presentation for his texts.

Indeed, it is not immediately clear what Hoccleve was assembling these poems for. The evidence of the circulation of these texts is also curious. HM 111 contains nineteen poems, all by Hoccleve; of these, thirteen are unique to this manuscript.[47] The other six are poems that seem to have circulated in rather different ways: one is an extract from Hoccleve's *Regement of Princes* (IMEV 2229), of which over forty manuscripts survive, but only one of which is otherwise an extract;[48] one is a lyric that appears elsewhere without attribution as a lyric, 'The Lamentation of the Green Tree,' in the Middle English prose translation of Deguileville, *The Pilgrimage of the Soul* (IMEV 2428); one is a brief lyric appearing elsewhere only in Bodleian Library, MS Fairfax 16, the famous mid-fifteenth-century collection of Chaucer and Lydgate; one, Hoccleve's 'Mother of God' is only found otherwise in two much later Scottish manuscripts, Bodleian Library, MS Arch. Selden. B. 24 (fols 130ᵛ-131ʳ) and Edinburgh, National Library of Scotland 18. 2. 8, fols 112ᵛ-115ʳ, in both of which it is ascribed to Chaucer. One brief lyric (IMEV 3831), Hoccleve's verse to the Duke of Bedford, appears elsewhere in BL, MS Royal 17 D XVIII. And the last, IMEV 2538, appears elsewhere in a disordered and excerpted form 'transformed into a general moral balade' in a copy that may derive from the poet himself.[49]

The situation in HM 744 is quite similar. The Hoccleve section contains twelve poems of which nine are unique; the other three are his very popular Epistle of Cupid (IMEV 666), his Miracle of the Virgin (IMEV 4122), and an imperfect copy of his Lerne to Dye (IMEV 3121). The first had a wide circulation. It appears in the major commercial compilations of the Oxford group, including Bodleian Library, MS Fairfax 16, and in Cambridge, Trinity College, MS R. 3. 20, the collection by John Shirley, and in the Scottish Chaucer manuscript, Bodleian Library, MS Arch. Selden. B. 24. The Miracle of the Virgin appears elsewhere in a Chaucerian context, as the Ploughman's Tale in Oxford, Christ Church, MS 152 and in Cambridge, Trinity College, MS R.3.21. Only the final poem, 'Lerne to Dye' reveals more distinct patterns of association primarily with Hoccleve's own works. It occurs elsewhere in Hoccleve's other holograph, Durham, University Library, Cosin V. III 9, as well as in BL, MS Royal 17. D. VI, which includes his *Regement of Princes* and BL, MS Harley 172 (a collection of poems by Lydgate, Burgh, and Idley). In addition, it also forms part of the distinct Hoccleve grouping discussed below in several Bodleian Library manuscripts and others in the Beinecke Library and in Coventry.

What the facts set out above reveal about the circulation of these texts in Hoccleve's Huntington collection? Presumably, like the Lydgate ones discussed earlier, they circulated in a piecemeal way as separate poems on loose sheets some of which 'leaked' into wider circulation, possibly without specific attribution to Hoccleve himself, who never seems to add identifying rubrics to his poems. This factor permitted the wider mis- or non-attribution of a number of these poems, over which Hoccleve had lost control, and which were circulating in a floating and appropriable state.[50]

It seems possible, however, that his general intention was not to circulate his Huntington holograph collection, at least in the form in which it now survives. The lack of attribution and decoration seem to suggest that it was not, at least at this stage, intended as a presentation copy. The lack of any evident systematic circulation suggests that it did not merge into the main stream of fifteenth-century book production, a fact that differentiates it from a number of other of Hoccleve's works and from from Hoccleve's other autograph manuscript, Durham Cosin. V. III. 9, the separate works in which seem to have circulated quite extensively, and which is fairly carefully and systematically decorated.

This potential for loss of distinct poetic identity in the Huntington Hoccleve holographs has some relevance to the final group of texts I wish to discuss. Once again, they are related to Hoccleve. There survives an assemblage of his poems that seem to have circulated, with unusual tenacity, as a group. It comprises five manuscripts, three in the Bodleian Library, MSS Laud misc. 735, Bodley 221, and Selden supra 53; one in New Haven, Beinecke Library, MS 493; and the Coventry Corporation manuscript, which consists of a sequence of Hoccleve's poems for the Countess of Westmoreland, either preceded or followed by his *Regement of Princes*.[51] All these manuscripts seem professionally produced, probably between the second and third quarters of the fifteenth centuries,and the predominance of Hoccleve suggests London as the most likely site of production; most of them seem textually related. Sandwiched into this sequence in all these manuscripts is Lydgate's Dance of Death. None of these manuscripts contain attributions.

The puzzle is the Lydgate. How does it come to be situated recurrently in a manifestly Hocclevean sequence? Lydgate's text is hardly a brief filler, useful for filling out a booklet or quire. (It runs, in its fullest forms to between 84 and 89 eight-line stanzas.) It is possible that the collocation was made on consonance of subject matter, particularly with Hoccleve's Lerne to Die. But while no more obvious reason presents itself, it seems to suggest that, within at least some professional book-producing circles, there was little sense of authorial distinctiveness, except with larger individual works like those of Chaucer, Gower, and Lydgate with which I began.[52]

Two factors emerge as common to most of the collections I have been discussing: attribution and decoration, both factors generally most conspicuous by their absence. They reveal only intermittently any coherent sense of the identity of the author and even more intermittently any inclination to signal that in distinctive ways. It may also be significant that most of these collections were seemingly non-metropolitan productions, ones for which regional factors, particularly affiliation to a religious house, may have provided the material means, if not the actual resources for such assemblages.

It follows then that the conception of the author's works was one that took some time to take root in English literary culture. It is not evidenced in any very systematic way in later medieval writers, those whose works overlap the beginnings of printing in England. Skelton's works survive during his lifetime only in scattered forms and there are no early collections of Dunbar, Hawes, or Surrey. Wyatt is a partial exception to this generalization, but the fundamental difficulty with collections like BL, MS Egerton 2711 or the Blage manuscript is determining how much of his corpus is contained in these collections.[53] It is only with print that the process of systematic consolidation of a vernacular author's achievement starts to take place, explicitly expressed, most appropriately, for the first time in the 1532 edition of 'The Works' of Chaucer.[54]

NOTES

1 T. W. Machan, *Textual Criticism and Middle English Texts* (Charlottesville, Va., 1997), p. 97.

2 Machan, pp. 99-135.

3 See *The Poems of Laurence Minot*, ed. by Joseph Hall (Oxford, 1887).

4 These poems, together with other works by Herebert, have been edited by Stephen Reimer (Toronto, 1987); they are described in the manuscript as 'in manu suo scripsit frater Willemus Herebert' (fol. 205ʳ).

5 See, for example, Maldwyn Mills, 'The Composition and Style of the Southern *Octavian, Sir Launfal* and *Libeaus Desconus*', *Medium Aevum*, 31 (1962), 88-109.

6 See G. Neilson, *Huchown of the Awle Ryale the Alliterative Poet: a Historical Criticism of Fourteenth Century Poems ascribed to Sir Hew of Eglintoun* (Glasgow, 1902); J. T. T. Brown, *Huchown of the Awle Ryale and His Poems: Examined in the Light of Recent Criticism* (Glasgow, 1902); and C. Reicke, *Untersuchungen über den Stil der mittelenglischen alliterierenden Geschichte 'Morte Arthure,' 'The Destruction of Troy,' 'The Wars of Alexander,' 'The Seige of Jerusalem,' 'Sir Gawayn and the Green Knight'* (Königsberg, 1906).

7 For the most recent attempt to establish common authorship for some of these poems see R. A. Cooper & Derek Pearsall, 'The *Gawain* Poems: a Statistical Approach to the Question of Common Authorship', *Review of English Studies*, n.s. 39 (1988), 365-85.

8 Sylvia Huot, *From song to book: the poetics of writing in Old French lyric and lyrical narrative poetry* (Ithaca, NY, 1987), especially Ch. 7, 'The Vernacular Poet as Compiler: The Rise of the Single-Author Codex in the Fourteenth Century'.

9 See Sandra Hindman, 'The Composition of the Manuscript of Christine de Pizan's Collected Works in the British Library: a Reassessement', *British Library Journal*, 9 (1983), 93-123.

10 For description see *The Complete Works of John Gower*, ed. by G. C. Macaulay (Oxford, 1899-1902), II, clvii-clix.

11 Formerly owned by the Countess of Sutherland; sold Christie's, 2 July 1975, lot 242 (+ pl. 8), the fullest modern description; see also Macaulay, I, lxxix-lxxxii.

12 A. I. Doyle & M. B. Parkes, 'The production of copies of the *Canterbury Tales* and the *Confessio Amantis* in the early fifteenth century', in *Medieval Scribes, Manuscripts, and Libraries*, ed. by M. B. Parkes & A. G. Watson (London, 1978), p. 195.

13 Various rubrics within the *Canterbury Tales* do refer to Chaucer, but these seem to reflect his presence within the narrative rather than as an authorial identity.

14 For a full description and a facsimile of this manuscript see *Geoffrey Chaucer: Poetical Works: a Facsimile of Cambridge University Library Gg. 4. 27* (Cambridge, 1980), introd. by M. B. Parkes & R. Beadle.

15 For discussion see the introduction to J. Boffey & A. S. G. Edwards, *Bodleian Library MS Arch. Selden B. 24: a Facsimile* (Cambridge, 1997).

16 See *Magdalene College, Cambridge MS. Pepys 2006: a Facsimile*, introd. by A. S. G. Edwards (Norman, Okla., 1985).

17 For details of these see A. S. G. Edwards, 'Selections from Lydgate's Fall of Princes: a Checklist', *The Library*, 5th series (1971), and Nigel Mortimer, 'Selections from Lydgate's *Fall of Princes*: a Corrected Checklist', *The Library*, 6th series, 17 (1995), 342-44.

18 They appear together in BL, MS Royal 18. D. II, Bodleian Library, MS Digby 230, and Cambridge, Trinity College, MS O.5.2.

19 They are joined in BL, Add. MS 5140 and MS Egerton 2864, Oxford, Christ Church, MS 152, Longleat MS 257, and Austin, University of Texas, MS 143.

20 The standard account remains E. P. Hammond, 'Ashmole 59 and Other Shirley Manuscripts', *Anglia*, 30 (1907), 320-48; see now also Margaret Connolly, *John Shirley: Book Production and the Noble Household in Fifteenth-Century England* (Aldershot, 1998), pp. 145-69.

21 See E. P. Hammond, 'Two British Museum Manuscripts: a Contribution to the Bibliography of John Lydgate', *Anglia*, 28 (1905), 1-28, and Connolly, pp. 178-81.

22 IMEV nos 2081, 3845, 253, 2833, 2791, 1025, 2802, 915, 401, 186, 2784 (in that order). For a

detailed description of this manuscript see *The Seven Psalms*, ed. by Alexandra Barratt, EETS 307 (Oxford, 1995), pp. xiv-xxi.

23 IMEV 2081, 3845, 2791, 915, 401, 186. On 2784 see above.

24 He describes IMEV 2081 (fols 194-6) as 'compiled & made by John lidgate late a monke of the house of Seynt Edmundus of Bury'.

25 On Fox see G. R. Owst, 'Some Books and Book-Owners of Fifteenth-Century St Alban's', *Transactions of the St Albans and Hertfordshire Architectural and Archaeological Society* (1929), 176-95.

26 Barratt points to his bequest, along with other bound books of 'a boke that is in quayers xxv, for the more parte wryte redy' (xx).

27 See Owst, 'Some Books and Book-Owners', 178-9.

28 Of the four poems in the booklet not ascribed to Lydgate three (2833, 1025, 2802) are unique to this collection; one (IMEV 253) in two others: BL, Add. MS 39574, fol. 52^v, and Bodl., Lat. lit. e.17, fols 51-3. IMEV claims incorrectly that 2833 is ascribed to Lygdate.

29 For example, on fol. 43^v where the name 'William Curteys' appears in a rubric another, early hand has added the identification 'abbas de Bury' above it. The earlier view that the opening initial contains Curteys's arms seems incorrect (I am indebted to Prof. Stephen Reimer for this point and for letting me see a draft of a forthcoming article on this manuscript).

30 Two poems, IMEV 22, 1967.5, were added later and are not included in the numbers given here.

31 These are IMEV 448, 529, 824, 1130, 2394, 2464, 2625, 2791, 2812, 3845, 4099, 4112, 4245.

32 Hamer records 29, but 1050/1 is not there.

33 In addition to those noted in n. 30 (i.e. those common to all three manuscripts) Jesus and Harley also share IMEV 175, 401, 447, 1019, 1294, 1814, 1865, 2156, 3503, 3673, 3798, 4243. Only three poems occur in Jesus and not in Harley or Laud: IMEV 854, 2233, 3632.

34 Susanna Greer Fein, 'A Thirteen-Line Alliterative Stanza on the Abuse of Prayer from the Audelay MS', *Medium Aevum*, 63 (1994), 61; see also *The Poems of John Audelay*, ed. by E. K. Whiting, EETS, o.s. 184 (Oxford, 1931), p. ix. It is not, however, certainly a closed collection: at the end appear two poems arguably not by Audelay (see E. G. Stanley, 'The Verse Forms of John the Blynde Awdelay', in *The Long Fifteenth Century. Essays for Douglas Gray*, ed. by Helen Cooper & Sally Mapstone (Oxford, 1997), pp. 99-121, especially 104-5), and a prose extract from Rolle, with a unique alliterative verse interpolation (on which see Fein).

35 The first now surviving is 'XI' on fol. 2^r.

36 Julia Boffey, *Manuscripts of English Courtly Love Lyrics During the Later Middle Ages* (Cambridge, 1985), p. 10.

37 Fols 60^v-65^v are ruled for a full page, although written only on the lower part of the page (with the exception of fol. 60^v, which is written only on the top part of the page. Fols 66^r-102^v are set out with only the lower part of the page ruled (fols 71, 100-102 are blank, apart from some later additions on fol. 101^v and the insertion – probably later – of music on fols 100^v-101^r). It should be said that the amount of the page that is ruled does vary on occasions (e.g. fols 88^v, 100^v extending considerably over more than half the page; but about half a page is the norm). The change in page use corresponds to a shift in verse form, to roundels in four or (more rarely) five-line stanzas.

38 For discussion of the significance of these blank spaces see Mary-Jo Arn, *Fortunes Stabilnes: Charles of Orleans's English Book of Love* (Binghamton, NY, 1994), pp. 106-9. She concludes that 'the theory that the spaces above each roundel were originally intended for music has no support' (p. 107).

39 Huot (cited above, n. 8), pp. 242-73.

40 Kathleen Scott will explore Charles's possible links to the Corpus manuscript in a forthcoming study; see also her discussion of Corpus 61 in *Later Gothic Illumination* (London, 1995), II, 182-5 (especially 183).

41 For manuscripts decorated at Clare see Kathleen Scott, 'Lydgate's Lives of Saints Edmund and Fremund: a Newly-Located Manuscript in Arundel Castle', *Viator*, 13 (1982), n. 68

42 For some account of this manuscript see A. S. G. Edwards, 'The Transmission and Audience of Osbern Bokenham's *Legendys of Hooly Wummen*', in *Late-Medieval Religious Texts and Their Transmission: Essays in Honour of A. I. Doyle* (Cambridge, 1994), pp. 157-68. The work itself is edited by M. S. Serjeantson, EETS o.s. 206 (London, 1938).

43 *The Early English Carols*, ed. by R. L. Greene, 2nd edn (Oxford, 1977), p. clv.

44 Greene, p. clv. It is interesting that there was evidently some knowledge of Ryman's verse in Kent in the early sixteenth century. A poem in a Kent manuscript, now Dublin, Trinity College, MS 490, contains an allusion: 'let eure Ryman take hyede how he doht leue / and not to ssyne hym sselff to geue'; see John Scattergood, 'Two Unrecorded Poems from Trinity College, Dublin, MS 490,' *Review of English Studies*, n.s. 38 (1987), 46-9.

45 For descriptions see C. W. Dutschke et al., *Guide to the Medieval and Renaissance Manuscripts in the Huntington Library*, 2 vols (San Marino, Calif., 1989), I, 144-7, 247-51. For discussion see John Bowers, 'Hoccleve's Huntington Holographs: the First "Collected Poems" in English', *Fifteenth-Century Studies*, 15 (1989), 27-49.

46 On these links see A. I. Doyle & M. B. Parkes, 'The production of copies' (cited above, n. 12), pp. 163-210, especially 182-4.

47 I disregard three poems of which post medieval transcripts exist either from this manuscript or from printed editions; these are IMEV 3407, 3788, and 4251.

48 For details of the 44 complete manuscripts see M. C. Seymour, 'The Manuscripts of Hoccleve's *Regiment of Princes*', *Transactions of the Edinburgh Bibliographical Society*, IV, part 7 (1974), 255-97, and A. S. G. Edwards, 'Hoccleve's *Regiment of Princes*: a New Manuscript', *Transactions of the Edinburgh Bibliographical Society*, V, part 1 (1978), 32. Neither of these mentions the selection in the Huntington manuscript or in BL, MS Royal 8. A. X.

49 See Marian Trudgill & J. A. Burrow, 'A Hocclevean Balade', *Notes & Queries*, n.s. 45 (1998), 178-80 (the quotation is from p. 180).

50 For an elegant illustration of the textual history of one of these poems see Trudgill & Burrow, 'A Hocclevean Balade'.

51 The Laud, Bodley, Beinecke, and Coventry manuscripts all contain (in order) IMEV 124, 299, 1561, 3121, 3582, 4072, 2591, 2229; in Selden varies this order only in that 2229 precedes 124. For some comments on the textual relationships between these manuscripts see A. I. Doyle & G. B. Pace, 'A New Chaucer Manuscript', *PMLA*, 83 (1968), 22-34, especially 24 and n. 25.

52 For valuable analysis of the thematic implications of the collocation of these works see N. E. R. Perkins, 'Counsel and Constraint in Thomas Hoccleve's *The Regement of Princes*', unpublished Ph.D. thesis, University of Cambridge (1998), pp. 195-9; for a suggestive attempt to situate this collocation historically see a forthcoming study by Lee Patterson in *Yale University Library Gazette*; I am indebted to both authors for permitting me to see their work in advance of publication.

53 See the discussion in Richard Harrier, *The Canon of Sir Thomas Wyatt's Poetry* (Cambridge, Mass., 1975).

54 See A. S. G. Edwards, 'Chaucer from Manuscript to Print: the Social Text and the Critical Text', *Mosaic*, 28 (1995), 1-12. For advice and comment of various kinds I am indebted to Professors John Burrow and Derek Pearsall and to Dr A. I. Doyle.

A NEW MANUSCRIPT BY THE HAMMOND SCRIBE

Discovered by Jeremy Griffiths

LINNE R. MOONEY

SOME TIME IN 1995 or 1996, Jeremy Griffiths found yet another manuscript written by the scribe originally identified by Eleanor Prescott Hammond at the beginning of this century and thus called 'the Hammond scribe'. Because I was then writing an article about other new manuscripts in this hand, Jeremy told me about his find; but I did not include it in my article because it was, I thought, an important discovery that Jeremy planned to publish himself. But apparently he was too busy with other pursuits to investigate this new attribution thoroughly, and I gave the manuscript only a cursory look at that time. Since his death, I have been looking into his discovery and have made some further finds of my own about it.

Hammond's original identification of the scribe who now bears her name was predicated on what now appears a limited portion of the œuvre, no more than six manuscripts:[1]

(1) London, British Library, Add. MS 34360. This book and the next two are miscellanies, including minor works of Chaucer and Lydgate.

(2) BL, MS Harley 2251.

(3) Cambridge, Trinity College, MS R.3.21, where the scribe copied most of one gathering, fols 34^r-49^v, his work being taken over by the main scribe in line 5 of the final page.

(4) BL, MS Arundel 59, fols 1-89, with Hoccleve's *Regiment of Princes*.[2]

(5) London, College of Physicians, MS 388 (*olim* 13), Chaucer's *Canterbury Tales*.[3]

(6) BL, MS Royal 17 D. XV, fols 167-301, another *Canterbury Tales*, in collaboration with another scribe and with this text bound together *c.* 1470-1530 with political tracts, including works of Sir John Fortescue. In part this showing was limited by Hammond's concentration on poetic texts associated with Chaucer and Lydgate.

In an extremely important article, A. I. Doyle added four further items to Hammond's listing:[4]

(7) Worcester Cathedral, MS F.172, a miscellany with very literal prose

translations of excerpts from the Bible and Apocrypha, decrees of the diocese of London, a 'Letter of Alexander', and religious prose (including Richard Rolle and William Flete).[5]

(8) BL, Cotton MS Claudius A.VIII, fols 175^r-97^v, Fortescue's *Governance of England*.

(9) the single leaf BL, MS Harley 78, fol. 3, with part of *Piers the Plowman's Creed*, which occasioned Doyle's discussion.

(10) the single leaf preserved in the guardbook Bodl., MS Rawlinson D.913, fol. 43, with a fragment of the English prose *Merlin*.

And Doyle has found two further books in the scribe's hand:[6]

(11) BL, MS Harley 4999, *Statutes of the Realm*, from 1 Edward III until the book ends incompletely in 18 Henry VI (1440).

(12) Cambridge, Trinity College, MS R.14.52, English prose translations of Latin treatises on science and medicine.

To these items, Richard Green made a further addition:[7]

(13) BL, MS Harley 372, fols 71^r-112^r, a large fragment from another copy of Hoccleve's *Regiment*.[8]

And in my earlier article on the scribe, I discussed the hand as found in:[9]

(14) Cambridge, Trinity College, MS O.3.11, a volume of English texts on London city, guild, and legal matters, similar to 'Arnold's Chronicle'.

The fourteen manuscripts or fragments include four books and three fragments with English literary works. Another manuscript includes English prose translations and didactic works, and another compiles English medicine and science. Fortescue's *Governance*, the Statutes, and the manuscript of London city texts are all related to governance, as are some of the texts in the Worcester compilation and some of the texts bound with the Royal *Canterbury Tales*. The two copies of Hoccleve's *Regiment* might be classed as either literary or governance-related.

Jeremy's new identification associates the scribe's work still further with texts connected with the practical interests of those committed to governance. It is BL, Add. MS 29901, which the Additional catalogue describes as 'Treatises on state ceremonial, heraldry, etc.', dating it simply 'fifteenth century'. Add. 29901 is a paper manuscript of small folio size, with a blank bifolium at the head, followed by five quires of sixteen leaves each; the second half of the final quire of fourteen leaves is blank.[10] The modern foliation '1-87' covers only the written leaves. There is no decoration, apart from underlining of headings in red, with some headings and words in the texts rubricated. The manuscript was conceived and written as a unit, the texts running over from one gathering to the next, with catchwords by the scribe, and a table of contents by the scribe at the end (fol. 87^r). The hand shows those same features of spelling and letter-formation which Hammond and Doyle have identified as this writer's idiosyncrasies.

The manuscript presents the following texts:

1. Fols 1^r-12^v: in Latin, the service of the lords ('Servicia dominorum') at

the coronation of a king of England, in this case the coronation of Richard II in 1377, titled in other manuscripts where it occurs 'Processus factus ad coronationem regis Ricardi II' or 'de officiis senescalli constabularii marescalli etc.'.

2. Fols 13^r-16^v: in Latin, the order of the service at the coronation of a king ('Solempnitas coronacionis'), in this case again for the coronation of Richard II.

3. Fols 16^v-17^r: in Latin, the funeral services of kings ('Exequie regales quum ex hoc seculo reges migrare contigerint').

4. Fols 17^r-25^v: in Latin, the 'modus tenendi parliamentum'.[11]

5. Fols 26^r-36^r: in Latin (fols 26^r-29^v) and French (fols 29^v-36^r), the duties of the Earl Marshall and Constable ('Officium marescali et constabularii Anglie tam tempore pacis quam guerre').[12]

6. Fols 36^r-37^r: in French, 'Ordinacio belli domini Regis Edwardi contra Scotos' or 'Les ordonnaunces de les troyz batailles et des deux eles du bataille du Roy [Richard II?] a son premier voiage en Escoce l'an de son reigne ixme', possibly the Ordinances of War made by Richard II at Durham in 1385.

7. Fols 37^v-39^v: in French, an account of the campaign of Edward I in Scotland in 1296.

8. Fols 40^r-47^v: in French, a treatise concerning the creation of heralds and the duties that pertain to that office, attributed to 'Iules Cesar'.[13]

9. Fols 47^v-55^r: in French, the founding of the Order of the Garter.

10. Fols 55^v-59^v: in French, the founding of the Knights of the Bath ('quant escuier vient a court pour receuoir l'ordre de cheuallier du Bain').

11. Fols 60^r-79^r: in Latin, the treatise on heraldry ascribed to Johannes de Bado Aureo, usually translated as 'John of Guildford', compiled at the instance of Anne, queen of Richard II.[14]

12. Fols 79^r-86^v: in Latin, another treatise on heraldry, 'Tractatus de insigniis et armis …', attributed to Bartholus de Saxoferrato and dated 1358.[15]

Whatever the general dispersal of these texts, Add. 29901 shows a significant overlap of contents with a narrow range of other books.[16] Two books show extensive agreement in the first ten contents items: BL, Cotton MS, Domitian XVIII contains eight of these texts (6 and 7 are lacking), while BL, Cotton MS, Nero D.VI has the first seven (substituting a similar French text on the duties of the marshal for our text 5). More distantly, Cotton Nero D.II includes items 8 and 9. It may be significant that Nero D.VI belonged to an Earl Marshall, Nero D.II to a King of Arms. And two heraldic books unknown to Sharpe, College of Arms, MSS L.6 and M.18, have the two concluding texts (MS L.6, our item 8 also).

The first four items of Add. 29901 record precedents for ordering coronations and royal funerals and for summoning parliament. These were all events conducted by the Steward, Constable, Earl Marshall, and Kings of Arms. Item 5 describes the duties of the Marshall and Constable. Items 8-10 describe the order of proceedings for the creation of Heralds, the foundation of the Order of the Garter, and the creation of Knights of the Bath, all instituted by the sovereign but overseen by the Earl Marshall in particular, the Constable, and/or the Garter King of Arms. According to Wagner, the Ordinances of War of 1385 (item 6) were the written foundation on which the Earl Marshall and Constable of England based their right of 'authority over the army in the field'.[17]

The treatise of Johannes de Bado Aureo (item 11), according to Wagner (p. 67), is the earliest explicit reference to Kings of Arms or Heralds having the right to grant arms, along with or instead of the crown (as was the custom on the continent). In stating that Kings of Arms and Heralds have this right, Johannes cites 'Bartholus', i.e. the final item of this volume. Bartholus de Saxoferrato was a famous jurist who served the Emperor Charles IV, father of Richard II's queen Anne. His 'Tractatus', according to Wagner, is 'the earliest-known treatise on heraldry' (p. 68).[18] Especially given the provenance of closely related books, this concentration of texts on rights and responsibilities of Earl Marshall, Constable, Garter, and other Kings of Arms implies that the Hammond scribe might well have undertaken this commission for one of these officials, or for the king.

The manuscript contains no names of early owners or indications of provenance. To improve on the Additional cataloguer and those, like Wagner, who could date the book only by its latest text (1399, Henry IV's creation of the Knights of the Bath for his coronation), Jeremy's identification of the scribe is crucial. From the other manuscripts in his hand, we have fairly concrete evidence that he lived and worked during the 1460s and 1470s, possibly into the 1480s. At least one of the other books he copied, although not commissioned for this owner, was the property of a later herald; Thomas Wall, Windsor Herald (and a Garter King of Arms 1534-6), signs the *Regiment of Princes* in Arundel 59, fol. 130[v], 'bought of henry at the tauerne within buschopsgate at London the yere of our Lord 1525 wyttenesse Robert Lytylbouring Saywell etc. the viii[th] day of May'.[19] I propose first to consider what light might be shed on the scribe's activities should we ascribe provenance of the book to one of the two contemporary Garter Kings of Arms. The two men who held the office in this period had careers as King of more than a quarter-century – John Smert from 1450 to 1478, John Wrythe from 1478 to 1504.

Although there is little information about the first of these men, John Wrythe seems to have taken an active interest in recording arms, and as Garter at the time of the incorporation of the College of Arms he was responsible for assembling the library of the College.[20] His activities in collecting and keeping books, both his own and those of the College, is mentioned more than once in the famous dispute in 1530 between his son, Thomas Wrythe, or 'Wriothesly', as he styled himself, who succeeded him as Garter (1504-34), and Thomas Benolt, Clarenceux King of Arms (1511-34).[21]

Wrythe seems to me the more likely of the two Garter Kings of Arms to have commissioned this book of precedents. He was originally Falcon King of Arms in the 1470s, then Norroy King of Arms for little more than a year (1477-8) before being advanced to Garter.[22] He was an innovator in styling English arms, having invented the practice of adding charges to indicate cadet status. He wrote some arms and texts about arms in BL, Add. MS 45133, as well as in College of Arms, MS M.3, in both of which there are also arms recorded by his son.[23] In addition, he was keeper of all the heraldic rolls and books, first at Coldharbour, the Thames Street residence given at its incorporation to the College of Arms (1484-5), then at his home (1485-1504).

In the dispute between Wrythe's son, Thomas Wriothesley, and Thomas Benolt, the former alleged that his father, who was Garter when the Heralds were granted a charter and college at Coldharbor, kept the library there.[24] At the accession of Henry VII, when the Heralds were turned out of Coldharbour by the Act of Resumption, Wrythe took the College library into his own keeping. Benolt claimed that at Wrythe's death his son had kept the library to himself, handing over only such copies of the precedents and rolls as he had made himself. In so doing, he had prevented the provincial Kings of Arms, like Benolt, from access to records that would prove their cases.

Wriothesley replied that at the time of his father's death he and his brother William, later York Herald, had turned over all of the College's books to Roger Machado, Clarenceux King of Arms. They had acted at their father's request, keeping only such books as had been his personal property, and they alleged further that the books of the College had remained at Blackfriars in Machado's keeping and had been transferred intact to successive Clarenceuxes down to Benolt, the present holder. These details evidence a collection of heraldic precedents in John Wrythe's time and their subsequent provenance at Black-friars in the possession of the Clarenceux Kings of Arms.

A further record suggests that Add. 29901 might be connected with this line of descent. First, by his will proved in May 1534, Benolt bequeathed all his books relating to arms to his friend Thomas Hawley, at the time Carlisle Herald and afterwards Clarenceux (1536-57). Hawley was given life-use of the collection, and it was to pass at his death to each subsequent Clarenceux 'as longe as they may Endure'. Benolt also stipulated that an inventory of the books be made and passed on with them.[25] This inventory was duly drawn up by Thomas Wall, at the time Windsor Herald, whom we have already seen as the owner of a 'Hammond scribe' manuscript. It survives in several copies, includ-ing College of Arms, MS Heralds, vol. 1, fols 139-81, perhaps the original.

This inventory includes several manuscript books whose single texts correspond with items in Add. 29901:

(a) item [16] 'a Booke of the fourme of Coronations of Kinges and burialles of divers estates made to be writtyn by T. Benolt', similar to Add. 29901, items 1-3.

(b) item [21] 'a Booke of Jehan de B[a]udo Aureo & Franciscus de Fossis writin in french', corresponding to Add. 29901, item 11, and, in spite of the difference in the language of the text, the title corresponding in part to the apparently unique title in the Add. 29901 contents table: 'cum Francisco de Foueis in distinctionibus armorum'.[26]

(c) item [22] 'a litell Booke writtyn in basterd hande & wel illuminyd concernyng the droites and custumes of the office of armes w^t many other goodly maters', possibly identical with Add. 29901, item 8.

(d) item 23 'a great Booke writtin in paper royall of the arbre de Batailles with divers other thinges notable', possibly identical with Add. 29901, item 6, if it is not simply Honore Bovet's work.[27]

I am suggesting not that these entries refer to Add. 29901 itself, but that books like these, in this case gathered in the library of the College of Arms from 1484, could well have served as the exemplars from which the Hammond scribe compiled our manuscript.

On the other hand, Add. 29901's emphasis on the duties and privileges of the Earl Marshall and the Constable may instead point to a holder of one of these offices as the patron responsible for the manuscript. Constables during the active career of the Hammond scribe were John Tiptoft, Earl of Worcester (1462-7 and briefly in 1470); Richard Woodville, first Earl Rivers (1467-9); Anthony Woodville, Lord Scales and second Earl Rivers (briefly in 1469); and Richard, Duke of Gloucester (1469-70, 1471-83, until his accession to the throne).

Tiptoft, the first of these Constables, took an active interest in arms, being responsible for a set of 'Ordinances, Statutes, and Rules' to be followed in all 'Jousts of Peace Royal'. These were drawn up in 1466 'by the kinges comandement at wyndesore', and are preserved in College of Arms, MS M.6.[28] He was also an author, responsible for the translation of Cicero's *De amicitia*, printed by Caxton in 1481 (STC 5293). More significantly, he also translated Montemagno's *De vera nobilitate*, printed by Caxton in the same volume.[29] He would also have been Constable at the coronation of Edward IV's queen, Elizabeth Woodville (1464), which could account for the precedence given to coronations as the subject of the first two items in the manuscript.

Richard Woodville, and especially his son Anthony, were also Constables with large libraries and literary interests. Although he was Constable for only a few months, Anthony would have expected to hold the office for life on the death of his father, it having been granted to his father and heirs in perpetuity. He also was an important literary figure of the 1470s, translating three works published by Caxton. Such a connection might point to a very small literary circle if, as I have suggested elsewhere, manuscripts written by one of the Hammond scribe's collaborators appear to have found their way into Caxton's shop as exemplars for his publications.[30]

Richard, Duke of Gloucester and later King of England, also took an active interest in arms and the right to bear them. He founded the College of Arms early in his reign and donated Coldharbour as its permanent site.[31]

The contents of Add. 29901 relate still more closely to the duties and responsibilities of the Earl Marshal. The Marshals had, and still have, special responsibility for coronations and funerals and direct responsibility over the Kings of Arms and Heralds. The office of Earl Marshal was hereditary to the Dukes of Norfolk by the middle of the fifteenth century, when it was held by John Mowbray VI, third Duke, then by his son John VII, the fourth Duke (Marshall 1461-76), who features in the Paston Letters.[32] After a gap John Howard, a distant relative of the then extinct Mowbrays, was created Duke of Norfolk and Earl Marshal at Richard III's coronation.

The Marshalsy was apparently vacant from the death of the fourth Duke in 1476 until the accession of Richard III. Richard himself was Constable at the time and may have fulfilled some of the duties of Earl Marshall as well, although Camden thought 'that the office was exercised between 1476 and 1483 by … Thomas [Grey], Marquess of Dorset'.[33] Other than Richard, who might have been interested in the attention given both offices in the manuscript, I find no particulars about these men to suggest a special interest in the written precedents for their offices.

What light does this new discovery shed on our knowledge of the Hammond scribe? In addition to the recognized Chaucerian affiliations of his work, we may now connect him with officers of Arms. This allows us to re-examine other manuscripts by the scribe. It may explain, for example, why BL, Harley 4999 records the Statutes from only the time of Edward III, since in those years a number of Statutes relating to the rights, privileges, and duties of the several armorial offices were promulgated. For example, 13 Richard II, cap. 2 (1389/90) deals with the rights and duties of the Constable.[34]

The heraldic contents may also help understand the Hammond scribe's fragment of *Piers the Plowman's Creed* in BL, Harley 78 discovered by Doyle. The text, a thirty-four line fragment, now occupies only the first leaf recto (fol. 3^r) of a bifolium. The other three sides, written in another hand which Doyle dates as 's. xv/xvi', record 'an all-but-complete copy of a letter (in English) under the signet of King Edward IV …, [a]ddressed to some person or body unspecified, … concern[ing] preparations for a campaign against Scotland in the first few months of 1481' (pp. 428-9). In this letter, we find again the concern with military campaigns in Scotland, which, as Doyle suggests, may have been recorded and kept as a precedent for similar occasions, like those recorded as items 6 and 7 of the Additional manuscript.

Doyle also suggests that the fragment of *Piers the Plowman's Creed* may contain 'subject matter of … special interest for the scribe or his director' (p. 434). The heraldic associations of Add. 29901 offer one explanation for this probably excerpted bit of text (lines 172-207 only). The passage, part of the speaker's visit to 'the prechoures' (154), describes the architectural details of what art historians consider 'almost certainly … the London house of Blackfriars'.[35] Blackfriars, as I have noted, was the site to which Thomas and William Wriothesley took the College of Arms books that had been in their father's keeping and gave them to Roger Machado. This was apparently considered their proper storage place in 1504. In fact, the wording of

Wriothesley's statement in his dispute with Benolt suggests that the Blackfriars chapter house was the Heralds' office. He and his brother had surrendered the books, he testifies, 'by the commaundemente of there father unto Machado Clarencius and to other of the offyce of armes then beyng present in the chapitre house at the Blake Frears in London'.[36] A poetic description of Blackfriars might then have been of special interest to Kings of Arms, Heralds, or their scribes.

This passage of *Piers the Plowman's Creed* also contains a reference to the Great Rolls on which the Kings of Arms recorded the arms of all the families and individuals of their regions:

> wyde wyndows Iwrought, Iwriten ful thikke
> A cheveron with sharpe shieldes, to showen aboute
> Mid markes of Merchauntis, medled bitwene
> Mo than twenty and mo, twyes Inombred.
> Ther nys non herawd that hath half suche a Rolle,
> Right as a Ragman had Irent hem newe.

Wagner cites the lines as evidence that such rolls were a normal feature of heraldic responsibilities before the Visitation of 1530.[37] Such a description would seem of obvious interest to Heralds or other officers of Arms.

Blackfriars was located in the parish of St Andrew-next-the-Wardrobe, just east of the juncture of the Fleet estuary and the Thames, within the City walls (expanded in the thirteenth century to allow more space for the house). It comprised a church, churchyard, cloister, library, chapterhouse, dorters, kitchen, frater, lower frater, anchorite's house, and other buildings, all described in *Piers*; it was used for several meetings of Parliament in the fourteenth century and one, that of 1450, in the fifteenth.[38] Blackfriars was also proximate to the King's Wardrobe, which was situated, ever since Edward III had purchased the property in 1359, across the street, St Andrew's Hill. The two enclaves were linked by a bridge over the street by the beginning of the sixteenth century. The Wardrobe's facilities included stables, courtyard, warehouse, workrooms, cistern tower, great hall, royal halls, chapel, treasury, kitchens, and chambers. John Stow, in his *Survey of London*, noted that 'The secret letters and writings touching the estate of the Realme were wont to be enroled in the kings Wardrobe, and not in the Chauncery, as appeareth by the records'.[39] Thus there was scribal activity and an archive in the Wardrobe also, presumably keeping copies of sensitive correspondence like the letter in Harley 78.

In the same neighbourhood were residences of some of the armorial officials I have named as possible patrons of Add. 29901. Along the river just east of Blackfriars was Baynard's Castle, owned in the fifteenth century by Humphrey, Duke of Gloucester (1390-1447) and thereafter by Richard, Duke of York, and his sons Edward IV and Richard III. A little further east along the Thames, but west of Queenhithe, was a large stone house adjoining Brook's Wharf or

Broken Wharf, called 'Broken Wharf Mansion', which belonged to a suc-
cession of Earls Marshal, including the Mowbrays, in the fourteenth and fifteenth centuries.[40] Finally, John Tiptoft, a Constable, was buried at Blackfriars.

Admittedly, one could find connections of all these men with other
institutions as well. But the connections among this manuscript, the Harley 78
fragment, armorial officers, and Blackfriars may point us toward discovering
more about the 'Hammond scribe'. Because the fragment in Harley 78 is an
excerpt from a longer work copied out separately, it indicates a personal
interest of the scribe or his patron more clearly than do complete volumes,
certainly written to specifications. Its focus on Blackfriars may help us to find
the 'Hammond scribe' at work on other texts that will identify him clearly. I
think we should follow Jeremy's lead in investigating manuscripts of the
Heralds, Earls Marshall, Constables, Blackfriars, and Wardrobe for further
examples.

NOTES

I am grateful to the editors for their revisions, corrections and bibliographical references.

1 For Hammond's final statement, see 'A Scribe of Chaucer', *Modern Philology* 27 (1929), 26-
 33. Hammond had earlier discussed in detail the first two manuscripts in the following list; see
 'Two British Museum Manuscripts', *Anglia* 28 (1905), 1-28, a study which remains the best
 published description.
2 For a description, see M. C. Seymour, 'The Manuscripts of Hoccleve's *Regiment of Princes*',
 Transactions of the Edinburgh Bibliographical Society 4, vii (1974), 255-97 at 264-5.
3 For this book and the next, see John M. Manly & Edith Rickert, *The Text of the Canterbury
 Tales*, 8 vols (Chicago, 1940), 1:439-46 and 476-84, respectively; and for the additions to
 Royal, Anthony Gross, *The Dissolution of the Lancastrian Kingship: Sir John Fortescue and the
 Crisis of Monarchy in Fifteenth-Century England* (Stanford, 1996), pp. 8-9.
4 'An Unrecognised Piece of *Piers the Ploughman's Creed* and Other Work by its Scribe,'
 Speculum 34 (1959), 428-36. Besides the identification of the new work, Doyle meticulously
 describes the most distinctive features of the hand (particularly at 429-30). Like Hammond,
 Green (n. 7 below), and myself (n. 9 below), he includes a facsimile.
5 For an instructive study of one typical text, see Thomas Hahn, 'The Middle English *Letter of
 Alexander to Aristotle*: Introduction, Text, Sources, and Commentary', *Mediaeval Studies* 41
 (1979), 106-60.
6 Doyle has generously allowed me to list the first of these manuscripts, whose discovery he has
 not published himself; for the second, see his 'English Books In and Out of Court from
 Edward III to Henry VII', in *English Court Culture in the Later Middle Ages*, ed. by V. J.
 Scattergood & J. W. Sherborne (London, 1983), pp. 163-81 at 177 n. 42. I gave an account of
 the contents of R.14.52 in *The Index of Middle English Prose Handlist XI: Manuscripts in the
 Library of Trinity College, Cambridge* (Cambridge, 1995), pp. 53-64. On the basis of the
 signature 'Quod Multon' in one text, the scribe has sometimes been referred to as 'Multon' or
 'the Multon scribe'.
7 'Notes on Some Manuscripts of Hoccleve's *Regiment of Princes*', *British Library Journal* 4
 (1978), 37-41 at 39-40.
8 See Seymour 266-7.
9 'More Manuscripts Written by a Chaucer Scribe', *Chaucer Review* 30 (1996), 402-7; for the
 contents, see *Index*, pp. 109-14.
10 Viz. ii (blank) 1-5^{16} 6^{14}. For the BL description, see *Catalogue of Additions to the Manuscripts*

in the British Museum in the years MDCCCLIV-MDCCCLXXV, 2 vols (London, 1877) 2:740-41.

11 *Parliamentary Texts of the Later Middle Ages*, ed. by Nicholas Pronay & John Taylor (Oxford, 1980).

12 See Vernon L. W. Harcourt, *His Grace the Steward and the Trial of Peers* (London, 1907), pp. 168-9.

13 See A. R. Wagner, *Heralds and Heraldry in the Middle Ages: an Inquiry into the Growth of the Armorial Function of Heralds*, 2nd edn (1956; rep. Oxford, 1960), p. 43. Here Wagner describes a French account of the duties of heralds, which he thinks was probably written by Nicholas Villart or Calabre, King of Arms of Anjou and Touraine, just after 1400. This discusses 'changes of custom and ceremony since the days when Julius Caesar or Alexander – he is uncertain which – first created heralds; for this, having lost his book, he has to rely on memory'.

14 See Wagner, *Heralds*, p. 67. Richard Sharpe, *A Handlist of the Latin Writers of Great Britain and Ireland before 1540* (Turnhout, 1997), p. 210, lists five manuscript copies.

15 Wagner, *Heralds*, p. 68, citing Bysshe, *In Nicholaum Uptonum notae* (1654), p. 13, says Bartholus died in 1356. But equally, he cites Anstis's *Register of the Order of the Garter*, which states that the text was completed by Bartholus's son in 1358.

16 For example, items 1 and 10 appear both in John Paston's 'grete boke', BL, MS Lansdowne 285, and its probable source, Pierpont Morgan Library, MS 775.

17 Wagner, *Heralds*, pp. 20-1, citing Nero D.IV, fol. 89ʳ, and Sir Travers Twiss, *Black Book of the Admiralty*, Rolls Series 55, 4 vols (1871-76), 1:453.

18 Bartholus does not, in fact, name the right of heralds and Kings of Arms to grant arms, but gives it to each family and individual, with disputes being settled privately or before a judge. In England disputes were settled in the Court of Chivalry, ruled over by the Constable and Earl Marshall. Johannes interpreted the lines from Bartholus; see Wagner, *Heralds*, p. 123 (Appendix A, # 13).

19 Doyle, 'Unnoticed', p. 432 n. 27.

20 See Anthony Richard Wagner, *English Genealogy*, 2nd edn (Oxford, 1972), p. 357; Wagner, *Heralds*, pp. 89, 92, 94-5, citing Anstis.

21 While Garter in 1490, Wrythe purchased a book of precedents, now College of Arms, MS M.3, from the widow of William Ballard, March King of Arms; see Wagner, *Heralds*, p. 108. To this, he apparently made additions, for which see the next paragraph. For Thomas Wrythe changing his surname, see Wagner, *Heralds*, p. 83; his brother William also adopted the spelling, and William's son, Thomas Wriothesley, was the first Earl of Southampton, grandfather of Shakespeare's patron.

22 See Arthur Charles Fox-Davies, *A Complete Guide to Heraldry* (London, 1925), p. 31.

23 See Anthony Wagner, *Heraldry in England* (Harmondsworth, 1949), pp. 13-14; Thomas Woodcock & John Martin Robinson, *The Oxford Guide to Heraldry* (Oxford, 1988), p. 66. For the two manuscripts, see Wagner, *Heralds*, pp. 112-13 and 108, respectively.

24 Wagner, *Heralds*, pp. 89 and 94, gives a full account of this dispute, citing and quoting Anstis. Benolt alleged that Wriothesley's claim that the provincial Kings of Arms must register their patents with him, as Garter, derived only from the time of Wriothesley's father.

25 See Wagner, *Heralds*, p. 110.

26 A garbled version of this ascription appears at Bodl., MS Latin misc. e.86, fol. iʳ, in a hand of s. xvii: 'compiled out of ye books of Francis de Loucis at the command of Anne queen to king Richard [3] 2'. The text so described appears to be a John of Guildford derivative, here ascribed to 'John Dade'. My thanks to Ralph Hanna for bringing this version to my attention.

27 Wagner, *Heralds*, p. 152 (Appendix F).

28 Woodcock & Robinson, p. 4. For a biography, see R. J. Mitchell, *John Tiptoft (1427-1478)* (London, [1938]), with an edition of the Montemagno (IPMEP 830). My thanks to Tony Edwards for this reference.

29 Such was his reputation for love of the martial arts and for literary interests that the trans-

lation of Caesar's *Gallic Wars* printed by Rastell (STC 4337, 1530) was usually attributed to him.

30 Rivers translated *The Dictes and Sayengis of the philosophers* (1477, STC 6826); *The morale prouerbes of Cristyne* [de Pisan] (1478, STC 7273); and *The Cordiale* (1479, STC 5758). See further my 'Scribes and Booklets of Trinity College, Cambridge MSS R.3.19 and R.3.21', in *Middle English Poetry: Texts and Traditions: Essays in Honour of Derek Pearsall*, ed. by Alastair Minnis (Cambridge, 2001).

31 On Richard and his books, see Anne F. Sutton & Livia Visser-Fuchs, *The Hours of Richard III* (Stroud, 1990) and *Richard III's Books* (Stroud, 1997).

32 See *Paston Letters and Papers of the Fifteenth Century*, ed. by Norman Davis, 2 vols (Oxford, 1971), # 65 etc.

33 Cited G. E. C[ockayne], *The Complete Peerage*, 2 vols (Stroud, 1987), 2:612.

34 Wagner, *Heralds*, pp. 21 and 122 (Appendix A [8]).

35 Doyle, 'Unrecognised', p. 434. See the most recent edition, *The Piers Plowman Tradition*, ed. by Helen Barr (London, 1993), pp. 67-70, 220.

36 Cited Wagner, *Heralds*, p. 95.

37 I cite lines 175-80 from Doyle's transcription of the fragment, pp. 435-6; Barr, pp. 220-1, misses here the probable allusion to *Piers Plowman* B 3.47-50, 59-70, as well as the (non-alliterating) heraldic specificity of line 176, as reported in the Hammond scribe's fragment (other copies read 'Schynen with schapen/scharpen scheldes'). See Wagner, *Heralds*, p. 51. The poem would imply that such documents were in use at a very early date, before 1395.

38 See *The City of London from Prehistoric Times to c. 1520*, vol. 3 of *British Atlas of Historic Towns*, Mary D. Lobel, gen. ed. (Oxford, 1989), p. 72. And for the King's Wardrobe, see p. 78.

39 *A Survey of London by John Stow*, ed. by Charles Lethbridge Kingsford, 2 vols (Oxford, 1908), 2:16.

40 See 'Baynard's Castle' and 'Broken Wharf Mansion' in *British Atlas*, pp. 65, 67-8; and Stow 2:11-12, on the latter.

BODLEIAN LIBRARY, MS ARCH. SELDEN. B. 24 AND DEFINITIONS OF THE 'HOUSEHOLD BOOK'

JULIA BOFFEY

THE IMPULSE to shoehorn manuscripts into particular categories has prompted a number of long-running scholarly debates, among which the various attempts to distinguish between 'miscellanies' and 'commonplace books' have figured with some regularity.[1] That the generic terms used in the taxonomy of manuscripts are sometimes susceptible to multiple or confused interpretation has been a further complication in the issue: do we all understand the term 'miscellany' to denote the same thing, to begin with? and, proceeding into the mire of sub-categorization, are we likely to be in a agreement about the features that might qualify a manuscript anthology (or miscellany, or commonplace book) to be a 'songbook' or a 'sermon notebook' or a 'minstrel collection'?[2] This essay proposes an exploration of just one of these codicological sub-categories: that of the 'household book'. It will attempt to isolate some of the different features which have prompted this definition, to explore its application to manuscripts like the Tollemache 'Book of Secrets', whose contents and compilation have been illuminated by Jeremy Griffiths's work,[3] and to extend its usefulness (and the different shades which its meaning may comprehend) in relation to some manuscripts of apparently rather different sorts.

The Tollemache 'Book of Secrets', a collection of texts notable primarily for their everyday usefulness, is clearly a 'household book' in the sense that it constitutes a repository of practical information of more or less domestic kinds – recipes and remedies and instructions on matters such as dyeing, fishing, arboriculture, and book production – which various members of a household may have wished to consult, or to have recorded, for different contingencies.[4] To trace the patterns of survival elsewhere of some of the texts incorporated in this manuscript leads to collections which may have been compiled in diverse ways, but are all linked by a common concern with the pragmatic usefulness of the materials they contain. The treatise on arboriculture associated with the name of Bollard, for example, which forms part of the 'Book of Secrets', is to be found in an instructive range of further contexts.[5] In London, British Library, MS Sloane 7 it is copied, in conjunction with 'Godfrey upon paladie', by one scribe, with the Middle English collection of medical receipts known as the *Liber de diversis medicinis*; with treatises on 'the man*er* off making of salues entretis', on urines, and on the pestilence; with a note on 'the v*er*tues of rosmaryn'; and with information on the evil and good days of the year. That the book continued in practical use is suggested by the number of culinary receipts which were added over the years in a variety of later hands. In BL, MS Sloane 686, the Bollard material, again with a version of 'tractatus Godfridi super Palladium', is copied in conjunction with a version of Walter of Henley's treatise on husbandry and with remedies for equine and human ailments. Oxford, Bodleian Library, MS Bodley 591 combines the information about arboriculture with texts on uroscopy, phlebotomy, herbs, and midwifery; and Bodl., Rawlinson C. 506, an extensive collection of medical and culinary treatises, extends from Bollard on trees to texts on dyeing, and on hawking and pisciculture.

Available information about the compilers and owners of collections like these suggests that the books enjoyed 'household' use in a range of domestic or communal contexts. This use could serve the semi-professional household needs which might have been those of a medical practitioner[6] or the more diverse interests of country landowners such as John Whittocksmead of Wiltshire, whose copious compilation is now Yale University, Beinecke Library, MS 163 (the so-called Wagstaff Miscellany).[7] The inhabitants or functionaries of religious houses also needed this material, often in collections where practical material was included with formularies or texts on legal matters. Some of the extant copies of the English version of Walter of Henley's treatise on husbandry are included in collections of this sort: BL, MS Harley 493, a mainly legal collection copied in the fourteenth century, was by the fifteenth century in use in the Franciscan house at Reading; BL, MS Harley 274 served during the same period as the reference book of an estate steward; BL, MS Harley 273 came in the fifteenth century into the hands of a certain John, associated with the royal household.[8]

Mode of production is often invoked as a feature which permits the construction of distinctions between commonplace books and miscellanies of different kinds, but it is a variable in relation to household books of this kind, whose common characteristics have to do with content and nature of use rather than with the methods by which they were compiled. A household book for practical use might be a fascicular production, drawing together components from different sources, or it might equally be a notebook copied by an individual and destined for personal use. Quality of production is another variable, for these manuscripts range from the scrappily amateur to the professionally finished, and comprehend, in relation to Helmingham books for example, both the workmanlike 'Book of Secrets' and two much more lavishly illustrated books of birds, beasts, plants, and embroidery patterns (now Bodl., MS Ashmole 1504; and the collection of Paul Mellon).[9] Similar distinctions in level of formality might be drawn between amateur household books which proffer advice on domestic management and the much more elaborately conceived sets of royal or aristocratic household ordinances typified by Edward IV's *Liber Niger*, or the *Ordinances at Eltham for Henry VIII*, drawn up in 1526.[10] The latter of these makes express provision for a copy to 'remaine and be kept in the compting house, for the better information of the head officers of the chamber and household, how they shall from time to time, see the same put in effectual execution'.[11]

One useful distinction between different kinds of household book would set apart practically-oriented collections from those that also contain 'literary' material, of however unsophisticated a kind.[12] These too were the products of households of different sorts. It is possible to identify what seem to have taken shape as family collections, like Robert Thornton's two manuscripts,[13] or Edinburgh, National Library of Scotland, Advocates' MS 19.3.1,[14] or Bodl., MS Ashmole 61, compiled by the scribe Rate.[15] At the same time, compilations like Cambridge, Trinity College, MS O. 9. 38, from Glastonbury,[16] or BL, Add. MS 60577, associated with St Swithun's Priory, Winchester,[17] served the needs of members of religious communities. In all of these, a certain amount of pragmatically informative material is amalgamated, in variable proportions, with texts which serve devotional or recreational purposes. Although these collections are the fruit of widely (sometimes bewilderingly) divergent compilational activity, their cohesiveness as anthologies serving the needs of specifically defined groups is usually apparent in some way: sometimes in the evidence of the directing presence of a single scribe; sometimes in the incorporation of material with specific family application.[18]

In the case of certain compilations like Aberystwyth, National Library of Wales, MS Porkington 10, some household application may be suspected but not proved. The texts here include domestic informational material (Bollard on trees; recipes for inks and for dyeing; prognostications and medical receipts) along with considerable amounts of pious and recreational reading. While the paper evidence and the scribal patterns, as most recently discussed by Daniel Huws,[19] suggest a 'makeshift team' engaged in 'concurrent activity' which may well have been centred on a particular household or community, the compilers have left no clear signs of their identity. The construction of the fourteenth-century Auchinleck manuscript (NLS, Advocates' 19. 2. 1) has been the subject of similar speculation.[20]

The considerably more focused literary anthologies of the late Middle English period (the so-called 'aureate collections' of R. H. Robbins's taxonomy)[21] may seem in every respect a long way from the household books discussed thus far. But there may be instances in which the contents and use of such manuscripts, even though relatively homogeneous, and lacking any of the informative or practically useful texts which often indicate household application, suggest a household provenance or function of not so different a kind. The compilation which is now Bodl., MS Arch. Selden. B. 24 offers one such instance.[22] This manuscript contains only verse: some of Chaucer's works – *Troilus and Criseyde, The Legend of Good Women, The Parliament of Fowls* and the lyric 'Truth' – together with works by Clanvowe, Hoccleve, Lydgate, and Walton, several of which are attributed to Chaucer. After these poems come a number of others of Scottish provenance, including *The Kingis Quair*, *The Quare of Jelousy*, *The Lay of Sorrow*, and *The Lufaris Complaint*, most of which survive only here. The collection as a whole is of an unusual kind in its combination materials from English and Scottish traditions. In the categories commonly used to designate Middle English manuscripts it is unquestionably a verse anthology of some kind: Robbins's designation of 'aureate collection' locates it as one of a number of 'large, well-written and often illuminated manuscripts of formal verse ... by Chaucer and especially by Lydgate, or their imitators, or by the Scottish Chaucerians'. But while, for Robbins's definition, the nature of the texts contained in the manuscript determined its kind and affiliations, it is equally possible to argue that aspects of its function and use might give it 'household' or 'family' application which warrant a different categorization.

Scrutiny of the early use made of the manuscript necessitates some consideration of the physical aspects of its compilation. It was put together in Scotland in several stages, the first of which was apparently the transcription of *Troilus and Criseyde*. After this, the collection was for some reason enlarged: a process which involved the copying of the rest of the Chaucerian poems now in the manuscript, and of most of *The Kingis Quair* – a text which survives only here, with a scribal note attributing it to King James I of Scotland. Significantly, whoever commissioned this phase of the manuscript's expansion was able to call again on the scribe who had already copied *Troilus* and to request from him the copies of the added material. Near the end of *The Kingis Quair* the work of this scribe ceases; a second hand then copied the ending of this poem and (possibly after an interval) the generally short, usually unique, Scottish texts. None of these later Scottish works is accompanied by any form of decoration beyond some elaborate penwork initials, whereas the earlier parts of the manuscript (the Chaucerian texts and the the first scribe's stint of *The Kingis Quair*) were apparently, after the transcription of *The Kingis Quair*, 'upgraded' with the addition of a programme of decoration. Probably at this stage too the first leaf of *Troilus* was cancelled and replaced by one that included both a demi-vinet and an historiated initial illustrating a passage from Book I of the poem.[23]

The activities of the main scribe of the manuscript, which contribute signally to attempts to date the rough period of its construction, are significant also in suggesting the volume's status as something resembling a household book. His hand was some time ago perceived to be identical to that of the so-called Abbotsford manuscript of Gilbert of the Hay, now Edinburgh, National Library of Scotland, MS Acc. 9253. It has more recently been identified in two further manuscripts: one containing Mirk's *Festial* and the *Quatuor sermones* copied from a Rouen edition of 1499, now in St John's College, Cambridge (MS G. 19); and another, now in the possession of the Earl of Dalhousie, which contains a number of historical texts in Latin and Scots.[24] Evidence from the watermarks about the date of Selden's construction is consonant with the dates proposed for the copying of these other manuscripts, and would also seem to confirm that the collection took shape over a longish period during which it was subject to various decisions about upgrading.

As it turns out, all the manuscripts attributable to the main scribe of MS Selden contain some evidence of early connection with members of the Scottish Sinclair family. In MS Selden itself, the arms of Henry, Lord Sinclair, were added at the end of *Troilus* (on fol. 118ᵛ), at some point after the text's transcription – presumably after 26 January 1489 when he assumed the title; further inscriptions on a leaf at the end of the manuscript (fol. 230ᵛ) make reference to other Sinclair family names. The Hay manuscript and St John's MS G. 19 both bear the names of Sir Oliver Sinclair (Henry Sinclair's uncle), and the former seems to have stayed in the Roslin branch of the Sinclair family until at least the mid-sixteenth century, when Sir William Sinclair of Roslin wrote his name in it several times. The Sinclair connections with the Dalhousie manuscript are indicated by its contents – items concerned with Norse and Scottish history – and specifically its inclusion of a Latin genealogy of the earls of Orkney (the Sinclairs) of which the Abbotsford manuscript preserves a Scottish translation.

That this scribe remained in an apparently close relationship with different members of the Sinclair family over what would seem to have been a number of years may indicate that he was specifically retained in some capacity rather than simply called on through commercial networks. Household affiliations of some kind could have determined the nature of his service. His activities on behalf of different Sinclairs, while in many ways comparable to those of William Ebesham for various members of the Paston family,[25] are distinctive in their range and duration, possibly indicating family service of a closer and more long-standing kind than that which Ebesham offered. In addition to the fact that the scribe worked on several manuscripts for the family over a period of time is the evidence that he could be called upon to enlarge or modify commissions that he had already executed. In MS Selden, for instance, his work was evidently done in several stages, possibly quite widely spaced: first he copied *Troilus*, then added a substantial number of further texts, and eventually recopied the first leaf of *Troilus* when it had to be reformatted to accommodate decoration and illumination. Intermittent and unsystematic tasks of this kind do not seem characteristic of commercially organized or professional scribal activity.

Even though MS Selden's texts have nothing of the practical usefulness of the 'household book' as it is usually conceived, its production would nevertheless seem to have depended on the interests and personnel available to a familiar audience over some not inconsiderable period of time. In other words, it might be defined as a book *in use* in a specific household, or group of households, possibly compiled without recourse to commercial networks. There are parallels, both in England and within Scotland, to such relationships between scribes and households or individuals. The fourteenth-century Ludlow scribe who copied BL, MS Harley 2253 seems to have served the members of an aristocratic or ecclesiastical Shropshire household,[26] while in the fifteenth century it has been suggested that certain of the copyists who contributed to the Findern manuscript (Cambridge, University Library, MS Ff. 1.6), were 'estate servants', retained in various capacities by this Derbyshire family.[27] The researches of Ralph Hanna and Thorlac Turville-Petre have much to suggest about the scribal and literary activities fostered by the household patronage of the Gloucestershire Berkeley family and some networks of households in the north-east Midlands.[28]

A still closer analogy to the circumstances in which MS Selden was produced is afforded by the context in which one scribe of the late fifteenth and early sixteenth centuries worked on behalf of members of the northern Percy family. To BL, MS Royal 18. D. II, a fifteenth-century manuscript of Lydgate's *Troy Book* and *Siege of Thebes*, with a number of miniatures, he added a number of later poems, some specifically associated with the Percys;[29] to Bodl., MS Arch. Selden. B. 10, which contained Hardyng's *Chronicle*, he added materials he copied from a printed book, de Worde's *Prouerbes of Lydgate* (1519).[30] A telling evocation of an environment in which commissions of this sort were executed is provided by John Skelton (whose elegy on a member of the Percy family, coincidentally, was among the later additions to Royal 18. D. II) as he envisages in *The Garland of Laurel* the household copying by one 'maister Newton' of a group of personalized verse tributes composed for the Countess of Surrey and her ladies.[31]

Similar forms of relationship within Scotland may have influenced the activities of certain scribes. The similarities between the hand of the Selden scribe and that of the better-known scribe James Graye, several times noted and indeed by some authorities taken as evidence that they were one and the same individual,[32] may hint at some connection between the compilation of MS Selden and the circle of William Schevez, Archbishop of St Andrew's, whose ecclesiastical household (in its widest sense) evidently encompassed book-making and book-collecting activities of various kinds.[33] Graye's connections with another of Schevez's functionaries, Magnus Makculloch, are attested in their collaboration on a copy of the *Scotichronicon* (now Edinburgh, Scottish Record Office, GD 45/26/48) in which Makculloch worked on the text and Graye on the rubrication; they worked separately for Schevez in other contexts, and each too on other miscellanies, Graye's now NLS, Advocates' MS 34. 7. 3, and Makculloch's Edinburgh, University Library, MS 205. The similarity between Graye's hand and that of the first, main Selden scribe could suggest some common background or training (as notaries public, for example)[34] or connection with a milieu common to both Schevez's household and the Sinclair family: clerics employed by Schevez may reasonably have had connections with those serving the chapel of Roslin, a Sinclair foundation of 1446 whose constitution in 1477 made provision for a prebendary with six other prebendary priests and three clerks.[35]

The illumination and decoration in MS Selden appear also to be the result of comparatively unsystematic activities. The work is fairly rough, added at a later stage rather than comprehensively planned in conjunction with the scribal labour, and seems likely to have been supplied from somewhat piece-meal local (or possibly itinerant) resources. At the point when the second scribe added the final section of *The Kingis Quair* and the shorter Scottish poems which follow it, the decorative resources of the earlier upgrading programme were no longer to hand. Similarly strategic use of local resources can be observed in other illuminated manuscripts produced in Scotland at this time, for example the Psalter and Missal which James Sibbald copied for the Arbuthnot family in the 1480s and 1490s, which are supplied with copious but roughly executed miniatures and illumination.[36] The fluidity of these local resources can be glimpsed in records such as that of a payment made in St Andrews at the king's command on 17 December 1497 to 'James graye ... that brocht ane paynted table to the king',[37] or those which preserve information about one of the few identifiable Scottish artists of the period, Sir Thomas Galbraith, who became a clerk of the Chapel Royal in Stirling, and could turn his energies from 'the singyn of a balld to the king in the mornyng' to the illuminating of a breviary.[38]

The contents of MS Selden might seem at first sight to offer little in support of the hypotheses offered here about its status as a family or household book. But family piety, or family connections of some less easily reconstructable kind, may well have been influential in their selection. *The Kingis Quair*, as the manuscript note about its authorship by James I of Scotland makes clear,[39] was of some significance to the Sinclair family: one of Henry Sinclair's grand-mothers was James's sister. Supply of exemplars through family circles may explain the late addition of the concluding section of *The Kingis Quair* and also the appending of the shorter Scottish poems, one of which concludes with an address to a 'Princes, full gracious and excellent' whose 'hie commaundment' is said to have provided the poem's occasion.[40]

The successive enlargements of the collection may plausibly reflect attempts to mark occasions which were of importance to the Sinclair family. One such may well have been the marriage of James IV and Margaret Tudor in 1503, the culmination of efforts to forge an alliance between Scotland and England which had been afoot in a variety of forms for over a decade.[41] The addition to the existing Chaucerian material of the Scottish texts may indicate an effort to address nationalistic and political issues by means of a cultural statement pursued even to the detail of the linguistic forms observed by the scribes.[42] In the light of other attempts to mark the alliance – Dunbar's composition of *The Thrissill and the Rois*; Sir Thomas Galbraith's illumination of the marriage treaty with roses, thistles, and marguerites; gifts to the bride of prestigious liturgical books[43] – it does not seem out of place to understand MS Selden as a volume which makes both familial and nationalistic statements.

In the senses that 'household' may be coterminous with 'family', MS Selden seems very likely to have been some kind of 'household' book. It is not a household book in the way that the Tollemache 'Book of Secrets' or a collection such as MS Porkington 10 are household books, but at the same time it is considerably more than an anthology of later Middle English and Scottish verse. Function and use, just as much as method of compilation or assortment of contents, might reasonably enter into whatever designation the manuscript is awarded. To consider some of its claims as a household book of course raises in turn further questions: what exactly constitutes a household, for example, and how far – in the case of a family with multiple branches, like the Sinclairs – might it extend? would 'household' have meant the same in England as in Scotland at this period? what exactly can be assumed about the 'use' of a collection of this sort? Following the lead of questions as they arise in relation to particular manuscripts may stand in the way of the precision one might crave in matters of codicological taxonomy, but in the end it may promise greater enlightenment.

NOTES

1 For further discussion of these difficulties, see A. G. Rigg, *A Glastonbury Miscellany of the Fifteenth Century: a Descriptive Index of Trinity College, Cambridge, MS o. 9. 38* (Oxford, 1968), pp. 24-6, and the review by R. H. Robbins in *Anglia*, 89 (1971), 140-3; Gisela Guddat-Figge, *Catalogue of Manuscripts Containing Middle English Romances* (Munich, 1976), pp. 25-8; Cameron Louis, *The Commonplace Book of Robert Reynes of Acle: an Edition of Tanner MS 407* (New York, 1980), pp. 99-103; Julia Boffey & John J. Thompson, 'Anthologies and Miscellanies: Production and Choice of Texts', in *Book Production and Publishing in Britain 1375-1475*, ed. by Jeremy Griffiths & Derek Pearsall (Cambridge, 1989), pp. 279-315. Some of the more general taxonomic issues are addressed in the essays comprising *The Whole Book: Cultural Perspectives on the Medieval Miscellany*, ed. by Stephen G. Nichols & Siegfried Wenzel (Michigan, 1996).

2 An influential discussion of some of these terms is to be found in *Secular Lyrics of the XIVth and XVth Centuries*, ed. by R. H. Robbins, 2nd edn (Oxford, 1955), pp. xv-lv.

3 *The Tollemache 'Book of Secrets': a Descriptive Index and Complete Facsimile*, with an introduction and transcriptions by Jeremy Griffiths, Roxburghe Club (London, 2000).

4 For a list of the contents, and fuller discussion, see Griffiths, *Descriptive Index*.

5 Borrowed in part from a Latin *Book of Trees and Wine*, attributed to Gottfried von Franken, with different forms of which both Latin and Middle English versions of the text were often copied. See *Geoffrey of Franconia's Book of Trees and Wine*, ed. by W. L. Braekman, *Scripta*, 24 (Brussels, 1989), and David G. Cylkowski, 'A Middle English Treatise on Horticulture: *Godfridus Super Palladium*', in *Popular and Practical Science of Medieval England*, ed. by Lister M. Matheson (East Lansing, Mich., 1994), pp. 301-29. The most recent listing of the manuscripts is that of George R. Keiser, *A Manual of the Writings in Middle English, vol. 10* (New Haven, 1998), pp. 3689-90, 3903-4.

6 See, for example, BL, MS Harley 1735, discussed by R. H. Robbins, 'John Crophill's Ale-Pots', *Review of English Studies*, n.s. 20 (1969), 182-89.

7 Described in Barbara A. Shailor, *Catalogue of Medieval and Renaissance Manuscripts in the Beinecke Rare Book and Manuscript Library, Yale University. Volume I: MSS 1-250*, (Binghamton, NY, 1984), pp. 216-23, and discussed by Keiser, *Writings in Middle English*, p. 3596,

and 'Practical Books for the Gentleman', in *The Cambridge History of the Book in Britain, III*, ed. by Lotte Hellinga & J. W. Trapp (Cambridge, 1999), pp. 470-94.

8 See Dorothea Oschinsky, *Walter of Henley, and other Treatises on Estate Management and Accounting* (Oxford, 1971), pp. 11-12 and following.

9 Nicolas Barker, *Two East Anglian Picture Books*, Roxburghe Club (London, 1988).

10 For a rudimentary list of these, see Keiser, *Writings in Middle English*, pp. 3681, 3894, and Laurel Braswell, 'Utilitarian and Scientific Prose', in *Middle English Prose: a Critical Guide to Major Authors and Genres*, ed. by A. S. G. Edwards (New Brunswick, N.J., 1984), pp. 337-87 (p. 371). General discussion of household ordinances is to be found in the introductory material to *The Household of Edward IV: the Black Book and the Ordinance of 1478*, ed. by A. R. Myers (Manchester, 1959).

11 *A Collection of Ordinances and Regulations for the Government of the Royal Household, made in Divers Reigns, from King Edward III to King William and Queen Mary*, ed. by Nichols (London, 1790), p. 161; quoted by John Scattergood, 'Skelton's *Magnyfycence* and the Tudor Royal Household', *Medieval English Theatre*, 15 (1993), 21-48 (p. 24).

12 See Griffiths, *The Tollemache 'Book of Secrets'*, introduction.

13 *The Thornton Manuscript, Lincoln Cathedral MS 91*, introd. by D. S. Brewer & A. E. B. Owen, 2nd edn (London, 1977), and John J. Thompson, *Robert Thornton and the London Thornton Manuscript: British Library MS Additional 31042* (Cambridge, 1987).

14 Philippa Hardman, 'A Mediaeval "Library In Parvo"', *Medium Aevum*, 47 (1978), 262-73.

15 Lynne S. Blanchfield, 'The romances in MS Ashmole 61: an idiosyncratic scribe', in *Romance in Medieval England*, ed. by Maldwyn Mills, Jennifer Fellows, & Carol Meale (Cambridge, 1991), pp. 65-87, and 'Rate revisited: the compilation of the narrative works in MS Ashmole 61', in *Romance Reading on the Book: Essays on Medieval Narrative presented to Maldwyn Mills*, ed. by Jennifer Fellows, Rosalind Field, Gillian Rogers, & Judith Weiss (Cardiff, 1996), pp. 208-20.

16 See Rigg, *Glastonbury Miscellany* (cited above, n. 1).

17 *The Winchester Anthology: a Facsimile of British Library Additonal Manuscript 60577*, with an introduction and list of contents by Edward Wilson and an account of the music by Iain Fenlon (Cambridge, 1981).

18 For further discussion of manuscripts of this kind, see Felicity Riddy, 'Mother Knows Best: Reading Social Change in a Courtesy Text', *Speculum*, 71 (1996), 66-86 (especially p. 81, n. 52).

19 'MS Porkington 10 and its scribes', in Fellows *et al.*, *Romance Reading on the Book*, pp. 188-207.

20 T. A. Schonk, 'A Study of the Auchinleck Manuscript: Bookmen and Bookmaking in the Early Fourteenth Century', *Speculum*, 60 (1985), 71-91.

21 Robbins, ed., *Secular Lyrics* (cited above, n. 2), pp. xxiii-xxvi.

22 A fuller account of much of the evidence discussed below prefaces *The Works of Geoffrey Chaucer and 'The Kingis Quair': a Facsimile of Bodleian Library, Oxford, MS Arch. Selden. B. 24*, with an Introduction by Julia Boffey & A. S. G. Edwards and an Appendix by B. C. Barker-Benfield (Cambridge, 1997); see also Julia Boffey & A. S. G. Edwards, 'Bodleian MS Arch. Selden. B. 24: the Genesis and Evolution of a Scottish Poetical Anthology' (forthcoming).

23 Plate I in the facsimile.

24 See the facsimile, pp. 6-12.

25 A. I. Doyle, 'The Work of a Late Fifteenth-Century English Scribe, William Ebesham', *Bulletin of the John Rylands Library*, 39 (1957), 298-325; G. A. Lester, *Sir John Paston's 'Grete Boke': a Descriptive Catalogue, with an Introduction, of British Library MS Lansdowne 285* (Cambridge, 1984), pp. 34-43.

26 Carter Revard, 'Richard Hurd and MS Harley 2253', *Notes and Queries*, 224 (1979), 199-202, and 'Three More Holographs in the Hand of the Scribe of MS Harley 2253', *Notes and Queries*, 227 (1982), 62-3.

27 K. D. Harris, 'The Origins and Make-Up of Cambridge, University Library MS Ff. 1. 6',

Transactions of the Cambridge Bibliographical Society, 8 (1983), 299-333. For some other suggestions about regional copying activities, see Boffey & Thompson, 'Anthologies and Miscellanies' (cited above, n. 1), and pp. 125-41.

28 Ralph Hanna III, 'Sir Thomas Berkeley and his Patronage', *Speculum*, 64 (1989), 878-916; Thorlac Turville-Petre, 'Some Medieval English Manuscripts in the North-East Midlands', in *Manuscripts and Readers in Fifteenth-Century England: the Literary Implications of Manuscript Study. Essays from the 1981 Conference at the University of York*, ed. by Derek Pearsall (Cambridge, 1983),

29 On this manuscript, see Kathleen L. Scott, *Later Gothic Manuscripts, 1390-1490*, 2 vols (London, 1996), ii, 282-5, and on the family's literary patronage more generally, Mervyn James, *Society, Politics, and Culture: Studies in Early Modern England* (Cambridge, 1986), pp. 83-90.

30 O. Pächt & J. J. G. Alexander, *Illuminated Manuscripts in the Bodleian Library, Oxford* , 3 vols (Oxford, 1966-73), iii, 96 and 101; M. B. Parkes, *English Cursive Bookhands* (London, 1969), plate 15 (ii).

31 *The Garlande or Chapelet of Laurell*, 1093-9, in *John Skelton: the Complete English Poems*, ed. by John Scattergood (Harmondsworth, 1983), p. 343. On Skelton's Howard patronage, and the possible identity of Newton, see Greg Walker, *John Skelton and the Politics of the 1520s* (Cambridge, 1988), pp. 5-34.

32 See John MacQueen, 'The literature of fifteenth-century Scotland', in *Scottish Society in the Fifteenth Century*, ed. by Jennifer M. Brown (London, 1977), pp. 184-208 (p. 201) for relevant bibliography. The identification seems to have been authoritatively quashed by N. R. Ker, *Medieval Manuscripts in British Libraries. II: Abbotsford – Keele* (Oxford, 1977), pp. 1-2.

33 George H. Bushnell, 'Portrait of a Bibliophile, IV: William Schevez, Archbishop of St Andrews, d. 1497', *Book Collector*, 9 (1960), 19-29.

34 John Durkan, 'The Early Scottish Notary', in *The Renaissance and Reformation in Scotland: Essays in Honour of Gordon Donaldson*, ed. by Ian B. Cowan & Duncan Shaw (Edinburgh, 1983), pp. 22-40.

35 Ian B. Cowan & David E. Easson, *Medieval Religious Houses in Scotland*, 2nd edn (London, 1976), p. 225.

36 The manuscripts are now in Paisley Museum. See N. R. Ker & A. J. Piper, *Medieval Manuscripts in British Libraries, IV* (Oxford, 1992), pp. 2-6, and William MacGillivray, 'Notices of the Arbuthnott Missal, Psalter, and Office of the Blessed Virgin,' *Proceedings of the Society of Antiquaries of Scotland*, 26 (1892), 89-104.

37 Michael R. Apted & Susan Hannabuss, *Painters in Scotland, 1301-1700: a Biographical Dictionary*, Scottish Record Society, n.s. 7 (Edinburgh, 1978), p. 113.

38 Rev. Charles Rogers, *A History of the Chapel Royal of Scotland, with the Register of the Chapel Royal of Stirling* (Edinburgh, 1882), p. li; Apted & Hannabuss, *Biographical Dictionary*, pp. 40-1.

39 'Quod Jacobus primus scotorum rex Illustrissimus', fol. 211^r.

40 *The Lay of Sorrow*, fol. 219^r.

41 Louise Fradenburg, 'Sovereign Love: the Wedding of Margaret Tudor and James IV of Scotland', *Women and Sovereignty*, Cosmos, 7, ed. by Louise Fradenburg (Edinburgh, 1992), 78-100.

42 Julia Boffey & A. S. G. Edwards, 'Bodleian MS Arch. Selden. B. 24 and the "Scotticization" of Middle English Verse' (forthcoming in *Rewriting Chaucer*, ed. by Barbara Cline & Thomas Prendergast).

43 See, respectively, Priscilla Bawcutt, *Dunbar the Makar* (Oxford, 1992), 92-103; *Accounts of the Lord High Treasurer of Scotland. II, 1500-1504*, ed. by Sir James Balfour Paul (Edinburgh, 1900), pp. lvii-lviii; L. MacFarlane, 'The Book of Hours of James IV and Margaret Tudor', *Innes Review*, 11 (1960), 3-21; and Janet Backhouse, 'Illuminated Manuscripts associated with Henry VII and Members of his Immediate Family', in *The Reign of Henry VII: Proceedings of the 1993 Harlaxton Symposium*, ed. by Benjamin Thompson (Stamford, 1995), pp. 175-87.

CAXTON'S SECOND EDITION
OF THE *CANTERBURY TALES*

N. F. BLAKE

THOSE WHO WORK on English incunabula accept that Caxton's first edition of the *Canterbury Tales* [Cx^1] was published *c.* 1476, shortly after his return to Westminster, and that consequently his second edition [Cx^2] which he claimed was published six years later must be dated to 1482, although these dates are not always recognized by those who write about Chaucer.[1] The dating of the first edition is based on the watermarks and the typography of the volume in relation to those found in Caxton's other early Westminster prints.[2] Cx^1 is a close congener of Cambridge, Trinity College, MS R.3.15 [Tc^2], as established by Manly & Rickert.[3] In the Manly & Rickert classification Cx^1 and Tc^2 are group **b** manuscripts and they suggested that Tc^2 was copied from the copy-text used for Cx^1. Cx^1 is also closely linked to Oxford, New College, MS D314 [Ne], which in its turn is closely linked with the **b** portions of the Helmingham manuscript [He], now Princeton Library, MS 100. Manly & Rickert thought there was a more or less hierarchical line from He to Ne to Cx^1 and then to Tc^2. Group **b** manuscripts are from a modern textual point of view corrupt, for they contain additions, omissions, and textual revisions. However, manuscripts of this type were not rare and it is hardly surprising that Caxton should have got his hands on one. Nevertheless, someone as deeply involved in the book trade as he was could surely have acquired another manuscript if he had wanted to. The question of whether Caxton was responsible for the spurious lines in Cx^1 was raised by Manly & Rickert, who took the view that he was not because Tc^2 was set up from Cx^1's copy-text and not Cx^1. Their view was rejected by Beverly Boyd, who argued that Tc^2 could have been set up from a broken-up copy of Cx^1 and that therefore Caxton may be responsible for some of the spurious lines in the text.[4]

Manly & Rickert did not consider Cx^2 in any detail because the relationship of Cx^2 to Cx^1 was being studied by their pupil, Thomas Dunn, who submitted his PhD thesis in 1939, followed by a published version in 1940.[5] Even before Dunn's study, the relationship of Cx^2 to Cx^1 had been studied by several scholars; for example, Kilgour thought that the manuscript used by Caxton to correct Cx^1 might have been London, British Library, Add. MS 35286 [Ad^3][6], a view not accepted by Dunn though he recognised its close relationship to Cx^2. For his part, he examined the relationship of Cx^2 to Cx^1 using the materials assembled by Manly & Rickert as part of the Chicago project. In view of the difficulty in obtaining copies of Dunn's study, it is necessary to review his conclusions at some length.

He notes first that in the prologue to his second edition Caxton gives the following account as to why he published it:

… of whyche bookes so incorrecte was one brought to me vj yere passyd/ whyche I supposed had ben veray true & correcte/ And accordyng to the same I dyde do enprynte a certayn nombre of them/ whyche anon were sold to many and dyuerse gentyl men/ of whome one gentylman cam to me/ and said that this book was not accordyng in many places vnto the book that Gefferey chaucer had made/ To whom I answerd that I had made it accordyng to my copye/ and by me was nothyng added ne mynusshyd/ Thenne he sayd he knewe a book whyche hys fader had and moche louyd/ that was very trewe/ and accordyng vnto hys owen first book by hym made/ and sayd more yf I wold enprynte it agayn he wold gete me the same book for a copye/… And he ful gentylly gate of hys fader the said book/ and delyuerd it to me/ by whiche I haue corrected my book/ as here after alle alonge by thayde of almyghty god shal folowe/ [a2^{r-v}]

In his thesis Dunn rejects most previous explanations of the relationship between Cx^1 and Cx^2 and claims:

… first, that Cx^2 was set up from a corrected copy of Cx^1. Second, I shall show that Cx^2 is a conflate text, and, third, that it is an edited text. Finally, I shall show that the source of the corrections in Cx^2 was a good manuscript that is not now known to exist. And as a by-product of this work, something of the quality of Caxton both as a printer and as an editor will appear. (p. 2)

He suggests that this 'good manuscript' (Dunn refers to it as Y – a usage retained in this paper) belonged to Manly & Rickert's group a, though it was not possible to identify a particular extant manuscript as Y.

Although Dunn had access to the Manly & Rickert material, his work was completed before their text was published. Hence, following their example he took as his base text of the poem Skeat's student edition (1895). This decision has considerable bearing on his statistics and how he approached the textual tradition. Dunn established that in composing Cx^2 Caxton did not alter the *Canterbury Tales* prose texts. All the prose lines missing in Cx^1 are also missing in Cx^2, and the prose texts in Cx^2 exhibit very few changes from Cx^1. Thus in the Tale of Melibeus Cx^1 and Cx^2 depart from the Skeat text 1475 times, but Cx^2 disagrees with Cx^1 in only 45 of these 1475 variants. In the two prose texts there are only 113 disagreements in the texts of Cx^1 and Cx^2. This is significantly different from the relationship of Cx^1 to Cx^2 in the poetic tales and even in the large number of variants which are found in manuscript versions of the prose tales. In other words, the prose tales in Cx^2 were set up direct from Cx^1 without any correction or editing by Caxton or a compositor. The only possible exception to this conclusion is the Retraction for which Cx¹ may have been compared against Y.

For the metrical portions of the work Cx¹ was also the copy-text. But they had been corrected against Y, though this was done in fits and starts. Corrections were also made to Cx¹ without recourse to a reading in Y. To support his case Dunn examined the unique variants that are found in Cx². As an example one may consider the case of the Wife of Bath's Prologue and Tale. Dunn found thirty-two unique variants, fifteen of which he considered insignificant because they consisted of the inclusion or omission of an 'unimportant word'. Four are typographical, for they correct old or introduce new printing errors. Eight are inversions, alterations of the tense of a verb and such like. That leaves only five which are worth considering and they are all found in the Prologue. They are reproduced by Dunn in this way:[7]

(1) 144　And lat us *usen hoot barley breed* Cx¹
　　　　And lat us wyves hoten barley breed Ad³ Bo² Ch Dd Ds El En¹ Gg Hg Ht
　　　　And lat *to* us *wyves hoten barley breed* Cx²

(2) 291　*to* olde dotard *shrewes* Cx¹
　　　　olde dotard shrewe Ad¹ Ad³ Bo² Bw Ch Cn Cp Dl Ds El En¹ En² En³ Gg Gl Ha² Ha⁴ Ha⁵ Hg Hk Ht La Lc Ld¹ Ld² Ln Ma Mc Mg Mm Nl Ph² Ph³ Ps Pw Py Ra¹ Ra³ Ry¹ Ry² Se Si Sl² Tc¹ To
　　　　to olde dotard *shrewe* Cx²

(3) 642　And me of olde *Romance talis* teche Cx¹
　　　　And me of olde *Romayn gestis* teche Bo² Cn Dd Ds El En¹ Ha⁴ Hg Ht Ma Py
　　　　And me of olde *Romaunce gestis* teche Cx²

(4) 645　*ones opyn* Cx¹
　　　　open heded Ad¹ Bo² Cn Dd Dl En³ Ha⁴ Ht Ln Ps To
　　　　open heveded Ad³ Ch El Ha⁵ Hg
　　　　ones opyn heded Cx²

(5) 848　make *the* for to morne Cx¹
　　　　make thyn herte for to morne Ad¹ Ad³ Bo¹ Bo² Ch Cn Cp Dd Ds El En¹ En³ Fi Gg Gl Ha² Ha⁴ Ha⁵ Hg Hk Ht La Lc Ln Ma Mc Mg Mm Nl Ph² Ph³ Ps Pw Ra¹ Ra² Ra³ Ry¹ Se Si Sl¹ Sl² Tc¹ To
　　　　make *the sore* for to morne Cx²　(p. 22)

Dunn offers the following explanations for these changes. In (1) Caxton made a mess of his copy-text in Cx¹ and in trying to make sense of this for Cx² he interpreted *lat* as 'leave to' and destroyed the relationship of this line to its context. In (2) for Cx² he saw that *shrewes* should be singular, but failed to see the phrase was an exclamation or a form of address and thus ended up with nonsense. In (3) he either did not know the difference between *Romaunce* and *Romayn* or else simply blurred the two texts uncritically. In (4) he conflated the two texts without crossing out *ones*, though it is possible he retained it deliberately. Dunn suggests that (5) is an example of editing without consulting the manuscript. Caxton realised Cx^1 did not have a good reading, but instead of looking at the manuscript he 'used an adverb which was a favorite with him – *sore* – and satisfied his conscience that he had done well' (p. 23). Dunn concluded from this study that one could postulate with confidence the readings which Caxton found in Y, which are uniformly superior to those in Cx^1 and other group **b** manuscripts.

Dunn next considered the different lines, both single lines and passages, and alterations in words or phrases between Cx^1 and Cx^2. In Cx^2 there are 277 lines, accepted by Dunn as genuine, which are not in Cx^1, though 62 of these replace spurious lines in Cx^1. A further 27 spurious lines in Cx^1 are deleted in Cx^2. This left 15 spurious lines in Cx^1 which were carried forward into Cx^2. Of the new lines considered genuine by Dunn no extant manuscript has them all, though Dd is the manuscript which has most, though other group **a** manuscripts are not far behind. As for changes to words and phrases he examined the relationship of Cx^2 to Cx^1 against a few manuscripts: Ad^3, Ch, Dd, El, En^1, and En^3. He concludes that El or Ad^3 shares the most readings with Cx^2. However, the interpretation and choice of the individual readings are not without difficulty, because the variation in the number of changes among the different manuscripts is usually quite small. He indicates that certain manuscripts could have provided all the extra variants in individual tales and prologues. The five which supply almost all the necessary changes to Cx^2 are Ad^3, Ch, Dd, El, and En^1, though no one manuscript provides all the changes. Dunn's overall conclusion is:

Caxton's method was to scratch out the wrong word or phrase of Cx^1 and to write in the correction from the new manuscript. But though he often changed a major word in the line, he frequently failed to change the context of the line to meet the requirements of the new word …

Chapter V revealed a considerable number of variants from Cx^2 to Cx^1 which showed that Caxton improved the readings of Cx^1 towards those of a better text which corresponded generally in quality to the best extant manuscripts. A substantial number of lines in Cx^2 reflect these improvements drawn from Y. In addition, Caxton found in Y a large number of lines now accepted as Chaucer's and more than any single extant manuscript could supply him. And generally where he has added these lines, they correspond in wording to the very highest authorities. (pp. 74-5)

It is time now to evaluate Dunn's study. One problem is that he used Skeat's student edition which he took to reflect the genuine *Canterbury Tales* and this affected his attitude to the text. Nevertheless, his general conclusions that Cx^2 is set up from a copy of Cx^1 which has been emended in some way, and that Cx^2 is a conflated text are not in dispute. The principal question which remains is by what process Cx^1 was emended to produce Cx^2. It follows that Cx^2 as a conflated text cannot belong to a single manuscript group. All one can do is identify the group to which Y belonged. In his thesis Dunn chose some examples to illustrate the changes made in Cx^2 and I listed those from the Wife of Bath's Prologue. But the way Dunn reproduces these readings is neither complete nor accurate. If one considers line 642, the impression he gives is quite misleading. This line shows a high degree of change in the transmission of the text, and these changes and the manuscripts which have them are not listed. Two manuscripts, Ii and Ne, show complete agreement with Cx¹. Others agree with Cx¹ in reading *Romaunce*, including Lc, Ld¹, Ln, Mg, Mm, Ph³, Ps, Ry¹, Sl², and To. Others have the readings attributed by Dunn to the original, but spell *Romayn* in different ways so that it is not clear what is meant. Thus Bw has *Romayns* and others, including En¹ and La, have *Romans*. Do these spellings represent the plural of *Roman* or the word *Romaunce*? The likelihood that Y had the line as found in Cx² is reasonably strong. Furthermore, Dunn does not represent the spelling of the manuscripts or incunabula accurately, for he seems to be interested only in the words. In line 144 the spellings *hote/hoot/ hoote/hoten/hete/hate* in the various manuscripts could influence how the scribes or compositors understood the text. He also fails to give the context of the lines, so his claim that line 291 makes nonsense is hardly just. Cx² reads:

> But folk of wyuys make none assay
> Tyl they be weddyd to old dotard shrewe.

The plural *shrewes* in Cx¹, which in these two lines is otherwise identical with Cx², gives way to the singular *shrewe* to rhyme with *shewe* in 292. The sense that people fail to test wives till they are married to an old, foolish wretch makes adequate sense, though it might be better with an indefinite article before *old*. The change in Cx² may not completely reflect the reading in Y, but to suggest it is meaningless is going too far. The data which Dunn supplies cannot be relied on as it stands.

In his analysis, Dunn takes added or omitted lines and passages together, but this may not be the clearest procedure to follow. Dd is the manuscript which shares the most lines with those corrected in Cx². Dunn's line count includes both individual lines and those occurring in passages. Thus a manuscript like Ch, which is similar to Cx² in most of the extra lines, differs from it because it omits five passages (B4060b-c, C297-8, F673-708, F1455-6, and F1493-6), which together account for most of the forty-eight lines which Dunn claims are found in Cx² but are missing in Ch. Apart from the two passages found only in Cx², Ad³, and El from the Franklin's Tale (F1455-6 and 1493-6), Ch also lacks the lengthy Squire-Franklin link. The count of forty-eight lines gives a some-what misleading impression, for it seems much larger than, say, Dd, which lacks only thirteen lines which have been added to Cx². But these thirteen lines in Dd are also principally found in five passages (A252b-c. C297-8, E775, F1455-6, and F1493-6), three of which are the same as those missing in Ch. Ad³, on the other hand, lacks twenty lines added to Cx² which are largely accounted for by only four passages. Furthermore, this count may be skewed because both Ad³ and Dd have missing folios and Dunn included in his calcu-lations lines in those passages now missing in Ad³ and Dd which he calculated had originally been present in these manuscripts. The differences between Ad³ or Ch and Dd are not perhaps as telling as the number of lines suggests. As for altered words and phrases, Ad³ shares rather more with Cx² than El does, though the difference is slight. What may be more significant than Dunn allows is that manuscripts like Ch and Ad³, both now accepted as related to Hg, could be close in the manuscript tradition to the possible source for many of the readings in Cx². In this connection, Garbaty has shown that de Worde had access to a good manuscript closely related to Hg and it is possible that this is the same manuscript used to correct Cx¹ for Cx² which remained in the workshop from 1482 to 1496.[8] This would depend on whether the story of a gentleman lending his father's manuscript to Caxton is genuine or merely a publisher's blurb. There is no suggestion in the Prohemye that Caxton returned the manuscript. Because of added tales and missing passages neither Ch nor Ad³ can be Y but, as both were copied rather later than the early *Canterbury Tales* manuscripts, their copy-texts or a related manuscript was more likely to be available shortly before Caxton published Cx².

Dunn suggests that Caxton carried out his work indifferently and possibly in a hurry so that Y was not used as copy-text. Dunn did not consider this editorial undertaking against any of Caxton's other editing. He refers to the compositor(s) only incidentally and never evaluates the different contributions of Caxton and the compositor(s). Equally, although his concern was simply to show the relationship between Cx¹ and Cx² and to identify, if possible, what manuscript Caxton used, Dunn set the tone for much future discussion. Cx²'s readings are not listed in the Manly & Rickert edition and it has been neglected in discussions of the poem's transmission, even though it had access to readings in a good manuscript. It remains possible that where Cx² differs from Cx¹ it might have a good reading in places where no extant manuscript shares Cx²'s form, because Y cannot be identified with any extant manuscript. The result of Dunn's study has been that little or nothing has been written on Cx² as a printed book, how it was set up, what it consists of and how these features may help us to understand its relation to Cx¹. In order to understand this book more closely, I propose to examine these features before returning to Y.

Cx² differs from Cx¹ in various typographical and layout features.[9] Many of these are simply the result of Caxton's greater experience at printing. Cx² has running heads, signatures, and woodcuts which are not found in Cx¹. It does not have catchwords. The woodcuts are of the various pilgrims and each corresponds to twenty lines of type.[10] Apart from the scene of the pilgrims at dinner, the woodcuts are equestrian portraits of single pilgrims, most of which are fairly stock figures. That for the Clerk is inappropriate since he carries a bow and arrows, and it may have been meant in the first instance for the Yeoman. Carlson notes that there are only three series of manuscript illuminations, El, Gg, and the Oxford fragments (i.e. Ma and Ph3). Of these it is the last with which Caxton's woodcuts have most in common and Carlson suggests that it is not unlikely that this manuscript passed through Caxton's hands, since the woodcuts were made specially for Cx² and must have been based on some model.

There are twenty-three different woodcuts, most of which are used more than once. In the General Prologue there are twenty different woodcuts. The same woodcut is used for the Merchant, the Franklin, and the Summoner, and another woodcut is used for both the Physician and the Parson. One woodcut introduces the five guildsmen, though it hardly seems appropriate for any of them. There are no woodcuts in the General Prologue for the (Second) Nun or the Nun's Priest since they do not figure prominently there. These two have new woodcuts for their tales. There is also no woodcut of Chaucer or of the Canon's Yeoman, neither of whom is described there. There is one for the Yeoman, though this is not used later for the Canon's Yeoman, who is represented at his tale by the woodcut of the Shipman. There is a woodcut of the pilgrims at their dinner in the Tabard, but there is no woodcut of the Host. If a pilgrim mentioned in the General Prologue tells a tale, the woodcut in the General Prologue (though this does not apply to the Franklin who for his tale is represented by the woodcut for the Manciple in the General Prologue) is used again, normally at the head of his/her tale rather than of the prologue introducing it. The woodcuts which are not re-used are those for the Yeoman, a guildsman, the Ploughman, and the pilgrims' dinner. New woodcuts in the body of the poem are found for the (Second) Nun, the Nun's Priest, and (?) Chaucer, which occurs twice, at the head of Sir Thopas and Melibeus. Altogether Cx² contains forty-seven woodcut images. In the General Prologue the woodcut of the Physician/Parson occurs twice in quire b (b4^v and b6^r) which one would expect if the pages of type were re-distributed quickly after printing, though the one of the Merchant/Franklin/Summoner appears in three neighbouring quires (a8^v, b2^r, and c1^v). The inclusion of woodcuts in Cx² would naturally mean that the arrangement and organization of its text were different from those in Cx¹, although there are many other features that would have had an influence. There are no woodcut initials. For large capitals the compositors inserted a guide-letter for a rubricator to draw the appropriate initial letter. There is no title-page to the volume.

Cx² has thirty-eight lines per page compared with only twenty-nine in Cx¹; Cx¹ uses type 2 while Cx² uses type 4* with type 2* for running heads. Both texts insert rubrics for tales or their parts within the text and neither contains any marginal glosses or rubrics. Cx² is, however, more expansive in its overall layout and it is clear that more attention had necessarily been given to layout when the text was set up. Perhaps the most significant feature of Cx² is that it has three series of signatures. They can be understood to divide the text into three parts as follows:

Part I a-t⁸, v⁶
Prohemye (a2^{r-v}), General Prologue (a3^r-c5^v with woodcut of the Knight), Knight's Tale (c6^r-g3^v), Miller's Prologue (g3^v-4^v with woodcut of Miller),

Miller's Tale (g5^r-h5^v), Reeve's Prologue (h5^v-6^v with woodcut of Reeve), Reeve's Tale (h7^r-i4^r), Cook's Prologue (i4^{r-v}), Cook's Tale (i5^r with woodcut of Cook-i6^r), Man of Law's Prologue (i6^r-7^r), Man of Law's Tale (i7^v with woodcut of Man of Law -l7^v), Merchant's Prologue (l7^v-8^r with woodcut of Merchant), Merchant's Tale (l8^v-n7^v), Squire's Prologue (n8^r), Squire's Tale (n8^v with woodcut of Squire-p1^v), Franklin's words (p1^v-2^r), Franklin's Prologue (p2^{r-v}), Franklin's Tale (p2^v with woodcut of Franklin-q6^v), Wife of Bath's Prologue (q6^v with woodcut of Wife of Bath-s2^r), Wife of Bath's Tale (s2^r-7^v), Friar's Prologue (s8^r), Friar's Tale (s8^v with woodcut of Friar-t5^v), Summoner's Prologue (t5^v-6^r), Summoner's Tale (t6^v with woodcut of Summoner-v6^v).

Part II aa-hh^8, ii^6

Clerk's Prologue (aa1^{r-v}), Clerk's Tale (aa2^r with woodcut of Clerk-cc3^r), Lenvoy de Chaucer (cc3^{r-v}), Verba Hospitis (cc3^v-4^r), (Second) Nun's Prologue (cc4^r-5^v), (Second) Nun's Tale (cc6^r with woodcut of (Second) Nun-dd4^v), Canon's Yeoman's Prologue (dd5^r-7^r), Canon's Yeoman's Tale (dd7^v with woodcut of Canon's Yeoman-ff1^v), Physician's Tale (ff2^r-6^r), Words of Host (ff6^{r-v}), Pardoner's Prologue (ff6^v-8^r), Pardoner's Tale (ff8^v with woodcut of Pardoner-gg7^v), Shipman's Tale (gg7^v with woodcut of Shipman-hh5^v), Verba Hospitis (hh5^v), Prioress's Prologue (hh6^{r-v}), Prioress's Tale (hh6^v with woodcut of Prioress-ii1^v), Prologue of Chaucer's Tale (ii2^r), Tale of Thopas (ii2^v with woodcut of 'Chaucer'-ii5^r), Words of the Host (ii5^v-6^r).

Part III A-K^8, L^6

Chaucer's Tale of Melibeus (A1^r with woodcut of 'Chaucer'-C4^r), Monk's Prologue (C4^v-5^v), Monk's Tale (C6^r with woodcut of Monk-E1^v), Nun's Priest's Prologue (E2^{r-v}), Nun's Priest's Tale (E3^r with woodcut of Nun's Priest-F3^v), Manciple's Prologue (F3^v-5^r), Manciple's Tale (F5^v with woodcut of Manciple-G1^r), Parson's Prologue (G1^r-2^r), Parson's Tale (G2^v with woodcut of Parson-L3^v), Retraction (L3^v-4^r).

There are blanks at a1 and L5-6. But where a new part begins, there are often empty spaces as well. The end of the Summoner's Tale on v6^v occupies only two lines, which are followed by the rubric ending the tale and that introducing the Clerk's Prologue 'And foloweth the Prologe of the clerk | of Oxenford'. These rubrics are followed by a gap of thirty lines. When the Clerk's Prologue beings on aa1^r this is introduced by the rubric 'Here begynneth the prologue | Of the clerke of Oxenford /' so that this prologue is introduced twice. The conclusion of the Words of the Host which conclude the Tale of Thopas on ii6^r occupy only ten lines and they are followed by the rubric 'Sequitur Chawcers tale', taken over from Cx^1. The rest of ii6^r and all of ii6^v are blank. The Tale of Melibeus opens on A1^r with a woodcut but no introductory rubric. The inclusion of the Prohemye in the first quire means it was written before the text was set up, so it was not an afterthought. But this means the reference to 'vj yere' between Cx^1 and Cx^2 in the Prohemye was written before the book was printed and consequently refers at the latest to the start of Cx^2's printing and not to its date of publication.

Although I have previously suggested that three sets of signatures probably indicate three separate compositors, we now know that Caxton had only two compositors to start with during his early years at Westminster.[11] Cx^1 was set up by two compositors working on two presses. There is nothing to suggest that this workshop staffing had changed by the time Cx^2 was printed. Consequently we need to look more closely at the question of the number of compositors used in Cx^2. There are significant differences in the length of the three parts. Part I contains 158 folios, part II 70 folios and part III 86 folios. The break between parts I and II seems designed to divide the text into two equal halves for two compositors, for part I has 158 and parts II and III 156 folios. Part III starts with the prose Tale of Melibeus. Even if it was considered beneficial to start a new quire with prose, this would not necessitate a new set of signatures. The division of the second half into two parts needs an explanation, and the most likely one is that it was more convenient for the second compositor to start his stint with the Tale of Melibeus rather than the Clerk's Tale, which means that part III was set up before part II. One reason might be the woodcuts in Cx^2. Part I begins with the General Prologue, which contains woodcuts of most pilgrims, but not one of Chaucer. If the second compositor started with Melibeus in part III, it would mean that one compositor would not need to wait for the other to finish with the woodcut of the Clerk since both would have used that woodcut in the early part of their stints if the second compositor started with part II, which opens with the Clerk's Tale. This would not prevent overlap in the use of woodcuts later on but it may not in itself be a sufficient reason for suggesting that part III was set up before part II. A consideration of other details may suggest additional reasons for this procedure.

Working from the description of the three parts given above, we notice immediately that the disposition of the woodcuts undergoes a change during the setting up of the text. To start with the woodcuts are crammed in. On folio c5^v, which ends the General Prologue and opens the Knight's Tale, eighteen lines from the end of the General Prologue are included. These are followed without a gap by the rubric 'Here begynneth the knyghtis tale' which is in its turn followed without a gap by the woodcut of the Knight, which extends one line below the bottom of what was the normal page of type. The tale itself starts on the following folio without any gap or rubric. In other words, one tale follows the next without a gap and its woodcut is inserted immediately if there is space for it. There is no attempt to space out the text or to start a new tale with its woodcut at the top of a new page. Where there is no room for the woodcut at the foot of the page, then it appears at the top of the next page as is true of the Man of Law's Tale on i7^v. But in these cases the rubric introducing the tale is joined to the rubric ending the prologue. In this case the rubric on i7^r reads 'Here endeth the prologue/ and begynneth | the tale of the man of lawe'. There is no introductory rubric on i7^v. A change can be noticed with the Merchant who follows the Man of Law. His prologue follows on the same page as the end of the Man of Law's Tale with a rubric introducing it, but at the end of the Merchant's Prologue on l8^r there is no rubric ending his prologue, but there is the woodcut at the bottom of the page. On the next page, l8^v, there is the rubric 'Here begynneth the marchauntes tale' which is followed by the tale after a one-line gap. The end of the Merchant's Tale and the start of the Squire's Prologue are noted by a rubric at the bottom of n7^v, but the prologue occupies n8^r. Although the prologue does not occupy the whole of the page, there is no rubric to conclude it; there is just a ten-line gap. On n8^v there is the woodcut of the Squire, followed by the rubric 'Here begynneth the squyers tale' with a one-line gap before and after it. However, these arrangements may have been dictated by different reasons. At the end of the Merchant's Prologue there is no rubric to close it (although there had been one in Cx^1) because the compositor wanted to squeeze in the woodcut at the bottom of l8^r. Since the prologue consists of eighteen lines and the woodcut occupies twenty, the compositor may have decided there was no room for any rubric. A rubric to open the tale is placed on l8^v at the head of the tale. A small gap after the Squire's Prologue (n8^r) is caused by lack of room for the woodcut of the Squire, but the compositor did not use it to include a rubric to end the Squire's Prologue, because there was no rubric here in Cx^1. He included a woodcut followed by the rubric to introduce the Squire's Tale on n8^v, which may have been a pragmatic solution determined to some extent by his new order of tales. With the Franklin's Tale we revert on p2^v to the system of having a joint rubric ending the prologue and beginning the tale, followed by the woodcut of the Franklin and the tale. On q6^v the rubric notes the end of the Franklin's Tale and introduces the Wife of Bath's Prologue and then has the woodcut of the Wife completing the rest of that page. A one-line gap before the rubric means that the woodcut drops one line below the level of the page. This is one instance where the woodcut comes before the prologue and not immediately before the tale, which may be due to the length of the Wife of Bath's Prologue. As for the Friar and the Summoner, their prologues end with a rubric, and on the next page the woodcut is followed by the rubric introducing the tale. This arrangement may have been caused by lack of space on the relevant folios, though it may also represent a development in the mise-en-page.

With part II this arrangement continues in that the rubric for the end of a prologue is separated from that for the beginning of the tale which is always placed after the woodcut. The woodcuts are often placed at the head of a page unless space allows it to be in the middle of a page, which is true of the Pardoner, Shipman, and Prioress. With part III this system continues with the difference that the rubric introducing a tale, although separated from that ending the prologue, always comes before (and not after) the woodcut.

There is then progression in the way the woodcuts and rubrics are handled. At first, the end of one narrative item and the start of the next are run into one rubric, but gradually that rubric is split up into its two parts and, finally, the second of the two parts may be put before or after the woodcut where it occurs. If part II was set up before part III one might have expected the rubrics in part II to appear before their respective woodcuts and those in part III after the woodcuts, for that would represent the normal progression in organization: a joint rubric with both end of prologue and start of tale followed by the wood-cut, then the separation of the rubric into end of prologue and start of tale as independent units so that the end of the prologue is on one page and the start of the tale rubric follows on the next one before the woodcut, and finally the rubric to introduce the tale placed after the woodcut. The relation of rubrics to woodcuts in Cx² thus offers a further reason for supposing that part III was set up before part II. There are other signs of a similar nature. Thus, in part I when there is a new paragraph in a continuous piece of couplet verse which is indi-cated by a large capital to be inserted by a rubricator, the compositor does not leave a blank line before the capital. This applies right through part I from the General Prologue (e.g. c3ʳ) until the Summoner's Tale (v3ᵛ). However, in part II there is a blank line in all equivalent situations as in the Canon's Yeoman's Tale (ee3ᵛ), the Pardoner's Tale (gg2ᵛ, gg3ʳ), and the Tale of Thopas (ii5ʳ). In part III the system is mixed. In the prose tales there is sometimes a blank (A2ʳ) and sometimes not (A2ʳ), but at the only place in couplet verse in part III where this situation occurs (Nun's Priest's Tale E6ᵛ) there is a blank. In one instance (Monk's Tale D3ᵛ) the compositor left a three-line blank before a large capital instead of the usual single-line gap. The development in this system may also indicate that part III was set up before part II.

There are running heads throughout the book and these show some in-teresting variations. They occur on both recto and verso of each folio. In part I the General Prologue has the running head 'Prologue', always spelt in this way. Elsewhere throughout part I the normal spelling of this word in running head and rubric is 'prologe' (although there is an exception to this in the rubric at the end of the Man of Law's Prologue) and the normal style is 'The X's tale' or 'The X's prologe'. Thus we find 'The knyghtis tale' and 'The Mylleres prologe'. The spelling 'Mylleres' occurs on g3ᵛ and g4ᵛ with 'prologe' and on g5ʳ with 'tale', but otherwise 'Myllers' with <s> rather than <es> is used. 'The Reues prologe' occurs on h6ʳ, but 'The Reues Prologe' with capital <P> on h6ᵛ. 'The Reues tale' is the standard pattern except on h7ᵛ and h8ᵛ where 'The Reues Tale' with capital <T> rather than <t> is found, as though the head had been carried forward in its composing stick from one sheet to the next. On i4ʳ where the Reeve's Tale ends and the Cook's Prologue begins, the running head is 'The Myllers tale', which again suggests that either some heads were carried forward in the composing sticks and then wrongly inserted elsewhere or they were never taken out of the formes. On i4ᵛ the head is 'The Cokis Prologe'. Although i5ʳ has the head 'The Cokis Tale', i5ᵛ has 'The Reues Tale'. The mistakes or changes in a head usually follow the quire organization and indicate how the text was set up. Thus there is a running head 'The marchauutes tale' with a turned <n> on m1^v, m2^v, m3^v, and m4^v, but there is a normal <n> on these folios' respective rectos and for the rest of the tale. On n8^r the running head is 'The squyer Prologe', which then gives way in the tale to 'The Squyers tale' except that on o5^r there is the erroneous head 'The squyers Prologe' a form which does not occur elsewhere and may have been prompted by the start of the second part of the tale on this page. On the remaining rectos of this tale Squire has a small <s> rather than the capital which is otherwise the norm. From q7^r until the end of quire r, the head is 'The Wyf of Bathe Prologe', but from s1^r that is changed to 'The Wyf of Bathes prologe' and the genitive in <s> continues in the heads throughout the tale.

With part II some changes occur in the heads. From now on and right through part III, each prologue has the head 'The Prologue' without the name of the pilgrim and each tale has the pattern 'The Tale of the X' rather than 'The X's Tale'. This is not true of the heads for the Clerk's Tale, which starts part II, and read 'The clerkis tale of oxenford' though with a varied use of capitals. This is, nevertheless, different from the pattern of 'The Wyf of Bathes Tale'. On bb6^v and bb7^v there is no space between *clerkis* and *tale* in the head. Although the rubrics of prologue and tale refer to the Second Nun, the heads refer to her simply in the form 'The Tale of the Nonne'. The words of the Host between the Physician's Tale and Pardoner's Prologue has the head 'The Prologue' (ff6^r). The Tale of Thopas has the head 'Of Syr Topas' throughout, though the name is spelt 'Thopas' in the text of the poem, but in part III the Tale of Melibeus has the head 'The Tale of Chaucer' or 'The Tale of Chawcer'. Parts II and III show a clear change from part I and this also represents some form of progression. However, there is some suggestion that this scheme may have had some influence in part I where some rubrics reflect it. Thus where Cx^1 has no rubric at the end of the prologue and the beginning of the tale of the Man of Law, Cx^2 has the rubric 'Here endeth the prologue/ and begynneth | the tale of the man of lawe' (i7^r). This is particularly interesting as this is the one occasion the spelling 'prologue' is found in a rubric in part I and where the formula 'The tale of X' is used. At the end of the Merchant's Tale, we find the rubric 'Here endeth the Marchauntes tale/ And | foloweth the prologe of the squyers' (n7^v). Here the formula 'The prologe of the X' is used and the occurrence of 'squyers' with final <s> may suggest the compositor had 'squyers prologe' in front of him as in Cx^1. The same formula is used to introduce the Wife of Bath's Prologue where we find 'And foloweth the prologe of the Wif of Bathe' (q6^v) though that is imitated from Cx^1.

In part I the Man of Law's Tale is the only one in stanza form, but no attempt is made to set complete stanzas on each page; the stanzas are broken up after any line and the rest of the stanza is set on the following page. But unlike the usage in Cx^1 the stanzas are separated by spaces. There are no divisions in this tale. The Squire's Tale is divided into three parts with rubrics, although the rubrics are not in Cx^1. These rubrics are in Latin so on o5^r we find 'Explicit prima pars | Et sequitur pars secunda' and similarly for the third part. In part II the Clerk's Tale has divisions with rubrics as in Cx^1, but the rubrics are expanded in Cx^2. Cx^2 repeats after E196 'Prima pars Grisildis' (aa4^r), but where Cx^1 has after E448 simply 'Secunda pars', Cx^2 has 'Explicit secunda pars | Et sequitur pars tercia' (aa8^r) – and so on through the rest of the tale. After E1176 Cx^1 has no sub-title, but Cx^2 has 'Lenuoye de Chaucer a | les marietz de n[ot]re temps' (cc3^r). Cx^1 has the rubric to end the Clerk's Tale after the 'Verba hospitis', but Cx^2 ends the tale before the 'Verba hospitis' and after E1212g has the new rubric 'Here enden the wordes of the hoost' (cc4^r). Similarly, after the Physician's Tale, Cx^2 has rubrics for both the Words of the Host and the Pardoner's Prologue, whereas Cx^1 incoporates both into the prologue. After the Shipmans's Tale Cx^2 has a new rubric 'Here endeth the wordes of the hoost' (hh5^v). After the Prioress's Tale, Cx^2 adds the rubric 'Here foloweth the prologue of | Chaucers Tale' (ii2^r) and after this prologue includes 'Here endeth the prologue' (ii2^r). After the end of the Tale of Thopas the rubric is 'The hoost Interrupteth his tale /' (ii5^r).

When Cx^2 was set up, the order of tales in Cx^1 was changed. The changes are not extensive. There are no added tales, such as Gamelyn or the Ploughman's Tale. There are only two new links, the Squire–Franklin link (F673-708) and the Nun's Priest's Endlink (B4637-52) which is incorporated as the first part of the Manciple's Prologue. In Cx^1 the order of fragments/tales was I–II–Squire–Merchant–III–Clerk–Franklin–VIII–VI–VII–IX–X. Since Y contained the Squire-Franklin link, some re-arrangement of tales was necessary. Caxton reversed the order of the Squire and Merchant and put the Franklin earlier in the sequence to follow the Squire to produce the order I–II–Merchant–Squire–Franklin–III–Clerk–VIII–VI–VII–IX–X. The Merchant's Prologue remains E1213-44, which is still wrongly situated because it contains a reference to Griselda of the Clerk's Tale, which has not yet been told. The Squire's Prologue remains the Man of Law's Endlink (B1163-90) with 'Squire' the speaker at B1179. Only the Squire–Franklin link is new in this re-arrangement. In Cx^1 F709-28 were described as the Franklin's Prologue and so this new link, which was strictly unnecessary as a link, is introduced as 'The wordes of the frankeleyns' (p1^v) where one may notice the use of the final <s> as in the rubric used in Cx^2 to introduce the Squire's Prologue (n7^v). In the Nun's Priest's Endlink the last line reads 'Sayd to another man as ye shal here', though this reading may already have been in Y. If it was it would explain why Fragment VIII was not put after the Nun's Priest's Tale, which is its usual position in group **a** manuscripts, though not those of Robinson's O Group. It allows for the Manciple, a male, to follow rather than the Second Nun as more commonly in the order. In Cx^2 various passages which are now considered spurious, such as the obscene additions at the end of the Merchant's Tale, are deleted and other passages are added, such as the additional twenty lines in the Nun's Priest's Prologue (B3961-80). The major changes to order and content are not extensive and are easily what could have been noted by Caxton on the copy of Cx¹ used as copytext, but the compositors could have used Y to insert the necessary passages. What is striking is that the Clerk remains separated from the Merchant, Squire, and Franklin, and their three tales still come before Fragment III even though the Merchant refers to the Wife of Bath in his tale. Caxton did not pay such close attention to the content of the poem, which detailed correction of all its lines might have led to, and this may possibly indicate that he was not responsible for the minor changes to the text. He was content to make major changes and probably to leave the minor textual changes to his compositors. It is to these minor changes which we must now turn.

In his stemmatic analysis of the Wife of Bath's Prologue on CD-ROM, Peter Robinson discusses the variants found in Cx², which are mostly shared by de Worde and Pynson.[12] In his work he divided the various manuscripts into groups which differ from those found in Manly & Rickert. These he labelled the O Group, consisting of Ad¹, Ad³, Bo², Ch, En³, Ha⁵, Hg, Ht, Ra³, and Tc¹, and the A, B, CD, E, and F Groups. The O Group is the one which preserves readings closest to Chaucer's original. The A, B, and CD Groups are not too dissimilar from the Manly & Rickert groups, but E contains four manuscripts, Bo¹, Ph², Gg, and Si, and F another four manuscripts, Bw, Ln, Ld², and Ry². When he examined Cx² against the variants characteristic of these groups Robinson found the following distribution:

Group	Group variants	Group variants in Cx²	
A	96	50	
B	168	110	
CD	153	5	
EF (shared)	61	2	
E	134	8	
F	99	3	
O	28	3	(pp. 108–9)

Since Cx¹ belonged to the Manly & Rickert group **b**, it is not surprising that Cx² shows a high proportion of Group B variants (about 60 per cent). When the Prologue is broken down into two-hundred line blocks, the level of variants from Group B remains constant at about two-thirds of the total. The only other group with a high number of variants reflected in Cx² is Group A, consisting of Cn, Dd, Ds, En¹, and Ma, with Cx² showing 50 of the possible 96 variants (approximately 50 per cent). When these variants are taken in two-hundred line blocks, one notices that the first four hundred lines show a much higher proportion of Group A variants (37 out of 58) than the last four hundred lines (13 out of 38) – a ratio of approximately two-thirds to one-third. Since Group B variants remained constant, this variation in Group A variants may suggest that as the corrector got further into a section of text he was less careful about making changes. However, since El seems to have changed its copy-text about line 400, it is possible that this change in the ratio of variants may reflect some special features in the choice of copy-texts in Group A manuscripts. These statistics relate only to variants characteristic for the whole group and do not isolate individual manuscripts. But Dunn showed that both Ad³ and Ch shared many readings introduced into Cx² with Y and they are both O Group manuscripts. How much one may rely on such broad figures remains debatable.

It is important to review some detailed textual material now available on the CD-ROM of the Wife of Bath's Prologue, for that may give us further information about the changes which were made or which were overlooked in the progression from Cx¹ to Cx². I choose a few lines for comment.¹³ At line 25 Cx² agrees with Cx¹ in reading, though with minor spelling differences, 'Of this noumbre very diffinicion'. The majority of manuscripts do not have *very* here, which is found only in the incunabula and in Tc², though Nl and Ph² have *the* and Dl has *and* rather than *very*. Many manuscripts read *Vppon* rather than *Of* at the beginning of this line. Apart from the incunabula, the manuscripts with *Of* are Cn, Ds¹, En¹, He, Ii, Ma, Mc, Ne, Ra¹, Se, and Tc², usually those manuscripts which fall into Robinson's Groups A and B, except for Dd. It is difficult to tell whether Y had *Of* rather than *Vppon*, but it is very unlikely it had *very*. But if corrections were being inserted in the copy of Cx¹ used as copytext for Cx², one would assume that the corrector here overlooked the differences between this line in Cx¹ and Y which almost certainly did not have *very*, and possibly not *Vppon* either. This line in itself would probably support Dunn's claim that Cx² was set up from Cx¹.

At line 30 Cx¹ and Cx² read:

> For wel y woot that myn husbonde   (Cx¹)
> Eke wel I woot he sayde that myn husbonde   (Cx²)

In this case the line as found in Cx¹ is replicated in most of those manuscripts which have *Of* as listed in the previous paragraph. The Cx² reading is a good one which is found in Ad³, Bo¹, Dd, Hg, Hk, Ht, Ph², Ra³, and Tc¹, a group which includes many of the O Group manuscripts. Other manuscripts have a different reading, though most are rather more like Cx² than Cx¹. The majority which have a slightly different reading agree with El in omitting *that* after *sayde*. Ch puts *that* before *he sayde*. If the corrector wrote his corrections in the margin of the text as suggested by Dunn, he must have made it quite clear where the corrections should go in the line.

At line 81 we find the following readings:

> He wolde wel euery wight were as he   (Cx¹)
> He wolde euery wyght were suche as he   (Cx²)
> He wolde wel that euery wight were swich as he   (Hg)

Here Cx² differs from Cx¹ in omitting *wel* and including *suche*. Most manuscripts read *swich*, for only Tc² agrees entirely with Cx¹, but many have different readings for *wel that*. These vary from omitting *wel* (which is the commonest reading) to replacing *wel that* with *not*. Only one other manuscript,

Dl, agrees with Cx² in the whole line. If there were a corrector he would have to indicate that *mel* be omitted, though he may have suggested an alternative for it which the compositor overlooked. It maȳ be easier to think of the compositor correcting the text and deciding that an addition in one part of the line deserved an omission in another.

A good example of where Cx² creates a new reading which is based on an imperfectly corrected version of Cx¹ is provided by line 100. The following readings may be noted:

> Hath meny a vessel of siluer and of gold   (Cx¹)
> Hath not euery vessel of siluer and of gold   (Cx²)
> He hath nat euery vessel/ al of gold   (El)
> Ne hath nat euery vessel/ al of gold   (Hg)

In this line two manuscripts, Ne and Tc², agree with Cx¹, and a further three, Ii, Nl, and Ra², refer to both silver and gold. All these manuscripts omit *Ne/He* at the beginning of the line and this feature is found in a further 27 manuscripts. It is possible that Y did not have initial *Ne/He*, but it is more likely that it had no reference to silver. Ra² reads *som of silver and som of golde* and Nl reads *Hath vessell som of sylvir & gold*. Ii reads *of syluer and golde*. The odds on Y reading something like this are small. We may assume that the corrector focussed on the first half of the line, rather than the second, and this approach is as likely to have been adopted by the compositor as by an editor. There are many other examples like this.

As one goes through the text one is struck by two features. First, there are a large number of changes, many of which are relatively trivial, and second the majority of these changes reflect, though they do not always reproduce exactly, readings in good manuscripts. There are equally a great number of places where the readings in Cx¹ and Cx² are the same. In many of these cases the readings are shared by other manuscripts and it is not easy to decide what Y read in most of them, despite Dunn's claim to the contrary. Dunn suggested that a corrected copy of Cx¹ was alone used as copy-text for Cx², because occasionally a correction within the line was inserted into the margin and wrongly added by the compositor to the front of a line. Mostly, however, the changes are inserted in their right place. The changes examined above do not prove that the corrections were made on a copy of Cx¹. There seem to me to be two possible alternatives for the minor changes made in Cx²: either the corrector (whether Caxton or someone else) went through Cx¹ indicating where changes should be made on that copy or the compositors used both the manuscript and Cx¹ as joint copy-texts. The type of mistake which Dunn claimed proved only a corrected copy of Cx¹ was used could as easily have been made by compositors using two copy-texts, a situation which he appears not to have considered. Misplacing an occasional word in the line or failing to take over all the text found in the manuscript are mistakes just as characteristic of someone using two copy-texts. If the corrector went through Cx¹ laboriously, then Caxton was a much more conscientious editor than we usually give him credit for. When all is said and done, it was a laborious job which did not have to be performed since compositors could cope with two copy-texts.

Dunn did note that corrections were not made to the prose tales from Cx¹ to Cx² and this could indicate that the difficulty of trying to collate prose from two copy-texts was too great. The absence of corrections here tells against the idea that Cx¹ was corrected as the copy-text, since there is no reason why a corrector going through a text should not treat the prose in the same way as the verse, if the intention was to create a more authentic text. After all, Caxton was quite happy to make considerable changes to other prose texts which he published, such as *Le Morte Darthur* and the *Golden Legend*. In setting Cx² the problem for the compositors in using two copy-texts would be twofold. The first is being able to cast off the right amount of text to be set on each page, for pages of text were not set in the order in which they appeared in the finished volume. This was not likely to be a great problem in the verse since extra or omitted lines could easily be noted and counted; and changes within a line would make no difference to the casting-off. This situation applied to parts I and II which are exclusively in verse, apart from the initial Prohemye. The problem of setting the prose from two copy-texts was avoided by using only one. The second is that if more than one compositor was working on the text at the same time, it would be impossible to use Y as a copy-text unless it was in an unbound state and could be distributed in quires or even bifolia to the compositors. Both these difficulties may be resolved. The evidence strongly suggests that only two compositors worked on Cx². This is indicated by the history of Caxton's press and developments in the *ordinatio* of Cx² which have been outlined above. The most reasonable explanation of this situation is that part III was set up before part II.

Apart from the matter of the woodcuts, another reason for setting part III before part II is that part III begins in prose for which the manuscript Y was not needed, because the prose is not corrected against Y. Hence the second compositor could have started on his work at the same time as or, if he was finishing setting another text, somewhat later than the first compositor. The second one would need to have access to Y in part III only for the tales of the Monk, Nun's Priest, and Manciple before he tackled the prose Parson's Tale. It is not possible to decide whether the decision not to use Y for the prose tales was purely pragmatic, i.e. dictated by the need for the second compositor to start his compositing before the first compositor had finished his stint using Y, or whether it was decided in advance on the assumption that some overlap was likely and should be avoided. The need to start with part III before part II suggests that the compositors also had access to Y and that the two compositors were, at least for some of the setting, working at the same time.

A possible scenario for the way Cx² was prepared is that, after studying Y probably somewhat cursorily, Caxton made decisions about the order of the tales and what passages to add or omit. He decided to leave detailed changes to the compositors who worked both from the annotated copy of Cx¹ for additional and omitted passages and from Y for detailed changes. The first compositor started with the General Prologue of part I and the second compositor started with Melibeus in part III because he did not need Y for the prose tale. The compositors may not have worked continuously on the poem, for they also set other texts during the production of this long text, and the second compositor may have started later than his colleague. There is evidence to suggest that Caxton did not make extensive changes to the poem and showed little concern for inconsistencies such as the Merchant's Tale referring to the Wife of Bath's Tale before it was told or the Merchant's Prologue referring to the Clerk's Tale as though that tale preceded his own. Caxton was interested in the broad sweep of the changes, but it is probable that the compositors introduced the more detailed changes. In his prologues and epilogues Caxton never refers to his workers or gives them any credit for their contribution to his printed books; the omission of any recognition of the compositors' contribution to Cx² fits in with that pattern. Although Wynkyn de Worde was apparently employed by Caxton from his return to England until his death, Caxton never refers to him in any way. The possible contribution of the compositors to the text of Cx² has been overlooked. The identification of Y is still uncertain. It may, as Dunn suggested, have belonged to the Manly & Rickert group **a**, though it should not be altogether ruled out that it would, if it had survived, have been a member of Robinson's O Group and perhaps related to a manuscript like Ad³ or Ch. Whether it was bound or not, the compositors clearly had strategies which enabled them to overcome whatever difficulties the copytext(s) presented.

NOTES

1 The sigils used for the manuscripts and incunabula of the poem are those found in most discussions of the poem; see *The Canterbury Tales Project Occasional Papers Volume I*, ed. by Norman Blake & Peter Robinson (Oxford, 1993), pp. 95-6 for a complete list.

2 See Lotte Hellinga, *Caxton in Focus* (London, 1982), p. 83.

3 John M. Manly & Edith Rickert, *The Text of the Canterbury Tales*, 8 vols (Chicago, 1940), especially vol. 2.

4 Beverly Boyd, 'William Caxton', in *Editing Chaucer: the Great Tradition*, ed. by Paul G. Ruggiers (Norman, Okla., 1984), pp. 21-5.

5 Thomas F. Dunn, *The Manuscript Source of Caxton's Second Edition of the Canterbury Tales* (University of Chicago PhD Thesis, June 1939). All quotations are taken from this thesis. The printed version was issued privately by University of Chicago Library in 1940.

6 M. Kilgour, 'The manuscript sources of Caxton's second edition of the *Canterbury Tales*', *PMLA*, 44 (1929), 186-201.

7 The corresponding line numbers in the CD-ROM of the Wife of Bath's Prologue for the line numbers used by Dunn are (1) 144; (2) 291; (3) 620; (4) 623; and (5) 822; see *The Wife of Bath's Prologue on CD-ROM*, ed. by Peter Robinson (Cambridge, 1996).

8 T. J. Garbaty, 'Wynkyn de Worde's "Sir Thopas" and other tales', *Studies in Bibliography*, 31 (1978), 57-67.

9 For descriptions of Cx¹ and Cx² see E. P. Hammond, *Chaucer: a Bibliographical Manual* (New York, 1908, rptd 1933), pp. 517-19 and Dan Mosser in Peter Robinson (1996).

10 On the woodcuts see David Carlson, 'Woodcut illustrations of the *Canterbury Tales*, 1483-1602', *The Library*, 6th series 19 (1997), 25-37, especially pp. 25-30.

11 See N. F. Blake, *Caxton: England's First Publisher* (London, 1976), pp. 61-3, and for the number of compositors used by Caxton see Hellinga (1982), pp. 59-62.

12 Peter Robinson, 'A stemmatic analysis of the fifteenth-century witnesses to *The Wife of Bath's Prologue*', in *The Canterbury Tales Project Occasional Papers Volume II*, ed. by Norman Blake & Peter Robinson (London, 1997), pp. 69-132.

13 The line numbers are those found in the CD-ROM lineation system, see Peter Robinson (1996).

THE ILLUSTRATION AND DECORATION OF THE REGISTER OF THE FRATERNITY OF THE HOLY TRINITY AT LUTON CHURCH, 1475-1546[*]

Kathleen Scott

THE FRATERNITY

The Fraternity of the Holy Trinity, given a royal licence in 1474 and founded in 1475 in association with a chantry at the parish church of Luton, was one of many such institutions in England in the fourteenth and fifteenth centuries. These fraternities or confraternities, which included both men and women in their membership, were of considerable importance in the social structure of towns but were actually founded for reasons of religious piety, primarily a fear of an afterlife in purgatory (or worse) and a belief in the role of the mass in achieving a more pleasant outcome in the afterlife. In 1389 the already numerous religious guilds were required by Richard II to record for the Chancery such items as their form of governance, the oath of entry, their customs, all feasts and assemblies, and their properties. The returns for 507 guilds have survived, leaving a reasonably clear picture of their founding purposes and activities.[1] Generally speaking, the main expenditure of these religious fraternities was to employ and maintain one or more chaplains for saying divine services, especially for the dead or for recently deceased members, and sometimes for the benefit of the living, especially for the good estate of the realm and the king and his family; and, indeed, the Luton Register[2] makes provision for two chaplains 'to syng dayly within the parish Churche of Luton … for prosperous estate of Kyng Edward iiii and Queen Elizabeth'. Members of such a fraternity might be expected to pay a fee at entry or to make gifts during the year, to attend mass on the feast day of the fraternity's name-saint, to donate extra candles on that day, wear livery at ceremonies, attend the funeral of a member, give offerings at mass, carry a torch at a funeral service[3] or in a Corpus Christi procession,[4] and attend an annual feast and meeting.

Another common reason for the foundation of a fraternity was for the provision of lights or candles on some or all feast-days, or before a particular image in the church to which the guild was attached, or for funeral services for a member (cf. Pl. 11).[5] The provision of candles seems to have something of an obsession, and a typical founding purpose would be that for the Fraternity of the Holy Cross, Amcotts, Lincolnshire, established in 1377-8 in order to maintain twenty-six wax candles to burn in the church in honour of the Holy Cross.[6] Candles are described as 'a costly indulgence' at this period, a fact that may explain fraternities taking on their provision as a *raison d'être*.[7] Only seldom were maintainance or repairs to the church with which the Fraternity was associated a concern; chaplains and candles were by far the most important business. Apart from soul-alms at the death of a member, there is also much less emphasis on the giving of alms or out-reach to the sick and poor than might be expected; but perhaps more charitable acts took place in practice than is evident from the 1389 returns.[8]

The Guild of the Holy Trinity at Luton church was founded by Thomas Rotherham, his brother John Rotherham, and others who had received permission from the crown in May 1474. John Lammer, the vicar of Luton church, Geoffrey Boleyn, mayor of London (although deceased), and Thomas Kipping, a draper of London and owner of a fine copy of the *Mirroure of the Worlde*,[9] are among those listed in gold lettering on the opening page of the Register, opposite the frontispiece, but following Edward IV, his queen Elizabeth, and his mother Cecily. Thereafter, the names of the master and wardens for each year were recorded, usually within a border, as well as the names of newly inducted members and their wives. The membership was diverse and by no means only local: it included several abbots of St Albans monastery (Pls 2, 4), and eventually Henry VII, Henry VIII, three of the latter's wives, as well as bishops, heads of other religious houses, canons, monks, merchants, and a physician and minstrel.[10]

In the absence of surviving statutes, the activities of Luton fraternity members have mainly to be assumed by comparison with the ordinances of other similar guilds. There probably were certain services that the membership was required to attend, as well as obligatory attendance at funerals of members and at an annual meeting and feast, when wardens would have been elected for the coming year. The account book of the fraternity, which survives, does not record an admission fee, nor does it suggest that funds were used for a school or given to the poor; but members were obliged to contribute to the annual feast,[11] and the accounts have many items relating to payments for wax tapers and for funerary hangings.[12] It is moreover certain that dead persons were admitted to the membership – probably on payment of a fee. The Luton guild is also known to have possessed its own hall 'at the hub of the town, dominating both literally and metaphorically the market place, from where the majority of members derived their livelihood'.[13] With its hall separated from the church, its well-to-do membership, and the presence of women, it is likely that there was also a certain social aspect to the fraternity activities, a side of life that does not inevitably negate the religious intentions.[14]

THE ILLUSTRATIONS OF THE FRATERNITY'S REGISTER

It is not unusual in English manuscript illustration of the later period to find the masterful together with the mediocre, and the Luton Guild Register is no exception. The frontispiece (Pl. 1), which is of exceptional artistic quality, is followed later in the manuscript by only two historiated initials (Pl. 2) and one small miniature in a modest style (Pl. 4). The selection of the frontispiece artist, who was certainly not English-trained, suggests a demand for a special commission by a knowledgeable patron or patrons, perhaps here with a specifically required artist. As far as the pictorial matter is concerned, the frontispiece shows an accurate sense of how it was appropriate to represent images of royalty before a religious icon, almost certainly following instructions given to the artist.

Although the frontispiece painting was commissioned by the fraternity at Luton to commemorate its founding, the imagery of its frontispiece served other important fraternity purposes. The iconography announces the social status of its membership – of the foremost possible rank and wealth in the realm: the king, queen, at least one royal relative, a bishop, apparent courtiers and high-ranking persons among local and regional citizenry. Few provincial parish guilds counted a reigning king and queen among their first members.[15] The frontispiece also demonstrates in visual terms the special devotion of Guild members to the 'holy and undivided Trinity',[16] members to whom, the picture suggests, the Trinity revealed itself. Marks sees the frontispiece as making a political as well as a pious statement in view of the reference on the opposite page (fol. 14ʳ) to the king's father, Richard duke of York, as 'veri et indubibitati heredis corone anglie'.[17] The miniature further speaks to the importance of the book itself: a volume that contained a visual preface of such artistic stature would be worthy of display in the hall, would indeed enhance the hall and the fraternity.

The retreat in subsequent miniatures to more mediocre pictorial work, to the linear uninspired work of much commercial English illustration of the later period (Pls 7, 8), happened as soon as the first important illustrative statement had been made in the frontispiece. After the magnificent beginning in 1475, no further miniatures were entered until the pages for 1499 and 1504, with little following illustrative matter of any kind. The Guild Register is, nevertheless, of considerable decorative importance because of its borderwork, which continued to be entered year by year and which now offers a record of the quality and style of illumination available at this latest period of manuscript production, when both printing and the massive importation of printed books were underway in England.

THE PICTORIAL SUBJECT MATTER OF THE REGISTER

The following listing gives the format, size, folio number, relevant year, pictorial subjects, and other representational images in the Luton manuscript, arranged as far as possible according to order of appearance, not by size or relative importance on the page. Unless otherwise noted, the miniatures are in coloured pigments, with some use of gold or gold wash. Heraldic subjects such as coats of arms are not listed as historiated initials, even though it is a site where crowned royal arms and supporters often occur (see Pls 3, 4).[18]

One full-page miniature: fol. 13ᵛ (Pl. 1), for 1475: (23.6 × 14.7 cm). The frontispiece miniature shows a bishop, with crosier, wearing a red mitre with infulae and a cope brocaded with a pomegranate design. He is kneeling at a *prie-Dieu*, very much in the foreground, with the arms of Rotherham twice on the hood of the cope, and holding an inscribed scroll ('Blessod: lord: in: trenete: Saue: all: thes: fretarnete'). The ecclesiastic is Thomas Rotherham, at this time bishop of Lincoln, in 1480 Archbishop of York, and from 1475 to 1483 Chancellor of England and trusted councillor to Edward IV. At left, Edward IV, crowned, in state robes with ermine collar and edging, also kneels at a *prie-Dieu*, with four tonsured clerics behind him, including three monks in red habits with raised cowls edged in white and four secular male figures. The secular males possibly include Edward, Prince of Wales (born November 1470), and Richard, duke of York (born August 1473). At right are Queen Elizabeth and other female figures in noble dress, one (just behind the queen) with a rosary at her waist and the arms of England on her robe. The identity of this person is not entirely clear: her youthfulness suggests that she is the princess royal, Elizabeth (born February 1466), who was nine years at the time, but since the queen and this figure are distinguished by black head-dresses, possibly the sign of a matron, and since Cecily is mentioned on the page opposite, Cecily Neville, mother of Edward IV, is perhaps the more likely identification.[19] All kneel in an attitude of prayer before an Image-of-Pity Trinity.[20]

In the iconic group God the Father, crowned and clothed in a red robe, supports the partly nude body of Christ, who displays the chest wound with his right hand and whose feet rest on a crystal tau-orb. The Father is seated on a gilt high-backed Gothic throne ornamented with finials and crockets, with a tapestry cloth attached to the back; the throne is surmounted by a canopy whose hangings of pink backed with a green lining are held open by angels. The Trinity is thus presented before a cloth or canopy of honour and seems in the act of being revealed to the high-ranking assemblage and members of the Fraternity. Through an open arch at left, there is a view of a city with street scene and at right of the interior of a church.

Two historiated initials: fol. 28ʳ (Pl. 2), for 1499: (5.1 × 6 cm) (left) an abbot (Thomas Ramrige, of St Albans) with crosier and mitre, with pomegranates on robe, kneeling at *prie-Dieu*, with inscribed scroll ('O blissid holy trinite Saue all thys fraternite'), with monk in black habit (Benedictine) behind; (right) a Crucifix-Trinity, with God the Father blessing; fol. 32ʳ, for 1504: (5.9 × 5.5 cm) (left) bishop (Galfridus Blythe, bishop of Lichfield) with

Pl. 1. Luton Art Museum, Luton Guild Register, fol. 13ᵛ (1475), frontispiece of Thomas Rotherham, Edward IV, Queen Elizabeth and others before an Image-of-Pity Trinity.

Pl. 2. Luton Art Museum, Luton Guild Register, fol. 28ʳ (1499), detail of historiated initial of Thomas Ramrige, abbot of St Albans, and a Benedictine, kneeling before a Crucifix-Trinity.

mitre and crozier and inscribed scroll ('O blissit trinite saue & kepe all thys fraternite'); (right) Crucifix-Trinity, with God the Father blessing.

Two marginal miniatures: fols 81ᵛ, 102ʳ, two stags with raised right leg.[21]

One marginal drawing: fol. 30ʳ, 1501-2: (6.4 × 10.2 cm at widest point) man in contemporary secular dress, with glaive, gesturing towards five rabbits in holes.[22] In pen and ink.

Ten small panels: (above coats of arms in large initials) respectively for the years 1510-19: fols 39ʳ, 41ᵛ, 44ʳ (Pl. 3), 45ᵛ, 47ʳ, 48ᵛ, 50ʳ, 54ʳ, 56ʳ, 58ʳ (varying in size between 2.1 × 1.8 cm and 2.6 × 2.3 cm), Crucifix-Trinity as crest.

Representations in borders: fol. 13ʳ, for 1475, squirrel eating nut; parrot with red collar;[23] fol. 14ʳ, for 1475, bird; man in cap, with sword; peacock in

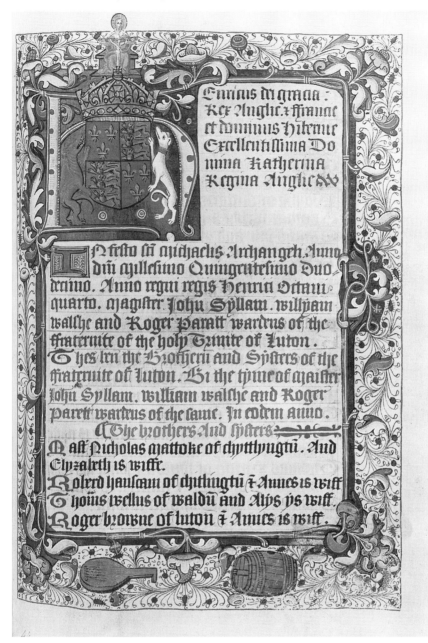

Pl. 3. Luton Art Museum, Luton Guild Register, fol. 44ʳ (1512), border page with arms in initial surmounted by a panel with Crucifix-Trinity; in lower border, a lute and tun, the punning badge of the town of Luton.

splendour; man (?Samson) wrestling with lion;[24] fol. 18^v, for 1480, green bird eating golden fruit; fol. 26^v, for 1496, man with spiked club and shield, battling dragon; long-beaked bird with raised wings; fol. 27^r, for 1497, green bird/(?)dragon grotesque; dog-like grotesque; fol. 28^r, for 1499, strawberries; peacock in splendour; winged dragon;[25] fol. 30^v, for 1502, parrot with red collar; bird; fol. 31^r, for 1503, dragon; fol. 34^r, for ?1508, crowned Tudor portcullis, with black feather (in margin); fols 93^r, for 1531, 97^r, for 1532, and 100^r, for 1533, gold fleur-de-lis. The borders between fols 41^v and 122^v contain a lute and tun as a visual pun or badge for Luton in the lower border or margin; see Pls 3, 4.

Two initials with cadels: fol. 95^v, for 1531, (in rose ink) profile face with tongue protruding; fol. 121^r, for 1545, (in red ink) profile face.

One miniature: fol. 97^r (Pl. 4), for 1532: (in two parts) at left (in unframed space), an abbot (Robert Catton, of St Albans) in cope, alb, and gloves and with mitre and crosier, kneeling, with monk in black habit (Benedictine) behind; in right border, another monk in dark blue habit (rector of the College of Bonhommes, Ashridge[26]), kneeling.

Unfinished border: fol. 33^r, sketch for an English border in two margins.

THE FRONTISPIECE: THE ICONOGRAPHIC CONTEXT IN ENGLAND

If one takes as the important iconographic elements in the Luton frontispiece (Pl. 1) a central iconic and devotional image, members of a royal family, members of an institution, and an ecclesiastic, then it is not possible to point to any surviving counterpart to the Luton miniature in English manuscript illustration. No other miniature, either chronologically preceding or subsequent to the Luton miniature, has a figure like that of Archbishop Rotherham which, by its size and central position before the devotional image, implies precedence over the royal family; the iconography is, to say the least, exceedingly unconventional. Rotherham is evidently conceived in this picture not merely in his estate as bishop but also as founder of the Guild and as representative of the membership; as such, he holds the scroll with an invocation to the Trinity to preserve the fraternity and all its membership and, as such, he figures uniquely in the composition of the scene. Rotherham's image may also suggest his involvement in commissioning the artist and/or largely paying for the illustration and decoration of the first bifolium, as well as his close advisory relationship with Edward IV. Only one other surviving English fraternity book of a later date, the Dunstable Guild Register, with iconographically similar if independent scenes, depicts representative guild figures.[27]

Because of the unusual nature of the Luton frontispiece, I intend to concentrate on it in this study (rather than on the other illustrations) and in particular to suggest partly an English and partly a continental context for the pictorial subject. In order to understand its emergence in the lower part of the scene as a confluence of traditional English images and in order to appreciate

Pl. 4. Luton Art Museum, Luton Guild Register, fol. 97ʳ (1532), miniature of Robert Catton, abbot of St Albans and a Benedictine, with another cleric kneeling in right border.

the roles, as far as they can be reconstructed, of Bishop Rotherham and of the artist in the upper part, we need to have some impression of the kinds of indigenous images that preceded the frontispiece of 1475. By way of considering its pictorial heritage, the frontispiece should be regarded from several different but sometimes overlapping perspectives: (i) those of a man and woman before an iconic image; (ii) of a family before such an image; (iii) of an ecclesiastic before an image; (iv) of royalty before an image; (v) of royalty with an institutional company; and (vi) of the devotional image itself used as the central object of such a scene. This brief survey of earlier subjects will not be exhaustive nor will it go back beyond *c.* 1390, even though such subjects, usually called donor scenes, had been in English book art since well before 1390.[28]

As an early instance, we may take an unusual scene from the Carmelite Missal[29] of the last decade of the fourteenth century, of a man and woman with patron saints, kneeling in devotion before the Virgin, who acts as intercessor between them and a Trinity as two Persons and Dove. Even at this time the scene is not particularly unusual in having both a male and female, offering devotion to a religious image,[30] but it is important to be aware of this theme in view of its future, more frequent representation.[31] A second type of scene takes the iconographic process one step further in preparing for the Luton frontispiece, that of a family before a religious icon. Family scenes are generally rare in English book art of the later period, and the scene from a York book of Hours (Pl. 5),[32] made between 1405 and *c.* 1415 for a branch of the Bolton family, is of special interest here because the icon is again a Trinity, albeit a Crucifix-Trinity, for which there seems to have been a particular enthusiasm in the fifteenth century, approaching the intensity of devotion to the Virgin. As we shall see, the Crucifix-Trinity is by far the most common mode of representing that pictorial theme, while the Image-of-Pity Trinity as in the Luton frontispiece is an extremely rare depiction in England.

Another pictorial element that can be isolated in devotional scenes before the Luton frontispiece is that of an ecclesiastic in piety before the Trinity. Like the kneeling male patron,[33] the kneeling ecclesiastic is also frequent in English book art, and I mention here only two examples: the well-known miniature in the Vernon manuscript (Pl. 6), of after 1382 and probably *c.* 1390-1400, of a cleric before a Crucifix-Trinity,[34] and a miniature of the same kind in a York missal with the cleric before a Crucifixion.[35] Apart from the Luton miniature, the most highly placed religious figure in such a scene is William Ashenden, abbot of Abingdon Abbey, placed just outside a Crucifixion miniature, with God the Father and Dove completing the Trinity above the cross.[36]

The only other theme relevant to the frontispiece that can be found in earlier depictions is that of royal figures in adoration before a religious image. On the whole, such scenes are not common, the most famous exception easily being the Wilton Diptych, with Richard II as a young man before the Virgin and Child and a host of angels.[37] Between this remarkable painting at the beginning of the century and representations of Henry VI in the late 1440s, there is only

Pl. 5. York, Minster Library, MS Add. 2, Hours, fol. 33ʳ, Bolton family before a Crucifix-Trinity.

Pl. 6. Oxford, Bodleian Library, MS Eng. poet.a.1, Vernon miscellany, fol. 265ʳ, cleric kneeling before a Crucifix-Trinity.

one apparently royal if ambiguous figure surviving in a devotional scene. The frontispiece of a book of Hours[38] made for Johanna of Navarre is thought to have been owned by a queen of England on grounds of an inserted miniature of a woman with English royal arms (faint) on her robe in a lower register, kneeling before the Virgin and Child and a Crucifix-Trinity together in a single upper register. Ambiguity about the meaning of the miniature arises because the figure also wears a nimbus for sainthood, and I know of no English queen of this period who would meet both qualifications.

Then, after 1445 and probably around 1450, we have a representation of Margaret of Anjou, queen of Henry VI, kneeling at a *prie-Dieu* before the Virgin and Child at the head of a prayer roll.[39] This roll and, not incidentally, the scene were almost certainly commissioned for Margaret's personal use, and the form in which she was represented would presuppose her approval of probably an acknowledged form in which to represent royalty under such circumstances. For King Henry, two devotional scenes survive, one each in the foundation charters of Eton and King's College, both dated March 1446, both by the same artist, and in nearly the same configuration.[40] In addition to demonstrating royal piety, these two miniatures, each of which extends around two margins of the document, introduce for the first time in England, so far as is now known, the concept of a royal figure together with (although in his own initial space, well separated from) a group of figures representative of the membership of an institution. Whether this pictorial concept was an *ad hoc* creation or derived from other earlier scenes in England or on the continent, we cannot be certain; but because it was employed on two important royal documents to royal foundations, it can be taken as an acceptable, probably even desirable, public image in the royal consciousness, such as it was at this time, of these matters.[41]

Of no less importance with respect to the version in the Luton frontispiece is a tinted pen drawing that accompanies the genealogical chronicle in British Library, MS Harley 318, fol. 8ᵛ. Both Henry VI and his queen Margaret are kneeling (without *prie-Dieu*), presented by Sts George and Margaret, before a Crucifix-Trinity (Pl. 7). Here at last, some time between their marriage in April 1445 and Henry's forced retirement in 1461, is an image with three of the Luton elements together in one scene: a man and woman, royalty, and a Trinity. The drawing is also important both in that it is the first known scene of a king and queen of England before a devotional image and in that it suggests not only that devotion to the Trinity had reached the high societal level of royalty but that it was, as it were, public knowledge to the point of being represented in a chronicle. It is also the only representation of which I am aware, since a miniature of 1326-7,[42] that makes an explicit connection between an English royal figure and St George, that is, the first known visualization in the fifteenth century of what came to be a national statement.

So at this point English book art had available all the iconographic components necessary to the Luton frontispiece, apart from the form of the

Pl. 7. London, British Library, MS Harley 318, genealogical chronicle, fol. 8ᵛ, Henry VI and Queen Margaret with patron saints, kneeling before a Crucifix-Trinity.

Trinity; these components were available for both Edward IV's accession in 1461 and his marriage to Elizabeth in 1464. If the iconography was employed even in a minor genealogical chronicle, an extremely popular text in the contemporary book-market, it is not entirely surprising to find another such scene surviving in a second chronicle, a roll in codex form: Oxford, Jesus College, MS B.114.[43] This time a more finished, fully tinted drawing shows Edward IV and his queen Elizabeth, in a composition that is very close to the Harleian miniature of Henry and Margaret, even to the same presenting saints, George and Margaret (Pl. 8).[44] We know that Edward or his agents were not averse to the use of propagandistic methods to confirm and promote his right to the throne, and we know that artists in his period picked up and employed scenes, especially from genealogical chronicles, some of which had been used perhaps more innocently for Henry VI. This miniature seems to be one of those, but, in view of the representation of Edward IV and Elizabeth in the Luton frontispiece, this drawing acquires more importance in retrospect and possibly indicates that Edward and his queen held the Trinity in a certain genuine devotion beyond propaganda.

It is probably clear that certain visual basics are established in the Jesus College drawing: the king and queen are presented in three-quarter view, kneeling at a prayer table, facing each other on the same pictorial plane, in an attitude of reverence or prayer, with the devotional image above and centred between them, and with the additional figures (saints) placed directly behind them. An important theme in both the Harley and Jesus drawings is, as I have said, that of portraying the king with the patron saint of England. Although this notion is not shown in the Luton miniature, this nationalistic theme, as we shall see, occurs again in much later panel paintings based on the same compositional structure.[45] It is not known whether the Jesus College manuscript was made for Edward and Elizabeth,[46] but the miniature, which is not likely to be merely a bald copy of Harley 318, may nevertheless have been devised with knowledge of the royal couple's (or at least Edward's) special devotion to the Trinity. The drawing may also be an indication of one manner in which Edward IV was pleased to be represented. Although we know from a fine genealogical roll in the Philadelphia Free Library,[47] of 1461 – before May 1464, probably made for Edward, that earlier in the reign the manner in which he was pictured was more oriented towards a justification and assertion of his claim to the throne, by 1468 – and certainly by 1475, the date of the Luton frontispiece – he may have wished for a more sedate public image and for piety to be recognized as an aspect of his court culture. The great window of the north-west transept of Christ Church Cathedral, Canterbury, formerly contained a similar representation: the uppermost tier of lights contained a Trinity (with saints) and the lowest depicted Edward IV and Elizabeth with their children, kneeling 'towards some central object of devotion',[48] i.e. the crucifix in the upper tier. The Jesus College miniature and the Canterbury glass may to some extent, together with king's close association with Thomas Rotherham,

Pl. 8. Oxford, Jesus College, MS B.114, genealogical chronicle, fol. 18ᵛ, Edward IV and Queen Elizabeth with patron saints, kneeling before a Crucifix–Trinity.

elucidate the willingness of the king and queen to become founder-members of a more or less provincial guild devoted to the Trinity.

By now it can be granted that much of the royal iconography of the Luton frontispiece could have been inherited from past pictorial concepts known in England. The frontispiece however augments the visual format of the Jesus College drawing; in addition to the person of Rotherham, several other new iconographic features are present: (i) a princess royal, either the mother of Edward IV or the eldest daughter of Edward and Elizabeth, Elizabeth; (ii) a figure probably representing the priest attached to the guild (behind the first hooded figure); (iii) male and female figures in aristocratic dress, representing either further children of the royal couple[49] or courtiers and ladies-in-waiting or, most probably, a mix of both;[50] and (iv) three males in a red religious habit, whose significance is not known. No other scene made for English royalty has yet been recognized to include the mother of the king, though several made after the Luton frontispiece show royal children (see below); nor does any such scene depict a cleric. A religious figure as patron appears in only one of the subsequent votive representations made of a British royal family with a theme similar to the Luton frontispiece. The Trinity panels by Hugo van der Goes, in the National Gallery of Scotland, Edinburgh, were commissioned by a cleric, Edward Bonkil, Provost of the Collegiate Church of the Holy Trinity, Edinburgh, and his portrait, together with angel musicians, is painted on the obverse of the wings.[51] The front wing panels show a king, James III of Scotland, and a queen, Margaret of Denmark, Queen of Scotland, presented by patron saints, with a young prince kneeling behind the king, presumably the eldest son, James IV. As in the Luton frontispiece, the three members of the royal family are in prayer before an Image-of-Pity Trinity. These panels, which were probably commissioned after the birth of the prince, James, duke of Rothesay, in March 1473, and possibly finished before the birth of a second son, probably in 1478,[52] are a remarkable parallel, given the proximity in date and similarity in iconographic theme, to the Luton frontispiece. They are almost certainly, however, not a direct source of the Luton iconography. The triptych was painted on the Continent, and the wing panels, which were 'often imitated, usually by artists who worked in Flanders', may have been begun while Van der Goes was still in Ghent.[53] The panels were apparently 'in the Netherlands for a fairly long time'[54] and were perhaps not at a very advanced stage of completion when the Luton frontispiece was made. Nevertheless, the communality of themes suggests strong interest among the reigning British monarchs to be presented before an Image-of-Pity Trinity, an interest of which donors such as Rotherham and Bonkil would have been aware, or perhaps even it was an interest aroused because of the donors' knowledge of Flemish art at this time. Otherwise the Crucifix-Trinity was the dominant pictorial mode of the century in England, one undisturbed on any other occasion by the Image-of-Pity type.

After the 1470s there is a lacuna in the survival (and perhaps the production) of this pictorial theme until the first part of the sixteenth century. The two surviving images from this later period are a manuscript frontispiece and a panel painting, both depicting Henry VII and his family. Oxford, Christ Church, MS 179, fol. 2ʳ, contains a petition of 1503 to Henry VII, requesting permission to establish a guild for French residents in London. A frontispiece precedes the petition and proposed statutes of the guild,[55] a full-page miniature of the royal family – king, queen, and children – kneeling before a scene of the meeting of Joachim and Anna at the gates of Jerusalem.[56] Henry VII and his queen Elizabeth of York, kneeling, face each other in an attitude of prayer, each over a *prie-Dieu*, with crowned children disposed by gender behind each.[57] The religious episode takes place under a massive Gothic gate and portcullis (echoing the Tudor badges in the border) on a different plane from the royal family but on its own continuous physical space. As part of a formal petition from Frenchmen in England, the frontispiece cannot be taken as an expression of personal royal devotion, but the petitioners or the artist must have had some sense of what would please or of what was acceptable. The frontispiece is enclosed by a broad border of four other religious scenes, of Tudor badges, and of royal arms and supporters; and the border was certainly calculated to conform with fashionable border design in other royal manuscripts of the period.[58]

The second occurrence of Henry VII's family in a similar kind of devotional setting is an anonymous panel painting of *c.* 1505-9 in the Royal Collection, Windsor Castle. The foreground plane is once more composed of facing king and queen, in three-quarter view, kneeling at prayer tables on which lie open prayer-books; but the effect has become more rigid through a linear rather than grouped disposition of the royal children.[59] Several new iconographic elements distinguish this painting from the previous scenes. The central iconic image – the battle between St George and the dragon – is proportionately larger than earlier such iconic subjects and takes place between a well-articulated landscape and the heavens above. The separation of realities is impressed on the viewer by the presence of two canopies that seem to hold down each royal group to the earthly realm, and especially by the presence of an angel who stands between Henry and Elizabeth and who, as mediator between the physical world and the divine, gestures between Henry and the religious episode above.[60] The active involvement of the angelic figure in the Windsor panel is comparable to that of the angels in the Luton miniature, who open the drapery to reveal the divine image of the Trinity; the Luton angels are also visual intercessors or enablers, both for participants in the miniature and for viewers of it. The Luton angels lend a dramatic sense to the miniature of an event at the moment of its happening: they seem to have just lifted the hangings to reveal the Trinity, and they continue to hold it in the manner of a cloth of honour. The Windsor angel was painted with the cruder, pointing gesture of a *nota bene* hand that tends to emphasize the archaic quality of the scene.[61]

The final English royal family scene of which I am aware appears in yet a different form in the Dunstable Guild Register of the Fraternity of St John the Baptist.[62] Leaves from this volume survive only for the years 1506-8, 1522, and 1525-41. On the leaves for 1522, the pictorial structure of the royal devotional scene has been broken up either by the artist or by the demands of currently fashionable page design into separate pieces: (i) with the religious icon (here John the Baptist in a landscape) placed in a rectangular miniature space where an introductory initial would normally have stood; (ii) with the figure of Henry VII kneeling before a *prie-Dieu* in a panel on the left border; and (iii) with members of the Fraternity in separate spaces divided by arches in the lower border (Pl. 9). The queen, Catherine of Aragon, is not even on the same page; she is placed opposite (Pl. 10) but in a corresponding position, with John the Baptist in a miniature above, and Fraternity members again below, separated by a royal coat of arms into two areas delineated by columns. The traditional set-piece is present but deconstructed into component parts – with a con-comitant loss of intensity. As Marks says, although 'more ostentatious', the decoration of the Dunstable Register is 'even more formulaic than the Luton book', emphasized, I feel, by this separation of pictorial elements into two borders and then further into a series of panels or spaces divided by columns.[63]

Over a period of forty-odd years, from 1468 to around 1510, the icono-graphic theme of a royal family kneeling in reverence before a devotional image was, then, rendered of three reigning British monarchs, Edward IV, Henry VII, and James III of Scotland. From an apparently modest (as surviving) beginning in the English coloured drawing of Harley 318 (Pl. 7), a manuscript not even certainly made for a member of the royal family, the pictorial concept came to wider public view in manuscripts made for confraternities and in panel paintings made for placement in church or palace. From a less accessible visual statement in the two manuscript drawings, the iconography came to be em-ployed by institutions or royalty for their own purposes, one of which would have been display and another the coupling of an image of the reigning monarch with an image of the national saint. Edward IV in the Jesus College drawing is commended by St George, patron of England, James III in the Trinity panels is presented by St Andrew, patron of Scotland, and Henry VII in the Windsor panel is commended to St George by an angel. This icono-graphic set-piece was conceived and became popular because it could exploit and perpetuate themes apparently important to the monarchy in this last medieval period. The chosen votive figure or scene may or may not always have revealed the personal piety of the reigning monarch, but he is always shown costumed in state robes and not in armour, that is, in his role as head of the realm, not its warrior-defender. In its later form the monarch is not only devout to a religious icon but is also in the company of a symbol of the state, thinly disguised, we might suggest, as a religious image. Not least, progeny of the monarch wait behind him to provide continuity of devotion to church and state. These images were probably consciously deployed as an alternative

The transcribed text within the image:

Oraÿ for the prosperous preseruation of the moste noble and Roÿall Estate of oure soueraÿne lorde kÿnge Henÿ the vuɩ. and Queue his quene.

and all theɩr progenɩtoɩs.

Pl. 9. Luton Art Museum, Dunstable Guild Register, fol. 5ᵛ, in a miniature space, John the Baptist; in the border, Henry VIII with guild members below.

174

Pl. 10. Luton Art Museum, Dunstable Guild Register, fol. 6ʳ, in miniature space, John the Baptist; in the border, Catherine of Aragon, with guild members below.

public depiction of the character of the reigning king, who would otherwise have been represented in documents and in law books, as well as on seals and coinage, either in armour on horseback or enthroned with sceptre and orb.

THE DONOR AND ORIGIN OF THE FRONTISPIECE

I now want to look at the production of the Luton frontispiece and, as far as possible, the roles in it of Edward IV, Thomas Rotherham, and the artist, who was indisputably continental and not an Englishman imitating foreign style. The composition of the scene, as a scheme of persons on a level below the religious icon, falls naturally into two registers, and the instructions given to the artist probably also embodied this register-like effect. In the lower register we recognize the traditional English pictorial usage; the main unusual aspect is the figure of Rotherham placed in a position of prominence over the king, bearing his coat of arms, with even the king not bearing his. The scroll and the words on it give Rotherham yet more importance as intercessor for members of the fraternity. The figure of Rotherham had to be the result of a special instruction, and who more likely than Rotherham himself? I feel reasonably certain that Rotherham took the commission for the frontispiece on himself, possibly selected the artist, probably gave instructions for its composition, and paid for it.[64] The recto of the frontispiece, fol. 13^r, with the title-page of the Register, also bears the arms of Rotherham in the introductory initial. Rotherham's well-documented interest in books and education might be another indication of his direct involvement. He is ranked among the great benefactors of Cambridge and Oxford universities, with the former receiving a gift of two hundred books from him.

When we return to the upper register of the Luton frontispiece, we are, however, in a non-English world, and I am less convinced that Rotherham gave precise instructions for this part of the miniature. He may have known of the continental form of the Image-of-Pity Trinity or may have simply given instructions for a Trinity and left the artist, whom he surely knew to be Flemish, to render what he knew. The continental origins of the subject cannot be sufficiently explored here, but a few earlier scenes from various media can at least be mentioned, perhaps to set a direction. Some versions of the Image-of-Pity Trinity were well known and probably to some extent responsible for the spread of the iconography in the Flemish arena; two of these are an altar of *c.* 1427-32, in the Städelsches Kunstinstitut, Frankfurt, and a Trinity in the Hermitage, Leningrad, both painted by the Master of Flémalle (?Robert Campion).[65] The standing postures in the former are closer to the York Corpus Christi glass (see below, p. 177), but in the latter both divine figures are seated, with Christ's body in a similar broken posture, under a tented canopy with curtains drawn back, similar to the form of the Luton miniature; the scene shows however no crystal orb. Another important Flemish representation is the central panel of the tapestries made for the Order of the Golden Fleece,

Bruges, in the second-third quarters of the fifteenth century, now in the Kunst-historisches Museum, Vienna.[66] A painting of *c.* 1440 by an anonymous artist contains other Luton elements, Christ's feet on a globe and angels supporting a cloth of honour.[67]

Certainly the only other similar renderings known at present for a British patron are the Trinity panels made for James IV of Scotland by Hugo van der Goes, after 1473 and probably before 1478. On stylistic grounds it has been suggested that the Trinity panels were done around 1475-6, almost at the time of the Luton frontispiece. Given the English interest in Flemish art and artists at this time, the concurrence of dates is probably synchronicity, not inter-dependence one way or the other. The central subject of the east window of Holy Trinity Church, York, is also worth mentioning in this context in that it also shows an Image-of-Pity Trinity, even if with God the Father and Christ both more or less standing and not enthroned. This window is connected with York guild of Corpus Christi, of which Thomas Rotherham became a member in 1489. The window itself, and I quote John Knowles, 'dates from about the year 1476'.[68]

As a brief afterword to this cluster of Luton-like images around 1475, I want to bring attention back to the earliest known analogy to the Luton frontispiece. The lower 'register' of some of the English counterparts might seem, from my discussion, to owe its origin and/or impetus to the obscure pen drawing in Harley 318 (Pl. 7); but this premise would turn the usual flow of influences back to front, that is, an insignificant image acting as cause of a more significant creation(s). It would however probably be more realistic to assume the exist-ence of a lost archetype of the royal family before a religious icon, a scene that was generally known or at least known to prominent patrons or artists of the period. Whatever the truth of this hypothesis, the pictorial subject was taken up during the reign of Henry VI and afterwards given considerable pictorial status as a mode of projecting both conventional royal piety and dynastic continuity through the presence of royal progeny. As sometimes happened in the later Middle Ages, the political and the religious found a common purpose and expression.

Lastly, as an inadequate but deep-felt tribute to Jeremy's talent and love of medieval English manuscripts, I want to close with the final passage of his talk concerning the Luton Register, given to the British Archaeological Association in April 1984:

'The final border and entry in the Register, that of 1546 ... contains no hint of the impending fate of the chantry and fraternities that were dissolved with them. ... At the time of its dissolution, the hall of the Luton Fraternity was apparently rented out ... [and] the chantry certificate [of dissolution] records that the guild had goods and ornaments worth only five pounds and no plate; it had been the most wealthy of the nine fraternities in Bedfordshire. The chantry certificate continues: "Ther hath no grammar nor precher ben found in the said Brotherhood syns the feast of St Michael the Archangel last past.

Item ther hath no money nor other profett ben paid to any porr person out of the said brotherhood at any time this five years intended to have continuance for ever. Also ther are resident two priests, the one priest John Johnson of the age of 60 years but meanly learned, not able to serve a cure. The other is called Robert Gregory of the age of 50 years, but meanly learned, not able to serve a cure and neither of them hath any other living but the said brother hood." Whatever the realities that lie behind these formulas, this passage has its own unavoidable simplicity.'

NOTES

*As long ago as 1983, Jeremy Griffiths and I planned to write a two-part study of the Luton Guild Register. Jeremy was to do the historical and social introduction as well as a description of the scribal hands and heraldry, while I was to describe the illustration and decoration. Jeremy and I were dilatory, and Richard Marks [see below n. 2] has in the meantime written an excellent study of both the Luton and Dunstable guild registers, which will now serve in place of Jeremy's contribution. I am most grateful to Richard Marks for sending me a copy of his study before publication and to Dr Elizabeth Adey, Keeper of Local History, for her kindness in allowing me to examine both manuscripts. I am also indebted to Chris Grabham for arranging for photographs of the two volumes.

1 H. F. Westlake, *The Parish Gilds of Medieval England*, London & New York, 1919, pp. 36ff.

2 The main literature with further bibliography concerning the Luton Register is in Sotheby's, *Catalogue of the Bute Collection of forty-two Illuminated Manuscripts and Miniatures*, London, 13 June 1983, lot 19, with seven plates (two in colour); J. Lunn, 'The Luton Fraternity Register', *Bedfordshire Magazine*, 19 (1984), 177-82; and R. Marks, 'Two Illuminated Guild Registers from Bedfordshire,' in *Illuminating the Book: Makers and Interpreters; Essays in honour of Janet Backhouse*, ed. by M. P. Brown & S. McKendrick (London, 1998), pp. 120-41. The Register is on parchment, of 130 fols + 3 flyleaves, with 26 lines of prose; it measures 28.6 × 20.5 cm at fol. 13^r. A calendar is on fols 1^r-6^v, with three-line gold KL initials on a rose and blue ground without a border or spraywork; fols 7^r-12^v are blanks; and the Register begins on fol. 13^r. Decoration, apart from the calendar, includes: text written in gold, silver, and blue; calligraphic ascenders; line endings; gold letters on a rose and blue ground with sprays of green-tinted feathering and gold motifs of pinecones and balls on fols 15^r, 16^r, 17^{r-v}, 18^r, 19^{r-v}, 20^{r-v}, 21^{r-v}, 22^{r-v}, 23^{r-v}, and 24^{r-v} (by the same hand); a two-sided border on fols 18^v and 32^v; and thirty-two 3- or 4-sided borders. See text above for list of illustrations.

3 See as an example of this practice the miniature with the service for the dead in London, British Library, Add. MS 50001, Hours of Elizabeth the Queen, fol. 55^v, in which mourners carry torches in addition to elaborate candlesticks with tapers placed at each end of the bier. Scenes with torches only are in, e.g. Cambridge, Trinity College, MS B.11.7, Hours, fol. 80^r; Fitzwilliam Museum, MS 2-1967, Hours, fol. 114^r; BL Add. MS 42131, Bedford Hours and Psalter, fol. 46^r; and New York, Pierpont Morgan Library, M 893, Hours and Psalter, fol. 60^r.

4 See M. Rubin, *Corpus Christi: The Eucharist in Late Medieval Culture* (Cambridge, 1991), pp. 243-71.

5 For the use of ceremonial lights during religious offices in England at this period, see J. C. Cox, *Churchwardens' Accounts from the Fourteenth Century to the close of the Seventeenth Century* (London, 1913), pp. 160-6.

6 Westlake (cited above, n. 1), p. 155.

7 E. M. Carus Wilson, 'The Overseas Trade of Bristol' in *Studies in English Trade in the Fifteenth Century*, ed. by E. Power & M. M. Postan (London, reissued 1966), p. 232. Miniatures in books of Hours accompanying the service for the dead invariably show the bier with tapers; some miniatures may show only the bier and candlesticks, omitting clerics and mourners

Pl. 11. London, British Library, MS Arundel 302, Book of Hours, fol. 77ᵛ. Service for the dead, with clerics, bier and candles.

rather than the candles. A miniature (fol. 77ᵛ) such as that in BL, Arundel MS 302, Hours, gives a real sense of the importance of candles to the rite for the dead (Pl. 11).

8 See Westlake, pp. 136-238, for a listing of the various foundation purposes of religious fraternities.

9 Oxford, Bodleian Library, MS Bodley 283; see K. L. Scott, *Later Gothic Manuscripts*, vol. VI of *A Survey of Manuscripts Illuminated in the British Isles*, gen. ed. J. J. G. Alexander (London, 1996), II, cat. no. 136, for further literature, and I, ills. 487-9, 494.

10 Lunn (cited above, n. 2), p. 180.

11 Lunn, pp. 179-80.

12 I owe the preceding information to Jeremy Griffith's unpublished talk on the Luton fraternity, given to the British Archaeological Association in April 1984. The Luton fraternity account book is in the Bedford County Record Office.

13 Marks (cited above, n. 2), p. 136 and passim for further comments on the economic and social position of the Luton fraternity.

14 For a description of the variation in such guilds in size and influence, see M. Keen, *English Society in the Later Middle Ages 1348-1500* (London, 1990), pp. 102, 103-4, 274-5.

15 The royalty (and nobility) were more commonly members of merchant guilds in London; the Skinners' Company, for instance, commemorated the induction *c.* 1473 of Edward IV's queen, Elizabeth, with a three-quarter page miniature (reproduced in Scott (cited above, n. 9), I, ill. 473, cat. no. 130) and inducted Queen Margaret, widow of Henry VI, into the Fraternity in 1475 (J. F. Wadmore, *Some Account of the Worshipful Company of Skinners of London* (London, 1902), p. 41; miniature reproduced in C. Meale, 'Patrons, buyers and owners: book production and social status', in *Book Production and Publishing in Britain 1375-1475*, ed. by J. Griffiths & D. Pearsall (Cambridge, 1989), pp. 201-38, fig. 21). The nobility are also frequently found as members of merchants' fraternities; the Skinners received Lord Fitzhugh in 1464 and John, Earl of Oxford, in 1478; and the guild of Corpus Christi, Goodramgate, York, also had high-ranking members such as Cecily, duchess of York, in 1456 and the duke and duchess of Gloucester in 1489 (J. A. Knowles, *Essays in the History of the York School of Glass-Painting* (London & New York, 1936), p. 169).

16 The 'sancte et indiuidue Trinitatis' of the introductory paragraph of the manuscript (fol. 13ʳ); no visual reference is made to the Blessed Virgin Mary, who shares in the Fraternity's name.

17 Marks, p. 134.

18 The initials historiated with royal coats of arms are on fols 14ʳ, 35ᵛ, 37ʳ, 39ʳ, 42ʳ, 43ʳ, 44ʳ, 45ᵛ, 47ʳ, 48ᵛ, 54ʳ, 56ʳ, 58ʳ, 70ʳ, 72ʳ, 77ʳ, 84ʳ, 87ʳ, 100ʳ, 104ʳ, 106ᵛ, 108ʳ, 110ʳ, 114ʳ, 115ʳ, 118ʳ, 120ᵛ, and 122ᵛ.

19 The second option is favoured by the Sotheby's cataloguer and by Marks, p. 122, pointing up the difficulty in identifying 'portraits'.

20 This particular type of Trinity is also called the 'Trinity of the Broken Body' by E. Panofsky (*Early Netherlandish Painting; Its Origins and Character* (Cambridge, Mass., 1953), I, pp. 335-6; II, pl. 310, fig. 468); and a 'Corpus Christi subject' by Knowles (cited above, n. 15), pp. 171, 172.

21 Reproduced in Marks, fig. 85. The posture of the stags may derive from a playing card motif; see A. H. van Buren & S. Edmunds, 'Playing Cards and Manuscripts: Some widely disseminated fifteenth-century model sheets', *The Art Bulletin*, LVI (1974), 12-30, fig. 6, the two of Deer.

22 J. Griffiths made this tentative identification of the implement.

23 Reproduced in Marks, fig. 81.

24 Reproduced in Marks, fig. 82.

25 Reproduced in Marks, fig. 83.

26 Identified by Marks, p. 122.

27 The Dunstable Register is discussed below, p. 173; see Pls 9 & 10. The frontispiece of the Register of the Guild of St Anne, Ghent, of 1477, in the Royal Library at Windsor Castle, attributed to the Master of Mary of Burgundy, may also be of interest in that it shows

member-figures in the lower border. Although in a continental manuscript, it has one member of the English royal family, Margaret of York (together with Mary of Burgundy) kneeling before a statute of St Anne (reproduced in G. Ring, review of O. Pächt, *The Master of Mary of Burgundy* (London, 1948), in *The Burlington Magazine*, 91 (1949), 86-7, fig. 26).

28 For a survey of some donor scenes in fifteenth-century English book art, see K. L. Scott, 'Caveat Lector: Ownership and Standardization in the Illustration of Fifteenth-Century English Manuscripts', in *English Manuscript Studies 1100-1700*, ed. by P. Beal & J. Griffiths, I (1989), pp. 19-63, esp. 21-2, pls 5-6, 10-14.

29 BL, Add. MSS 29704-5, fol. 193ᵛ; reproduced in M. Rickert, *The Reconstructed Carmelite Missal: An English Manuscript of the late XIV Century* (London, 1952), p. 115, pls D (colour), XXXIII; for another manuscript example, see Oxford, Keble College, MS 47, Hours, last quarter of 14th century, fol. 9ʳ, man and woman praying before Virgin and Child; reproduced in L. F. Sandler, *Gothic Manuscripts 1285-1385*, in Alexander, *Survey* (cited above, n. 9), 1986, I, ill. 387 (cat. no. 146).

30 See Sandler, I, ills. 77, 199, 248.

31 See, for example, BL, Royal MS 2.A.xviii, Beaufort Hours and Psalter, fol. 23ᵛ; reproduced in Rickert (see n. 29 above), pl. LI; and in Scott, I, ill. 161. See also Bodl., MS Lat. liturg. f. 2, Hours, *c.* 1400, fol. 2ᵛ, with a scene of a man and woman in adoration of the Transfiguration (reproduced in O. Pächt & J. J. G. Alexander, *Illuminated Manuscripts in the Bodleian Library Oxford*, III: British, Irish and Icelandic Schools (Oxford, 1973), no. 795, pl. LXXVII; and Philadelphia, Free Library, MS Widener 3, Hours, made *c.* 1470-80, on the continent for an English patron, John Brown, with a man and woman kneeling before a Mass of St Gregory.

32 York, Minster Library, MS Add. 2, Hours and prayers, fol. 33ʳ; reproduced in Scott, I, ill. 138 (cat. no. 33).

33 See, for example, BL, Arundel MS 109, Missal, before 1446, fol. 262ᵛ, a male patron kneeling before a Crucifix-Trinity.

34 Bodl., MS Eng. poet.a.1, miscellany, fol. 265ʳ; reproduced in Pächt & Alexander, III, no. 676, pl. LXX; A. I. Doyle, *The Vernon Manuscript: A Facsimile of Bodleian Library, Oxford, MS. Eng. poet.a.1* (Cambridge, 1987); and Scott, I, ill. 3 (cat. no. 1).

35 San Marino, Huntington Library, HM 1067, fol. 148ᵛ; reproduced in C. W. Dutschke, *Guide to Medieval and Renaissance Manuscripts in the Huntington Library* (San Marino, 1989), fig. 94.

36 Bodl., MS Digby 227, fol. 113ᵛ; reproduced in M. Rickert, *Painting in Britain: the Middle Ages*, (Harmondsworth, 2nd edn, 1965), pl. 186; Scott, I, ill. 382 (cat. no. 101a).

37 See D. Gordon, *Making and Meaning: The Wilton Diptych*, with C. M. Barron, A. Ray, & M. Wyld (London, 1993).

38 Paris, Bibliothèque nationale, MS n.a 1.3145, fol. 3ᵛ; reproduced in F. Avril & P. D. Stirneman, *Manuscrits enluminés d'origine insulaire VIIe-XXe siècle* (Paris, 1987), pl. XCVI (cat. no. 219).

39 Oxford, Jesus College, MS 124; reproduced in J. J. G. Alexander & E. Temple, *Illuminated Manuscripts in Oxford College Libraries, The University Archives and the Taylor Institution* (Oxford, 1985), no. 564, pl. XXXII.

40 The charters show Henry VI before a conflated image of the Assumption and Coronation of the Virgin. The King's document is reproduced in J. J. G. Alexander, 'William Abell "lymnour" and 15th Century English Illumination', in *Kunsthistorische Forschungen Otto Pächt zu seinem 70. Geburtstag*, ed. by A. Rosenauer & G. Weber (Salzburg, 1972), pp. 166-72, fig. 2. The King's charter is distinguished from the other by showing the figure of a bishop-saint who stands next to the Assumption, making a gesture of intercession towards the kneeling king. The devotional subjects in these documents would relate to the institutions, not to the king.

41 The charter of Henry VI of 19 August 1444 to the Leathersellers' Company, London, should also be noticed, even if the king is not in the act of devotion. Here he is again in the initial space, isolated from the merchant classes, handing a charter to five groups of citizens who kneel below on swatches of earth. This charter is reproduced in full by W. H. Black, *History and Antiquities of the Worshipful Company of Leathersellers* (London, 1871), at rear; and in part

by G. Unwin, *The Gilds and Companies of London* (London, 1927), facing p. 162. See also the reproduction in Sotheby's, *Western Manuscripts and Miniatures*, London, 19 June 1990, lot 70, of the introductory initial to a document of June 1485, containing a Virgin and Child, adored by a group of Cistercian nuns and the abbess at a *prie-Dieu*. The nuns are drawn outside of the initial in the margin; and the initial is surmounted by a royal crown with lion supporters, recording the virtual presence of King Richard III. The text is of royal letters patent to the Cistercian nunnery of Esholt, West Yorkshire.

42 Oxford, Christ Church, MS 92, Walter of Milemete, *De nobilitatibus, sapientiis, et prudentiis regum*, fol. 3ʳ; reproduced in Sandler (cited above, n. 29), I, ill. 217 (cat. no. 84).

43 The miniature (fol. 18ᵛ) is in the part of the copy before an inscription with the date 1468 (fol. 25ʳ): 'Deo gras. qd. sc'psit dns Thomas Hasulden/Anno dni millmo CCCCmo sexagesimo octauo;' reproduced in Alexander & Temple, no. 587, pl. XXXIV.

44 There is something rather touching about the semi-circular workaday chair used for the 'throne' of the Trinity in Harley 318 – in contrast to the iconographically standard platform-bench of the Jesus College miniature (cf. Pls 7 and 8).

45 The main distinction in visual themes between this drawing and the Luton frontispiece (as well as other later images of its type) is the extensive use of inscribed scrolls in the drawing.

46 For the books of Edward IV, see A. F. Sutton & L. Visser-Fuchs, 'Choosing a Book in Late Fifteenth-century England and Burgundy', in *England and the Low Countries in the late Middle Ages*, ed. by C. Barron & N. Saul (New York, 1995), pp. 75-6, 78, 79-81.

47 Rare Book Department, MS European 201; reproduced in Scott, I, ill. 393 (cat. no. 104).

48 G. McN. Rushforth, *Medieval Christian Imagery as illustrated by the painted windows of Great Malvern Priory Church Worcestershire* (Oxford, 1936), p. 375. The window is known partly through remains and partly from a 17th-century polemical tract; the section of the tract concerning the Canterbury window is printed in full in M. H. Caviness, *The Windows of Christ Church Cathedral Canterbury*, Corpus Vitrearum Medii Aevi, Great Britain, vol. II (London, 1981), p. 253.

49 Edward IV and Elizabeth had three boys and seven girls. Since three male figures, two with gold collars, are shown behind the religious personages, the first two would seem to represent royal children. Margaret, however, died eight months after her birth on 10 April 1472, and three other daughters, Anna, Catherine, and Bridget, as well as one son, George, were born either in or after 1475, when the frontispiece was made.

50 Royal children in a devotional scene (below the Virgin and Child adored by the Magi) had been rendered *c.* 1360 in a wall-painting made for St Stephen's Chapel, Westminster. This painting shows Edward III and his family, kneeling, wearing heraldic surcoats and bearing identifying labels (see F. Hepburn, *Portraits of the Later Plantagenets* (Woodbridge, 1986), pp. 90-1; a copy of the paintings made by J. T. Smith in 1807 is reproduced by J. J. G. Alexander, 'Painting and Manuscript Illumination for Royal Patrons in the Later Middle Ages', in *English Court Culture in the Later Middle Ages*, ed. by V. J. Scattergood & J. W. Sherborne (London, 1983), pls 3, 4).

51 See C. Thompson & L. Campbell, *Hugo van der Goes and the Trinity Panels in Edinburgh* (National Galleries of Scotland, 1974), for a study of these panels and for reproductions of them and related Continental scenes; and for Bonkil, pp. 13, 37-9.

52 The uncertainties associated with these dates are explained by Thompson & Campbell, pp. 55-6.

53 Thompson & Campbell, p. 57.

54 Ibid.

55 Because three scribes are involved in this manuscript of only seven folios, it may have been made in two or three stages: the petition in 1503 by Hand A (to mid-page on fol. 2ᵛ); the ordinances by Hand B, fols 3ʳ-6ʳ; [blank = fol. 6ᵛ]; and a list of names of masters of the guild 1503-1517 by Hand C (fol. 7ʳ). Although by two scribes, the petition and ordinances are a logical unit and may well have been made at the same time, with the masters' names compiled at the later date of *c.* 1517.

56 Reproduced in Alexander & Temple (cited above, n. 39), no. 823, pl. LVI. Three boys (Arthur, Henry, and Edmund) had been born by 1503; and although four are shown, only two girls (Margaret and Mary) had survived infancy. If the dead could join fraternities, perhaps they could also be rendered in paintings. For further discussion of this manuscript, see Marks (cited above, n. 2), n. 18.

57 The rendering of Henry VII's face is particularly sensitive and may show elements of a portrait. I have not entered into the thorny area of portraiture with respect to any of the royal figures in this study.

58 See especially the Quadripartite Indentures: BL, Harley MS 28, *c.* 1504-5, fol. 1ʳ; Harley MS 1498, dated 1503, fol. 1ʳ; London, Public Record Office E 33/2, dated 1504; Bodl., MS Barlow 28, dated 1504, fol. 1ʳ; and MS Rawl. C. 370, dated 1504, fol. 1ʳ. See also BL, Royal MS 12.B.VI, *Liber de optimo fato*, probably made for Henry VII; and Westminster Abbey Library, MS 39, prayer book of Margaret Beaufort, mother of Henry VII, early 16th century.

59 Reproduced in Hepburn (cited above, n. 50), fig. 62. Three young men are again shown behind Henry and four young women behind Elizabeth. The royal family are referred to as 'donors' (p. 93). The royal figures are in fact more integral thematically than donors. The picture also states that, even if commissioners of the panel, the family is still subject in their piety to the sanctity of the national emblem of the saint. Hepburn has a useful discussion of the place of these figures, whom he sees as 'little more than royal symbols', in the history of English portraiture.

60 The princess and castle of the St George legend are as usual situated in the landscape of the background.

61 A 'Magnificat' window in the transept of Woburn Abbey, probably complete by late December 1501 (Rushforth (cited above, n. 48), p. 369), showed in its original state Henry VII in armour, Elizabeth of York (now lost), and their heir, Arthur, Prince of Wales, with three courtiers behind him, kneeling at prayer tables; all looking in one direction. Here the images of the royal family are more likely to commemorate a donation and to serve a local political purpose, a symbolic 'taking possession' of Malvern (Rushforth, p. 375) rather than to display royal piety or special devotion to the Virgin.

62 This register is also in the Luton Art Museum, Wardown Park, Luton. For further information concerning the manuscript, see Marks, pp. 123-7, figs 87-90.

63 Marks, p. 127.

64 Marks, p. 130, thinks it is likely that the costs of the first leaves were 'borne personally by the president during his year of office', since the guild accounts do not indicate any payments for writing or decoration of the register.

65 Panofsky (cited above, n. 20), II, pl. 93, fig. 207; and II, pl. 95, fig. 210.

66 G. Schiller, *Iconography of Christian Art*, II: The Passion of Jesus Christ, trans. by J. Seligman (Greenwich, Conn., 1972), fig. 783.

67 Schiller, fig. 771; and Schiller reproduces other subjects of this type. See also Keble, MS 35, prayers, in German, 15th-16th centuries, fol. 3ʳ, reproduced in colour in M. B. Parkes, *The Medieval Manuscripts of Keble College Oxford* (London, 1979), pl. III, which has all the Luton elements, apart from the globe; and see also the sculpted oak image of Father and Son from ?Brabant, second half of 15th century, in the Musée Diocésain, Liège, reproduced in *Flanders in the Fifteenth Century: Art and Civilization*, exhibition catalogue (Detroit, 1960), no. 93, p. 257.

68 Knowles (cited above, n. 15), p. 169; Cecily, mother of Edward IV, had also been inducted some years earlier. For the Image-of-Pity Trinity, see Knowles, Pl. XLV(C).

THE BOOK AND THE BROTHERHOOD

Reflections on the Lost Library of Syon Abbey

VINCENT GILLESPIE

ON 21 APRIL 1420 five priests, twenty-seven sisters, two deacons, and three lay brethren were solemnly professed as the first members of the English Bridgettine house, to be known as the monastery of Saint Saviour and Saint Bridget of Syon, of the Order of Saint Augustine.[1] Among their number was Thomas Fishbourn, soon to be elected first Confessor-General, and a priest whose monastic trajectory epitomizes many of the distinguishing features of this power-house of late-medieval spirituality. Fishbourn's involvement with the King's royal foundation of Syon goes back at least as far as January 1416, when he was a member of Bishop Stephen Patrington's committee of inquiry into various constitutional disputes at the nascent house. This committee met at the command of, and apparently in the presence of, Henry V, and drew up the *Articuli Extracti* to resolve disagreements between the King's initial nominees as Abbess and Confessor-General (neither of whom was still involved in the order by the time of the solemn professions in 1420).[2]

The confirmation of Fishbourn's election as Confessor-General in 1421 must have seemed like a judicious and highly satisfactory outcome to a difficult, protracted and troubled birth, for he drew together two important strands in the abbey's early history. Through his links (still not altogether clear) with the abbey of St Alban's, he represented the strong influence of that house on the early life and early legislation of Syon (not least on the committee set up to devise the Syon additions to the Rule of St Saviour for both sisters and brethren, and through the advice and guidance of Abbot John Whethampstead in the stormy early years of the house following the death of Henry V in 1422 and the papal bull of the same year in which Martin V outlawed double orders).[3] Through his links with the king (the *Martiloge* describes him as 'regis fundatoris confessor et consiliarius'), he reflected and embodied Henry's devotion and commitment to his new foundation. Thomas Gascoigne, sometime Chancellor of Oxford University, benefactor and regular visitor to Syon and source of well-informed gossip on the early years of the house and on the cult of Bridget in England, praised Fishbourn as 'valde Deo devotum', claiming that before his entry into religion 'fuit magnus armiger et denotus in boria Angliae'.[4] Fishbourn also typifies another characteristic of the brethren in his donation or bequest of at least eighteen books to their library at or before his death in 1428.[5]

A little over a year after the first professions, Henry V drew up his last will at Dover on 10 June 1421 and, after signing and sealing it, left England for the last time.[6] His twin foundations of Syon and Sheen were still much in his mind. In his will, he included St Bridget in the list of saints to whom he looks for assistance. To both foundations he leaves the sum of 1000 pounds to be spent on their construction 'de lapidibus uel saltem tegula vocatur "bryk"'. But his benefactions reveal that it was to Syon that his fatherly interest turned most readily. He leaves the abbey his three-volume glossed Bible and 'omnes libros nostros modo existentes in custodia sua', with the exception of the great Bible owned by his own father which he wishes passed on to his successors.[7] Royal books were, then, according to the will, already in the care of Syon before the King's death. Henry leaves his books of meditation and those useful for preaching the Gospel to be divided equally between Syon and Sheen, stipulating that the preaching books should all go to Syon because the brethren there are required to preach and the Carthusians are forbidden so to do. On 26 August 1422, only five days before his death, Henry added a codicil specifying again that Syon should have all the preaching books and instructing that neither house should possess duplicate copies of any work. The royal library had, in fact, recently been augmented by the addition of some 110 books captured after the siege of the Market of Meaux earlier in 1422.[8]

This royal benefaction ought to be seen as the founding collection of the Syon abbey library (or libraries, as it is clear that there were separate collections for the sisters and the brethren, probably in addition to collections of liturgical and other books needed for the office of the order).[9] But, as with much of the history of this richly fascinating and challenging collection, nothing is quite as simple as it looks. The surviving catalogue of the library of the Brethren, drawn up and partly revised by Thomas Betson in the very early years of the sixteenth century, makes no mention of the royal books.[10] These would surely have been a prized possession as a benefaction from a founder who stands first in memory in the order's *Martiloge*, dating in its earliest form from 1431, well within living memory of the first professions and of the King's death. But the *Martiloge* fails to make any mention of the king in connection with gifts of books. Indeed early benefactions to the library are not specifically mentioned in the *Martiloge* until the record of a community decision reached in 1471, where the status of proto-benefactors goes instead to Thomas Grant, canon and precentor of St Paul's (who died in that year) and to his parents. It may be that the library at Syon was not the intellectual treasure-house in the first half century of the house's existence that it was later to become.[11]

Quite what happened to those royal books destined for Syon is unclear. Maybe they suffered the fate of the remainder of his books which were left to the University of Oxford, which was still, in 1437, vainly petitioning Duke Humfrey for his help in securing their delivery. They seem never to have arrived, and many of the books captured at Meaux went instead to King's Hall, Cambridge. The failure of the bequest is odd, especially as one of the executors was Henry Fitzhugh, who had first conceived the plan of bringing a house of Bridgettines to England and had visited the mother house of Vadstena in 1406 to arrange the first abortive plantation, located outside York. (Fitzhugh is himself commemorated in the *Martiloge*, second only to Henry in the pecking order of prayer.) It may be that the clause in Henry's codicil instructing that all books not otherwise bequeathed should remain with the king's son 'pro libraria sua' somehow overrode the main bequest.[12]

But Henry's benefaction, whether executed or not, draws attention to one of the main reasons why a relatively small number of brethren (no more than thirteen priests, four deacons, and eight lay brethren when the house was at full size, compared to the sixty nuns in the other house, the whole community of eighty-five meant to represent the apostles (including St Paul) and the disciples) should have required a library at all. Nominally the order followed the Rule of St Augustine, in obedience to papal decrees concerned at the proliferation of private religions in the fourteenth century. In practice, the order observed the *Regula Salvatoris* (miraculously revealed and dictated to Bridget), with special additions for both the brethren and sisters negotiated and developed as customary practice in the English house through dialogue with Vadstena. In February 1425, after various political alarms and excursions, Fishbourn persuaded Pope Martin V to issue the bull *Mare Anglicanum* which gave Syon a large measure of constitutional independence from Vadstena and from the General Chapter of the order.[13] But although Syon developed some idiosyncratic customs (particularly in regard to the power of the local bishop (in Syon's case, London) and over the election of the abbess by the nuns alone), the house observed the spirit and most of the letter of the rule. Chapter 15 of the *Regula Salvatoris* requires priests to expound the Gospel in the vernacular every Sunday at Mass in the presence of all the nuns, and to preach publicly at all major feasts. They were also to accept confessions, and had the canonical status of minor penitentiaries.[14] That the preaching office of the brethren was taken seriously is suggested by the provision in the vernacular *Additions* for the brethren which allowed a preacher three days' remission from choir duties 'to recorde hys sermon'.[15] Indeed seven Syon brethren are recorded in Betson's index to his catalogue as having had their sermons preserved in the library at some point, six of whom are credited with no other form of literary output. Several further entries in the catalogue record donations by named brethren of anonymous sermons, and these may camouflage more of their own compositions. Unlike many contemplative orders, the Syon brethren were expected to have a decisive and effective pastoral programme and to offer spiritual guidance and leadership. This was integral to the order's self-perception, and explains why Syon became, from early in its history, such a place of resort for those seeking spiritual direction across the social spectrum from Margery Kempe to Margaret Beaufort; from Thomas Gascoigne to Thomas More; from Margaret Duchess of Clarence to Elizabeth Barton, the Fair Maid of Kent.

Books must have been an important part of the intellectual life of the brethren. The *Regula Salvatoris* allowed books to be received 'as many as be necessary to doo dyuyne office and moo in no wyse', and also provided that 'Thoo bookes they shalt haue as many as they wylle in whiche ys to seruen or to studye'.[16] The pattern of recruitment, especially in the later years of the fifteenth century and into the sixteenth century, shows a high percentage of graduate entrants, and some very high-powered academic recruits, including several former heads of house at Oxford and Cambridge. Many of these men brought all or part of their books with them on profession (some made selected donations to their *alma mater* on resignation). Stephen Sawndre, for example, fifth Confessor-General from 1497 to his death in 1513, was previously a fellow of Pembroke Hall, Cambridge, and left three books to them on his resignation, probably to join Syon; Betson's catalogue records eighteen of his books in the brethren's collection. John Trowell, who left Merton College, Oxford, as vice-Warden in 1491, left Merton three books and gave Syon twelve.[17] Even in its early years, when the library seems to have been less substantial and wide-ranging, the house benefited from the generosity of its brethren. The core of the early library was the magnificent collection of at least one hundred and eleven volumes given by John Bracebridge, who had enjoyed a successful career as a grammar master in Lincoln diocese before resigning in 1420, perhaps to become one of the original professed priests.[18]

Many of the identified donors to the library were priest-brethren of the order, though benefactions from at least two lay brethren are also recorded. External gifts to the library came from academics, nobility, the printer Wynkyn de Worde (who seems to have had a close spiritual and commercial relationship with the house), and secular clergy. Early donors of property and money in-cluded Queen Catherine of Valois (widow of Henry V), John Duke of Bedford (Regent after Henry's death, who took over the role of protector of Syon and laid the foundation stone when the convent moved up river in 1426 to its final home opposite Sheen at Isleworth), the Hungerford and Boleyn families, and several well-placed and wealthy merchants and/or their relicts. Powerful friends included bishops and ecclesiastics such as Cardinal Beaufort, Richard Clifford, and Henry Chichele.[19] Margaret Duchess of Clarence, an early noble lay donor to the library, struck up a close relationship with one of the early brethren Symon Wynter (d. 1448) who translated for her the life of St Jerome and seems to have acted as her confessor.[20] Of the over 1400 volumes recorded in the final recension of Betson's library catalogue, only 200 have not been specifically assigned to a donor (and in some of these 200 cases the donor's name may have been erased). So the development of the library at Syon was heavily indebted to the generosity of its own brethren and of their admirers and supporters.

The death in 1471 of Thomas Graunte, a priest of St Paul's cathedral, whose twenty-six donations recorded in the catalogue constitute a substantial collection of multi-work miscellany manuscripts, prompted the addition of special provision in the *Martiloge* for benefactors to the library. The service of the dead with nine readings and a requiem mass are to be said for those who provide books for 'librarie sororum vel librarie fratrum' or who provide books for common use. On the brethren's side, the service is to be said by the priest brother who currently holds the deputed office of *custos librorum* or *librarie*, a post whose existence is confirmed from other documentary sources, notably the Library Ordinances of 1482.[21] The 1471 document implies the existence of at least three collections of books at Syon: the library of the sisters, the library of the brethren, and the collection of books held for common (and probably liturgical) use. But earlier Syon documents imply the emergence of a book culture early in the life of the house: the vernacular *Additions* to the Rule for the Sisters and for the Brethren, dating from the first half of the fifteenth century (though surviving only in much later copies), both include specific prescriptions against the mistreatment of books and require silence in what is explicitly called 'the lybrary'.[22]

It is important, however, when assessing the nature and size of book holdings at Syon, to remember not only that there were at least these three collections, but also that books could and probably did move between them and that the catalogue of the brethren's library as it survives today represents a snapshot, or a series of snapshots, of the holdings as they were in one of the house's collections at one phase in its relatively short history.[23] For reasons to be outlined below, it is unlikely that Betson's catalogue, or the additions and alterations made to it after his death, represent a summative account of the collective holdings amassed in a century of considered accumulation. Rather the evidence suggests that the collection was labile, fluid, and strikingly responsive to changes in fashion, focus, and need among its users.

Books arrived in both houses and libraries at Syon from external benefactors; they arrived with priests entering the order as brethren; but, judging by the donations attributed to the brethren in Betson's catalogue, they also continued to arrive for the use of those brethren after they had entered the order. In the early years after the first professions, Syon sought guidance from the mother-house at Vadstena on a number of procedural and constitutional points. Vadstena replied in a series of *responsiones* dating from 1421 and 1427. *Responsio* 132 allows brethren to receive books *after* they have been professed.[24] This seems particularly to have been the case in the late fifteenth and early sixteenth centuries, a period of great growth in the size of the collection, when a number of the brethren had arrived not only with substantial and impressive academic reputations but also with substantial and impressive academic libraries. Late donors to the collection include at least one head of a Cambridge college: Edyman, Master of Corpus, in 1515. J. Watson, Master of Christ's from 1517 to 1531, was a correspondent of the noted Syon brother and eventual martyr St Richard Reynolds, himself the most substantial donor of books to the later collection, with 94 volumes attributed to him in the catalogue.[25]

Syon embraced the potential of the printing press early. Books printed in the 1460s and early 1470s are easily identified in the surviving catalogue.[26] As so many of the later accessions to the brethren's library were printed books, and because Betson established the practice of recording the *secundo folio* of nearly all the books he catalogued (a practice continued in the post-Betson recension of the catalogue) it is possible in some cases to identify donations associated with particular priest-brethren which cannot have come into the house with them on their profession because their publication post-dates that profession. Betson's good curatorial habit of including the *secundo folio* for each pressmark is invaluable, as it usually allows discrimination between the various early printed editions of a particular work to pinpoint the precise edition that found its way into the library at Syon. Such acquisitions were, of course, in keeping with the permissive tone of the *Regula Salvatoris* with regard to books for study.

Stephen Sawndre, Confessor-General from 1497 to 1513, resigned his Cambridge fellowship in 1478. He perhaps brought with him what is now D30 (the Cologne 1475 edition of Augustine of Ancona's *De ecclesiastica potestate*) and D35, the Venice 1477 edition of the *quodlibets* of Scotus edited by Thomas Penketh. But he must have subsequently acquired or been given C17 (the Venice 1491 edition of Antonius Andreae's *quaestiones* on the *Metaphysics* of Aristotle) and A10 (Perotti's *Grammaticae* and of his *Ars epistolandi*, whose *secundo folio* agrees with the editions of Paris 1488 and Lyon 1492).

Richard Terenden, a Fellow of New College, Oxford, in 1473, has books printed in Nuremberg 1475 (H41), Venice 1480 (T54), Nuremberg 1484 (K49-51), 1485 (L46), Nuremberg 1487 (E60-64), Strasbourg 1490 (M99), Nuremberg 1498 (T66), and Strasbourg 1501 (T62), some of which will certainly have been acquired after his profession. He seems to have been systematically acquiring new printed books for over twenty years. Among his acquisitions are some significant books: the four-volume Bible with the postills of Nicholas of Lyre, printed by Koburger in Nuremberg 1487; the 1490 Strasbourg edition of the *Legenda aurea*; and several canon law texts such as the Strasbourg 1501 edition of Durandus's *Rationale diuinorum officiorum* and the 1498 Nuremberg edition of the *Summa Angelica* of Angelo de Clavisio.

Richard Reynolds, a prolific donor to the collection, had been a Fellow of Corpus Christi College, Cambridge, and is recorded as donor of books printed after his profession at Syon in 1513, such as the Paris 1516 edition of Jacques Le Fèvre's commentary on the *Ethics* and *Politics* of Aristotle (now C1); or his Venice 1516 edition of Bessarion (C5). His copy of the sermons of Gabriel Biel (R38) has a *secundo folio* which agrees with Hagenau editions printed in 1510 and 1519, so it is unclear if he acquired it pre- or post-profession, but his copy of Johannes Raulyn's quadragesimal sermons (S24-5) was the Paris 1519 edition, and his copy of Raulyn's penitential sermons must post-date the *editio princeps* in Lyon 1518. His copy of Thomas Ringstead's commentary on the book of Proverbs was in fact the Paris 1515 edition that attributed the work to Robert Holcot (G23), while his copy of Petrus de Natalibus's *Cathologus Sanctorum* was the Lyon 1514 edition (M85).

Another substantial late donor to the collection was John Fewterer, Fellow of Pembroke Hall, Cambridge, still active in Cambridge as late as 1515, and Confessor-General during the troubled years leading up to the suppression (he died in 1536), whose donations included the massive nine-volume edition of Jerome edited by Erasmus and printed in Basel 1516 (H49-53) and Iohannes Oecolampadius's index to the Erasmus Jerome (H54) which was not published until 1520, and predated his election as Confessor-General by only three years. It is likely that he acquired both after joining the brethren. He gave also two volumes of the Basel 1521 edition of the works of Bede (I2-3). Fewterer in particular seems to have actively acquired printed books well into the mid-1520s, when the upkeep of the surviving catalogue seems to have been abandoned (or was perhaps transferred to another catalogue, of which no trace survives). His copy of the works of Fulgentius and Iohannes Maxentius (O43) has a *secundo folio* that agrees with the editions from Hagenau 1520 and Cologne 1526. If it was the latter, this would make this the latest dateable accession to the catalogue, but even the earlier edition would post-date his arrival at Syon. Other donors in the 1520s included Henry VIII, who gave a copy of his 1521 *Assertio septem sacramentorum aduersus Martinum Lutherum* (O23), and one Langton, probably not a member of the community as his name does not occur in the *Martiloge*, who gave the Erasmus New Testament para-phrases (Basel 1522: H57), his paraphrases on the Acts of the Apostles (Basel 1524: I54), and Theophylact of Constantinople's *Enarrationes in quattuor euangelia* (Basel 1524: H58). Another post-1520 accession was the Basel 1521 edition of Tertullian (N43), with no donor identified in the catalogue (perhaps a purchase for the community). But it is probably significant that there are relatively few recorded donations of post-1515 editions (Betson died in 1516), and very few recorded donations by brethren after 1520. Accessions or purchases may gradually have stopped being recorded in the 'Betson' catalogue. Indeed several volumes have survived which were known to have been owned by Fewterer in Syon but which are not recorded in the catalogue in its final phase.[27]

An earlier confrater, Lawsby, who died in 1490, presumably acquired his copy of the pseudo-Bonaventuran *Meditationes vitae Christi* only shortly before his death as the *secundo folio* given by Betson agrees with the edition printed in [Paris] and dated by *ISTC* [*c*. 1490] (*GW* 4743).[28] Thomas Westhaw, third Confessor-General, had been a Fellow of Pembroke Hall, Cambridge, in 1436, and had previously been professed as a Carthusian of Sheen in 1459 before transferring to Syon where he became Confessor-General from 1472 to his death in 1488. Among his gifts were several collections (or *Sammelbände*) of

Cologne editions all printed in the early 1470s, and therefore likely to have been acquired during his time at Syon.[29]

The networking and academic reputation of the sixteenth-century brethren may have placed them at the forefront of the new learning in England and helped them to identify, target, and acquire or receive by gift many of the new editions and studies that flooded out of Europe's presses at this time. But the development of the manuscript collection in the earlier years of the house also shows signs of deliberately targeted acquisition. The donor of A30, an incomplete copy of the *Catholicon* of Balbus, is entered by Betson as 'Syon', perhaps indicating a purchase on behalf of the community (or possibly an internal transfer from one of the other collections). Similarly Q62-3, a copy of the *Sermones Meffreth* in three parts, first printed in Basel 1483, has Syon as the donor. As Syon was not formally allowed to accept gifts of money (although sums are recorded in the *Martiloge*, perhaps as valuation of land or gifts in kind), and as all financial surpluses had to be disposed of at each year's end it seems possible that gifts of books would have been encouraged, especially in return for the kinds of external pastoral and spiritual duties undertaken by some of the brethren.[30]

The benefactions of Margaret Duchess of Clarence may well fit into this pattern. One of her gifts was a large Bible, once E1 in the Syon library and now London, British Library, Add. MS 40006. This book was already 150 years old when, at the expense of Margaret, 'devenit iste liber ad fratres monasterii de Syon ad [...] eiusdem domini symonis wynter fratris eiusdem monasterii' (fol. 16ᵛ). I have already mentioned the pastoral relationship that existed between Margaret and Symon Wynter and this may be reflected in this donation, perhaps for his use but maybe also at his instance. Although the crucial word describing his role in the acquisition or receipt of the book is now illegible in the manuscript, it is likely that Simon's role in instigating the purchase of this fine large second-hand volume was driven by a perceived need for books of this kind by the community in its early years.[31] In addition to books given by the brethren, some books were acquired second-hand. An entry in the index to the catalogue relating to a now-erased description of M48 describes the work as '*Reynerus* in suo libro qui dicitur liber beate Marie de Saltreya'. The work in question is the *Summa* or *Pantheologia* of Rainerius Iordanis de Pisa, which survives elsewhere in the collection (D25-9 and D85-6). But the attribution to 'beate Marie de Saltreya' reads more like an original *ex libris*, suggesting that this volume may have been acquired second-hand after having previously been in the collection of the Cistercian Abbey of the Blessed Virgin Mary at Sawtrey (Huntingdonshire). The kinds of complication that could arise in such transactions are suggested by B40, a vernacular translation of the *Compendium medicinae* of Gilbertus Anglicus. In Betson's catalogue, the name of Thomas Westhaw, third Confessor-General, has been erased as the donor of the volume. Betson's catalogue records his donation of nearly fifty books. B40 is now Glasgow, University Library, Hunterian MS 509, and the book has the *ex libris* inscription of John Sperhawk. In Sperhawk's will of 1472, he leaves 'to the house of Syon where Master Thomas Westhaw presides 26*s*. 8*d*. to be distributed … and the book of medicine he wrote with his own hand'. The erasure of Westhaw as donor of this volume probably reflects uncertainty or scruple as to who was the actual donor to the house, and suggests that the chain of benefaction and transmission by which books reached the library was not always transparent.[32]

A similar case arose when Thomas Jan or Jane (d. 1500), canon of St Paul's and archdeacon of Essex, gave a book to Syon on condition that Richard Terynden had the use of it in his life, suggesting that some system of earmarking volumes was in use. Jan is noted in the *Martiloge* as a generous benefactor of the house 'qui absque mercede temporalium aliquali graues labores gratissimosque fauores cum donariis librorum ceterumque beneficiorum monasterio huic de Syone exhibuit incessanter'.[33] Despite this, he is not listed in the catalogue as a donor. There was an entry in the catalogue describing a copy of the book he gave for Terynden's use: K48, which is now a blank erasure, is noted in the index as containing Jacobus Philippus Bergamensis's *Supplementum Chronicarum*, and ultra-violet examination confirms that this work was originally entered in K48, amid a series of books listing Terynden as donor (K47, 49, 50, and 51). Perhaps the book was erroneously entered, and remained in Terynden's possession, though the issue is complicated by the donor's name for this volume being apparently visible under ultra-violet light as Reynolds. What does seem clear, however, is that books eddied round the community in formal and informal collections and circulations, and it is unlikely that the catalogue reflects the limits and extent of book ownership among the brethren.

Another surviving Syon book, Oxford, Bodleian Library, MS Bodley 630, features in Betson's catalogue as N64. Still in its original vellum wrapper, and with the characteristic tags used in Syon to facilitate access to the constituent works of a compendious portmanteau volume (as so many of the earlier books at Syon were), the manuscript contains on an end flyleaf a fifteenth-century note of 4 marks and 2 pence as the 'precium libri'. On the front flyleaf is the note:

Hunc librum librarie fratrum de Syon Johanna Buklonde relicta Ricardi Buklonde ciuis et piscariis Londiniensis dedit fratri Rogero Twiforde et ceteris fratribus de Syon ad orandum pro ea et pro anima dicti Ricardi.

Joan Buklonde (d. 1462) was one of those powerful and influential London widows that we are beginning to learn more about, and she and her husband (who had died in 1436) are entered into the Syon *Martiloge*'s list of benefactors and special friends to the value of thirty pounds.[34] The request for prayers in Bodley 630 is, as we have seen, explicitly legislated for in the *Martiloge*'s precriptions for benefactors to the library. She gives the book to the brethren in general, but specifically to Roger Twiforde by name. Had Roger served as confessor or spiritual director? Did he perhaps have special use of the book before it passed into the communal collection? In the catalogue, however, Buklonde is recorded as the donor, whatever role Twyford had played in its acquisition for Syon or early use of the volume after its arrival. This may be because she specifies that the book is given to 'librarie fratrum', whereas the Sperhawk benefaction was more vague. Unless recording practices changed therefore, these manuscript cases do not altogether explain the acquisition and donation of volumes by brethren after their profession, though they offer valuable evidence of the terms and conditions of lay benefaction to the library in its manuscript phase.

The Buklonde gift is interesting in other respects as well. Despite Joan's status as a significant benefactress of religious houses, it is unlikely that Bodley 630 represents a personal possession of the donors. Dating from the first half of the fifteenth century, and entirely in Latin, it contains over fifty separate works in its 280 folios. Most are short, mainly eremitical and confessional, with substantial meditative and homiletic materials from (or ascribed to) Augustine and Bernard. Given the presence of a contemporary price, the 'professional' quality of its execution, and the vocational nature of its contents, I would suggest that this is not a gift from the Buklonde's personal collection, but rather a commision or a sponsored purchase made on the second-hand market of a volume that had been identified as of use to the house or to Twyford himself. That it had such value and use is suggested by the fact that it survived the later re-organization of the catalogue and the deletion and de-accessioning of many manuscript books.

Random benefaction is a recurrent problem for all institutional libraries, and unwanted duplication of marginal texts must have been a common complaint of monastic librarians as it is of their modern-day college successors. Henry V certainly seems to have been well advised – perhaps by someone with experi- ence of monastic libraries- when he stipulated that Syon and Sheen should not receive from his bequest any volumes that duplicated existing holdings. This was a prudent move when donating to two newly-founded houses both seek- ing to improve and extend their library collections. It is, of course, a different problem for service books, where a new and growing house may have had some problems supplying its needs: Syon, we know, initially used second-hand generic Sarum service books which were subsequently adapted and edited for Bridgettine use.[35] But academic and monastic libraries may always have been victim of the well-intentioned but misguided gift: yet another *Speculum peccatoris*; yet more copies of the *Meditationes* of *ps.* Augustine or *ps.* Bernard. So targeting benefactors for potential purchases or as sponsors for building projects was probably as much a part of monastic life in the middle ages as it is of academic life today. Donor recognition, in terms of prayers and masses for benefactors, was less tangible but perhaps more tempting than today's packages. Moreover, just as modern academic libraries often aspire to (but rarely achieve) a steady-state condition, it is unlikely that monastic libraries could be allowed to grow unfettered.

At Syon, as I have suggested, the library seems to have come into prominence only slowly, and it is only after the *Martiloge* donor recognition package of 1471 that the pace began to quicken. Although Thomas Graunte, the proto-benefactor, and the other early donors gave manuscripts to provide a basic collection, it is perhaps not accidental that the increased visibility of the library in the extant records coincides with the advent of printing. Building work on the library at Syon is recorded in 1479-80 as part of a programme of works throughout the abbey.[36] This may have been to improve the accommodation of a growing collection and it may also have been in response to a growing trickle of printed books that seems already to have been finding its way into the collection. Westhaw gave collections of Cologne prints from the early 1470s; Steyke gave early printed editions from the 1470s and early 1480s (N44, 45, 48, 50, 52, 53, &c.); Frynge gave a copy of the Paris 1478 edition of Albertus de Eyh's *Margarita poetica* (A67); Wilcockes gave several works of Bessarion in their Rome 1469 printing (B55); Richard Whytford gave the Louvain 1474 edition of Petrus de Crescentiis' *Ruralia commoda* (C44) (though of course he was not professed until much later); Trowell gave the [Strasbourg 1477-8] edition of Vincent of Beauvais' *Speculum doctinale* (C46); Terynden gave the Nuremberg 1475 print of Thomas Aquinas's *Catena aurea*; examples could be multiplied.

The 1482 Library Ordinance recognizes the 'greete hurtte and notable dayly Enpayremente of oure singler tresour Bokes of oure Queeres and libraries for defaute of byndynge, wrytynge and notynge of Quayres', referring graphically to the wear and tear on the mansucript collection after half a century of communal use.[37] Provisions for the care of service books in particular are regularly found in the sacristan's account rolls between 1506 and 1536, and a layman, Thomas Raille, was apparently employed from 1482 onwards in the tasks of binding and copying with the title of 'keper of þe ... Brethernes locutorie'.[38] This is another sign of increased curatorial activity in library matters in the final quarter of the fifteenth century. It may be accidental or significant that the previous year (1481)Thomas Betson had resigned his position as rector of Wimbish in Essex, probably to enter the community at Syon. Raille and Betson were still at work in the library when the extant account rolls begin in 1506: indeed this is likely to have been a period of increased activity as the first recension of Betson's catalogue dates from this period, and its design and composition, the re-arrangement of the holdings, and the addition of the descriptive book labels to the library stock must have been a time-consuming and complex task.[39]

Some surviving Syon books do show that care was taken in their repair and renovation. The manuscript of the *Additions* for the brethren and the Book of Signs (formerly St Paul's Cathedral and now in the Guildhall library), partly written by Thomas Betson and otherwise probably corrected by him, has a particularly extensive set of repairs to the upper right quadrant of a series of leaves culminating on fol. 10 where the whole top quarter has been replaced, reruled, and rewritten.[40] BL, Add. MS 5208, once M72 in the brethren's library, is recorded in Betson's catalogue with the following contents:

M 72   *vestibus*

Regula sancti Augustini. ¶ Regula sancti Saluatoris. fo. 4°. ¶ Hugo de sancto victore super Regulam sancti Augustini. fo. 12. ¶ Frater Nicholaus Trivet de Ordine predicatorum super Regulam sancti Augustini. fo. 35. ¶ Dialogus quidam inter Racionem & animam. fo. 111. ¶ Regula de 6 anniuersariis habendis in Syon per annum. fo. 122.

The same contents are listed on fol. 1ᵛ of the manuscript, which must have been in Syon for some considerable time as items 4 and 5 are in the hand of the liturgist Clement Maidstone who died in 1456. Although the catalogue and the list of contents in the mansucript agree, the actual manuscript itself has the first two items in reverse order, the *secundo folio* does not match that given in the catalogue, and the foliation is aberrant. The answer to this riddle is Thomas Betson, who, perhaps half a century after Maidstone's stint in the book, recopied fols 3ᵛ to 19ᵛ of the manuscript as it now survives, supplying the *Regula Augustini* and the *Regula Sancti Salvatoris* but in reverse order to that found in the catalogue and flyleaf lists of contents. Betson, presumably in his role as librarian, was forced to replace earlier material which had been damaged or rendered somehow unusable and, for some reason, found himself unable or unwilling to reproduce the original order so that his stint does not tally with the foliation recorded in the catalogue.[41] But the catalogue foliation resumes in the manuscript at fol. 12, precisely at the point that the catalogue and manuscript list of contents say it will be found.

Similar care should have been taken with all the books in the various libraries, for the instructions for episcopal visitations require the Bishop of London to enquire: 'quomodo custodiuntur et reperantur libri studiales inter fratres et si inter eos habeatur Inventorium seu Registrum eorundem librorum'.[42] This requirement to look after and repair the books, and most notably to maintian a *registrum* or inventory of them, strikingly focuses on the 'libri studiales' rather than on the service books to which most other surviving evidence relates. It has long been clear that the catalogue first published by Mary Bateson in 1898 and now being re-edited by me with full bibliographical identifications of the constituent works and, wherever possible, indications of editions of printed books present in the collection, is just such an inventory or register. But, given its relatively late date – it is first written by Thomas Betson, one of the four deacons of the order, early in the sixteenth century, certainly in the first decade – it seems inevitable that earlier inventories and registers must have existed, if only to fulfil the visitation injunctions. No such earlier registers survive, nor do any obvious signs of earlier cataloguing, pressmarks, or other indications of curatorial activity that can be said with any confidence to predate Betson's period as *custos librarie*. There is a reference in Betson's description of one of John Bracebridge's early manuscript donations (M14) to '¶ Quoddam

Registrum de libris. fo. 118', which might refer to a registrum of the Syon books, but is perhaps more likely to be a list of Bracebridge's own substantial collection of over a hundred books dating from his time as a grammar master. Similarly one of Weston's books (O12) contains a '¶ Registrum cum exordio & fine quorundam librorum originalium doctorum multorum. fo. 260', but this probably refers to a reference listing of patristic works. The absence of *ex libris* marks, curatorial marks, or earlier pressmarks on surviving Syon books suggests that Betson's task in drawing up the new *Registrum* was largely undertaken *ab initio*, and the skill and ingenuity of his design and execution of the new catalogue served the community well.

It is not clear when Betson gave up his work on the catalogue, or if he continued to supervise the work of the other scribe whose hand appears in the manuscript. He may have handed over during the first decade of the century. The main stint of copying the new catalogue was completed around 1504, but some of the later additions are also in Betson's hand so he seems to have remained involved after this date. Even after his hand is replaced in entries into the catalogue, and even after his death in 1516, the collection continued to grow with the addition of new printed books. Some of these were added on blank pressmarks in Betson's catalogue; others were simply not catalogued (as we have seen, some surviving books owned by John Fewterer (d. 1536) do not feature in the catalogue at all). Books continued to be added to the catalogue at least until the mid-1520s, but Betson's meticulous standards of description, layout, and detail were not uniformly sustained by those responsible for later additions.

Betson was a remarkable librarian, and perhaps a passionate one. In his sole surviving published work, *A Ryght Profytable Treatyse*, printed by Wynkyn de Worde in 1500, his parting shot is a colophon that reads '¶ Lerne to kepe your bokes clene &c.'. To gauge from the thirty or so books surviving from the Brethren's library, his descriptions in the catalogue were notably accurate (though not always exhaustively complete). He notes details such as a change in the pattern of quiring in a manuscript (L33).[43] He is so meticulous at listing the works in a printed *opuscula* of Thomas Aquinas (D95) that it is possible to identify it precisely as a very rare *c.* 1488 low countries printing of 70 *opuscula* rather than the much more common 71 or 73 *opuscula*. He reports in his description of Richard Rolle's *Melos amoris* in M27 that 'dicitur manu propria hunc scripsisse librum'. He corrects false attributions in mansucript copies of popular works, as in P30 which he correctly identifies as Odo of Cheriton's *Sermones dominicales*, noting 'tamen intitulatur in Rubrica secundum M. Willelmum de Montibus'. He produced an index to the collection as he catalogued it that is so detailed that it allows modern users greater insight into the holdings. R7, for example, is described in the catalogue as 'Centum sermones beati augustini ypponensis Episcopi' without further elaboration. The index, however, lists 105 sermons attributed to Augustine in this pressmark, often providing the Incipit. So far I have managed to positively identify nearly eighty of these, and this would have been impossible without Betson's index. The index often adds crucially elaborative detail that allow the modern editor to clinch an identification or to link several occurrences of the same work.

Betson's catalogue already contains significant numbers of printed books even in its first recension, and it may be that his custodial activity was partly prompted by the increasing tide of printed books that necessitated revision, expansion, and rearrangment of whatever inventories or *registra* preceded him. At the latest after his death in 1516, other hands took on the role and at some point in the 1520s the catalogue seems to have been abandoned.[44] New marginal library marks added by a hand later than Betson's suggest that there may have been some intention to rearrange the collection to bring cognate materials more closely together. These added pressmarks might suggest that the Betson catalogue was being marked up for eventual absorbtion into a new *Registrum*. There is room for doubt about whether this was ever executed: only one of the surviving books carries any sign of the 'new' pressmarks. However, it does not seem ever to have been common practice at Syon to put press- or library marks in their books or on the book labels, even in the heyday of Betson's time as librarian.[45]

As it survives today, the catalogue offers remarkable evidence of the continuing efforts to accommodate and incorporate new accessions and to re-order and perhaps dispose of older, superseded, or less useful volumes. This gives a fascinating insight into the life of a major monastic collection as it embraced the change from script to print. The revisions and re-orderings carried out to the catalogue after Betson's time as librarian left behind them incomplete traces of new and old holdings. Some entries were erased altogether and replaced with new entries (invariably of printed books); other entries were moved elsewhere in the collection. Some sections – notably the canon law section T – were subjected to wholesale rebuilding. Some of the erased or redeployed volmes were removed from Betson's index of authors, but many others were not. Some sections were carefully weeded, others not. Some books disappeared altogether, others merely had their classmark erased. The last erased classmark in the index occurs in the list of the works of Hugh of St-Victor, suggesting that the process of purging the index was less than half completed before being abandoned.

We thus have several strands of information that can tell us about the contents of the collection at different stages of its development. The catalogue as it now stands describes the collection probably as it was in the 1520s, after revision, deaccessioning, and addition of new volumes. This catalogue is a hybrid of Betson and later additions. Behind this layer of the catalogue, however, it is possible to reconstruct some of the erased and deaccessioned volumes. Some of the erasures are at least partly readable under UV light and, when checked against the only partly updated index, it is possible to reconstruct these ghost volumes that were part of Betson's original census of the collection in the early 1500s. These two strata will both be included in the new edition of the catalogue.[46] A further strand of information is the addition of the new set of marginal pressmarks which suggest that a wholesale re-arrangement of the collection was at least proposed, the effect of which would have been to group cognate material more closely and perhaps more coherently together. A conspectus of the 'Betson' pressmark and the new marginal press-mark is now complete and will be included in the new catalogue.[47]

The items removed and apparently not reassigned elsewhere in the collection are interesting and potentially significant. It is, though, impossible to say with confidence whether such removals from the catalogue were the result of deliberate withdrawal of stock; the recognition of irredeemable loss through loan or damage; or the result of the texts being superseded, perhaps by printed editions or more comprehensive holdings. The truth is probably a combination of all these factors, though I suspect that printed editions of collected *opera* seriously lessened the utility of some of the older mansuscript miscellanies of patristic materials, and that printed canon law, with its superior finding aids and cross-referencing, rendered older manuscript collections less attractive. Lawyers, in my experience, always want the newest edition of everything, and the rearrangement was carefully and thoughtfully executed with few books disappearing altogether (though a canonical miscellany is replaced by a printed *Summa angelica* in T18). Thus the collection of English episcopal legislation that was originally in T22 is replaced by a printed vocabulary of canon law terms, maybe because its functions were now catered for by the multiple copies of Lyndwood's *Provinciale* which remained in the collection. Both older copies of the Ottobonian constitutions are discarded, as are two copies of the con-stitutions of Iohannes episcopus Eboracensis (the work either of John Kempe or John Thoresby). Given Syon's later prominence in the debate over the King's divorce, the wholesale restocking of their canon law library proved to be both good librarianship and political prescience. Indeed it seems likely that this was one of the most heavily used sections of the library in the twenty years prior to the dissolution. It certainly helps explain why people like Thomas More made such use of the collection.

Elsewhere in the catalogue, some authors attested in the index seem to have disappeared from the collection altogether. Bernardus Silvestris, who in Betson's catalogue was represented in three separate books, no longer features in the catalogue in its final recension. The only copy of William of Conches (in C18 alongside Bernardus Silvestris) disappears to be replaced by a volume of Aristotelian *problemata* whose *secundo folio* agrees with editions printed in Venice in 1501 and 1505, the gift of John Fewterer. The only copy of Claudian goes, as does a copy of the Revelations of Elizabeth of Hungary in English. John Howden's thirteenth-century poem the *Philomela*, influential on the development of the English cult of the name of Jesus, goes to be replaced by the 1516 London edition of the *Nova Legenda Angliae*, given by its printer Wynkyn de Worde. Both copies of Matthew of Vendôme, the only copy of Petrus Riga's *Aurora*, most of the works of Ovid (with the exception of the morally correct but textually discredited *De vetula*): all these go. But the balance is partly offset by the arrival of a printed text of the *Metamorphoses* given by the future 'wretch of Syon' and former Fellow of Queen's College, Cambridge, Richard Whytford. Also lost is a copy of 'Astrolabius poeta', perhaps Abelard's verses to his son, and an English *Consolation of Philosophy* (probably Chaucer's translation), though Boethius is still well represented in other copies including one with the influential glosses of Nicholas Trevet. A manuscript copy of the sermons of Bernadino of Sienna goes, to be replaced by a printed copy of the same at R65. A manuscript copy of Pseudo Denys the Areopagite's mystical theology is discarded, but a printed copy of his complete works is added at D118 in the edition of Strasbourg 1501 which contains among much else no less than four Latin versions of the mystical theology in the translations of Sarracenus, Grosseteste, Ambrosius Traversari, and Marsilio Ficino. Randomly scattered copies of Aristotle disappear to be replaced by consolidated humanist editions and commentaries. Noted printed humanist accessions include the *opera* of Vergil (in one of three 1490s editions all sharing the same *secundo folio*: A62); and two copies of the great Venice 1493 edition of Ptolemy, Zael, Bethen, and Messahala (B47 and B55); the *opera* of Plato (C7, the Venice 1491 edition, containing thirty-nine works and a life of Plato by Ficino) and Plotinus (C3, the Florence 1492 edition with Marsilio Ficino's commentary).

One of the most comprehensive purges was, by accident or design, carried out on the works of John Wycliffe. Four out of the six manuscript copies of Wycliffe's works, scattered in miscellanies throughout the collection and offering some important attestations of rare works by him, such as a previously unknown commentary on Aristotle's *Metheorum* (C15: now also attested from a catalogue in the *Carolinum* library in Prague[48]), and a letter from Wycliffe to John of Gaunt (K37) do not survive into the catalogue's final version. The view taken of him may be deduced from Betson's index entry for one of these lost texts: 'de sacramento altaris cum aliis de quibus cavendum est' (S6, fol. 11ʳ). But two copies of William Woodford's fourteenth-century attack on Wycliffe's views survive the collection's reorganization. D75, given by William Catesby who died in 1510, also contains other anti-Wycliffite texts.

In fact D75 is a particularly good if dizzying example of the kinds of confusion into which the later catalogue descended. D75 can be identified by contents and *secundo folio* with BL, MS Harley 42, which contains the labels characteristic of Syon books, listing contents, donor, and *secundo folio*. It is a feature of Betson's labels (which were originally nailed to the back cover of the books under a sheet of horn) that they do not contain pressmarks. But Harley 42 has on a flyleaf the pressmark of **d41**, which is the secondary marginal shelfmark assigned to D75 as preparation for the reorganization of shelfmarks after Betson's time as librarian. D41 itself is occupied in Betson's catalogue by the *Summa de virtutibus* attributed to Alexander of Hales in the edition from Paris 1509, the gift of John Fewterer. However, the index allows the partial reconstruction of another set of texts bearing the shelfmark D41, including the *Celestial Hierarchies*, Hugh of St Victor's commentary on that text, and a collection of ecclesiatical opinions *de provisionibus ecclesiarum*. There are, then, potentially three volumes with the Syon pressmark of D41: the original texts recovered from the Index, Fewterer's copy of the 1509 printed *Summa* (which itself has a marginal shelfmark in the catalogue of d8 implying that it was intended to move it), and Harley 42, alias D75, alias D41. It is hardly surprising that it seems to have become hard to keep track of the books.

The Betson catalogue was originally classified into an alphabetical sequence of broad thematic coherence, though this was eventually diluted by new accessions into vacant shelfmarks. Within these alphabetical sections, some trends emerge. Section A, containing grammar-school reading texts and editions of classical authors, is strikingly modernized by accessions from brethren touched by the beginnings of the new learning in England: Richard Reynolds, Curson (a brother at the dissolution in 1537), Richard Whytford, Stephen Sawndre, and John Steyke who died in 1513. Older grammatical reading texts are replaced by new humanist editions. In A49, Geoffrey de Vinsauf's *Poetria nova* is replaced by Richard Reynolds's copy of the Paris 1511-12 edition of Lucan. In A63 Leyland's grammar text is replaced by the Paris 1496 edition of the *Metamorphoses* with the commentary of Raphael Regius, given by Richard Whytford. The most emblematic substitution is the replacement in A70 of an archetypal collection of grammar-school reading texts (Cato, Avianus, Pamphilus, Horace, Maximian, Statius, and Claudian) by Richard Reynolds's copy of the *Silvae* of Iodocus Badius Ascensius in the Lyon 1492 edition. The end of section H (commentaries on scripture, mainly New Testament) has been blitzed to accommodate multi-volume monuments of the New Learning, most from the period after Betson's death in 1516: the Paris 1517 edition of Ludolph of Saxony; the nine-volume 1516 Erasmus Jerome; the 1520 index to that edition; Erasmus's 1519 New Testament; the 1519 edition of his *Annotationes* on the New Testament, the 1522 edition of his paraphrases on the evangelists; and the Basel 1524 edition of Theophylact of Constantinople's *Enarrationes* on the New Testament.

Section N offers some tantalizing juxtapositions. N26 had been a very traditional collection of *pastoralia*, including catechetic texts by Grosseteste and Richard Wetheringsett, Grosseteste's pastoral constitutions for Lincoln diocese, the sentences of Isidore, and the *ps.* Augustine *Duodecim gradibus abusionem*. It was replaced by a collection of printed texts including the Paris 1511 edition of Mapheus Vegius and Pynson's 1511 London edition of John Colet's 'oratio ad clerum in convocatione'; the volume's donor was Richard Reynolds. Of the 98 items in section O, nothing survives of the older 'Betson' holdings after O54; and O59 to the end of the section is entered over erasure, suggesting the wholesale reshaping of the section to accommodate large multi-volumed printed editions, including the *opera* of Gerson, Bonaventure, and Augustine.

Section N contains also what appear to be several collections of printed tracts, or *sammelbände*. For example, N62 opens with Thomas Aquinas's *De articulis fidei et ecclesiae sacramentis* in the edition by Ulrich Zel printed in Cologne *c*. 1470, and most of the remaining contents were printed by the same printer in the same year, or in Cologne about the same time. The donor was Thomas Westhaw who became Confessor-General in 1472 and died in 1488. N44 has a collection of works by Augustine, all printed by Bartholomaeus de Unkel about 1482, given by Steyke who died in 1513. N65 contains a collection of works by Jean Gerson, all printed by Johann Sensenschmidt and Andreas Frisner in the early to middle 1470s, again the gift of Westhaw. Other collections in section N gather together Cologne prints from a number of printers all appearing within a year or so of each other and probably acquired as a collection of fascicules. Syon had good links with stationers, booksellers, and printers in Westminster and the city: in the sixteenth century, several brethren (most notably Richard Whitford, the recipient of a dedicatory epistle from Erasmus in his 1506 edition of Lucian; and John Fewterer) kept the presses supplied with devotional and didactic works in English.[49] But it was a two-way relationship: the supply of *sammelbände* and their other extensive holdings of continental printed books suggests that Syon may have been a good market for the output of new overseas editions.

Perhaps the most mysterious effect of the post-Betson rearrangement of the catalogue is the disappearance of nearly all the works attributed to the Syon brethren themselves. In H34 Nicholas the Deacon's sermons on Matthew chapter 1 are replaced by Fewterer's Basel 1494 edition of Thomas Aquinas on John. Symon Wynter's alphabetical collection of 'materia predicabilis' in L41 gives way to Lawsby's gift of a manuscript copy of the *Rosarium Theologiae*, the reduced version of the alphabetical Wycliffite *Floretum*: very much a change of like for like; preaching aid for preaching aid; manuscript for manuscript. The sermons of Richard Bellyngham are removed without replacement from P34 and 35; likewise those of Thomas Bulde in P42 and R19. Hugo Damlett and Roger of Syon, both donors of books (the former not certainly a brother), both have their sermons deleted. The only Syon priest whose work survives into the final recension of the catalogue is Symon Wynter, with four volumes of *sanctorale* and *temporale* sermons, two copies of a vernacular sermon on the famous Syon pardon, and commentaries on Marian antiphons. Why is this? Were their works buried with them? Were home-grown sermons deaccessioned into the library of the sisters for improving reading or into some other intermediate collection? Although the reasons are murky, the policy is clear and ruthlessly applied. [50]

Certain broad trends are discernible in the growth and development of the collection of the Syon brethren as witnessed by the Catalogue. Script gives way to print, or is at least increasingly heavily outnumbered; manuscript miscelanies gave some way to collected *opera*; *antiqui* give way to *moderni*; humanist learning shows signs of supplementing if not entirely supplanting the old wisdom; secular learning in science and classical languages continues into the sixteenth century (though Greek texts are thinly represented); vernacular materials remain scarce (less than two dozen items in total). The catalogue offers an unrivalled insight into the intellectual milieu of the house on the brink of the Reformation. It paints a picture of a scholarly and spiritual community, many of whom, like Jerome in the life written by Symon Wynter, had turned from 'bokys of Poetys and Philysophres' to 'holy bokys'. According to Wynter, Jerome's influence on two heathens so changed them that 'levynge all þe vanytees of þe worlde [they] went yn-to þe monasterye', while two young Romans saved from execution by Jerome 'castynge from theym all wordly bysynesse, entred yn-to þe monasterye … entendynge to prayere and to penaunce and to holy lyuynge'.[51] The trajectory described by Symon Wynter is exactly that followed by many of his colleagues and successors. Betson's catalogue in its various stages of upkeep and neglect allows us a glimpse of the intellectual footsteps they trod in and left behind them.

NOTES

1 The information is drawn from the Syon *Martiloge* in London, British Library, Add. MS 22285, fol. 14ʳ (*De prima fundacione huius monasterii*), and fol. 6ᵛ (lower margin). The date of 5 February 1520, given in G. J. Aungier, *The History and Antiquities of Syon Monastery, the Parish of Isleworth and the Chapelry of Hounslow* (London, 1840), p. 38, is incorrect. According to the *Martiloge* (fol. 14ʳ, also on fol. 5ᵛ), the foundation stone at the first site was laid on 22 February 1415. In this article, obit dates for brethren and terms of Confessors-General are calculated by reference to the *Martiloge*. I am grateful to Dr Claes Gejrot for these references and for sending me a draft of the new edition of the *Martiloge* that he is undertaking with Dr Virginia Bainbridge.

2 *Martiloge*, fol. 3ʳ. The *Articuli Extracti* are preserved in Uppsala, University Library, MS C. 6, fols 78ᵛ-80ʳ. M. B. Tait, *The Brigittine Monastery of Syon (Middlesex) with special reference to its monastic uses*, unpublished D. Phil. thesis (Oxford, 1975), p. 58. Fishbourn was apparently a cousin of Richard Clifford, Bishop of London, who (as Visitor of the house) confirmed the election of Joan North as first Abbess and Fishbourn as first Confessor-General during a visitation on 5 May 1421: BL, Cotton MS, Cleopatra E. II, fol. 352ʳ; Aungier, p. 525.

3 A very useful account of the political turmoil of the house in the 1420s is given by F. R. Johnston, 'Joan North, First Abbess of Syon, 1420-33', *Birgittiana*, 1 (1996), 47-65, which highlights the role played by Whethampstead and John Duke of Bedford in securing from Martin V in 1425 the *bulla reformatoria* known as *Mare Anglicanum*. Fishbourn had visited Rome to lobby on behalf of the nascent house. William Heyworth, Abbot of St Alban's, had sat on Patrington's committee in 1416 along with Fishbourn (who may have been a hermit at St Alban's, but is described in the documents simply as 'priest'). The committee to draw up the *Additions* probably worked in the second quarter of the fifteenth century (and certainly between 1425 and 1473) and was made up entirely of Benedictines and Cistercians, including Hugo Eyton, subprior of St Alban's: *The Incendium Amoris of Richard Rolle of Hampole*, ed. by M. Deanesly (Manchester, 1915), pp. 91-130. Four versions survive of the Additions to the Rule for the English Syon: BL, MS Arundel 146 (in Middle English, for the sisters); London, Guildhall Library, MS 25524 (in Middle English, for the Brethren); Cambridge, St John's College, MS A.11 (a fragmentary Latin text for the brethren); and a post-medieval Latin version produced in Lisbon in 1607. The first three are edited or reproduced by James Hogg, *The Rewyll of Seynt Sauioure and Other Middle English Brigittine Legislative Texts*, vols 2-4 (Salzburg, 1978-80). For discussion, see R. Ellis, *Viderunt eam filie syon: the Spirituality of the*

English House of a Medieval Contemplative Order from its beginnings to the present day, Analecta Cartusiana, 68 (1984), cap. 3 (The Syon Additions). Fragments of the Rule and Additions were more recently identified among the manuscripts still in posession of the sisters: N. R. Ker & A. J. Piper, *Medieval Manuscripts in British Libraries*, 4 (Oxford, 1992), pp. 348-9.

4 *Loci e Libro Veritatum: Passages from Gascoigne's Theological Dictionary*, ed. by J. E. Thorold Rogers (Oxford, 1881), pp. 169-70. In the same passage, Gascoigne praises Symon Wynter, another early brother, as 'devotus religiosus in monasterio Syon in Anglia.' Fishbourn seems to have been Steward of St Alban's, and one of the St Alban's chronicles suggests in an entry for 1428 that he was previously 'vitam solitariam ducens'; Deanesly, *Incendium Amoris*, pp. 114-15.

5 *Martiloge*, fol. 3[r]. The provisions for prayers for dead founders were agreed by the community in 1431: first in the list stands Henry V ('huius monasterii fundator[is]'). N. Beckett, 'St. Bridget, Henry V and Syon Abbey', in *Studies in St. Birgitta and the Brigittine Order*, ed. by J. Hogg, Analecta Cartusiana, 35:19 (1993), 2, 125-50.

6 P. & F. Strong, 'The Last Will and Codicils of Henry V', *English Historical Review*, 96 (1981), 79-102; Becket, 127-8. Bridget is included in the list of saints from whom suffrages are requested at the beginning of the will (Strong, 89).

7 Henry had already spent substantially on the fabric of his new foundations: see R. W. Dunning, 'The Building of Syon Abbey', *Transactions of the Ancient Monuments Society*, n.s., 25 (1981), 16-26.

8 K. B. McFarlane, *Lancastrian Kings and Lollard Knights* (Oxford, 1972), Appendix C: 'Henry V's Books', prints a list of the books taken after the siege of the Market of Meaux, apparently from one of the town's religious houses, which he suggests might have been destined for Syon or Sheen. The books passed initially into the personal custody of the Treasurer, John Stafford, only finding their way into the Treasury itself in 1427, when this list was made. Initially some and subsequently all were given to King's Hall, Cambridge, where they are noted by 1440. No reason for over-riding the provisions of the will and its codicils is given.

9 A surviving 1482 ordinance for the making of books refers to 'the kepers of the libraris of the bretherne and [Sys]terne Sydes there', printed by R. J. Whitwell, 'An Ordinance for Syon Library, 1482', *English Historical Review*, 25 (1910), 121-3. The 1471 addition of an obsequy for donors to either of the two libraries is recorded in the *Martiloge*, fols 4[r-v] and 17[v]-18[r]. The *Martiloge* also grants prayers for the souls of benefactors of books for 'common use'. The standard (and masterly) discussion of the Syon libraries is now C. de Hamel, *Syon Abbey: the Library of the Bridgettine Nuns and their Peregrinations after the Reformation*, Roxburghe Club (Otley, 1991).

10 The catalogue is now Cambridge, Corpus Christi College, MS 141. It was edited by M. Bateson, *Catalogue of the Library of Syon Monastery Isleworth* (Cambridge, 1898). Mary Bateson's edition is an impressive and remarkable document, especially in the number of early printed books she was able to identify by their *secundo folio*. In re-editing the catalogue for the *Corpus of British Medieval Library Catalogues*, I am conscious of still relying on her scholarship and judgement, which have withstood the intervening century with their integrity and acumen unsullied. On Thomas Betson, see A. I. Doyle, 'Thomas Betson of Syon Abbey', *The Library*, fifth series, 11 (1956), 115-18. Betson probably entered Syon in or around 1481 and may have been involved with the library up to his death in 1516.

11 *Martiloge*, fol. 17[v]: (*De exequiis pro benefactoribus librariarum.Capitulum 7*). The decision is dated 7 September 1471, and grants prayers 'inspeciali pro anima magistri Thome Graunte et pro animabus Iohannis et Helene parentum eius. In generali vero pro animabus eorum omnium qui librarie sororum vel librarie fratrum aliquam vel aliquos libros ad communem usum eorundem pro Dei honore ampliando contulerunt.' De Hamel discusses the early phase of the house's libraries, suggesting their probable reliance on the second-hand market (on which more below).

12 For the petition to Duke Humfrey, see Strong, 94, n. 12. On the King's Hall books, see note 7 above. On Fitzhugh, see *Martiloge*, fols 3[r] and 15[v]. On the abortive York plantation, see now

M. Hedlund, 'Katillus Thornberni: A Syon Pioneer and His Books', *Birgittiana*, 1 (1996), 67-87. On Henry's codicil, see Strong, 100.

13 Tait (cited above, n. 2), cap. 4; Johnston, 47-53. On the order's general difficulties in the 1420s, see H. Cnattingius, *Studies in the Order of St. Bridget of Sweden I: The Crisis in the 1420s* (Uppsala, 1963).

14 *Regula Salvatoris*, ed. by S. Eklund, Den Heliga Birgitta Opera Minora 1, Samlingar utgivna av Svenska Fornskriftsällskapet, Andra Serien, Latinska Skrifter, 8:1 (Lund, 1975), cap. 15, section 174, p. 121. For the passage in the E text, see cap. 13, section 171 (Eklund, pp. 161-2). On the complex development of the rule and its manifestations in England, see Ellis, *Viderunt Eam Filie Syon* (cited above, n. 3), cap. 1. On their penitential authority, see Johnston, 56, citing *Liber Privilegiorum Monasterii Vadstenensis*, ed. by E. Nygren (Hafniae, 1950), p. 236. The preaching office of the Syon brethren has been carefully and thoughtfully studied by S. Powell, 'Preaching at Syon Abbey', *Working Papers in Literary and Cultural Studies*, 29 (Salford, 1997); see also her 'Syon, Caxton and the *Festial*', *Birgittiana*, 2 (1996), 187-207, which discusses Syon's possible involvement with printed sermons. Tait, p. 214, notes that Bonde, Fewterer, and Reynolds all served as university preachers at Cambridge before joining the order.

15 The Syon Additions for the Brethren (Guildhall manuscript) record in a short chapter headed 'Of the offices of the prechours' that 'Eche of the prechours schal besyde the sermon day haue thre hole days at lest oute of the quyer to recorde hys sermon', ed.by Hogg (cited above, n. 3), 3. 122.

16 Cambridge, University Library, MS Ff. 6. 33, fols 62^v-63^r, reproduced by Hogg, 2. 49-50. For the Latin text (II version), see cap. 21, sections 227-8: 'Libri quoque, quotquot necessarii fuerint ad divinum officium peragendum, habendi sunt, plures autem nullo modo. Illos autem libros habeant, quotquot voluerint, in quibus addiscendum est vel studendum' (Eklund, p. 127). The E version, cap. 18, sections 227-8, is substantially the same (Eklund, pp. 204-5).

17 Sawndre: *BRUC*, 507; Trowell:*BRUO*, 1910.

18 Aungier (cited above, n. 1), p. 52; Bateson, p. xxiii; Tait, p. 246, traces his career as a grammar master in Lincoln diocese. Entered in the *Martiloge* for 27 March (fol. 6^r), he is described as 'sacerdotis et bachalarii in theologia'; he was apparently the only graduate among the brethren in the 1428 election for the second Confessor-General.

19 See the list of 'Nomina specialium benefactorum et amicorum' in the *Martiloge*, fols 70^r-71^v; Aungier, passim.

20 On Margaret's links with Syon (and those of other noble benefactors), see G. R. Keiser, 'Patronage and Piety in Fifteenth-Century England: Margaret, Duchess of Clarence, Symon Wynter and Beinecke MS 317', *Yale University Library Gazette*, 60 (1985), 32-46. One of Margaret's gifts, a copy of Symon Wynter's *Sanctilogium Salvatoris*, originally items M1 and M2 in Betson's catalogue, was copied by Stephen Dodesham, later a Carthusian scribe of some productivity, though this may have been completed before his entry into religion, when he may have worked as a professional scribe: A. I. Doyle, 'Book Production by the Monastic Orders in England (*c*. 1375-1530): Assessing the Evidence', in *Medieval Book Production: Assessing the Evidence*, ed. by L. L. Brownrigg (London, 1990), pp. 1-21, esp. pp. 14-15. Some of her other gifts were purchased on the second-hand market; see below.

21 *Martiloge*, fol. 17^r; Whitwell (cited above, n. 9), 121-3. De Hamel has suggested (pp. 60-1) that Graunte was donating books to various institutions well before his death (including the copy of Bridget's *Revelations* now in BL, Add. MS 22572, given to Canterbury College, Oxford, and suggesting an (unsurprising) interest in the cult of the saint during his lifetime), but the entry in the Syon *Martiloge* dated 27 September follows close upon his death on 8 July 1471 (not 1474 as some sources report it).

22 Whitwell, 121; Hogg, 4.72 (the Additions for the Sisters). The relevant entries are usefully collected by M. C. Erler, 'Syon Abbey's Care for Books: Its Sacristan's Account Rolls 1506/7-1535/6', *Scriptorium*, 39 (1985), 293-307.

23 As will be explored below, and in more detail in the new edition of the catalogue, Betson's

original register of books was added to until the mid-1520s, and radical re-arrangement was begun by the erasure of old entries and the insertion of new (largely printed) texts into the vacated library marks. Later still, preparations were made for a wholesale re-ordering of the collection, perhaps in expectation of some change in its physical location or the manner in which it was stored. So even the single register that survives today probably witnesses at least three distinct phases of library development, re-ordering, and curatorial activity within no more than a quarter of a century.

24 Despite the degree of autonomy allowed to the house by *Mare Anglicanum* in 1425, Syon seems to have kept in close touch with the mother-house throughout the 1420s. Robert Belle and Thomas Sterington visited Vadstena in 1427, when they received a bone of St. Bridget: *Martiloge*, fol. 1ʳ. On this visit, the *Diarium Vadstenense* reports that they raised further questions regarding the rule: 'In die parasceves venerunt de Anglia duo fratres ordinis nostri petentes et reportantes raciones super aliquibus punctis regule', *Diarium Vadstenense: the Memorial Book of Vadstena Abbey*, ed. by C. Gejrot (Stockholm, 1988), p. 186. The colophon in BL, MS Harley 612 (s.xv med.), the important Syon copy of the *Revelations*, defences, and other para-legislative materials, reports that the accuracy of the text of its exemplar was confirmed for these same brethren by a Swedish notary during the same visit: de Hamel, pp. 57-8.The *responsiones* are preserved in Stockholm, Riksarkivet, MS A. 20, fols 164ff.; Tait, cap. 3.

25 Edyman gave a copy of the Paris 1513 edition of *Liber trium uirorum et trium spiritualium uirginum*, ed. by Jacques Le Fèvre d'Etaples, which included the *Pastor* of Hermas, Hildegard of Bingen's *Scivias*, the life of Elizabeth of Schönau, and Mechtild of Hackeborn's *Liber spiritualis gratiae*. Another copy of the same edition was at M107, given by Selby (the different *secundo folios* are taken from different pages of the same edition). On these links see Tait, pp. 338-9.

26 In addition to the Cologne *Sammelbände* discussed elsewhere in this chapter, see, for example, A45: Cicero, Venice 1470; B55: Bessarion, Rome 1469; K15: Valerius Maximus, [Strasbourg *c*.1470]; N66: Bernardino of Siena, Cologne *c*.1470; O11, Ambrose, Cologne *c*.1470. It should be noted, however, that some of these early prints will have entered Syon in the personal libraries of brethren professed after this period. Nevertheless, the 'printed' quality of the Syon collection is striking. M. C. Erler, 'Pasted-in Embellishments in English Manuscripts and Printed Books', *The Library*, sixth series, 14 (1992), 185-206, comments (204) that Syon 'appears to be the only English religious institution whose espousal of the new technology of printing is extensive enough to be described as adapting a continental model', both in relation to its own publications and its familiarity with continental printing though its library.

27 e.g. Merton College, Oxford, 76 b. 11 (a Hebrew Concordance printed in Venice, 1524) and Oxford, Bodleian Library, 8 A 11 Th (a copy of the Venice 1509 *opuscula* of Agepetus, with other works on the psalms by Reuchlin (Tubingen 1512) and Nicholas Denyse (Paris 1509), with the name of John Fewterer on the title-page, and with characteristic Syon tags and nail holes on the lower board corresponding to the usual position of the Syon book label). A copy of the Hagenau 1501 edition of Pelbàrt Temesvári, *Stellarium Coronae beatae Mariae uirginis* with a Syon label on the lower board, giving the donor as Curson, is now in the collection of Dr A. I. Doyle. It appears not to have been in the catalogue in any of its recensions.

28 As Lawsby died in 1490, the *GW* dating for this volume of 1485 might be preferable.

29. Where it is possible to identify the first item in a catalogue entry as agreeing with the *secundo folio* of an early printed book, the new edition of the catalogue (sometimes following Mary Bateson's lead) has explored the printing history of the other items to see if the volume may have been *sammelband*. Among Westhaw's books, the most likely examples are N60, N61, N62 (all Cologne), and N65 (Nuremberg). Grene's donation of N41 may also be a Cologne *sammelband*. On *sammelbände* generally, see S. Corsten, *Studien aum Kölner Fruhdruck* (Cologne, 1985); P. Needham, *The Printer and the Pardoner: an Unrecorded Indulgence printed by William Caxton for the Hospital of St. Mary Rounceval, Charing Cross* (Washington, 1986), discusses the Rosenwald Sammelband of Caxton editions.

30 cf. de Hamel, pp. 59-60, 88, who also notes that John Duke of Bedford marked his laying of the foundation stone for the new site at Isleworth by giving the house 'duos pulchros libros officii sororum et unam legendam' (p. 64); *Martiloge*, fol. 14ᵛ.

31 De Hamel makes a similar point, pp. 59-60, commenting that the purchase was unlikely to have been expensive. Indeed the decoration of the book was augmented after arrival in Syon. But its importance lies not in intrinsic value but in the demonstration of 'targeted acquisition'.

32 His will is printed in *Somerset Record Society*, 16 (1901), 222-5, esp. p. 224. I owe this reference, and much other information on Syon books, to the kindness of Dr Ian Doyle. Sperhawk was Prebendary of Ashill, Somerset, from 1451 to 1474, and his will was proved 4 February 1474. He left a book with works of Augustine to Hugo Damlett, another donor to the Syon library, as well as donations of money to the Carthusians. In a discriminating move reminiscent of Henry V's will, he leaves books to the university library in Cambridge, but specifies that if they already have the 'librum originalem' upon the Old Testament, it should pass to Pembroke College library or (if they also already have it) to Queen's College library.

33 *Martiloge*, fol. 72ʳ Jan's gift to Terynden survives as Xanten, Stiftsbibliothek, 3970B [Inc] 241.

34 *Martiloge*, fol. 70ᵛ: '19. Johanna et Ricardus Boklande ad valorem xxx librarum'. On Joan, see J. Stratford, 'Joan Buckland (d. 1462)' in *Medieval London Widows: 1300-1500*, ed. by C. M. Barron & A. F. Sutton (London, 1994), pp. 113-28. Richard Buckland, one-time treasurer and vice-chancellor of Calais, was a councillor and executor of the will of John, Duke of Bedford (another 'special friend' of Syon). Joan left service books and a large psalter in her will (Stratford, p. 126), but Bodley 630 is not mentioned there, strengthening the case for seeing it as an instigated purchase on behalf of the Syon community. Joan was part of a London circle that included clerics keen to improve the provision of grammar schools in London (Stratford, p. 122). For discussion of other women who were 'special friends' of Syon, see M. C. Erler, 'Syon's 'special benefactors and friends': some wowed [*sic*, wonderfully] women', *Birgittiana*, 2 (1996), 209-22.

35 The fullest account is now de Hamel, passim.

36 Dunning (cited above, n. 7), 18, reports that £467 8s. 3½d. was spent on the new church, the brethren's cloister, the chapter house and the library in the year from October 1479.

37 Whitwell, 122.

38 Erler, 'Care for Books' (cited above, n. 22), 298. Raille's duties at Syon are discussed in detail by de Hamel, pp. 83-91.

39 Many of the purchases in the account rolls discussed by Erler would have been pertinent to this curatorial activity, particularly purchases of horn and nails, used to cover the descriptive book labels placed on the lower boards of Syon books: Erler, 'Care of Books', 303, reports entries for 'pynnes for to Register bookes', and the Syon Rules and Additions require the maintenance of a *Registrum* of the books, which the surviving catalogue is clearly meant to be. Horn is reported in purchases between 1528 and 1530, which is after activity on the surviving catalogue ceased. This suggests that, although the surviving register was not being maintained, curatorial activity was continuing on the collection. None of the surviving Syon books, however, has curatorial signs that differ from the system established by Betson, though as Syon book labels did not show pressmarks or library numbers, this does not mean that the library was not reorganized by his successors as *custos librarie*.

40 See my fuller description of the repair in Hogg, 3. ix-x.

41 It will be remembered that the Bridgettines were formally established under the Rule of St Augustine, and followed Bridget's own *Regula Salvatoris* as customary law. This probably accounts for the original order of the items in M72. But it may be that Betson felt that in recopying the first two items he could now safely give priority to the special Rule of his own community.

42 Cambridge, St John's College, MS 11 (A.11), fol. 45ᵛ; Hogg, 2.144. Similar provisions appear in the vernacular Additions (Aungier, p. 278), but only this Latin version specifies books 'inter fratres'.

43 Now Cambridge, Trinity College, MS B. 15. 2 (339), which has an unbroken sequence of

quire signatures, and is regularly quired in twelves. It is noted at the beginning of quire e, however, that 'continet xvi folia' (fol. 49ʳ). In the catalogue entry for B24, Betson describes an 'Antidotarium Nicholai in cuius medio inseruntur medicine in minoribus quaternis' (Bateson, p. 15).

44 No edition printed after 1524 has been positively identified from *secundo folio*. Mary Bateson suggested that editions from 1526 and later were in the collection, but in all the cases known to me it has been possible to antedate the *secundo folio* in earlier printed editions. The latest currently known are H58 (Theopylact of Constantinople, Basel 1524) and K64 (Eusebius, Strassburg 1524).

45 BL, MS Harley 42 is described in the catalogue as D75, with the added marginal pressmark of d41. Uniquely, d41 is written on fol. 1*ʳ of the manuscript. Only one of the surviving Syon books that I have seen includes the 'Betson' shelfmark on its lower board: Bodl., MS Auct. D. 3. 1, a thirteenth-century Bible given by Richard Billyngham, descibed in the catalogue as R1, has r 1 written large on its lower board below and distinct from the usual book label.

46 Mary Bateson recovered some 'lost' volumes from the Index in Appendix IV of her 1898 edition, pp. xxix-xxx. Dr. Doyle examined the erasures under ultra-violet light in the 1950s and has kindly made available to me his notes, which I have been able to supplement a little with more recent ultra-violet examination.

47 In some cases it appears that large multi-volume editions were intended to be interspersed by smaller volumes in the new sequence. Perhaps this was to allow easier removal of large folio volumes from shelves by 'spacing' them with smaller books. The nine-volume Erasmus edition of Jerome (Basel 1516), for example, is H49-53 and has the Oecolampadius 1520 index added at H54. In the new library marks, these volumes would occupy 164-76, with each volume assigned an even number only. L51-3, the Nuremberg 1489 edition of Bersuire's *Repertorium Morale*, is re-assigned to m16, m18 and m20.

48 F7 (fol. 63ʳ) in a sxv² list of books from Hedvika's College, printed in facsimile *Katalogy Knihoven Kolejí Karlovy University*, with introduction by J. Bečka & J. Benda (Prague, 1948). I am grateful to Professor Anne Hudson for this reference and for much assistance with Wycliffite materials in Syon.

49 For discussion, see e.g., Powell, 'Syon, Caxton and the *Festial*' (cited above, n. 14); J. T. Rhodes, 'Syon Abbey and its Religious Publications in the Sixteenth Century', *Journal of Ecclesiastical History*, 44 (1993), 11-25; G. R. Keiser, 'The Mystics and the Early English Printers: the Economics of Devotionalism', in *The Medieval Mystical Tradition in England: 4*, ed. by M. Glasscoe (Cambridge, 1987), pp. 9-25. The foundational survey of this material remains James Hogg's 'The Contribution of the Brigittine Order to Late Medieval English Spirituality', *Spiritualität Heute und Gestern*, 3, Analecta Cartusiana 35 (1983), 153-74.

50 As noted above, some anonymous collections of sermons by Syon brethren may have survived into the later recensions of the catalogue. For a fuller discussion of Syon sermons and preaching, see Powell, 'Preaching at Syon Abbey'.

51 New Haven, Yale University Library, MS 317, fols 17ᵛ-18ᵛ, quoted by Keiser, 'Patronage and Piety', 40 (cited above, n. 20).

ROBERT HARE'S BOOKS[1]

ANDREW G. WATSON

ROBERT HARE'S NAME is found in manuscripts and printed books in many libraries: at the present I know of forty-six manuscripts that belonged to him (plus five untraced) and sixty-eight printed books (plus thirty-three untraced).[2]

Who was Robert Hare?[3] He was the second of three sons of Sir Nicholas Hare, Master of the Rolls, who died in 1557. The date of Robert's birth is not known but since he matriculated as a fellow-commoner of Gonville Hall, Cambridge, in 1545 we may suppose that he was born around 1530. He took no degree but in the manner of his time entered the Inner Temple, his father's Inn of Court, as a student in February 1547/8. In 1555 he was one of the gentlemen who bore the bannerols at the funeral of Anne of Cleves, ex-queen of Henry VIII, and three years later was in the service of William Paulet, 1st Marquis of Winchester. With Winchester's support he was admitted Clerk of the Pells and held that office until his resignation around 1571. In 1562 he was elected to represent Dunwich in Suffolk in the parliament that met in the following year. The remainder of his life was spent in antiquarian pursuits of which the main beneficiary was the University of Cambridge.

From that bare outline we can recognize the position that Hare held in society: he was of a respectable landed and legal family, he was a civil servant in the capital, and he was known at court. He knew, and was known by, at least some of the right people. Indeed he was just the kind of man whom one would expect to be interested in old records and manuscripts. There is, however, a further factor to take into account: he was a recusant and was from time to time in trouble for his religious beliefs. In 1577 he and his brothers Michael and William and two other men appeared in the return for the Inner Temple in the Diocesan Return of Recusants for England and Wales and are said to have 'not of a longe tyme continued emongst us but [to be] publykelye noted to be verie backward in religion'. In 1578 he appeared in a list of names and addresses of certain papists in London as one who repaired to a house occupied by Lord Chidiock Paulet (a brother of the Marquis of Winchester) whose name immediately preceded Hare's name in the list. This house was in Spitalfields,

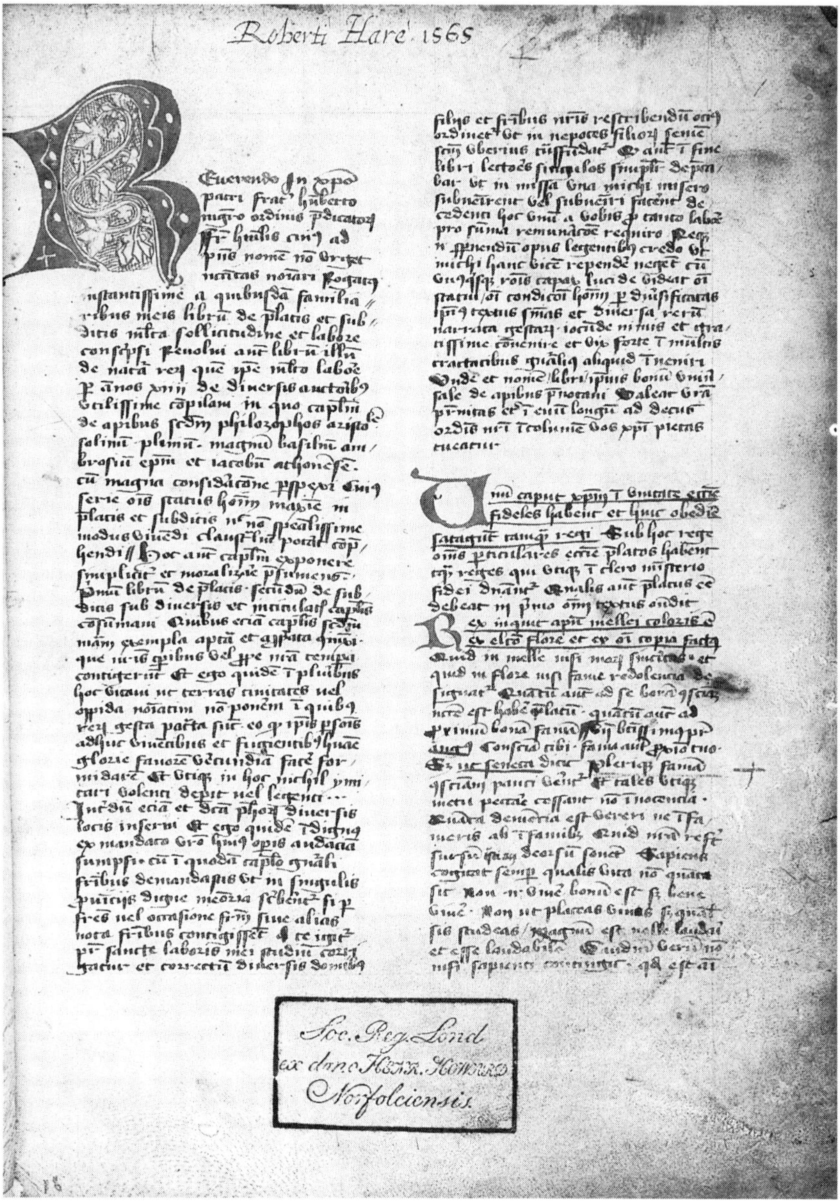

Pl. 1. London, British Library, MS Arundel 141, fol. 1ʳ, with Robert Hare's signature. Reproduced at 69 per cent.

a hotbed of adherents of the old faith.[4] In 1600, too, according to the *Dictionary of National Biography*, he was again in some trouble, probably for religious reasons.

So much for the basic facts about Hare's life. Before turning to details of what books he owned, let me deal with the sources of our knowledge. First, there are the books themselves, in which Hare often wrote 'Roberti Hare', sometimes with the date, sometimes with 'ex dono so-and-so', sometimes preceded by 'Liber' or 'Sum liber'. His writing is usually large and clear, firm rather than elegant, and perhaps not very distinctive.[5] For a facsimile, see p. 210. Inscriptions of one kind or another in his hand are in thirty-five manuscripts and fifty-eight printed books. There are occasional *ex dono* inscriptions recording his gift to someone else. The great majority of his books that have been recognized through these inscriptions are in London, Oxford, and Cambridge, with the odd one in Dublin, Manchester, Norwich, New York, and Philadelphia, but while that pattern of distribution is more or less what one would expect one has to remember that these are the places where most of my own discoveries have been made and where my informants have reported from and others may still turn up. It has to be said, however, that the current indexing of Neil Ker's *Medieval Manuscripts in British Libraries* has brought no more Hare manuscripts to light.[6]

Apart from inscriptions in Hare's books, the main record of them is a list of volumes that Hare gave to the library of Trinity Hall, Cambridge, in *Warren's Book* (see n. 1 above). William Warren, born in 1683, was a fellow and eventually vice-master of Trinity Hall, and his book, still in the college Archives, is a collection of materials for its history. On pp. 271–3 of Dale's edition is 'A Copy of ye catalogue of Books which Mr Hare gave to our Library', to which a colophon adds 'A note of those bookes whiche M^r Ro: Hare hath gyven to Trin: Hall Library by Wille delyvered me [i.e. John Cowell, the Master] by hym selfe, to be safely kept, in Hylary Term anno domini 1604'. Unfortunately neither the colophon nor the list itself is free from ambiguity, the problem with the will being Cowell's statement that the books were 'gyven … by Wille' in 1604. That cannot mean 'by testamentary bequest' for Hare's will (for which see below) became effective on his death in 1611, and in any case says nothing about manuscripts and of the printed books only that they should be sold. Writing a century later, Zacharias von Uffenbach, who visited Cambridge in 1710, gave both 1603 and 1605 as the date[7] but the former is contradicted by Cowell, who was in a position to know, and the latter is suspect since Arthur Agarde borrowed the present Trinity Hall MS 1 from Hare himself as late as November 1604 (see p. 216 below). The difficulty disappears, however, if we take 'by Wille' to mean not that the books were delivered under the terms of Hare's will but that they were delivered according to his desire (or willingly), a usage recorded in the *Oxford English Dictionary* (will sb^1. 16). As for the list, it is quite difficult to reconcile it with what is now in the library. It contains sixty-eight titles of which six are identifiable as manuscripts (one in two volumes) and the rest as printed books. Most of the printed books are certainly in the library to this day but some have strayed and a few are untraced. Of the books that are certainly manuscripts all are still in the library except the two-volume Bible (no. 47), but there are also in the library another seven Hare manuscripts not listed by Cowell (MSS 2, 5, 11, 12, 16, 24, and 30, nos 8, 10, 12, 13, 14, 16, and 18 below). No explanation for this discrepancy is known and one can suggest only that they may have been retained by Hare and given by him at a later date.

With these sources, we have to make what sense we can of Hare's collecting – when, whence, what, and why did he collect, and what happened to the books on his death. Just over sixty dates of acquisition are noted in the books – in 1548, one manuscript; in the 1550s, seven manuscripts and six or seven printed books; in the 1560s, ten or eleven manuscripts and ten printed books; in the 1570s, three manuscripts and fifteen printed books; in the 1580s, three to five manuscripts and four or five printed books; in the 1590s, one manuscript and two printed books; in the 1600s, one manuscript. We can supplement these by his *ex dono* inscriptions – one in 1566 and two in 1568 – and of course the publication date of a contemporary printed book provides the earliest possible date for its acquisition. The absence of dates in manuscripts in the later years may result from diminishing interest on Hare's part, but the relatively large number of dates of acquisition of manuscripts in the 1550s and 1560s may well reflect their greater availability then, before the increasing number of late-sixteenth-century collectors had become active. Unsupported by a precise date of acquisition, a *terminus ante quem non* provided by the publication date of a printed book is equivocal but examination of them shows a sufficiently similar pattern to Hare's acquisition of manuscripts, with the peak years in the 1560s and 1570s, to suggest that opportunity, or affluence, or interest, or a combination of all three, provide a simple explanation.

Identifiable sources of Hare's manuscripts, especially medieval institutional sources, are also very sparse and even if we know the original source we cannot be sure how close Hare himself was to it. Two manuscripts are from St Albans Abbey, the present Cambridge, St John's College, MS 183 (no. 4 in the list below) and Trinity Hall, MS 2 (no. 8). Both belong to the group obtained for that house by Abbot Simon (1167-83) but although we know that Trinity Hall MS 2 was bought by Hare in 1570 we do not know whether they came to him from the same source and what that may have been – surely not, at this date, from the Abbey itself but more likely, since he paid for Trinity Hall MS 2, from one of the rather mysterious booksellers who were selling old manuscripts at this time.[8] Very interestingly, at least two manuscripts came from the Royal Library – the present Bodleian Lib., MS Laud Misc. 684 (no. 43) in 1559 and BL, MS Harley 1197, fols 402-13 (no. 29) in 156(?)3.[9] One manuscript, Hare's most famous, Trinity Hall MS 1 (no. 7), came from St Augustine's Abbey, Canterbury. As long ago as 1965 I listed this manuscript as one that was possibly owned, if we are to believe John Bale, by William Carye, the London clothworker who owned other manuscripts and died in 1573,[10] and since Hare and Parker owned CCCC MS 467 (no. 1) I suggested (fortunately 'very tentatively') that Matthew Parker may have owned Trinity Hall 1 too after Carye. The sequence of owners would then have to be Carye, Parker, Hare, Trinity Hall. But it seems most unlikely that Parker would have parted with such an important Canterbury manuscript and I now regard Carye's ownership as unproven and Hare's immediate source as uncertain. Two manuscripts of Hare's came from Syon Abbey by means unknown: St Paul's Cathedral MS 5 (no. 37), rules for brethen of Syon, and an untraced Brigittine psalter (no. 50) which Hare gave to the Court of Pells in 1568. The manuscript which is now BL, Cotton MS, Cleopatra B. IX (no. 23) was acquired by Hare in 1588 and part at least, a calendar, is from Abbotsbury Abbey in Dorset. It bears a damaged name which I take to be that of the owner between the abbey and Hare – 'Georgius ?De la Corte'. And that is the sum total of English provenances. There is, however, a little (but interesting) evidence of Hare's acquiring books on the Continent. In 1551 he acquired Trinity Hall MS 3 (no. 9), Thomas Netter's *Doctrinale*, previously owned by the Carmelites of Ghent, and Trinity Hall MS 12 (no. 13), Boethius' *De consolatione*, of north French provenance; and in 1565 he acquired BL, MS Arundel 141 (no. 22), Thomas de Cantimpré's *De apibus*, owned by the Friars Minor of Dordrecht. Only their provenance suggests (but probably correctly) that Hare acquired these books on the spot, but four printed books are free of doubt since they bear the place as well as the date of acquisition, viz. Trinity Hall, F. VII. 25 (no. 78), Platina's *De vitis pontificum*, bought by Hare in Louvain in 1563; Trinity Hall, F. VIII. 12 (no. 79), Lipomanus's *Historiae de vitis sanctorum*, bought in Paris in 1564; Trinity Hall, F. I. 28 (no. 60), Jerome's *Vitas patrum*, bought in Paris in 1565; and the untraced copy of William of Newburgh's *Rerum anglicarum libri quinque*, bought in Douai in 1567 (no. 147). Although seven continental books is not much to draw conclusions from, together they suggest that the Roman Catholic Hare may have been abroad in and around 1551 during the reign of the Protestant Edward VI. Since he was elected a member of parliament in 1562 his later and longer period abroad seems unlikely to be on account of his recusancy.

Of books with evidence of only personal ownership prior to Hare's we have even fewer examples. CCCC MS 467 (no. 1), John Grandison's *Vitae S. Thomae Cantuariensis*, came to Hare 'ex dono Johannis Swyfte auditoris', presumably a professional acquaintance (d. 1570) of Hare's since he was an auditor in the Court of Augmentations and later of the Exchequer. Trinity Hall MS 17 (no. 15), a very fine copy of Roger Dymmok's *Contra xii haereses Lollardorum* written for presentation to King Richard II, was given to Hare in 1588 by Anthony Roper, grandson of Sir Thomas More. To that meagre number can be added the donors of four printed books: Trinity Hall Inc. 1 (no. 64), a Bible printed by Schoeffer in Mainz in 1472, was 'ex dono Stephani Tenant clerici 1558' (but I cannot identify the donor); Trinity Hall Inc. 28 (no. 55), a

Fasciculus temporum printed in Louvain in 1475, is 'ex dono Rogeri Amyce armigeri xxi° die Septembris 1557' (pretty certainly the Essex, London, and Suffolk man of that name whose will was proved in PCC in 1574, PCC 32 Martyn); Trinity Hall F.1. 30 (no. 66), Ludolphus Carthusiensis on the psalms, was bought from one Richard Johnson in 1574; BL 698. d. 1 (no. 102), *The apologie of Fridericus Staphylus*, a copy of the English translation of which, published in Antwerp in 1565, was given to Hare by the translator, the Catholic controversialist Thomas Stapleton). Although the meaning of the four-time repetition of the name Robertson/Robynson in Westminster Abbey Library's copy of Catharinus's *Opuscula* (no. 108) remains obscure it is not impossible that before Hare acquired it in 1552 the book was owned by Thomas Robertson or Robinson, Marian dean of Durham, d. 1561.

Leaving for a moment further consideration of what Hare acquired, and why, I turn to the short-term fate of his books, i.e. what happened to them during his lifetime or soon after his death. From our perspective, interested as we are almost entirely in his books, we are surely entitled to be astonished by the brevity of the reference to them in his will.[11] After many bequests to relatives, friends and servants he continues: 'And my will is that all my prynted bookes shalbe sould and the money therof risinge to be deuided into fower partes wherof two partes I giue to John Pendred my seruante before mentioned the thirde parte to my other twoe seruauntes ... and the fourthe parte to my sayed twoe maydes ...'. He also bequeaths his pictures of kings, queens, bishops, and other great personages. Manuscripts are not mentioned but it is of great interest that by implication he distinguishes them from printed books as being no longer in his possession.

Even during his lifetime Hare had been disposing of some books. In 1566 he wrote in the manuscript that is now Bodleian, MS Barlow 21 (no. 40), Ps.-Augustine, etc., 'Liber Henrici Spelman quondam Roberti Hare 1566'. Since the great Sir Henry Spelman was born *c*. 1564 this is presumably a gift to his father, also Henry. The two manuscripts now at Hare's old college, Cambridge, Gonville & Caius, MSS 391-2 and 717 (nos 2 and 3) (historical transcripts by Hare and a chronicle roll), were given by him in 1568 and in that same year he gave the Brigittine psalter referred to above to the Court of Exchequer for the swearing of oaths. His biggest gift was, of course, that made to Trinity Hall (see p. 211 above), probably the result of his friendship with the master, Dr John Cowell,[12] but it is clear that not all of his manuscripts were included in this. Some may have remained in Hare's hands. By 1612 Henry Savile of Banke owned the one-time Dordrecht manuscript that is now BL, MS Arundel 141 (no. 22).[13] By 1621 Sir Robert Cotton owned BL, Cotton MS Julius C. II (no. 26), a list of the archbishops of Canterbury from Augustine to Reginald Pole, which is entered in his 1621 catalogue.[14] A few manuscripts appear in other collections later in the century but we lack any knowledge of where they were in the interim: the present Cambridge, St John's College, MS 183 (no. 4) reached the college via Thomas, Earl of Southampton, in 1635; three manuscripts that Archbishop Laud gave to the Bodleian were part of his first donation and came to the Library in 1633 (MSS Laud Misc. 206 and 684 (nos 42 and 43)) and 1634 (MS Laud Misc. 707 (no. 44); Thomas Howard, Earl of Arundel, d. 1646, who owned Henry Savile's Dordrecht manuscript, presumably owned the present College of Arms, MSS Arundel 19 and 39 (nos 31 and 32). An unknown W. Cockburn bought the untraced printed William of Newburgh (no. 147) in 1635. It is perhaps surprising that only two of Hare's manuscripts (nos 5 and 6) are known to be in a Cambridge library that was growing rapidly in Hare's time and just after – that of Trinity College. One of these, MS B. 2. 18 (61) (no. 5) passed through Matthew Parker's hands (probably directly from Hare) and reached Trinity by gift of Thomas Neville, Master of Trinity and Dean of Canterbury, *c*. 1611-12, but the other, MS B. 10. 12 (223) (no. 6), did not reach the college until around 1700 and nothing is known about its whereabouts during the preceding century. Although some of the five or six books now in Lambeth Palace Library and others elsewhere bear a few indications of ownership before they reached their present locations, these too all date from too long after Hare's time to be significant, but it is possible that Westminster Abbey, whose library was also growing in the early seventeenth century, may have acquired its four Hare books at that time.

What then did Hare collect and why, and what more can that tell us about the man? It requires only a brief perusal of the list of Hare's manuscripts and printed books to gain an impression that his acquisitions were very miscellaneous in subject-matter. I see no signs of the pattern that one finds in the libraries of Dee, Parker, or Cotton, whose interests were so consistent and whose determination to indulge those interests were so strong, that each of these collections has a character of its own.[15] Putting it another way, if one is searching for a text or for a manuscript whose location one cannot recall, one can say with reasonable confidence that it is or is not the kind of thing that is likely to be in one of these three great collections. But no such impression comes from Hare's. Admittedly it is small, but if his means or opportunities were limited one might think that that might introduce a special character to his collection. One's impression is, in fact, of an interest in acquiring at least the manuscripts for their own sake. Even if one allows for the fact that as medieval manuscripts usually contain several texts a collector might well find himself in possession of a good many he did not want, his possession of the *Historia scholastica*, the *De apibus*, Plutarch, Grosseteste, Honorius, Terence, saints' lives, service books, anti-Lollard tracts, and so on combine only to give an impression of random acquisition. If we knew more about Hare's historical work (as distinct from his antiquarian interests, about which there can be no reasonable doubt) we might be able to get some idea of how he used them, but evidence from the books is virtually non-existent and indeed it is difficult to see how some of his texts could have been relevant to historical work of any kind, whether the collections on Cambridge and Oxford for which he is best known or the only other work attributable to him, the *Treatise on Military Discipline* in

BL, Cotton MS, Julius F. V (no. 27). As one might expect, however, there is some evidence for his contacts with other antiquaries, and their references to him are respectful. In a letter to John Stow which can be dated to before 1 March 1575, Henry Savile of Blaithroyde (Henry Savile the Elder), asks to be commended to 'good Master Hare', and in another letter Savile asks Stow to ask Hare about a book that has gone missing in transit.[16] (Since there is a reference in Savile's letter to the imminent publication of Lord William Howard's edition of Florence of Worcester's chronicle, the latter letter can be dated to 1592.) In an address to the Society of Antiquaries in 1604, Arthur Agarde, as recorded by Thomas Hearne,[17] stated that 'Mr Robert Hare, that worthy antiquary', had lent him 'a large booke of St Augustines ...', i.e. the celebrated Elmham manuscript now Trinity Hall MS 1 (no. 7). But Hare was not a member of the Society of Antiquaries himself. Indeed, although Agarde, a prominent Antiquary, spoke well of him, Hare seems to have been not even on the fringes of that body, if we can judge from the fact that Linda Van Norden, in her 1946 thesis on the Society[18] did not find it necessary to demolish a case that he *should* be considered a member: unlike one or two others, one of whom was Sir Walter Cope (on whom see below), there seems to be no suggestion from any source that Hare was a member. Since he was known to members, it seems to me to be odd that he was not, and if his religion was an obstacle one has to wonder how John Stow came to be a member despite having had his books searched while under suspicion of recusancy. Nor, oddly, is Hare included in the list of owners of medieval manuscripts that John Joscelyn, one of Archbishop Parker's secretaries, drew up for Parker's use *c.* 1565.[19] Although about 120 works by medieval British writers are included, the list of names of owners runs to less than thirty persons, with some curious omissions. John Dee is one, by the 1560s well known in Cambridge and at court as the owner of many books, and if Joscelyn's list should have included anyone it should surely have been him. Robert Hare, known to the Parker circle, may have been an oversight but it is possible that in the 1560s his still modest collection of manuscripts included few of the historical texts that were the object of Parker's greatest interest.

It seems to me, therefore, as one who is interested in post-Reformation collectors primarily because of what can be learned from them about their manuscripts, that as a collector of medieval manuscripts (and the owner of a respectable library of printed books) Hare is of interest rather than import- ance. Thomas Dackombe, monk and later minor canon of Winchester, had only about two dozen manuscripts (as far as we know) but many are from Winchester and he wrote his name and the price he paid on them very soon after the cathedral had ceased to be a cathedral priory, that is at what is surely the most crucial time in the history of that library and its books. Although some annotations suggest that he was sympathetic to the old religion he clearly had no intention that the books should be restored to their former owners, so we have interesting evidence of a mid-sixteenth-century attitude to these matters.[20] John Twyne of Canterbury is an even more interesting man – the first of at least three generations of historians, schoolmaster, mayor, and Member of Parliament for Canterbury, occupying a religious position which seems very unclear. He was literally within reach of the great hoard of Canterbury manuscripts at a time when they were most vulnerable.[21] The Saviles of Halifax, father and son, acquired books over a period of sixty years, and the scale and topographical consistency of their collecting (i.e. largely from north of England monasteries) give them considerable importance.[22] Parker, Dee, and Cotton were large-scale collectors and used their books for identifiable and consistent purposes.[23] Investigation of Sir Walter Cope's collecting activities led me to say much the same about him but since over forty of his two hundred or so manuscripts reached the Bodleian in its earliest years, their previous co-existence in the Cope library provided useful evidence about some provenances of an important collection.[24] Having devoted some time to Hare I feel that I know nothing about individual manuscripts that I was not in a position to discover before and that no picture emerges of his collection. I have, however, been surprised to learn of so many survivors of his library of printed books (and have some faith in the discovery of more)[25] and am sure that his importance as a benefactor to and in the University of Cambridge is great enough to justify examination of them. From that a more positive impression of the man and his books might emerge.

   In the following list the order is 1-46 Manuscripts, traced; 47-51 Manuscripts, untraced; 52-119, Printed books, traced; 120-52 Printed books, untraced; 153-57, Rejected. Note that the large number of printed books has led to their being listed in very summary form. Unless Hare's *ex libris*, with or without a date, contains evidence of earlier provenance and/or price or other significant information, it is omitted and replaced by an obelus (†) before the pressmark which indicates that Hare's name is in the book, and by a double obelus (††) before a date, if any, which indicates that the date is Hare's. A paraph (¶) before a pressmark indicates that Hare's signature, or occasionally initials, is lacking. Ownership of the printed books before and after Hare is noted only exceptionally.

MANUSCRIPTS: I, TRACED

1   Cambridge, Corpus Christi College, MS 467. John Grandisson, *Vita Thomae Cantuariensis*, s. xv[in]. On verso of first parchment endleaf: 'Liber Roberti Hare ex dono Iohannis Swyfte auditoris'. Owned by Parker but (*ex info* Timothy Graham) showing no evidence that he or his circle were interested in the contents. Swift was an Auditor in the (second) Court of Augmentations and from 1554 until his death in 1570 7th Auditor of the Exchequer (W. C. Richardson, *History of the Court of Augmentations 1536-1554* (Baton Rouge, La., 1961), p. 280; J. C. Sainty, *Officers of the Exchequer* (List and Index Society, Special Series, 18, 1983), p. 121. (I am indebted to Nigel Ramsay for these references.)

2 Cambridge, Gonville & Caius College, MSS 391-2. Transcripts, partly in Hare's hand. MS 391 art. 1 was copied by him in Trinity Hall MS 30, below.

3 Cambridge, Gonville & Caius College, MS 717. Chronicle Roll, anno 1447. At head of text: 'Collegio de Gonevile et Caius dono dedit Robertus Hare armiger anno domini 1568'. *DMC*, no. 253, pl. 247.

4 Cambridge, St John's College, MS 183 (G.15). *Novum Testamentum*, 1167 × 1183. On fols 1 and 9: 'Roberti Hare'. 'Hunc libellum fecit dominus Symon abbas \de/ Sancto Albano quem qui abstulerit ana<thema> sit'. *DMC*, no. 306, pl. 80.

5 Cambridge, Trinity College, MS B. 2. 18 (61), pt 2, fols 104-12. *Vita S. Ricardi Cicestrensis*, s. xiv. On the first leaf is 'Hare' in red Parkerian crayon, the most likely meaning of which is that Parker acquired the book from Hare, just as 'Twyne' written in red crayon in MS Corpus 161 probably indicates that Twyne was Parker's source for it.

6 Cambridge, Trinity College, MS B. 10. 12 (223). Bonaventura, *Vita Christi*, s. xv[1]. On fol. 1[r], erased: 'Roberti Hare 1548'. Given by John Laughton, MA, fellow and University Librarian, 1686-1712. On stamped leather binding are initials 'MA'. An origin 'probably in Northern England' is suggested by K. L. Scott, *Later Gothic Manuscripts 1390-1490: a Survey of Manuscripts Illuminated in the British Isles*, ed. by J. J. G. Alexander, 6; 2 vols (London, 1996), II, no. 62: her plate (I, no. 248) reproduces fol. 9 and colour plate (I, no. 10) reproduces fol. 43.

7 Cambridge, Trinity Hall, MS 1. Thomas of Elmham, *Historia abbatiae S. Augustini Cantuariensis*, anno 1414. On fol. 1[r]: 'Liber iste quondam spectauit ad coenobium beatorum Apostolorum Petri et Pauli siue Augustini iuxta muros ciuitatis Cantuarie. omnibus monachorum spoliatis, et in usum regium conuersis, idem liber fortuito peruenit ad manus magistri Roberti Haer, qui dedit eundem Collegio siue Aule Sancte Trinitatis Cantebrig. ibidem tuto et secure custodiendum. Hac tamen conditione ut si imposterum (fauente deo) monasterium illud reedificare contingeret: Tunc magister et socii collegij siue aule sanctetatis predicte, eundem librum monachis eiusdem cenobii restitui facerent. Quoniam ad eos de iura pertinere debet.' This is not in Hare's hand but, after the receipt of the book in Trinity Hall (for the date of which see p. 211 above), may have been added on the basis of a lost inscription by Hare which, if written many years before, would account for the inexplicably optimistic notion that the St Augustine's, Canterbury, community might be re-established. (The only other explanation for that would seem to be that the inscription was added to please an aged donor who was perhaps out of touch with reality). For a suggestion that before Hare the manuscript may have belonged to William Carye see A. G. Watson, 'Christopher and William Carye, collectors of monastic manuscripts, and "John Carye"', *The Library*, 5th series 20 (1965), 135-42, at 139; but see also p. 213 above, where doubt is expressed about Carye's ownership. *WB*, no. 1; *DMC*, no. 390, pl. 200, q.v. for other reproductions.

8 Trinity Hall, MS 2. Radulphus Flaviacensis, *Super Leviticum*, 1167 × 1183. On fol. 391[r]: 'Liber Roberti Hare precium .x. solidorum anno christi M.D.lxx.'; 'Hunc librum fecit fieri dominus symon abbas sancto albano quem qui ei abstulerit aut titulum hunc deleuerit anathema sit.' *DMC*, no. 391, pl. 81.

9 Trinity Hall, MS 3. Thomas Netter of Walden, *Doctrinale contra Wiclevistas*, anno

1500. On fol. 1ᵛ: Iste liber est < > uiri Domini Roberti Hare Angli'; fol. 1ʳ, 'Roberti Hare 1551'. Written for the Carmelites of Ghent: for scribal inscription see *DMC*, no. 392 (pl. 348 shows a later inscription). *WB*, no. 37.

10   Trinity Hall, MS 5. Augustine, *De civitate Dei*, etc., s. xv. On fol. 1ʳ: 'Roberti Hare 1552'. Christ Church Canterbury provenance, suggested in Trinity Hall catalogue, is rejected by Ker, *MLGB*.

11   Trinity Hall, MS 10. Vincent de Beauvais, *Imago mundi*, s. xv. On fol. 1ʳ of text is Hare's name. According to the Trinity Hall catalogue the manuscript was written at Bruges, but no evidence is provided. *WB*, no. 36.

12   Trinity Hall, MS 11. Petrus Blesensis, *Epistolae*, s. xv. On fol. 1ʳ: 'Liber Roberti Hare 1565'.

13   Trinity Hall, MS 12. Boethius, *De consolatione philosophiae*, in French, anno 1406. On fol. 1ʳ: 'Roberti Hare 1551'. On fol. 145ᵛ: 'Ce liure appartient a noble damoyselle mademoiselle quiercheuille [Durevie de Querqueville, Normandy] qui se trouvera cy luy Rende' (s. xvᵉˣ). For scribal colophon see *DMC*, no. 393, pl. 194.

14   Trinity Hall, MS 16. *Theologica*, s. xv. On fol. 92ᵛ: 'Liber Roberti Hare precium xxᵈ primo die Junii anno domini millesimo quingentesimo sexagesimo'. Hare's name is also at the front of the book.

15   Trinity Hall, MS 17. Roger Dymmok, *Contra XII haereses Lollardorum*, anno 1395. On front pastedown is 'Roberti Hare Londini 12° die Junij 1588 ex dono Domini Anthonij Rooper': he was the grandson of Sir Thomas More. On fol. 1ʳ: 'Roberti Hare'. This is the presentation copy for King Richard II and a very fine manuscript: see *DMC*, no. 394 and pl. 178. A. H. Lloyd, *The Early History of Christ's College Cambridge* (Cambridge, 1934), pp. 9-10, provides evidence for ownership after Richard II – John Wilok, John Carpenter (d. 1441), and (by the latter's bequest) William Byngham, rector of St John Zachary, London. *WB*, no. 43.

16   Trinity Hall, MS 24. Stephen Langton, *Super XII prophetas*, s. xiii. On fol. 1ʳ: 'Roberti Hare, 1562'. Christ Church Canterbury provenance, suggested in Trinity Hall catalogue, is rejected by Ker, *MLGB*.

17   Trinity Hall, MS 25. Ranulph Higden, *Polychronicon*, s. xiv. On fol. 1ʳ, partly cut off: 'Roberti Hare, 1586'. Possibly the *Polychronicon* listed as *WB*, no. 35, but that is in English and not said to be a manuscript.

18   Trinity Hall, MS 30. *De vita et morte domini W Bateman, Norwicensis episcopi*, s. xvi. On fol. 1ʳ: 'Roberti Hare'. Copied by Hare from his manuscript now Gonville and Caius College, MS 391 (no. 2 above), art. 1. See *WB*, pp. 7, 11.

19   University Archives, Hare A.i-ii; B.i-iii; C.i-iv. *Liber privilegiorum et libertatis alme universitatis Cantabrigiensis*. Copies by professional scribes of transcripts by Hare relating to the University, compiled from the University's records and other sources. Presented to the University by Hare in 1587. MSS A.i-ii are on vellum, very elaborately decorated, with frequent depictions of Hare's coat of arms and a dedicatory epistle with his notarial signature. MSS B.i-iii are the Registrary's copy, on paper and lacking the dedicatory epistle. MSS C.i-iv are the Vice-Chancellor's copy, with vellum title pages but the text on paper. Hare's arms appear frequently. The relationship of the sets is very difficult to establish; in the present context it may be safe to say that Hare presumably owned the A and B sets (A being derived from B), at least to the extent of commissioning and perhaps handling them. Although his arms are in C, it seems uncertain that that ever passed through his hands. (I am greatly indebted to Elisabeth Leedham-Green for instructing me in such facts as can be established. The summary and interpretation are, however, mine.)

20 Cambridge, University Library, MS FF. vi. 11. Thomas Scrope of Bradley, OCarm, *De institutione fratrum Carmelitarum ordinis*, s. xiv. Inside front cover: 'pertinet ad Vniuersitatem Cantebrige ex dono Roberti Hare'.

21 CUL, MS Ff. vi. 13. Michael of Cornwall, *Invectiva contra magistrum Henricum Abrincensem*, s. xiii/xiv. Fol. ii^v: 'Dono Roberti Hare 1594'.

22 London, British Library, MS Arundel 141. Thomas de Cantimpré, *De apibus*, s. xv. On fol. 1^r: 'Roberti Hare 1565' (see Pl. 1). On verso of first flyleaf: 'Liber conventus fratrum minorum in dordraco [Dordrecht]'. No. 236 in A. G. Watson, *The Manuscripts of Henry Savile of Banke* (London, 1969). With bookstamp 'Soc. Reg. Lond. ex dono Henr. Howard Norfolciensis'.

23 BL, Cotton MS, Cleopatra B. IX. *Treatise of chess*, in French; etc., s. xiii^{ex}. On fol. 4^r: 'Roberti hare 1588'. On fol. 59^r the calendar, at 12 Oct., has 'Dedicacio ecclesie beati petri allddesbyrie' and, at 16 Oct., 'Obiit dompnus rogerus abbas huius loci': from the Benedictine abbey of Abbotsbury, Dorset. On fol. 2^r: 'Memorandum quod ego Georgius De la corte huius libri sum possessor', s. xvi. Wills of two members of a de la Court family, resident in the precinct of Blackfriars, London, are PCC 2 Daughtry (1576) and 13 Daughtry (1577).

24 BL, Cotton MS, Faustina C. III. Robert Hare, *Collectanea de academia et villa Cantabrigiae*. Paper, ss. xv, xvi. A collection of original documents and transcripts in a number of hands, the basis of Hare's *Collectanea* in Cambridge University Archives, Hare A.i-ii; B.i-iii; C.i-iv.

25 BL, Cotton MS, Faustina C. VII. Robert Hare, *Collectanea de academia et villa Oxoniae*. Paper, ss. xv, xvi. Apparently not the basis of a formal copy: see Oxford Historical Society, 30 (1895), p. 195. On a front flyleaf is a note initialled by Sir Frederic Madden, 'This volume was formerly in the Old Royal Library binding.'

26 BL, Cotton MS, Julius C. II, fols 92-6. *Series archiepiscoporum Cantuariensium ab Augustino ad Ricardum Pole, 1555*. Paper, s. xvi^2. Listed in Cotton's catalogue in BL, MS Harley 6018, fol.116^v by 1621 as 'Series Archiepiscoporum Cant. per Robertum Hare' but there is nothing in the manuscript to confirm this, whether Hare as author or Hare as donor. The hand, a good sloped secretary, may however, be the hand of Cotton Julius F. V. below.

27 BL, Cotton MS, Julius F. V. R. Hare(?), *Treatise on military discipline*. Paper, s. xvi^{med}. On fol. 1^r: 'Roberti Hare 1556'. On fol. 55^v: 'Scriptum et finitum per me Robertus Hare Vltimo die Junij .1557'. As these Hare inscriptions are not in the same, secretary, script as the text, which is perhaps that of a professional writer (cf. that of Cotton Julius C. II, fols 92-6 above), it is evident that the date at the beginning is not the date of acquisition but perhaps the date when composition or copying of this fair copy began, or conceivably, when Hare began to compose it. It is not identifiable in Cotton's 1621 catalogue in BL, MS Harley 6018.

28   BL, MS Egerton 826. *Paternoster; Ave Maria*, etc. s. xv. On fol. 1ʳ: 'Robert Hare'. Fol. 1ʳ: 'James Orchard Halliwell No. 219'.

29   BL, MS Harley 1197, fols 402-13. Johannes Vossius, *Encomium in laudem Thomae Wolsey*, s. xvi^med. On fol. 402ʳ: 'Roberti hare 156(?)3 [1583?]'. The book was presented by the author to Cardinal Wolsey. James Carley, in a letter, has remarked that some of Wolsey's manuscripts went to the Royal Library on his death and that although this one is not found in the 1542 Westminster inventory of that library there is a possibility that Hare could have had it from there. A link between Hare and the royal household would be William Paulet, Marquess of Winchester, in whose service he was, or his recusant brother Lord Chidiock Paulet: for his connection with Hare see Nancy Pollard Brown (cited above, n. 5), pp. 130-1. If William Paulet was the connection the uncertain date of Hare's acquisition will be more probably 1563; if Lord Chidiock was, 1583 is more plausible.

30   BL, MS Lansdowne 390. Transcript of deeds of foundation and endowment of the Hospital of St John and St Katherine, Heytesbury, Wilts., by Margaret, widow of 2nd Lord Hungerford (d. 1459) and others, 1472, s. xv^ex. On fol. 1ʳ is stuck a strip of parchment probably cut from a preliminary leaf that was discarded when the book was rebound: on it is 'Roberti Hare precium xijᵈ 13 Aug. 1579 Londini.' On the granting of a licence to found and on the Hospital see *VCH Wilts.* 3 (1956), 337-40.

31   London, College of Arms, MS Arundel 19. *Chronicle of London to 1451*, s. xv^med. On fol. 1ʳ is 'Roberti Hare'.

32   London, College of Arms, MS Arundel 39. *Treatise on English kings' rights to the crown of France*, etc., s. xviⁱⁿ. On fol. 1ʳ is 'Roberti Hare 1563'.

33   London, Lambeth Palace Library, MS 156. Petrus Comestor, *Historia scholastica*, s. xii. On the first leaf of a preliminary quire: 'Roberti Hare 1566'. On the verso of the last leaf is the caution of Simon Denham 'in cista cecestrie', Oxford, 1480, and renewal by St[ran]gwysh, 1482. These men are probably Dr Simon Dunham, fellow of Lincoln College 1471 etc., in 1501 a Norfolk rector, and George Strangwysche (Strangways), rector of Lincoln College, 1480 (*BRUO*). Later owned by Abp. Richard Bancroft, d. 1611, founder of the Library.

34   Lambeth Palace, MS 186. *Psalterium*, s. xv. Fol. 1ᵇ, 'Roberti Hare 1563, Refugium meum dominus'. Later owned by Abp. Richard Bancroft, as no. 33 above.

35   Lambeth Palace, MS 341. Petrus de Monte, *De virtutum et vitiorum inter se differentia*; etc., s. xv^ex. Fol. 1: 'Roberti hare 1576'. Later owned by Abp. Richard Bancroft, as no. 33 above.

36   Lambeth Palace, MS 463. Battista Agnese, Portolan atlas, s. xvi^med, a copy of National Maritime Museum, MS 33.9921C/P12 which was made in 1555. On the pastedown: 'Roberti Hare 1564'. Written in very fine and delicate script with good illumination. On fol. 1ʳ are the royal arms of England: probably a presentation or commissioned copy. Gold-stamped leather binding over wooden boards with small compass set into inside of back board. Later owned by Abp. Richard Bancroft, as no. 33 above. Listed but not described in M. R. James's catalogue of the Lambeth manuscripts (as no. 156 below): for contents see H. R. Wagner, 'The Manuscript Atlases of Battista Agnese', *Papers of the Bibliographical Society of America*, 25 (1931), 2-110, at 94-5 (no.

LVII, previously at Westheim bei Augsburg), and D. Howse & P. Bittings, *An Inventory of the Naval and Astronomical Collections of the National Maritime Museum, Greenwich* (1973), section 6-21.

37   London, St Paul's Cathedral, MS 5. *Rules for Syon*, in English, s. xvi^{in}. On fol. iv^v: 'Liber Roberti Hare', 'Robert Hare', and an erased date, perhaps 1580. Written for the use of the brethren of the Bridgettine community at Syon.

38   New York, Pierpont Morgan Library, MS M. 100 (Clare, Giffard and Vescy Psalter), *c.* 1290-1300. On fol. 1^r: 'Roberti hare 1561'. L. F. Sandler, *Gothic Manuscripts 1285-1385: Survey*, V, ed. Alexander (cited above at no. 6) (London & Oxford, 1986), II, no. 12, tentatively ascribes it to the diocese of London.

39   Norwich, Norfolk and Norwich Record Office, Hare deposit. *Magnus annulus (Opus paschale)*, s. xvi. Antiquarian collections by Hare, with obits added by other members of the Hare family. It descended via a collateral branch of the family to Sir Thomas Hare, Bart., of Stow Hall, Stow Bardolph, Norfolk and was deposited with other records by his descendents in 1942. For a description of the contents see *Proceedings of the Society of Antiquaries of London*, 4 (1859), 258-60.

40   Oxford, Bodleian Library, MS Barlow 21 (*SC* 6459). (1) A poem on the Creation beg. 'Omnia disponens nusquam metam sibi ponens' (Walther, *Initia*, 13258); (2) Ps. Augustine, *Tractatus 3 de baptismo, PL*, 40, col. 1213. On p. 1: in Hare's hand, 'Liber Henrici Spelman quondam Roberti Hare 1566': the recipient must be Henry Spelman, father of Sir Henry Spelman, the jurist. On p. iv: 'Liber Tho: Barlow Coll. Reg. S[ocii] ex dono ... domini Clementis Spelman Henrici ... filii et scacarii sue fisci regis baronis'. On p. vii Barlow added his date of acquisition, 22 July 1659. It came to the Bodleian by his bequest in 1691. On fol. v^r: 'R. Fanshawe' (s. xvii).

41   Bodleian, MS Gough Eccl. Top. 2 (*SC* 17678). *Extract from* Valor Ecclesiasticus, *Rochester – Hereford*. Paper, s. xvi^i. On the back pastedown: 'Liber Roberti Hare 1607'.

42   Bodleian, MS Laud Misc. 206. Robert Grosseteste, *De septem vitiis*; Honorius Augustodunensis, *Elucidarium*; etc. Paper, anno 1495. Fol. 1^v: 'Liber Roberti Hare.' Whittawed leather binding over wooden boards with remains of clasp for strap. Probably written in Oxford, in the diocese of which the scribe, Thomas Halle, fellow of Lincoln College, was a rector until his death (*BRUO*, II, p. 853). *DMO*, no. 599, pl. 792.

43   Bodleian, MS Laud Misc. 684. Plutarch, *Life of Paulus Aemilius*, translated by Henry Parker, Lord Morley, s. xvi^{med}. On front pastedown: 'Liber Roberti Hare 1559'. Wooden boards, covered with worn buff velvet. Presented by Morley to Henry VIII and acquired from the Royal Library by Hare perhaps via William Paulet (for whom see no. 29 above). See also J. P. Carley, 'Presentation of manuscripts from the collection of Henry VIII: the case of Henry Parker, Lord Morley', in *Order and Connexion: Studies in Bibliography and Book History*, ed. by R. C. Alston (Woodbridge, 1997), 167, 175. Pächt & Alexander, III, no. 1184. *WB*, 272.

44   Bodleian, MS Laud Misc. 707. Galfridus de Vino Salvo, *Poetria novella*; etc. Paper, s. xv. On fol. 4^r: 'Roberti Hare'.

45   Bodleian, MS Rawlinson A. 398. Bonaventura, *Vita Christi*, s. xv^{med}. Fol. 1^r: 'Roberti hare. 1553'.

46   Bodleian, MS Selden supra 55 (*SC* 3443). *Vita Edwardi regis et confessoris*, s. xv^{med}.

Fol. 9ʳ: 'Roberti hare 1552' (illustrated in H. R. Luard, *Lives of Edward the Confessor*, Rolls Series, (1858), pl. [3]).

MANUSCRIPTS: II, UNTRACED

47 'Biblia Sacra manuscripta in duobus voluminibus', *WB*, no. 38.

48 BL, MS Lansdowne 254, art. 20 (now fols 201-18) is headed 'This is an Index of a Ms of Clarenceux Lee now in the custody of Mʳ Hare'. The contents of the manuscript are evidently heraldic and the reference is to Richard Lee or Leigh, Clarenceux king of arms, d. 1597. The Lansdowne manuscript is a collection of papers of various dates concerning topics which were of interest to and discussed by members of the Elizabethan Society of Antiquaries. This item and no. 49 below, which is in the same hand, date from the first quarter of the 17th century, after 1617, and the headings, also in the same hand, from later in that century. It is not clear whether 'in the custody of', and 'in the hands of' in no. 49 indicate permanent ownership by Hare.

49 BL, MS Lansdowne 254, art. 21 (now fols 219-24) is headed 'An abridgment of a Ms of ffellowe Norroy now in the hands of Mr Hare'. The contents of the manuscript are heraldic and the reference is presumably to Sir Richard St George, Norroy king of arms 1604-23, a member of the Elizabethan Society of Anriquaries. See no. 48 above.

50 Bridgettine Psalter (cf. Kal., 28 May, 7 Oct.). Inscription on first flyleaf records that it was given by Hare, Clerk of the Pells, October 1568, to the Court of Exchequer for oath-taking. Sotheby sale 14 Dec. 1932, lot 413 (John Meade Falkner sale) to Marks & Co. for £27 (*MLGB* Supplement). Not subsequently traced. From Syon Abbey.

51 Psalter, 'no. 267 in a bookseller's catalogue' reported by Kathleen Scott, inscribed 'R. Hare, 1568'. This is evidently no. 267 in a J. & J. Leighton sale catalogue, undated and variously ascribed to 1912 and 1914, but the description does not mention the date 1568. Not subsequently traced, but if the Leighton description is correct the absence of Syon provenance and any mention of Hare's gift of the book to the Court of Exchequer shows that it was distinct from no. 50 above.

PRINTED BOOKS: I, TRACED

[Nos 56-97, all now at Trinity Hall, are recorded in *WB*, 271-2;
the others have been traced elsewhere.]

52 †Cambridge, Trinity College, C. 7. 6⁴. Baldwin, archbishop of Canterbury, *De altaris sacramento sermo* (Cambridge, 1521), *STC* 1242. Later signature on title-page of Fran: Brooke. Part of a pamphlet volume (date span 1521-93) with no sign of Hare's name on other components. Given to Trinity by John Laughton.

53 †Cambridge, Trinity Hall, Inc. 6 (B. III. 23), Bernardinus de Bustis, *Rosarium sermonum* (Hagenau, 1500), Hain *4164, *GW* 5808). ††1559. *WB*, no. – . *EPB*, no. 6.

54 †Trinity Hall, Inc. 26 (B. V. 24). Terence, Works, in Latin and French (Paris, n.d.) (Hain 15435). *WB*, no. – . *EPB*, no. 26.

55 †Trinity Hall, Inc. 28 (D. I. 15), W. Rolewinck, *Fasciculus temporum* (Louvain, 1475) (Hain 6920). ††1557. 'Ex dono Rogeri Amyce armigeri'. Amyce is probably the

'Roger Amyce esquier, Colnewake, Essex; London, Welleshall, Suffolk'. whose will was proved in the Prerogative Court of Canterbury in 1574. *WB*, no. 62. *EPB*, no. 28.

56 ¶Trinity Hall, Inc. 5 (D. II. 29), Hartmann Schedel, *Das Buch der Chroniken und Geschichten* (Nuremberg, 1493); Hain 14508; *BMC*, II, 437. *WB*, no. 2.

57 †Trinity Hall, F. I. 5, Eusebius Pamphilus, *Historiae ecclesiasticae scriptores Graeci* (Basel, 1570) Adams, E1097. *WB*, no. 4.

58 †Trinity Hall, F. VIII. 6, Laurentius Surius, *De probatis sanctorum historiis*, 6 vols (Cologne, 1570-5); Adams, S2103 (Trinity Hall copy). ††1580. *WB*, no. 5.

59 †Trinity Hall, F. I. 29, Capgrave, *Nova legenda Angliae* (London, 1516); *STC* 4601. *WB*, no. 6.

60 Trinity Hall, F. I. 28, Jerome, *Vitas patrum* (Lyon, 1507); Adams, J145. On title-page: 'Liber Roberti Hare Angli Parisiensis 1565. precium 6 sous'. *WB*, no. 7.

61 ¶Trinity Hall, L. VI. 22, (1) Asser, *Aelfredi regis res gestae* (1574), *STC* 863. (2) Thomas Walsingham, *Historia brevis* (1574), *Ypodigma Neustrie* (1574); *STC* 25004-5. *WB*, no. 9.

62 ¶Trinity Hall, L. VI. 23, Matthew of Westminster, *Flores historiarum* (1570); *STC* 17653. *WB*, no. 10.

63 †Trinity Hall, E. I. 28, Leandro Alberti, *Descriptio totius Italiae* (Venice, 1556); Adams, – . On title-page: 'Londini mense iulio 1572 precius viii^s Roberti Hare'. *WB*, no. 28.

64 Trinity Hall, Inc. 1 (C. IV. 12), *Biblia* (Schoeffer, Mainz, 1472) (Hain 3052, *GW* 4211). †1558. On flyleaf: 'Liber Roberti Hare ex dono Stephani Tenant clerici'. In a blind-stamped binding with crowned rose, fleur-de-lys and portcullis. Probably *WB*, no. 40, 'Biblia Sacra antiquissimae Impressionis'. *EPB*, no. 1.

65 ¶Trinity Hall, F. I. 3, George Bullock, *Oeconomia concordantia* (Antwerp, 1572). *WB*, no. 41.

66 Trinity Hall, F. I. 30, Ludolphus Carthusiensis, *In psalterium expositio* (Lyon, 1518). Adams, L1674. Inside front cover, 'Liber Roberti Hare quem emit a Richardo Johnson 1574'. *WB*, no. 42.

67 ¶Trinity Hall, A. IV. 12, Ambrosius Calepinus, *Dictionarium* (Venice, 1576); Adams, C216. *WB*, no. 44.

68 †Trinity Hall, G. II. 21, Augustine, *Confessio Augustiniana* (Dilingen, 1569). Adams, A2178. ††1573. *WB*, no. 46.

69 †Trinity Hall, M. I. 24, John Acton, *Constitutiones legitime seu legatine regionis anglicani* (Paris, 1504); *STC* 17108. ††1578. *WB*, no. 48 (a conflated entry which includes no. 70 below).

70 †Trinity Hall, *M. I. 24, W. Lyndwode, *Provinciale* (Antwerp, 1525); *STC* 17111; Adams, L2117. ††1578. *WB*, no. 48 (a conflated entry which includes no. 69 above).

71 †Trinity Hall, J. II. 33, Ciprianus Leovitius, *De eclipsibus 1554 usque 1606* (Augsburg, 1556); Adams, L519. ††1560. *WB*, no. 49.

72 †Trinity Hall, F. VII. 24, John Fisher (Roffen.), *De veritate corporis et sanguinis Christi in Eucharistia* (Cologne, 1527). Adams, F534. ††1573. *WB*, no. 50.

73 ¶Trinity Hall, L. III. 14, John Bale, *Scriptorum illustrium maioris Britannie catalogus* (Basel, 1549); Adams, B136. *WB*, no. 11.

74 †Trinity Hall, L. VI. 1, Henry Savile, *Rerum Anglicarum scriptores* (1596), *STC* 21783. ††1596. *WB*, no. 3.

75 †Trinity Hall, J. III. 12, Conrad Gesner, *Bibliotheca instituta* (Zürich, 1574); Adams, G514. ††1574. *WB*, no. 12.

76 ¶Trinity Hall, E. I. 18, Philipp Lonicer, *Chronicorum Turcicorum tomus …* (Frankfurt am Main, 1578); Adams, L1455. *WB*, no. 14.

77 †Trinity Hall, L. VI. 16, Hector Boethius, *Scotorum historiae* (Lausanne, 1574); Adams, B2309. ††1575. *WB*, no. 16.

78 Trinity Hall, F. VII. 25, Bartolomeo Platina, *De vitis pontificum* (Cologne, 1562); Adams, P1420. On title-page: 'Roberti Hare Louanij 26 Octobris 1563. precium ij^s viij^d'. *WB*, no. 17.

79 Trinity Hall, F. VIII. 12, Aloysius Lipomanus, *Historiae de vitis sanctorum* (Louvain, 1564); Adams, L744. On title-page: 'Roberti Hare Angli precium lxv ss(?) 1564 Parisiis'. *WB*, no. 18.

80 †Trinity Hall, F. I. 22, Roverus Pontanus, *Rerum memorabilium libri quinque* (Cologne, 1559); Adams, P1881. ††1576. *WB*, no. 21.

81 †Trinity Hall, F. 1. 21, Michael Bucchinger, *Historia ecclesiastica* (Louvain, 1560); Adams, B3016. *WB*, no. 23.

82 †Trinity Hall, E. 1. 24, Johannes Nauclerus, Tomus primus [secundus] *Chronicon* (Cologne, 1564); Adams, N73-4. ††1572. *WB*, no. 25.

83 †Trinity Hall, G. I. 6, Bernardinus de Breitenbach, *Peregrinatio in terram sanctam* (Mainz, 1486), Hain 3956; *GW* 5075. ††1563. *WB*, no. 27.

84 †Trinity Hall, F. VII. 33, Daniele Barbaro, *Aurea in quinquaginta psalmos doctorum Graecorum cathena* (Venice, 1569); Adams, B1511. ††1581. *WB*, no. 51.

85 †Trinity Hall, F. VIII. 13, Giacomo Sannazaro (attrib.), *Speculum passionis Christi* (Paris, 1509). Adams, S327; Petrus de Natalibus, *Catalogus sanctorum* (Lyon, 1519). Adams, N48. *WB*, no. 53 ('per Jacobum San[…]').

86 †Trinity Hall, E. I. 8, Georg Eder, *Oeconomia Bibliorum* (Cologne, 1568); Adams, E66. ††1597. *WB*, no. 54.

87 ¶Trinity Hall, H. III. 32, G. Chaucer, *Works* (1598). *WB*, no. 61. *STC* 5077-9.

88 ¶Trinity Hall, F. VI. 12, (1) J. Raulin, *Itinerarium Paradisi*; (Paris, 1512); Adams, R183; (2) Council of Constance, *Libellus apostolorum nationis Gallicane (defensiuus conclusiones in consilio Constantien.) …* (Paris, 1512); (3) N. de Clamanges, *De lapsu et reparatione iustitie* (Paris, 1512). *WB*, no. 63. Spierinck binding.

89 †Trinity Hall, F. VI. 27, J. Raulin, *Opus sermonum de adventu* (Paris, 1518); Adams, R186. *WB*, no. 64.

90 ¶Trinity Hall, F. V. 32, John Fisher (Roffen.), *Contra Lutheranae assertiones* (London, 1558); *STC* 13078-9. *WB*, no. 68.

91 †Trinity Hall, B. V. 28, Virgil, *Opera Vergiliana* (Lyon, 1517). Adams, V468. ††1567. *WB*, no. – .

92 †Trinity Hall, F. VI. 31, Petrus Galesinius, *Martyrologium S. Romanae Ecclesiae* (Venice, 1578). Adams, G136. ††1588. *WB*, no. – .

93 †Trinity Hall, F. I. 31, Richard Rolle of Hampole (attrib.), *Speculum spiritualium* (Paris, 1510). Adams, S1558. ††1558, ††1588. *WB*, no. – .

94 Trinity Hall, G. II. 8, Thomas Aquinas, *Enarrationes* (Paris, 1546). Adams, A1480. On title-page: "Liber Roberti Hare precium iijs iiijd Westmonasterii 1569 xvii marcii'. *WB*, no. – .

95 †Trinity Hall, F. VI. 10, Petrus Canisius, *Commentariorum de verbi Dei corruptelis liber primus* (Dilingen, 1571). †† 'Lond. 1571'. Adams, C517; *WB*, no. – .

96 †Trinity Hall, F. VI. 30, Palladius, bp. of Aspona, *Historia Lausiaca* (Paris, 1570). Adams, P104. ††1571. *WB*, no. – .

97 †Trinity Hall, F. VII. 17, Johannes Viguerius, *Institutiones theologicae* (Paris, 1554). Adams, V767. *WB*, no. – .

98 †Cambridge, University Library, Syn. 8. 56. 11. (previously D*. 14. 38²), Myles Hogarde or Huggarde, *The Displaying of the Protestantes* (London, 1556), *STC* 13557.

99 †CUL, Syn. 8. 56. 13 (previously G*.14.37⁵), C. Tunstall, *A letter written ... unto Reginald Pole* (London, 1560), *STC* 24321.

100 †CUL, Q*. 11. 35 (sel.), Robert Wakefield, *Kotser codicis ... quo probatur coniugium cum fratria carnaliter cognitum illicitum omnino* (London, ?1533), *STC* 24943.

101 †Dublin, Archbishop Marsh's Library, N1. 4. 9, Hieronymus Rubeus, *Historiarum libri x Gothorum* (Venice, 1572). ††1573. Adams, R843.

102 London, British Library, 698. d. 1. Fridericus Staphylus, *The Apologie of Fridericus Staphylus. Intreating of the true understanding of Holy Scripture* (Antwerp, 1565), *STC* 23230. 'Liber Roberti Hare ex dono authoris 1564 [*sic*]', i.e. the gift of the translator, Thomas Stapleton, the Roman Catholic controversialist (1535-98; *DNB*).

103 BL, C. 27. a. 4., Abraham Fleming, *A straunge and terrible wunder ... in the parish church of Bongay, Norwich, 1577, in a great tempest. With the appearance of an horrible shaped thing*, [n.p., 1577]. 'Roberti Hare' on title-page, illustrated in J. H. Bloom, *Early Suffolk Tracts 1473-1650* (London, 1921), p. 80, no. 338, *STC* 11050. 4.

104 †London, Lambeth Palace Library, II. 6. 6. *The Myrroure of our lady* (London, 1530), *STC*, 17542. ††1558.

105 †Lambeth Palace, 1486. 8, Rabbi Samuel, *Contra iudeorum errores* (Antwerp, 1486), Hain 14267; *BMC* 9. 188. The volume also contains *Sermones super particulis antiphonae salue regina* (Alost, 1487), *BMC*, IX, 126. The binding is of Netherlandish pattern. Whether this means that the book came to Hare in this binding or that he had it bound when he was on the Continent it suggests that he owned both works.

106 †Lambeth Palace, 1488. 6 (4), George Marshall, *A compendious treatise in metre declaring the firste originall of sacrifice* (London, 1554), *STC* 17469. This and the following item were probably separate in Hare's time; the binding is Abp Bancroft's.

107 †Lambeth Palace, 1488. 6 (5), *Stella clericorum* (Paris, Anthoine Caillaut, *c.* 1500). ††1551. This and the preceding item were probably separate in Hare's time; the binding is Abp Bancroft's. The edition has not been identified: it has the acrostic containing Caillaut's name found in other editions, is quired a⁶ b⁴, and has 46 lines to the page.

108 †London, Westminster Abbey, C. D. 81, Ambrosius Catharinus, *Opuscula* (Lyons, 1542). Adams, C1095. ††1552. Blind-stamped binding over boards by the London binder I.R., Oldham, *EBSB*, Rolls AN. n(1) with Fp. a(1), used 1537-42. On a flyleaf is 'for Mastar robertson | for doctor Robynson | for Master Robynson | for Mastar robynson' in a good italic hand of s. xvi^med but perhaps only a pen trial: for a

Robertson/Robinson to which this might refer see *DNB*, s.v. Robertson (Robinson), Thomas, fl. 1520-61, MA and D.Th. of Oxford, appointed dean of Durham by Queen Mary in 1557.

109 †Westminster Abbey, T. 1. 34, *Breviarium Romanum* (Lyons, 1556). Adams, – .

110 †Westminster Abbey, Gal. I.1.54. John Jewel, bp, *The true copies of the letters betwene Iohn Bisshop of Sarum and D. Cole upon occasion of a sermon preached 1560* (London, [1560]), *STC* 14612.

111 †Westminster Abbey, Gal. G. 6. 26, Franciscus de Mayronis, *Decalogi seu decem preceptorum domini explanatio* ([Paris, 1519]). Adams, M947. ††1556. In blind-stamped binding over boards, too rubbed to be identifiable but evidently English.

112 †Manchester, John Rylands University Library, 15415. Richard Whitford, *The Pype, or Tonne* (London, 1532), *STC* 25421. ††1572.

113 †Oxford, Bodleian Library, Ashmole 1215 (15), Richard Whitford, *A Werke for Housholders* (Southwark, 1531?), *STC* 25422.3.

114 †Bodleian, 4° Z. 74 Jur. (*SC* 27860), John Caius, *De antiquitate Cantabrigiensis academiae* (1568). *STC* 4344. With manuscript notes by the author.

115 †Oxford, Christ Church, f. 8.12. Cunradus Hubertus (John Cheke), *Historia vera* (Strasbourg, 1562). Adams, C1433. ††1589. 'Jo. Fleming Merton 1568 praet' 16^d'; 'Ro: Burton 1615:': no. 847 in N. K. Kiessling, *The Library of Robert Burton*, Oxford Bibliographical Society, ns 22 (Oxford, 1988).

116 †Oxford, University Archives, N.E.P supra 20*. Brian Twyne, *Antiquitatis Academiae Oxoniensis apologia* (1608). *STC* 24405. On the title-page is an ornamental 'r:h.'. The few annotations are not certainly in Hare's hand but it may well be he who wrote the running titles.

117 †Peterborough Cathedral [at CUL], Pet. E. 6. 60, Thomas More, *Apologye*, 1533, *STC* 18078. A written date '1533' is not Robert Hare's.

118 †Peterborough Cathedral [at CUL], Pet. A. 4. 8, Edmund Bonner, *A profitable and necessary doctryne*, 1555, *STC* 3282. ††1567.

119 †Philadelphia, Rosenbach Foundation and Library, Inc. H 491.Walter Hilton, *Scale of Perfection* (London, 1494), *STC* 14042. ††1558.

PRINTED BOOKS: II, UNTRACED

[Nos 120-45 are recorded in the list of books in *WB* that Hare intended to give to Trinity Hall; the others are recorded in miscellaneous sources.]

120 Matthew Paris, *Historia*. *STC* 19209-9a.

121 Matthew Parker, *Catalogus cancellariorum in academia Cantabrigiensis* (London, 1572); *STC* 19292.

122 Paulus Aemilius, *Historia*, Adams, A231-42, of which A239 (Paris, 1555) is at Trinity Hall but bears no sign of Hare's ownership.

123 Froissart, *Chronica*; Adams, F1064 etc., *STC* 11396-9 (London, 1523-80). (Trinity Hall 1611 edn is a replacement.)

124 Laurentius Surius, *Tomus primus [– quartus] conciliorum omnium* (Cologne, 1567-86), 4 vols. Adams, S2097-2102.

125 Thomas More, *Opera* Louvain, 1565, 1566, 1566; Adams, M1749-51, *STC* 18094-6 (London, 1551-96).

126 Francesco Guicciardini, *Historiarum sui temporis libri viginti* (Basel, 1567); Adams, G1523.

127 Polydorus Vergil, *Historia*, *STC* 24654-8 (1546-*c.* 1560) or Basel 1534. Adams, V446 (at Trinity Hall but lacking indication of Hare's ownership).

128 Sebastian Muenster, *Cosmographica* (Basel, 1559); Adams, M1911.

129 Martin Du Bellay, *Commentariolum de rebus Gallicis* (Frankfurt am Main, 1574, 1595); Adams, D998-9. *WB*, no. 19.

130 Marianus Scotus, *Chronica* (Basel, 1559); Adams, M582. *WB*, no. 20.

131 *Rerum Britannicarum historiae a diversis authoribus collecta*, ed. by H. Commelin (Heidelberg, 1587); Adams, S819 (at Trinity Hall). *WB*, no. 22.

132 Flavius Josephus, *Opera* (Basel, 1567 etc.); Adams, J366 etc. *WB*, no. 30.

133 Simon Schardius, *Germanicarum rerum quatuor celebriores vetustioresque chrono-graphici* (Frankfurt, 1566); Adams, G488. *WB*, no. 32.

134 Valerius Anselmus Ryd, *Catalogus annorum* (Berne, 1540, 1550); Adams, R984-5. *WB*, no. 33.

135 *Biblia sacra*, ed. Johannes Benedictus (Paris, 1541); Adams –. *WB*, no. 38.

136 *Thesaurus Christianae religionis ab Alfonso Guerrero*. Alfonso Alvarez Guerrero, *De iure ac potentate Romanorum pontificum* [containing the text of *Thesaurus*] (Cologne, 1586); Adams, A854. *WB*, no. 52.

137 Johannes Ebser, bp of Chiemsee, *Onus ecclesiae* (Cologne, 1524, 1531); Adams, E20-1. *WB*, no. 55.

138 Johannes de Burgo, *Pupilla oculi* (Rouen, 1516; Adams, B3304 (at Trinity Hall)), also other edns. *WB*, no. – .

139 *Liber statutorum universitatis Bononiensis*. Perhaps *Statuta et privilegia almae Universitatis Juristarum gymnasii Bononiensis* (Bologna, 1561). *WB*, no. 58.

140 *A devuout treatyse called the Pylgrimage of perfection* (London, 1526); *STC* 3277. *WB*, no. 59.

141 *Ciceronis opera cum commento*; Adams, C1638-42 (Paris, 1527, 1539; Basel, 1540; Lyons, 1540-1. *WB*, no. 60.

142 Henricus Boort, *Fasciculus morum* (Deventer, *c.* 1495: *GW* 4934), (Cologne, 1517: Adams, B2462). *WB*, no. – .

143 Johannes Franciscus de Pavinis, *Baculus pastoralis* (Paris, 1503, 1508, 1514; Adams, P527-9). *WB*, no. 65.

144 Franciscus de Mayronis, *Decalogi seu decem preceptorem domini explanatio* (Paris, 1519); Adams, M947. *WB*, no. 66.

145 Nicholaus de Aquavilla, *Sermones dominicales* (Paris, 1513, 1517, 1519: Adams, N237-9). *WB*, no. 67.

146 †W. Carew Hazlitt, *Roll of Honour* (London, 1908), made a note in his own copy, now BL, 1655/4, that Robert Hare owned a copy (inscribed 'Roberti Hare, 1572') of Thomas More's *Utopia*, in English, 1556, i.e. *STC* 18095, 18095.5.

147 †Bloomsbury Book Auctions SC 138, 10 May 1990, lot 101. William of New-burgh, *Rerum anglicarum libri quinque* (Antwerp, 1567). Adams, W187. It bears a 'note of acquisition by Robert Hare at Douai for 18 pence in 1567 and by W. Cockburn for 3 shillings in 1635'. Sold to 'Mandl'.

148   †Christie SC 17 Nov. 1976, lot 232. William Camden, *Reges, reginae, nobiles et alij in ecclesia collegiata B. Petri Westmonasterii sepulti* (London, 1600). *STC* 4518. Later owners include Thomas Astle (d. 1803).

149   †E. P. Goldschmidt, Catalogues 101 (1953), no. 65; 107 (1955?), no. 41, and Supplementary catalogue 1 (1957), no. 15, note that 'the autograph of Robert Hare ... is on the title' of J. Morocurtius, *Brunonias, Hugonias, Threnodia adversus Lutheranos* (Antwerp, 1540). Copies are recorded in W. Nijhoff, *Nederlandsche bibliographie van 1500 tot 1540. Mid medewerking van M. E. Kronenberg* (The Hague, 1919 –), fasc. 9 (1919), nos 1547-9.

150   †Sotheby, SC 28 March - 8 April 1927 (Christie-Miller (Britwell) sale), lot 829. Gildas, *De calamitate excidio et conquestu Britanniae* (Antwerp?, 1525?); Adams, G614 suggests Paris?, *c.* 1525. *STC* 11892 ('Not an *STC* book'). Hare's signature is on the title-page. 'Ro: Robinson' was also an early owner.

151   †Sotheby, SC 9 Nov. 1960, lot 392. Mechthild of Hackeborn, *Liber gratiae spirituales* (Venice, 1522). Some marginal notes are probably Hare's. 'The binding by John Reynes (Rel. 5 HHH.2 and Oldham HE 21) must date from between 1522 and 1532 when Reynes was using the royal arms panel in this state'. Sold to Maggs for £58.

152   †Quaritch, *SC* 98/16 (1988), lot 1, previously Sotheby, SC 22-23 June 1998, lot 2 (library of the late John Bensusan Butt). Aelfric, *A testimonie of Antiquitie*, 1566?, *STC* 159.5. 'Among the ownership captions on the title-page are those of Robert Hare, 1586 ..., W. Stonehouse and Ralph Thoresby'.

REJECTED

153   Arundel Castle, MS s.n., John Lydgate, *Lives of S. Edmund and S. Fremund*, suggested by Kathleen Scott (*Viator*, 13, 1982), 335-66 at 344-5 and fig. 14, on the grounds that initials 'RH' are found at the ends of stanzas as added decoration to the text. It is impossible to say that the very plain initials are not Hare's but there is no known example in his books of his using his initials in this way and he is only one of a number of possible persons suggested by Scott. Present evidence does not, therefore, justify acceptance of his ownership.

154   Trinity Hall, MS 28, is recorded by M. R. James in the Introduction to his catalogue of the Trinity Hall manuscripts (as no. 156 below) having belonged to Hare. He says nothing to this effect in his description of the book, which bears no evidence of Hare's ownership, and was probably confusing it with MS 30, no. 18 above.

155   Edmonton, University of Alberta. A reference to 'a copy of Spenser' in Edmonton in a review by John Durkan in *The Library*, 5th series, 28 (1973), pp. 259-61, states that it was owned by 'Hare'. After checking his notes Dr Durkan tells me that the owner was one J. Hare of Trinity College, Cambridge.

156   London, Lambeth Palace Library, MS 185, Hildebert, *Sermones*, s. xii/xiii. According to the index of M. R. James, *A Descriptive Catalogue of the Manuscripts in the Library of Lambeth Palace: the Mediaeval Manuscripts* (Cambridge, 1932), Robert

Hare's name is on fol. 1^b of this manuscript, but that is not mentioned in the text of the catalogue and there is no sign of Hare in the manuscript. Lambeth MS 196, unindexed, is, however, Hare's and is presumably the book that James intended to refer to.

157 Lambeth Palace, MS 761, *Vita S. Edwardi*, s. xiii. In his catalogue (as no. 156 above), James writes: ... 'Fol. iii^b: a title of s. xvi and a note (perhaps in the writing of Robert Hare): 'This Booke was left by Islip (sometime Abbot of Westminster) as he was visiting the lands of his own monastery in Gloucestershire ...'. James then gives a reference to *The History of Westminster Abbey by John Flete*, ed. by J. A. Robinson (Cambridge, 1909), pp. 24-9, which bear inscriptions copied by Hare in his own manuscript now Cambridge, Corpus Christi College, MS 491. The inscriptions have no relevance to the Lambeth manuscript but presumably explain why James makes a connection with Hare. They could be relevant only if the hand on fol. iii^b were Hare's, but it is not. On fol. 1^a is an erased inscription, but what can be seen is not in Hare's hand.

1 Jeremy Griffiths was interested in Robert Hare as a collector of medieval manuscripts and acquired a copy of an important source for the study of Hare's library, *Warren's Book*, ed. by A. W. W. Dale (Cambridge, 1911). He lent it to me in 1988 and turned the loan into a gift in 1989 as being likely to be more used by me than by him, and it therefore seems appropriate that in this memorial volume I should justify his hope that I would eventually turn my attention to Hare. Originally I had intended to limit my investigations to manuscripts, and the number of printed books that have come (and may continue to come) to light has been both welcome and disconcerting. For reasons of space I have abbreviated my descriptions of the printed books (see p. 217 below) but after some hesitation I have included Hare's autograph manuscripts, which provide some evidence for the nature and quality of his antiquarian work.

2 In 1992 I gave a short talk about Hare in Cambridge and I am grateful to members of the audience, David McKitterick and David Riley, who later told me of additional Hare books. Subsequently Nigel Ramsay added a good number. I am pleased to acknowledge the usefulness of several relevant lists of Trinity Hall books sent to Dr McKitterick by Mrs Lavinia Hinton, formerly Sub-Librarian at Trinity Hall, and passed on to me. Long before that Ian Doyle and Kathleen Scott had been urging me to 'do' Hare and they have continued to keep me informed of discoveries. More recently the researches of Mildred Budny and Timothy Graham in the Parker Library at Corpus Christi College, Cambridge, which show that Hare's activities impinged on those of other antiquaries in Cambridge and elsewhere, have encouraged me to action. Tony Edwards spent a lot of his time, and saved a lot of mine, examining Hare's printed books in Trinity Hall Library, in which he had the help of Andrew Lacey, Assistant Librarian. I am most grateful to both of them.

3 This paragraph is based on the article by Thompson Cooper in the *Dictionary of National Biography*.

4 For the Diocesan Return see *Publications of the Catholic Record Society*, 22 (Miscellanea 12) (1921), p. 105. The Spitalfield list is printed in *Calendar of State Papers Domestic, Elizabeth, Addenda 1566-1579* (London, 1871), pp. 550-1. By a happy chance the Spitalfields community is dealt with by Nancy Pollard Brown (with brief mention of Hare) in an article which passed through Jeremy Grifffiths' hands – 'Paperchase: the dissemination of Catholic texts in Elizabethan England', in *English Manuscript Studies*, I, ed. by Peter Beal & Jeremy Griffiths (Oxford, 1989), pp. 120-43.

5 Another facsimile of his inscription, in Oxford, Bodleian Library, MS Selden supra 55, is in *Lives of Edward the Confessor*, ed. H. R. Luard (Rolls Series 3, 1858), pl. 3. *Ex libris*

inscriptions in two Westminster Abbey books, T.1.34 and Gal. G. 6.26 (nos 109 and 111), acquired in his early years, are, however, in a very beautiful italic script which he may well have learned in Cambridge: see A. Fairbank & B. Dickens, *The Italic Hand in Tudor Cambridge*, Cambridge Bibliographical Society Monograph 5 (1962).

6 N. R. Ker, *Medieval Manuscripts in British Libraries*, 4 vols (Oxford, 1969-92) (vol. 4 with A. J. Piper). At the time of writing, the first run through the index of owners has been completed.

7 Z. C. von Uffenbach, *Merkwürdige Reisen* (Ulm, 1754), pp. 44-7, (at 47, 46); English edition by J. E. B. Mayor, *Cambridge under Queen Anne* (Cambridge, 1911), pp. 123-98 (at 166, 165).

8 Mysterious because so little is known about them but the few fully authenticated instances and sheer probability are adequate confirmation of the existence of this trade. The present BL, Cotton MS, Vespasian A. X was 'bowght vppon a stall in London' by John Dee in 1574 (M10 in R. J. Roberts & A. G. Watson, *John Dee's Library Catalogue* (London, 1990)); Simonds D'Ewes's accounts contain occasional entries of manuscripts purchased from booksellers (see A. G. Watson, *The Library of Sir Simonds D'Ewes* (London, 1966), List H *passim*); one Stephen Pott(s), *bibliopola Londinensis*, occurs in 1610 and 1628 (see R. W. Hunt, 'St John's College donors', in *Studies in the Book Trade in Honour of Graham Pollard* (Oxford, 1975), pp. 63-70, at 68, 70).

9 Identified as Royal books by Professor James Carley. To these can almost certainly be added BL, MS Cotton Faustina C. VII (no. 25), which bears Sir Frederic Madden's note that it was formerly in the Old Royal Library binding.

10 A. G. Watson, 'Christopher and William Carye, collectors of monastic manuscripts, and "John Carye"', *The Library*, 5th series, 20 (1965), 135-42 (at 139). For Bale's record of Carye see *Index Britanniae Scriptorum: John Bale's Index of British and Latin Writers*, ed. by R. L. Poole & Mary Bateson (Oxford, 1902), reissued with a new introduction by C. Brett & J. P. Carley (Cambridge, 1990), *passim*.

11 PCC Prob. 1/118, dated 1 July 1611, proved 6 November 1611.

12 This was not Hare's only benefaction during Cowell's mastership: in 1597 the college acquired an estate at Walpole St Peter through a bequest of an earlier master, William Mowsse (Mouse, Mosse), d. 1588, whose executor Hare was, supplemented by a contribution from Hare (*VCH: Cambridgeshire and the Isle of Ely*, III (1959), p. 367).

13 For the date 1612 see A. G. Watson, *The Manuscripts of Henry Savile of Banke* (London, 1969), p. 13: Savile's 'A' catalogue, in BL, MS Add. 35213, fols 5-32, which includes BL, MS Arundel 141, must date from before 1612 since its eighth item, now Bodleian, MS Bodley 581, was bequeathed by Thomas Twyne to the Bodleian in that year.

14 BL, MS Harl. 6018, fol.116ᵛ.

15 On these collectors see Roberts & Watson, *Dee*; R. I. Page, *Matthew Parker and his Books*. Sandars Lectures in Bibliography, 1990 (Kalamazoo, Mich., 1993); C. G. C. Tite, *The Manuscript Library of Sir Robert Cotton*. Panizzi Lectures, 1993 (London, 1994).

16 Both letters are printed in John Stow, *A Survey of London*, ed. by C. L. Kingsford, 2 vols (Oxford, 1908), I, pp. lxviii, lxxii-iii, from BL, MSS Harley 374, fol. 24 and Harley 530, fol. 1 respectively.

17 Thomas Hearne, *A Collection of Curious Discourses*, 2 vols (London, 1771), II, p. 160.

18 Linda Van Norden, 'The Elizabethan College of Antiquaries', unpublished Ph.D. thesis, University of California, Los Angeles, 1946.

19 The list is in BL, Cotton MS, Nero C. III, fols 208ᵛ-12. For an edition see T. Graham & A. G. Watson, *The Recovery of the Past in Early Elizabethan England: Documents by John Bale and John Joscelyn from the Circle of Matthew Parker*, Cambridge Bibliographical Society Monograph 13 (1998), pp. 61-109.

20 A. G. Watson, 'A sixteenth-century collector: Thomas Dackomb, 1496-*c*. 1572'. *The Library*, 5th series, 18 (1963), 204-17.

21 A. G. Watson, 'John Twyne of Canterbury as a collector of medieval manuscripts', *The Library*, 6th series, 8 (1986), 133-51. I am glad to take the chance to correct a silly last-minute

error: the newly-discovered will mentioned on p. 145 is that of John, not Brian, Twyne.

22 For the Saviles see n. 13 above.

23 For them see n. 15 above.

24 A. G. Watson, 'The manuscript collection of Sir Walter Cope (d. 1614)', *Bodleian Library Record*, 12, no. 4 (1986), 262-97.

25 This is strengthened by the last-minute discovery (thanks to Richard Ovenden) of two Hare printed books in Westminster Abbey Library, a visit to inspect which led to the finding of two more there (nos 108-11).

ADDENDUM

At the last possible minute of the last possible hour seven more of Hare's printed books have come to my notice, in the draft of *The Library of Humphrey Dyson* (*c. 1582-1633*), which is in preparation by Alan H. Nelson, University of California, Berkeley, for publication by the Oxford Bibliographical Society. They are as follows: (1) BL, *The edict of the French king, for the appeasing of the troubles of his realm*, 1573 (*STC* 5039); (2) BL, David –, *A summe of the Guisian ambassage to the bishop of Rome*, 1579 (*STC* 6319); (3) BL, Francis, duke of Anjou, *The protestation of the most high and mightie Prince Frauncis*, 1575 (*STC* 11311); (4) BL, Henry IV, king of France, *The declaration of the king of Nauarre ...*, 1585 (*STC* 13106); (5) BL, Henry III, king of France, *The edict or proclamation ...*, 1576 (*STC* 13091); (6) Folger Library, William Harrington, *The commendacions of matrimony*, 1528 (*STC* 12800); (7) Folger Library, Reginald Pole, *Libri duo*, Rome, 1562 (Shaaber P196).

All of the above bear Hare's name, and no. 6 also his date 1551.

On Dyson see *Dictionary of National Biography, Missing Persons* (1993).

AN AUGUSTAN EPISODE IN THE HISTORY OF THE COLLECTION OF MEDIEVAL MANUSCRIPTS AT LONGLEAT HOUSE

Kate Harris

THE CURRENT CATALOGUE of the Marquess of Bath's manuscripts dates from 1864 and includes both medieval and more modern materials, as well as items which would now more commonly be assigned to a catalogue of archives: what follows draws on research undertaken in the course of a long-overdue attempt to replace this unpublished Victorian account in respect of the one hundred or so medieval manuscripts at Longleat House. The essay will include, among other things, discussion of manuscripts no longer at Longleat and (a not unconnected matter) the Chaucer editor, John Urry. I shall miss Jeremy Griffiths's ready sympathy over this diversion from the desired rapid preparation of the new descriptive catalogue of the Longleat medieval codices.

The history of the manuscript collection at Longleat begins just before the House itself was built by Sir John Thynne, steward to Protector Somerset: MS 258, like the Caxton Boethius also still in the collection, was used by the builder's uncle, William Thynne, as copy-text for the first edition of Chaucer's collected works which he published in 1532.[1] The last major accession occurred in 1941 when the future 6th Marquess of Bath inherited the small but very distinguished (showy) collection, dominated by late medieval manuscripts, formed by the plutocratic nineteenth-century bibliophile, Beriah Botfield.[2] MS 258 is not listed in 'Sir John Thynnes bookes at longeleate', a list of eighty-five manuscripts and printed books drawn up in September 1577 (the Boethius is number 26). Nine medieval manuscripts (chronicles very much predominant) still in the collection are recognizable in the list. However, it is a 'tricky' document from which to make generalizations, because it is not a complete account of Thynne's holdings at the time. (The 'at longeleate', I have discovered from examining related contemporary or near contemporary materials, is intended as a crucial distinction – there is ample evidence that Thynne's books and archives went where he needed to make reference to them and moved as and when his needs changed.) The list is 'tricky' also on a simpler level – it is a fair copy of an ill-written original (the surnames were clearly impenetrable to the transcriber on occasion).[3] Thus the recorded copy of Gower's *Vox Clamantis*, one of three further medieval manuscripts listed but not surviving in the collection (number 85) is entered as 'Johannes [blank] vox clamantis'.

Also not surviving in the collection are item 3 'An olde wrighten biblle in lattin laking the beginning of Genesis and of Exodus' and the late-fifteenth-century collection listed under item 34 and still recorded in the 1702 catalogue of the manuscripts in the collection of the 1st Viscount Weymouth at Long-leat.[4] This last highly idiosyncratic volume is the more interesting because it is identifiable elsewhere. The entry in the 1577 list records a volume in which the following works are 'all bounde together':

Cato in inglishe and lattin verse, preceptes of [blank] in verse in inglishe | A discription [blank] of earthe and the nature of man wrighten in | verse in inglishe, what vertues he muste haue that [blank] in verse in inglishe ./ | An historie of two marchauntes in inglishe verse, prouerbes of wisdom in | inglishe verse | Brute the croniklle of England in englishe the kinges from brute | allmoste vnto Edwarde the fourthe raigne | Certaine prayers callid the xv oos in inglishe verse, the proces of the biblle | of englishe pollyrye [sic], exhortinge all englande, to keepe the sea (enironid) | wrighten in englishe verse. Liber de moralibus philosophorum in inglishe ./

This same volume, then bearing the shelfmark IX D 69, is listed in the catalogue of 1702 as follows:

In hoc Volumine continentur .1°. Catonis disticha Latinè & Anglicè.| 2°. Statio puerorum ad mensam. 3°. A prayer of the Crosse.| 4°. a poem how life is most loved. 5°. What vertue he must have | that will hear the Masse .6°. A history of two Merchants| in Engl. verse vpon Vellum. 7°. The proverbs of wisdome.| 8. A Chronicle of England call'd Brute, in English ending at the Coronation of K. Edward yᵉ 4ᵗʰ. 8°. The 15 O's .9°. The | Bible of English policy exhorting England to keep the Sea. | 10°. An account of some antient Philosophers.

This is identical with the volume which is now Oxford, Bodleian Library, MS Rawlinson poet. 32, an unusual manuscript made up of six booklets, some parchment, some paper, and dating from the second half of the fifteenth century (the *Brut* it includes is dateable in or after 1461). Rawlinson opens fols 3ʳ-29ᵛ with *Cato Major*, Benedict Burgh's version of Cato's *Distichs* (*IMEV* 854); at fols 30ʳ-31ᵛ occurs John Lydgate's *Stans puer ad mensam* (*IMEV* 2233); at fols 31ᵛ-32ʳ 'A prayer of the Crosse', the same poet's 'a pon a crosse naylid I was for the' (*IMEV* 3845); at fols 32ᵛ-35ʳ the B version of 'Erthe upon Erthe' beginning 'whan life is most louyd' (*IMEV* 3985); at fols 35ᵛ-37ᵛ 'The XXX virtues of the Masse', beginning '.XXX. vertewis schal haue he' and comprising thirty-one quatrains and two concluding six-line stanzas (*IMEV* 3573); at fols 38ʳ-53ᵛ Lydgate's *Fabula duorum mercatorum* (*IMEV* 1481, now ending defectively); at fols 54ᵛᵃ-55ʳᵇ 'Prouerbis of wysdom' (*IMEV* 3502, including *IMEV* 1416); at fol. 55ʳᵇ 'þe .X. comawndmentes' (*IMEV* 176); at fols 55ᵛᵃ-56ᵛᵃ the *Brut* opening with a table of all the kings of England from Brute to Edward IV (*IPMEP* 374, this item is specifically described as con-cluding with the coronation of Edward IV in the 1702 catalogue); at fols 169ᵛ-

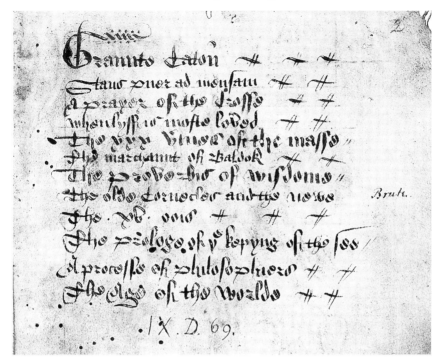

Pl. 1. Oxford, Bodleian Library, MS Rawlinson poet. 32, fol. 2ʳ (detail). Reproduced by permission of the Bodleian Library, Oxford.

172ᵛ, not Lydgate's *The Fifteen O's* (*IMEV* 2394), but the thirty-four stanza rhyme royal version beginning 'O Ihesu Crist of euerlastyng swetnes' (IMEV 2469); at fol. 172ᵛ the couplet 'Aman [*sic*] without mercy of mercy shall mysse | He shall haue mercy that mercyfull ys' (*IMEV* 77); at fols 173ʳ-193ʳ the *Libel of English Policy* (*IMEV* 3491); and at fols 194ʳ-204ʳ the anonymous abbreviated English version of Guillaume de Tignonville's *Dits moraulx*, the *Liber de Moralibus Philosophorum* (*IPMEP* 591 C). It is difficult to imagine that another manuscript with identical content was ever produced, but if the identification should be held to admit any doubt at all, it only has to be mentioned that Rawlinson poet. 32 bears the shelfmark 'IX. D. 69.' in the hand of Viscount Weymouth's librarian, the non-juror George Harbin, immediately below the table of contents on fol. 2ʳ (see Pl. 1).[5]

When Thomas Thynne, shortly afterwards to be created 1st Viscount Weymouth, unexpectedly succeeded his cousin, murdered in Pall Mall in 1682, it seems that he inherited no more than a manuscript collection formed at a period still as it were 'in touch' with the Middle Ages. The group of volumes concerned, with the significant exception of those books associated with the

Pl. 2. View of the Old Library, Longleat House. Reproduced by permission of the Marquess of Bath, Longleat House, Warminster, Wiltshire.

Chaucer editor, William Thynne, seem largely to have been bought as reading copies or, like MS 96, John Bellenden's translation of the *Historia Scotorum* of Hector Boece, otherwise acquired as reading copies. MS 96 is inscribed by Sir John Thynne at the beginning:

ffounde in Edenburghe at the wyninge | and burninge therof / the vij[th] of Maye | beinge Wednisdaye / the xxxvj[th] yere [1544] | of the R< >igne of *our* soueurayn Lorde | Kinge Henry the eight p*er* | Ion Thynne

   There is evidence that a number of the medieval manuscripts were acquired quite late, that is that they cannot belong to the 'core collection' formed in the sixteenth century. MS 52, a Florentine Josephus copied and signed by the notary Ser Amanzio di Nicolo Berti and in a contemporary binding with the Medici arms, for instance, has a note of ownership by Sir Thomas Playters, baronet of Sotterley in Suffolk dated 20 December 1707.[6] Much more importantly, there is ample evidence of the 1st Viscount's self-conscious attempt to create a great library. The Old Library is the only one of the several important interiors created for Weymouth to survive at Longleat (see Pl. 2) – also from this period were the Best Gallery, a vast picture-gallery forming the approach to the Library on the top floor of the south front, a long gallery to the east on the floor below overlooking the renowned baroque garden created for him by George London, and a chapel in the west wing rising through the basement and ground floors. The Old Library still houses Weymouth's books in their seventeenth-century presses and is still hung with the set of portraits of suitable literary and learned subjects copied for his patron by Thomas Robinson:[7] the room originally (again suitably) accommodated also the portrait of Sir Philip Sidney formerly belonging to the poet's sister at Wilton, but now given more prominence elsewhere in Longleat House.[8] Less clear but emerging are the more precise impulses and intentions behind Viscount Weymouth's specific purchases of medieval manuscripts.

His collecting activity may have been quite well known to contemporaries: to Dr Thomas Guidot of Bath he was a focus for the bequest in 1703 of the 'Liber rubeus Bathoniae', MS 55, a miscellany, a library between two covers, probably belonging originally to a Bath commissary court official and having a table of contents dated 1428. The volume is in a contemporary binding, the front board most unusually including a socket for balance and weights, and the back probably having originally an enamel crucifix – the book has the gospel lections which would qualify it for use as an oath book. The collecting activity was something Weymouth seems to have wanted to transmit to posterity, and Longleat accordingly became a hot-house for a younger generation of collectors, amongst them his nephew Thomas Thynne of Old Windsor who was, for a short time before his early death on 24 April 1710, Weymouth's heir. Two undated lists largely of incunabula and sixteenth-century volumes bought for him and a third fragmentary list in the same hand survive in the Longleat archive, one headed 'Bookes Bought at Venice for Thomas Thynne Esqr.' and another 'Bookes bought for Mr Thynne':[9] the latter concludes with a manuscript item, a Petrarch manuscript ('Petrarcha M.SS. bella & Anticha. Carta Pergamina – 4.°'), now number 252B in the collection. A binding bill of 13 January 1710 relating to this copy of the *Canzoniere* helps with the dating of the acquisition.[10]

Besides the stray volumes already mentioned, just over thirty extant medieval manuscripts are listed in the catalogue of 1702. The scale and rate of the acquisitions of the 1st Viscount Weymouth only started to become clear to me when the number of the Longleat manuscripts previously owned by the legal historian, Sir Henry Spelman (d. 1641), a friend of Sir Robert Cotton and member of the Society of Antiquaries, became apparent. Amongst them was the stunning copy of the *Pupilla oculi*, Longleat House MS 24, illuminated by the master of the frontispiece in the manuscript of Chaucer's *Troilus and Criseyde*, Cambridge, Corpus Christi College, MS 61.[11] The Spelman sales relevant here took place on 28 November 1709 and 26 January 1710 (another took place in 1820).[12] I am reasonably certain so far of recognizing as many as nineteen Longleat books in the sale catalogues, and one other no longer in the collection but certainly purchased at this time by Weymouth, which I will be mentioning again shortly. Books bought at the Spelman sales and still in the collection (usually not as decorative as MS 24) are highly various and include a Martyrology of the Carmelite Convent in Oxford (MS 16), a Hebrew/Latin dictionary with Hebrew Psalter and Grammar (MS 21), a Guido Faba manuscript (MS 286), a Wycliffite Bible (MS 3), a Middle English sermon collection (traditionally called *Postils of the Gospels*) with *Pore Caitiff* and the *Abbey of the Holy Ghost* (MS 4), Nicholas Upton's *De officio militari* (MS 250), a copy of Christine de Pizan's *Livre des faits d'armes et de chevalerie* (MS 252), two texts copied by William Ebesham, *Objectiones et argumenta contra et pro privilegiis Sanctuarii Westmonasteriensis* and *Tractatus de sanguine Christi precioso* (MS 38),[13] and the collection, including Lydgate's *Siege of Thebes* and Chaucer's *Knight's Tale* and *Clerk's Tale*, inscribed by Richard III before he became king (MS 257).[14]

It is particularly useful, however, to turn to a single post-medieval manuscript, Longleat House MS 259, to illuminate the intellectual life lying behind Weymouth's manuscript purchases. This is a collection of verse by Waller, Godolphin, and Cowley, which is followed (fols 47ʳ-78ʳ) by a borrowing list, 'Books lent out of my Lord's Library', largely in the hand of the librarian, George Harbin, and relating to the period 28 July 1700 - 24 April 1718. There are also some autograph entries by borrowers themselves, users like Bishop Thomas Ken, who had been under Weymouth's protection since he was deprived of his See of Bath and Wells in 1691: he enters on fol. 47ᵛ for instance 'To yᵉ Bᵖ: yᵉ Hist: of Ethiopia – Nov: 14ᵗʰ: [1701]' and on fol. 49ᵛ '[John] Goodman on yᵉ Prodigall 4° Tho: Bath', the loan datable to the late summer of 1703. Most of the entries in fact are not dated but can be dated roughly using the closest dated entry; nearly (but not quite all) are crossed through, showing that the volumes in question had been returned. Fol. 66ᵛ has a number of entries in the hand of Humfrey Wanley, the palaeographer and Anglo-Saxonist, one of them dated 3 October 1709: by this time Wanley is usually thought to have been in the service of Robert Harley, Earl of Oxford: they had been first introduced as early as April 1701 and Wanley's resignation from his position as Secretary to the SPCK in June 1708 certainly suggests that he was confident of a secure appointment elsewhere. The first occurrence of his hand in the Longleat borrowing list is undated but clearly only slightly earlier than the second: it reads –

> Don Quixote Vol .I. 8ᵛᵒ. H Wanley. Restor'd.
> Don Quixote. Vol.II. 8ᵛᵒ. H Wanley Restor'd.

The dated entry, referring to Sir Robert Naunton's *Arcana aulica*, an account of the chief courtiers of Elizabeth I, which had remained unpublished during the author's lifetime, reads –

> Sʳ Rob. Naunton's Arcana Aulica. 16ᵗᵒ. H. Wanley. Restor'd.
> Oct.3. 1709. Madam Higgins has Boethius de Cons. Philos. in English (VII.W.442.)

Wanley's hand also appears in another entry (fol. 67ʳ) referring to 'Dugdales Baronage 2 Volls.' sent to the Viscount Weymouth on 12 October 1709.

For reasons still unclear, Wanley was a guest at Longleat between 31 July and 3 November 1709. He records in a letter to his wife dated 12 September 1709:[15] 'My Lord is very kind to me, and I hold forth now and then a merry Story at table, before all the Lords & Ladies, as if I were among my Equals'. Some four years after Wanley's sojourn at Longleat, Weymouth is known to have given material encouragement to Wanley's projected edition of the Dunstable Chronicle, the Chronicle of Benedict of Peterborough, and the Lanercost Annals, an edition which Wanley never saw come to completion, interrupted as it was by Weymouth's death on 28 July 1714; Weymouth gave the editor one hundred pounds for this project and promised as much again for the dedication, agreeing further to take fifty copies of the published work.[16] Although Thomas Hearne recorded in his diary for 26 August 1721 that Wanley 'told me that he did formerly by way of Specimens of Hands in all Ages my Lord Weymouth had from him, and that he hath no design of doing more that way, & that he hath no time to print anything', it has been realized by scholars only very recently that Wanley's famed 'Book of Specimens', survives in the Longleat collection:[17] it is Longleat House MS 345 and is depicted in the Society of Antiquaries' portrait of its creator.[18] It was described by Heyworth, the editor of the palaeographer's letters (of course, from documentary sources only), as 'a collection of dated documents and of alphabets derived from them, designed to show the development of writing and to serve as a palaeographical aid in the dating of manuscripts' and includes items destroyed or damaged in the Cotton fire of 23 October 1731. Dr Parkes refers to Wanley as 'the greatest English palaeographer' and, basing his estimation on the specimens published by George Hickes in his *Thesaurus* of 1705, writes:[19]

These specimens reveal his incredible palaeographical skills: meticulous observation, but directed by a creative, imaginative curiosity which sought to identify every movement of the fingers (and the rhythms) with which scribes had executed a wide range of different scripts. Wanley did not draw or trace these specimens but wrote them. Comparison of his specimens, even at second hand through the published engravings (a medium unsympathetic to other reproductions), with the original manuscripts reveals that they are more like replicas than other examples of facsimile script.

In his letter of 11 August 1697 to his patron (and landlord) Arthur Charlett, Master of University College, Oxford, describing his book of specimens Wanley wrote:[20] 'I shall for the future take specimens from no books but what have dates, as most of those in small letters have; or other certain marks whereby we may know the true age of the books …'. Its pragmatic function is defined rather more waspishly by the scribe himself in his letter to Charlett:[21] 'with such a Collection a man may soon learn to read the MSS, which would have done well, if many who have published old authors, could have done'.

Wanley clearly trafficked in books for the 1st Viscount Weymouth and for the latter's family after the Viscount's death. According to Dugdale, Longleat House MS 38 already mentioned 'was purchased by the celebrated Humphrey

Wanley (Lord Oxford's librarian), at the auction of Sir Henry Spelman's Manuscripts, for Lord Weymouth'.[22] Wanley's close involvement in this sale is demonstrated by London, British Library, MS Harley 7055 which contains, mounted on fols 232-9, twenty-six leaves from a small pocket book in which he compiled his own 'Catalogue of the MSS. in the Library of Sir. Henry Spelman, sold by Auction by John Harding who bought them, December 20, 21, & 22 .A.D. 1709.': as might be expected the entries for each lot, if very brief, are much better informed, more accurate, and more precise than the descriptions in the published auction catalogue.[23] Further, according to a letter to his wife of 3 October 1707, Wanley had hopes of selling his portrait of Sir Robert Cotton from the collection of Sir Symonds d'Ewes to Weymouth.[24] Weymouth also employed Wanley as a record agent at the Tower: his letter of 7 July 1709, which opens with reference to Wanley's impending sojourn at Longleat ('I have too great a value for yr merit, not to reioys that I am like to see you sooner, than you first mentioned …'), directs Wanley to employ his 'knowledge of Records' in furthering Weymouth's interests in Bodenham Devereux in Herefordshire and Bratton in Wiltshire.[25]

BL, MS Harley 6686 (Law Precedents, 33 Elizabeth I-5 James I) and MS Harley 6687 A-D from 1572, originally a thick octavo copy of Littleton's *Tenures* but now divided into four volumes, were given on 6 August 1715 to the Earl of Oxford's library by 'Madam Thynne', that is Grace Stroud, widow of Weymouth's son, Henry Thynne.[26] Harley 7055 preserves on fol. 48[r-v] a memorandum drawn up by Wanley as late as 11 April 1718 of books and other items to be seen and sometimes also acquired apparently by Edward Harley on a journey to Salisbury, Wilton, Longleat, Bath, Wells, and Oxford: it evidences considerable familiarity with the Longleat House archive and opens:[27]

Memorandums, 11 April 1718.

To see the MSS. in the Cathedral Library of Sar*um*. particularly, the two Old Psalters. To see the Earl of Pembrokes Pictures at Wilton near Sar*um*.
To see M[r] Harbins Collection of Letters of M[r] Henry Savil, &c. & some of His Curious Printed Books.
To see the Library, & certain Antiquities at Long Leat. (which last may be had, I believe, for asking).
To desire M[r] Harbin to procure all. Letters & Papers, written by, or relating to the Lady Arabella, to be fairly transcribed | (each upon a distinct Paper, in folio;) in Order to be regularly placed among, & Bound up with Your own.
To desire M[r] Harbin, to procure Your Lordship from Prior Nash (so called) the Oldest Register of Sar*um*: Iohn Wy-|cliffes Trialogus, in MSS. and what other Antiquities he hath, or had.
To Borrow that Register of Hereford which is in the Library at Long Leat, for M[r] Iames Hill.
To induce the B*isho*p of Bath & Welles to bequeath to your Lordship those Ten Rentals of His Dioces, which I was in-|strumental in procuring him from the Late Lord Weymouth: together with His own Collections concerning the History of | Cathedral Churches.

To enquire in & about Bath, (besides viewing the Walls;) what Antiquities are in Private Hands.

At Oxford, in the Museum.

The fine Gilded MS. I think is numbered 1262; if not, rather, that marked 1511.

In the Bodleyan Library.

⌈Barocc.3.⌉ Observe the marginal scholias of Aretas …

However, it is the entries in Wanley's diary for 3, 4, and 6 May 1715 (not least because of the amount of money involved) which most catch the attention.[28] The first reads: 'The Secretary Related that the fine Prayer-book, which the late Lord Weymouth bought at the Price of £100; is now come into the possession of Sir Robert Worsley; who (having been asked) is willing to sell it to my Lord at the same price.' (Sir Robert Worsley of Appuldurcombe on the Isle of Wight was the husband of the 1st Viscount's only daughter and only surviving child, Frances Thynne.)[29] Wanley records that the volume was accordingly delivered on 4 May: 'Mr. Harbin brought the fine Primer … & delivered the same to my Lord Harley that it might be shewn to my Lord of Oxford.' It seems that the volume was not purchased at this point: Wanley's entry for 6 May reads: 'My Lord Harley was pleased to Order that the Primer above-mentioned be redilivered to Mr Harbyn for Sir Robert Worseley; it being judged too dear at £.100. and his Lordship having another book, yet finer than this, in his View.'

The manuscript concerned appears to have been BL, Add. MS 18850, the Bedford Hours. It was finally purchased by the future 2nd Earl of Oxford (for £100) in December 1717, as his surviving letters in Add. MS 70470 attest. He writes urgently on the subject from Wimpole to Wanley in London on 7 December 1717: 'I desire you will take the first opportunity to find Mr Harbin and enquire of him if the Fine Prayer Book that was my Lord Weymouths be to be disposed of and what will be the price of it, and if it be gone who has it, I desire you will not fail to send me an answer to this by Teusdays Post.' His letter of 12 December shows that a deal had been struck and that the manuscript was eagerly awaited in the country (the letter is otherwise taken up with Harley's transactions with the bookseller Nathaniel Noel, but the subject uppermost in his mind is very clear) :

I thank you for your last letter which gave me such a particular account of the Fine prayer Book, I am very much obliged to Sr. Robert Worseley for his kind expressions. I desire you will go to him with my Humble service and thanks as soon as you can after you have received this, I have enclosed you a note for one Hundred and Twenty pounds one Hundred for ye Book the other twenty as I shall direct. I desire you will have a Box made for the Book and very carefully packed up, and that it may be sent to me by the Huntingford coach which comes out next Teusday morning … I desire you will not fail to do this: I desire a letter from you by Saturdays post of this affair. I shall send to Huntingford on purpose for the Box. … I repeat it again that the fine prayer Book must be sent without fail.

Sir Robert Worsley received payment on 14 December as is evidenced by his signed receipt of that date in Add. MS 70487 (no. 50) – 'Receved of M^r. Wanley ye sum of One Hundred Pounds for A Manuscript illuminated Primer which I deliverd him'. News of the successful purchase (with notice of 'two Wardrobe Books' also received from Worsley) was acknowledged on 15 December and the manuscript finally arrived at Wimpole on the seventeenth: Harley concludes a letter of this last date, otherwise occupied with the binding of some of his collection, ' I have just now received the Box with the Book ...'[30]

Longleat House MS 259 also has rising twenty entries relating to books borrowed by John Urry: the loans are datable roughly to the period after 2 August 1704 down to 26 November 1712. Urry's use of the library is not to be explained, then, solely by the needs of his edition of Chaucer and, be it said, his need to raise subscriptions for the same.[31] His Chaucer appeared in 1721: the work having finally been revised by Timothy Thomas (with a life of the poet by John Dart) after Urry's death on 18 March 1715. As the preface to the edition recalls (sig. i2^r): 'About the latter end of the Year 1711, some Persons well acquainted with Mr. Urry's Qualifications ... proposed to him to put out a new Edition of Chaucer. ...'

Urry (like the 1st Viscount Weymouth) was of Christ Church, matriculating in 1682: he was deprived of his studentship on the accession of William III for his refusal of the oath of supremacy. These two reasons alone may be enough to explain his becoming a recipient of Weymouth's patronage. I note further as possibly deserving investigation that the Thynne pedigree includes an Urry marriage: the 1st Viscount's second cousin, Mary, is recorded as having married one 'Urrey of London'.[32] Urry appears on fol. 52^r of the borrowers' list, borrowing Thomas Guidot's *De thermis Britannicis* of 1691: the entry reads 'Mr Urry Dr Guidot on the Bath 8vo'. The nearest dated entry (2 August 1704) concludes fol. 51^r. The next entry (fol. 54^r 'Formulare Anglicanum') includes the date of return, 2 April 1705, and is also in Urry's own hand rather than Harbin's. More interestingly Urry appears as a frequent borrower of Gavin Douglas's translation of the *Aeneid*, in both a printed edition and a manuscript copy (Longleat MS 252A is the volume concerned). (As the preface attests, Urry was one of the editors of the edition of Douglas published in Edinburgh in 1710 with the title *Virgil's Aeneis, Translated into Scottish Verse*, whilst Weymouth was one of the subscribers: his copy is still on the shelves at Longleat.) On fol. 64^v in MS 259 is an autograph entry for 16 August 1708, 'Bp Douglas translation of virgile | in Print & MS to J Urry', and on fol. 69^r a similar entry for 17 July 1711 referring to the same loans but concluding with an additional note '1711 Nov*ember* ye 2 returnd Mr Harbin Present'. Such additions to entries occur only in the case of loans to Urry: another on fol. 69^v, referring to Inigo Jones *The most notable antiquity of Great Britain, vulgarly called Stone-heng* of 1655, reads similarly '15 Oct*ober* 1711 Stonhenge by | Inigo Jones & vindicated by Webb borrowd | by J Urry, Nov*ember* ye 2^d returnd 1711 present Mr Harbin. the above M*entione*d G Dougl MS & print'. On fol.

72^r, at some point before 19 November 1712, he is found borrowing 'an old edition of Chaucer fol.' and Caxton's edition of the Boethius translation. Harbin's careful wording of the final entry relating to Urry bespeaks I believe a decision taken over the librarian's head and perhaps contrary to his own judgement: the entry in question on fol. 72^v reads –

Nov. 26th [1712] Mr Urry carried wth him to | Oxford (with my Lord's leave) a MS on | vellom, 4to, in wch are some Poems of Chaucer | Item. Caxton's edition of Chaucer's Transla- | tion of Boethius. fol. | Item. An antient Printed edition of Chau | cer's works. fol. restored

Only the last entry is crossed through, though at least the copy of Caxton's Boethius, like MS 258 cast off for the printing of William Thynne's 1532 Chaucer edition, is still in the library.

As is well known, the preface to Urry's Chaucer includes his 'Catalogue of the MSS. made use of in this Edition', a list of fourteen manuscripts (by no means all the volumes which he consulted): Timothy Thomas follows the catalogue with notice of seven more manuscripts omitted from the editor's list. It is worth recalling that Weymouth and family and employee figure in both the catalogue and the omissions. The preface records (sig.k1^v) that George Harbin, Weymouth's librarian, acted as intermediary with Mr Yarborough to facilitate the loan of a *Canterbury Tales* manuscript belonging to Edmond Canbey of Thorn in Yorkshire (Phillipps 8136, now Switzerland, Cologny, Foundation Bodmer, cod. 48), and also (sig.k2^r) that the widow of Henry Thynne, son of the 1st Viscount, lent Urry a *Canterbury Tales* manuscript 'purchased by her, which had belonged to Mr. Long a Prebendary of the Church of Exeter' (this is the Duke of Northumberland's copy at Alnwick Castle which includes the *Tale of Beryn*), whilst the 1st Viscount himself lent a copy of the *Troilus*. This is the additional item mentioned earlier as recognizable in the Spelman sales catalogues – it is now San Marino, Huntington Library, MS HM 114. Timothy Thomas records 'this I found amongst Books and Papers left by Mr. Urry' and notes in the preface that he made use of the manuscript in his work on the glossary, citing the book as 'MS. Sp.' on the strength of the presence of Spelman's signature on the first leaf. He concludes his mention of the manuscript (sig.li^r): 'I have since been informed that it belonged to the late Lord Viscount Weymouth, from whom it is probable Mr. Urry borrowed it not long before his Death; which might be the reason that no notice is taken of it in that Catalogue he left of the MSS. which he had seen and perused.'

Urry's edition was greeted with unanimous contempt: his editorial method, encompassing as it did quite radical intrusions into the text to achieve conformity with his concept of the regularity of Chaucer's metre, was questioned by Richard Rawlinson even before publication, and did not inspire confidence in Timothy Thomas, a fact he made reasonably plain in the edition itself: this probably did little to enhance the volume's chances as a saleable commodity in the market place.[33] Tyrwhitt's view that the Chaucer text produced by Urry was 'by far the worst that was ever published' is a distinction still accorded to the edition. This, however, was for the future: it is quite possible that Weymouth's interest in the Chaucer edition was in some sense even proprietorial – one of the portraits he commissioned for his library at Longleat House portrays Chaucer (Pl. 2).³⁴ Weymouth's manuscript collection was fortunately to have a shelf-life much beyond that of the Chaucer edition he sponsored and, as he could not have foreseen, much beyond the other grand projects with which he was concerned and which provide a further and wider context for the manuscript collecting activity which has been the subject of this essay.

NOTES

1 See James E. Blodgett, 'William Thynne (d. 1546)', in *Editing Chaucer: the Great Tradition*, ed. by Paul Ruggiers (Norman, Okla., 1984), pp. 32-52, and Robert Costomiris, 'Bodleian MS Tanner 346 and William Thynne's Edition of Clanvowe's "Cuckoo and the Nightingale"', *The Library*, 6th Series, 20 (1998), 99-117: see also Brian Donaghey, 'William Thynne's Collected Edition of Chaucer: Some Bibliographical Considerations', in *Texts and Their Contexts: Papers from the Early Book Society*, ed. by John Scattergood & Julia Boffey (Dublin, 1997), pp. 150-64.

2 The antiquary Beriah Botfield (d. 1863), a Roxburghe Club member and heir to a Shropshire ironworks fortune (his seat, however, was at Norton Hall, near Daventry in Northamptonshire), collected incunabula, Bibles, and fine illustrated natural history books, as well as medieval manuscripts. For Botfield's printed books recently leaving the Longleat collection, see Christie's sale catalogues, *Highly Important Printed Books and Manuscripts*, 23 June 1993 (lots 51-69) and particularly *Highly Important Books from Beriah Botfield's Library*, 30 March 1994 and the discussion contained in John Collins' article, 'The Botfield Sale, 30 March 1994, London, Christie's', *Bulletin de Bibliophilie*, 1 (1994), 218-23.

3 I am approaching completion of an edition of this book-list which is among the Thynne Papers at Longleat: the edition includes identification of the items listed and notice of those volumes which still survive at Longleat (well over a third of the books come into this last category). For some account of the analogous case of Sir John Thynne's acquisition and storage of archive material, see my introduction to Kate Harris & William Smith, *Glastonbury Abbey Records at Longleat House: a Summary List*, Somerset Record Society, vol. 81 (Taunton, 1991). The 1577 list makes no mention of the two copies of Piers Plowman associated with Sir John Thynne, London, British Library, Add. MS 10574 and Oxford, Bodleian Libary, MS Laud Misc. 581 (see C. David Benson & Lynne S. Blanchfield, *The Manuscripts of Piers Plowman: the B-version* (Cambridge, 1997), pp. 61, 63, 83, 85).

4 Longleat House archives, 1st Viscount Weymouth, 240, 01/01/1702, a shelflist of the library including the manuscripts at 'Classis IX' (shelves B-F).

5 It was Thomas Ken, the non-juring Bishop of Bath and Wells, who had first (very cautiously) recommended Harbin to Lord Weymouth as a household chaplain (Longleat Thynne Papers XIX fol. 18ʳ: 'The Bishop of Ely [that is the Bishop's fellow non-juror, Francis Turner] mentions to me one Mr Harbin, who was his owne Chaplaine heretofore, an excellent scholar, & as far as I could observe, of a brisk, & chearfull temper, however, I was unwilling to engage your Lordshippe to take him, without a previous triall, & I haue told ye Bishop that your Lordshippe should make experiment of him for a quarter of a yeare, before he fix'd in your family …'.): in the event Harbin's service at Longleat was long – he was to became tutor to the 2nd Viscount Weymouth who succeeded as a minor in 1714.

6 Amanzio's protocols run 1450-99. MS 139 at Holkham Hall, an Italian translation of Augustine's *De cura pro mortuis*, is also signed on fol. 31ᵛ by this scribe, 'Amantius scripsit': see

further Albinia de la Mare, 'New Research on Humanistic Scribes in Florence', in *Miniatura Fiorentina del Rinascimento 1440-1525*, ed. by Annarosa Garzelli (Florence, 1985), pp. 425-6 n. 20 and, for a listing of the manuscripts copied by the scribe, *ibid.*, Appendix I, p. 595 2A.

7 Thomas Robinson the portrait painter of 35 Golden Square in London: for notice of the portraits for the Old Library in Robinson's letters to Weymouth of 1, 10 and 13 June 1704, see Thynne Papers XXV fols 276ʳ, 293ᵛ, 296ᵛ (the last reports 'I have almost finished the Pictures of Mʳ Butler & Hobs. Mʳ Betterton has promisd me to send up his Original of Shakespeare that I may Copy it for your Lordship ...'). Humfrey Wanley in a letter of 3 October 1709 written at Longleat records (BL, Add. MS 70482, otherwise Portland CCCCXXXII, Welbeck Wanleyana, BL Loan 29/258) 'Here ha's been one Mr Robinson a Painter, who live's in Golden Square; he doe's all the business that this Noble Family ha's in his Way, and is a very Good sort of a Man.' For Wanley's presence at Longleat see further below pp. 238-41.

8 For this portrait and its provenance see Roy Strong, 'Sidney's Appearance Reconsidered', in *Sir Philip Sidney's Achievements*, ed. by M. J. B. Allen, Dominic Baker-Smith, Arthur F. Kinney, & Margaret M. Sullivan (New York, 1990), pp. 3-32: see further Henry Woudhuysen, 'A "Lost" Sidney Document', *Bodleian Library Record*, 13 (1990), 353-9.

9 Longleat House archives, 1st Viscount Weymouth, 240, 01/01/1710.

10 'Mr Steel the book-Binders Bill' (Longleat House archives, 1st Viscount Weymouth, 240, 13/01/1710), includes '1 petrarck in 4.° Red: turky Exterord' priced at 12s. which seems to correspond with MS 252B. The bill also includes a very significant number of incunabula and Aldine publications.

11 For this manuscript see my paper 'The Patronage and Dating of Longleat House MS 24, a Prestige Copy of the *Pupilla oculi* illuminated by the Master of the *Troilus* Frontispiece' (delivered as part of the Seventh York Manuscripts Conference 1-3 July 1994 and forthcoming in *Prestige, Authority and Power: Studies in Late Medieval Manuscripts*, ed. by Felicity Riddy), which seeks to date the volume to 1415 and associate it with Henry, 3rd Baron Scrope of Masham, executed for complicity in the Southampton plot 5 August 1415: a survey of the illuminator's oeuvre by Dr Kathleen Scott, 'Limner-Power: an English Book Artist of c.1420', is to appear in the the the same publication.

12 *Bibliotheca Selectissima: being the Library Of the Late Sir Edmund King, M.D. ... Also the Library of that Eminent and Learned Antiquary, Sir H.S – ...*, sold for the bookseller John Harding, 28 November 1709 and *Bibliotheca Selectissima: Pars altera: Being the Remainder of the Library of That Eminent and Learned Antiquary Sir H.S. ...*, sold for Harding by Edmund Curll, 26 January 1710 (both sales took place at the Temple Change in Fleet Street). Though I have checked the copies in the British Library, Bodleian, and Christ Church and though Dr Ian Doyle and Robert Babcock have been kind enough to examine the copies at Durham and Yale for me, thus far I have traced no catalogue preserving evidence of the identity of buyers at the sales.

13 For Ebesham's opus see A. I. Doyle, 'The Work of a Late Fifteenth-century English Scribe, William Ebesham', *Bulletin of the John Rylands Library*, 39 (1957), 298-325, and Linda Voigts, 'A Handlist of Middle English in Harvard Manuscripts', *Harvard Library Bulletin*, 33 (1985), 87-9. For Weymouth's acquisition of MS 38 see further below pp. 239-40.

14 On MS 257 see most recently Anne Sutton & Livia Visser-Fuchs, *Richard III's Books* (Stroud, 1997), pp. 279-80: see also the same authors'. 'Richard III's Books: II. A Collection of Romances and Old Testament Stories', *The Ricardian*, 7 nos 95-7 (1986-7), 327-32, 371-9, 421-36.

15 BL, Add. MS 70482 (unbound correspondence: formerly Portland Papers CCCCLXXXII, Welbeck Wanleyana, BL Loan 29/258).

16 *Letters of Humfrey Wanley, Palaeographer, Anglo-Saxonist, Librarian 1672-1726*, ed. by P. L. Heyworth (Oxford, 1989), p. 285, n.2. Wanley describes the project in a letter to Robert Harley dated 15 October 1713 (*ibid.*, p. 285): 'I am now actually engaged in the Publication of some of our English Historians, in Two Volumes in Folio; towards which work I have already gotten near two hundred Sheets of Paper written mostly by my own Hand and which I hope to see

come forth into the World with as much Reputation as any Book of the like Kind hath here mett withal.' For Wanley's 'Proposal for Printing a Volume of Old English Historians, from my Lord's Library' see *ibid.*, Appendix VII, pp. 484-5. He originally planned to include with the chronicles and annals, illustrative material in the way of notes, charters, seals, manuscripts, and epitaphs, as well as a glossary and index. For Wanley's transcripts see BL, Harley MSS 3666 and 4886, and for John Elphinstone's transcription of the Lanercost Annals, undertaken for Wanley, Harley MSS 3424-5. The transcripts of the Dunstable chronicle and that of Benedict of Peterborough were finally published by Thomas Hearne in 1733 and 1735 respectively.

17 Simon Keynes, 'The reconstruction of a burnt Cottonian manuscript: the case of Cotton MS. Otho A. I', *British Library Journal*, 22 (1996), 113-60. Thanks are due to Dr Keynes on several counts: first for being a scholar punctilious enough to enquire, in the face of the general assumption that it did not survive, whether the 'Book of Specimens' was 'simply sitting somewhere on your shelves' (private letter of 30 April 1996), and subsequently for liberally supplying many references and copies relating to Wanley and Spelman: noting that the layout of the 'Book of Specimens' derives from Mabillon's *De re diplomatica*, Dr Keynes gave a paper 'Humfrey Wanley and his "Book of Specimens" ' at the International Congress on Medieval Studies, Western Michigan University, Kalamazoo on 8 May 1998. A facsimile edition of MS 345 is now projected.

18 The portrait by Thomas Hill is reproduced as the frontispiece to Heyworth's edition of Wanley's letters.

19 M. B. Parkes, 'Archaizing Hands in English Manuscripts', in *Books and Collectors 1200-1700: Essays Presented to Andrew Watson*, ed. by James P. Carley & Colin G. C. Tite (London, 1997), p. 127.

20 *Letters of Humfrey Wanley*, p. 69.

21 *Ibid.*, p. 71.

22 William Dugdale with additions by John Caley, Henry Ellis, & Bulkeley Bandinel, *Monasticon Anglicanum a new edition enriched with a large accession of materials* (London, 1817, reprinted Farnborough, 1970), I, p. 276 n.m. (treated under Westminster, the manuscript is referred to as 'The Register of this Sanctuary').

23 Many of the Longleat volumes would not be identifiable or would be wrongly identified if the printed sale catalogue alone was used: MS 257 (folio lot 58), for example, is listed in the printed version merely as (p. 56) 'Chaucer's Works, with other Poetry, [Vellum]', while Wanley describes the manuscript at MS Harley 7055, fol. 234^r, as 'Seige of Thebes. [Whilome as old stories tellen us.] – Arcite & Palamon – Grisild full of Pacience – <u>Incip.</u> There is at y^c west side of Italie, <u>with Chaucers lenvoye</u> | – Ipomedon a Romance in Prose, imp*erf*. – History of y^c Old Test. in Old English Verse, wants some leaves at beginn – s*criptus* c*irca* t*empus* Henrici 6.'

24 *Letters of Humfrey Wanley*, p. 232, n. 27n.

25 BL, Harley MS 3782, fols 178^r-179^r: 'I have a great Neighbour at Bodenham who by power & art has almost outed me, & from beeing my Tenant will scarce allowe me to bee a poor Freeholder under him … What I desire is y^t you would search in the Tower for any Inquisitions or other Charters concerning Bodenham D'Evereux and take Copies of what you thinke materiall either for information, or support of my Right … Probably you will finde a great deale of stuff not of much use …'. See further Weymouth's letter to Wanley 19 July 1709, Harley 3782, fol. 180^r, following the conduct of the search.

26 *The Diary of Humfrey Wanley 1715-1726*, ed. by C. E. Wright & Ruth C. Wright, 2 vols (London, 1966), I, pp. 13-14: the entry for 6 August 1715 reads 'The Secretary brought in 4 thick octavo books, partly written & partly printed, relating (chiefly) to our Common Law. Those three which are in Covers of Velvet, &c. are supposed to be of the Hand of the Lord Chief Justice Sir Edward Coke: and that the notes of the other, being in Parchment-Cover, are written by Sir William [*sic, recte* George] Stroud, Father to Madam Thynne, who gave them all four to the Library.'

27 Fol. 45 contains a related list headed 'At Oxford, your Lordship may please to see'. The

collection relating to Arbella Stuart mentioned on fol. 48ʳ is part of the Longleat Talbot Papers, purchased by the 1st Viscount in 1712.

28 *Diary*, pp. 10, 11.

29 He was the elder brother of the Henry Worsley, 'a man of scholarly tastes, generous in lending manuscripts', who appears in Wanley's letters (*Letters*, p. 13, n.7, p. 16 relating to the loan of what is now MS Harley 1666 to Wanley). A letter from Henry Worsley to Wanley on fol. 218ʳ in Harley MS 3782 suggests that George Harbin acted as an intermediary between them: 'Mʳ. Harbin told me yᵉ other day, you had a mind to treat with me abᵗ my Mˢˢ. I desire yᵉ favor of you to drink a dish of tea with me to morrow Morning abᵗ. nine a clocke …'.

30 Add. MS 70470 (unbound correspondence) is otherwise Portland CCCCLXX and Loan 29/249. Add. MS 70487, part of a collection of Wanley miscellanea, is otherwise Portland CCCCLXXXIV and Loan 29/259. Heyworth briefly mentions the evidence recorded in the receipt *ibid.*, p. 11, n.2. For an account of the later history of the manuscript see A. N. L. Munby, *Connoisseurs and Medieval Miniatures* (Oxford, 1972), pp. 158-9. The volume finally left the collection of the 2nd Duchess of Portland, Margaret Harley (daughter of the second Earl of Oxford), in 1786: its many owners before it entered the British Museum in 1852 included the Duke of Marlborough who bought the book for £687 15s. in 1815.

31 Two bifolia of printed receipts (eight receipts in all) for the 'first Payment to the Subscription, for the Works of JEFFERY CHAUCER; To be deliver'd in Quires to the Bearer hereof …', all signed by the editor, John Urry, survive in the Longleat archive (1st Viscount Weymouth 240 01/10/1711).

32 Beriah Botfield, *Stemmata Botevilliana* (Westminster, 1858), p. 59.

33 On Urry's edition see William L. Alderson, 'John Urry (1666-1715)', in *Editing Chaucer* (cited above, n. 1), pp. 93-115, excerpted from William L. Alderson & Arnold C. Henderson, *Chaucer and Augustan Scholarship* (Berkeley, 1970).

34 On the possible source of the Chaucer portrait see Thynne Papers XXV, fols 268-9 letter of the actor, Thomas Betterton, to Colonel Finch 25 May 1704: 'I have at Reading beside Shakespears, a Head of Chaucers, as big as yᵉ Life, and I think no ill one. I haue Sʳ Iohn Suckling, and Fletcher. If my Lord pleases to haue any of these Coppy'd for him, and you (Sʳ) will do me ye honor to send me his Lord.ᵖˢ commands, they shall be punctually obey'd …'.

A LIST OF THE PUBLICATIONS
OF JEREMY GRIFFITHS

A. S. G. Edwards

1981

Review of K. V. Sinclair, *French Devotional Texts of the Middle Ages: A Bibliographic Manuscript Guide* (Westport, 1979), in *Analytical & Enumerative Bibliography*, 5: 109-12.

1982

'A Re-examination of Oxford, Bodleian Library, MS Rawlinson C. 86', *Archiv*, 134: 383-8.

1983

St John's College, Cambridge, MS L. 1. Introduction by R. Beadle & J. Griffiths. Norman, Okla.: Pilgrim Books.

'*Confessio Amantis*: the Poem and Its Pictures', in *Gower's Confesio Amantis: Responses and Reassessments*, ed. by A. J. Minnis. Cambridge: Boydell & Brewer, pp. 163-77.

Review of Kathleen L. Scott, *The Mirror of the World* (Roxburghe Club, 1980) in *The Book Collector*, 32: 235-8.

1985

'[Contribution on Osborn MS fa. 1 of Gower's *Confessio Amantis* to] Marginalia', *Yale University Library Gazette*, 59: 174.

Review of *The Miller's Tale* (Variorum Chaucer, vol. 10, part 3), ed. by T. W. Ross in *Studies in the Age of Chaucer*, 7: 237-42.

Review of *English Court Culture in the Later Middle Ages*, ed. by V. J. Scattergood & J. W. Sherborne (London: Duckworth, 1983) in *Medium Aevum*, 54: 299-301.

Review of Rowan Watson, *The Playfair Hours: a Late Fifteenth-Century Illuminated Manuscript from Rouen* (London, 1984) in *The Ricardian*, 7: 183-5.

1986

'The Culture of the Court, the Culture of the Country', *Medieval English Studies Newsletter* (Tokyo), 14 (July): 1-3.

Review of *Fifteenth-Century Studies*, ed. by R. F. Yeager (Hamden, Conn., 1984), in *The Ricardian*, 7: 296-8.

1989

Book Production and Publishing in Britain, 1375-1475, ed. by Jeremy Griffiths & Derek Pearsall. Cambridge: University Press.

'The Manuscripts', in *Lollard Sermons*, ed. by Gloria Cigman. Early English Text Society 294. Oxford: University Press, xi-xxix.

Review of Laurel Braswell, *A Handlist of Manuscripts Containing Middle English Prose in the Douce Collection, Bodleian Library, Oxford* (Cambridge, 1987), in *Studies in the Age of Chaucer*, 11: 191-4.

1989-95

English Manuscript Studies, 1100-1700, ed. by Peter Beal & Jeremy Griffiths. Vols 1-5. Vols 1-2: Oxford: Blackwell, 1989-90; Vols 3-5: London: The British Library, 1992-5.

1990

Review of S. Schutzer, *Medieval and Renaissance Books in the Library of Congress* and Margaret M. Manion, Vera F. Vines, & Christopher de Hamel, *Medieval & Renaissance Manuscripts in New Zealand Collections* (London, 1989), in *The Times Literary Supplement*, 15 June: 650.

1991

'Croatia's D-I-Y Division', *The Independent on Sunday*, 29 September: 32-3.

1992

Speculum Peccatorum. 'The Mirror of Sinners' printed in London by Wynkyn De Worde c. 1509-10. With an Introduction and Translation by Jeremy Griffiths. Roxburghe Club.

'A Newly Identified Manuscript Inscribed by John Shirley', *The Library*, 6th series, 14: 83-93.

Review of C. W. Dutschke *et al.*, *Guide to Medieval and Renaissance Manuscripts in the Huntington Library* (San Marino, 1989), in *Medium Aevum*, 54: 299-301.

1993

The De Croy Hours. Sheffield: Ruskin Gallery.

1994

'"Loose Sheets and Idle Scribblings": the Case Against Shakespeare's Lleweni Connection', *The New Welsh Review*, 25: 52-7.

'The Covehithe Pendant: a Newly-Discovered Anglo-Saxon Pendant of Latticed Reticulated Glass', *Journal of the British Archaeological Association*, 147: 128-32.

'Chaucer: Life & Times on CD-ROM', *Medieval English Studies Newsletter* (Tokyo), 31: 22-3.

1995

'Book Production Terms in Nicholas Munshull's *Nominale*', *Art into Life: Collected Papers from the Kresge Art Museum Medieval Symposia*, ed. by Carol Garrett Fisher & Kathleen L. Scott. East Lansing: Michigan State University Press, pp. 49-71.

Introduction to *The Medieval and Renaissance Manuscripts of St John's College, Oxford*. Reading: Research Publications, pp. 5-7.

'Unrecorded Middle English Verse in the Library at Holkham Hall, Norfolk', *Medium Aevum*, 64: 278-84.

'Manuscripts on the Schøyen Collection Copied or Owned in the British Isles before 1700', *English Manuscript Studies*, 5: 36-42.

'Thomas Hingham, Monk of Bury and the Macro Plays Manuscript', *English Manuscript Studies*, 5: 214-19.

'New Light on the Provenance of a Copy of *The Canterbury Tales*, John Rylands Library MS Eng. 113', *Bulletin of the John Rylands Library of Manchester*, 77: 25-30.

1996

'John Capgrave', Robert Flemming', 'Thomas Chaundler', Christopher Urswick' in *The Dictionary of Art* (Grove), 5. 668-9, 6. 518, 11. 167, 31. 750-1.

'A Mid-Fifteenth Century Book-List and Inventory from East Dereham, Norfolk', *Norfolk Archaeology*, 42: 332-9.

Review of Peter Brown & Elton D Higgs, *A Handlist of Manuscripts Containing Middle English Prose in the Additional Collection, British Library, London (10001-14000)*, O. S. Pickering & Susan Powell, *A Handlist of Manuscripts Containing Middle English Prose in Yorkshire Libraries and Archives*, James Simpson, *A Handlist of Manuscripts Containing Middle English Prose in Parisian Libraries*, & S. J. Ogilvie-Thomson, *A Handlist of Manuscripts Containing Middle English Prose in Oxford College Libraries*, in *The Library*, 6th ser., 18: 56-8.

Review of *Catalogue of the Pepys Library at Magdalene College, Cambridge*, Vols II.i-ii, III. ii, V.i, in *The Library*, 6th ser., 18: 68-70.

1997

Review of *New Science Out of Old Books*, ed. by R. Beadle & A. Piper, in *Ricardian*, XI, no. 138: 147-50.

Review of *The Towneley Plays*, ed. by Martin Stevens & A. C. Cawley, in *Notes & Queries*, n.s. 44: 253-4.

Review of M. Tidcombe, *Women Bookbinders, 1880-1920*, in *The Library*, 6th ser., 19: 274-6.

1998

'An Unrecorded Copy of *The First Scottish Prophecy* in Middle English Verse from the Library of Sir Thomas Phillipps', *Notes & Queries*, n.s. 45: 432-4. (with I. Taavitsainen).

Review of *A Millennium of the Book*, ed. by Robins Myers & Michael Harris, and *Antiquarians, Book Collectors, and the Circle of Learning*, ed. by Robins Myers & Michael Harris, in *The Library*, 6th ser., 20: 68-9.

2000

Katherine Tollemache's Book of Secrets. Edited with an Introduction by Jeremy Griffiths. Roxburghe Club, forthcoming.

INDEX

INDEX OF MANUSCRIPTS